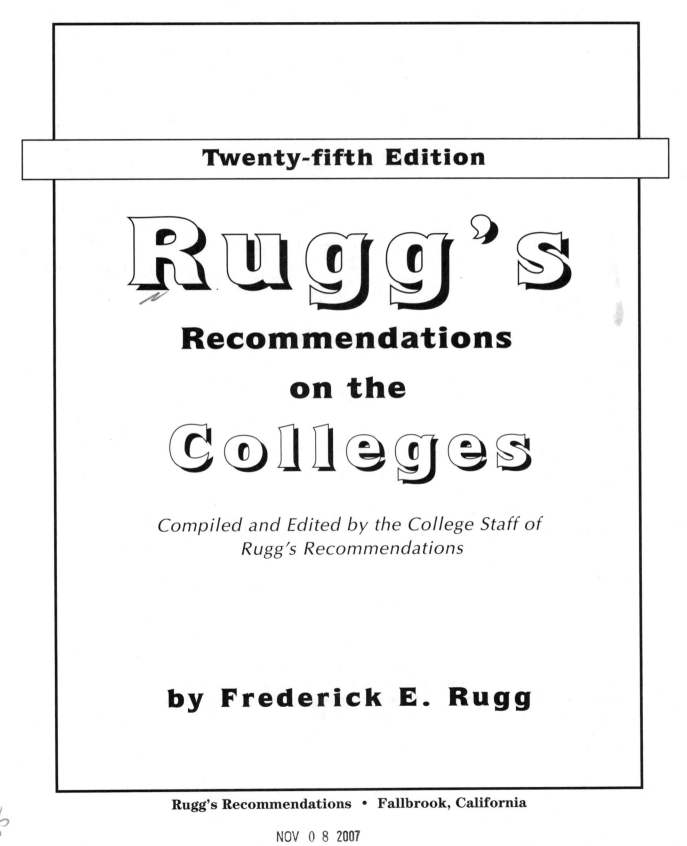

Twenty-fifth Edition

Rugg's
Recommendations
on the
Colleges

*Compiled and Edited by the College Staff of
Rugg's Recommendations*

by Frederick E. Rugg

Rugg's Recommendations • Fallbrook, California

To
Barbara, Betsie, and Sue

TABLE OF CONTENTS

SOME NOTES FROM THE AUTHOR

WHY THIS BOOK?

As a secondary school college counselor, I heard the following question from a student or parent almost daily: "Can you please give us a list of quality colleges where one can major in psychology (or engineering or business or whatever)?"

For many years I pulled out the college handbooks and came up with a list of hundreds of colleges for each category and spent too much time with the student sifting through the multitude of schools, trying to narrow down the huge list.

I thought about a way out of this dilemma for a long time. People from Harvard would find an easy solution. They might tell the parents and student not to worry about a college major—just go to a fine liberal arts college (like Harvard) and everything will fall into place. After all, it's not the major and professors that count, it's the wonderful student body that makes a great college great. Right?

Well…over the years, I had trouble convincing parents of the merits of that argument. I guess they realize that all good universities are not good in every field.

Today, there's just so much pressure on young people to line up their careers and pick their occupations in life early. Career education seems to start in kindergarten these days. I've noticed that many parents pick right up on it and give Johnny the business if he hasn't chosen his career by the sophomore year of high school or earlier. No matter what I told Johnny and his parents, they still wanted a list of "the quality colleges with a good psychology (or whatever) department."

This book lists the quality departments at quality colleges and it will make the school counselor's job easier. For example, a public school counselor can use it constantly in January when juniors (and sometimes sophomores) line up outside his/her office, asking for a list of colleges to "go with" their PSAT scores. Probably a prep school counselor, a junior and community college transfer counselor, or a librarian might even find more use of this guide for college majors. Since this book is for the aid of the counselor, it is, then, also a guide for students and their parents in the college admissions process.

WHY THESE 1100 COLLEGES?

From our experience in the college admissions process, we have chosen 1100 quality four-year colleges (out of over 2000 that offer bachelor degrees) to study. We began with the 275 colleges that have survived the careful screening process involved in the granting of a Phi Beta Kappa chapter. The Phi Beta Kappa schools are listed in Appendix A. These colleges received chapters for superior undergraduate performance in the liberal arts and sciences.

To this list were added 825 colleges—schools that our staff felt are as good (or better) as several of the Phi Beta Kappa colleges or have excellent specialized programs. We should also note that, in general, the more well-respected the college, the more departments and majors were included. Berkeley is listed under 37 departments while some others only under one. The typical school in the study was noted with 9 departments. A departmental page averages 175 recommended colleges.

HOW IT'S DONE

Over the years, college students have been surveyed - the number well into five figures. If you want a straight answer, the young folks seldom waver. We also receive monthly evaluations from secondary school counselors around the country. Some colleges submit to us departments at their schools that they consider "hidden gems". They also send us departments they consider their "strongholds". Weekly, a variety of college personnel lobby for a certain program at their university. Also, almost every week we get "tipped off" on a great department at a college at workshops I present around the U.S.A. on the college admissions process. Almost every year since 1977 I've added 300 departments to my list. This year the number is over 750.

What can eliminate a department or stop its consideration? No balance. For example, too many professors from the same alma mater in a department, or too many professors in a department graduating from that very college. If the average college in America gives out 6% of it's degrees in, say, the field of Psychology, and the department in question is at a 5% level, this sets up a "red flag", too.

HOW DO YOU USE THIS BOOK?

If you know what you want to major in at college—great!—just look it up. In most cases, you will find each departmental section organized into three groups of colleges:

Group I—Most Selective Colleges

Colleges here are among the 100 most selective colleges in America. They accept very few students with high school averages below 80 (top prep schools can, of course, lower this figure significantly) and College Board scores below 1800 (New SAT-1) and 27 (on the American College Test).

Group II—Very Selective Colleges

Many of the students at these colleges have "B" averages (80-90), and College Board scores between 1650 and 1800 (New SAT-1) and ACTs between 24 and 26.

Group III—Selective Colleges

Although these colleges are, in general, easier to get into than Group I and II colleges, please keep in mind that they are, in our opinion at least, among the top 1100 colleges in the country. Many students at these colleges have College Board scores just under 1650 (New SAT-1), or just under 24 on the ACTs.

Now that we have an idea of the group breakdown, a student may need help deciding from which group(s) to select his/her colleges. The guidance counselor can help here—having knowledge of colleges and a student's grade point average, class rank, board scores, etc. Most students will want to start with a group of 8 to 10 colleges from the departmental major page. This "major page" is a starting point. Schools can be added to the student's list by his/her counselor—from the counselor's own knowledge of the student, and knowledge of other colleges that might "fit" the student. Schools can be eliminated from a student's list after reviewing the college catalogs (see Appendix F—The Get Going Form), checking out undesirable features (city vs. rural setting, etc.), visiting the colleges, and other personal preferences. If the student does not have a major in mind, he or she should go to a typical liberal arts (e.g., English or Math) page to get started. I've also included a letter code system for the college's enrollment figure. The enrollment letter appears beside each college name with the following code:

XL = Extra Large Enrollment (over 20,000 students)
L = Large Enrollment (from 8,000 to 20,000 students)
M = Medium Enrollment (from 3,000 to 8,000 students)
R = Moderate Enrollment (from 1,000 to 3,000 students)
S = Small Enrollment (under 1,000 students)

SOME PARTING SHOTS

I don't care to go into the argument of "Picking a college because it has a great Mathematics Department" vs. "Picking a school because the school overall is great (Yeah Harvard!) and you'll probably change your major anyway." The fact of the matter is that parents, career educators, and other educators are telling 16-year-olds (and younger) to have a career and a major all mapped out and I bet will continue to do so. I'm sure high school counselors will continue to be asked to help Suzy find a list of quality schools with "excellent majors in mathematics." Personally, I see nothing wrong with a high school senior, who loves mathematics, trying to pick a quality school where the math department at that institution is ranked by its students as one of the top majors at that school and is generally recognized as being top notch by college counselors. If Suzy changes her mind after a year or two, she's at least given it a good shot with a premier math department. And chances are excellent that if she changes her major, it was because another outstanding department at that school helped her grow and reassess her career goals. She'll probably stay with that department for her new major. No harm done.

A few other comments on this book and some random thoughts...

1. Some state universities, like Penn State, are very competitive for out-of-staters. A university such as this may be in Group II for in-staters, but, in reality, is a Group I school for "outsiders."

2. In general, a college that is competitive is that way for all majors—but there are some departments that are exceptions. For example, engineering is a tough major and must be considered "Group II" at a "Group III" school.

3. A knowledgeable observer of the college scene will note that some competitive "alternative" colleges do not appear in this work, e.g., Hampshire College (MA), St. John's (MD). The jury is not unanimous on these progressive schools, and they are not included in this book except under "Miscellaneous Majors Pages."

4. A few majors in this book, such as engineering, have not been broken down into subdivisions (Civil, Electrical, Mechanical, etc.). Students will have to research these majors more fully. Well, what's wrong with that? Good to have the youngsters doing some hard work and research on the college admissions process. Foreign Languages, however, is broken down.

5. Every year a few more colleges close their doors. Today, colleges are under pressure to compete and "Be Hot." We need a college guide to weed things out a bit, a consumer-oriented handbook. We hope this helps.

6. Don't overlook the good small liberal arts college. Too many large universities are too impersonal. But some kids love a big school. Some thrive in the anonymity of a huge lecture hall.

7. Keep in mind that weak departments at Harvard, Yale, Stanford, Princeton, etc. might be equal to or better than the strongest departments at many colleges and universities.

8. This book is an aid for counselors, parents, and kids—nothing more. It is not a guide for the colleges to compare themselves one with the other.

9. Do not be surprised if you discover that the best of the more expensive schools are actually least expensive—because they have financial aid, the part-time jobs, etc. They're able to meet a student's financial need in many cases.

10. Students should discuss with their counselors the socioeconomic factors of the colleges they are considering. Will the college of your choice have several students enrolled with your socioeconomic background? And, please get in your college visits.

11. When you visit a college, seek out the students who attend and ask them the following question: "When you sign up for classes, do you get 100% of your choices, or only 4 out of 10 courses, or...?" Also, does the faculty seem to be there, to like to talk to you, to meet and greet you? Or are they not to be found?

12. Most states have a "flagship" university, the leader of the system (e.g., The University of North Carolina at Chapel Hill). In this book it is listed as just "No. Carolina." The other members of the University system are listed as follows: No. Carolina (Asheville), No. Carolina (Charlotte), No. Carolina (Greensboro), No. Carolina (Pembroke), No. Carolina (Wilmington).

13. Some colleges do a great job with private school youngsters, others do a fantastic job with public school youngsters. Some colleges are outstanding with both groups. A very fine college with an outstanding record with public school youngsters is Virginia's Roanoke College.

14. A tip for the high school senior: Don't ease up in your senior year. Take a tough course load with courses such as Physics. College admissions people aren't stupid. The first thing they look at when they review your high school record is the quality of your high school courses.

15. To parents and counselors: Hang tough. The pieces will finally fit.

16. Keep in mind that a starter list of colleges to consider for your daughter #1 may be a terrible list for your daughter #2.

17. I received a phone call from a community college instructor in the Mid-West. He also consults with companies recruiting college graduates, and has found my lists to be the best. He said to me on the phone, "The true test of any college guidebook or college list is, 'Does the information work?' So if the best information comes from college janitors, you go after college janitors."

18. I give an apology now to many of the top secondary prep schools in the country. Many of you may not be happy with my recent emphasis on adding departments to the Cal States, the Mass States, Connecticut States, Pennsylvania States, Michigan and Illinois States, etc. But the public school counselors and parents need these recommendations and they are over 90% of my customer base.

19. Some more thoughts on the college visit. I have never known someone to visit two college campuses, and then to report that both the colleges are equal, and that the visitor has no favorite of the two. NEVER. So visit. If you can't visit during the school year, visit during the college's vacation(s). If you cannot do that, please have the student visit the college's website, the department page in question, e-mail professors, e-mail or write admission and/or financial aid. Again, have the student do it.

20. This book is not perfect. It has never claimed to be perfect. Our study is not scientific. It has never claimed to be. But it is a good place to start and represents tens of thousands of contacts. I'll repeat that. We have never claimed to be perfect. There is no expert in the field. There never will be. The field is too big. We've even moved to many parts of the country to try to put together "the big picture." We do our best.

Frederick E. Rugg

San Diego County, California
January, 2008 (25th Edition)

SOME NOTES ON THE TWENTY-FIFTH EDITION

The twenty-fifth edition contains over 1000 entry changes since the twenty-fourth edition. All 100 plus majors have been revised. Arabic and Public Relations - these two majors have been added.

The "Average SAT-1/Average New SAT/ACT Total/Recommended majors" pages are included mainly because of counselors' requests. School counselors wanted average score comparisons and an index of colleges showing recommended majors. In all cases, SAT Total Scores are noted and the equivalent ACT score is provided. These scores are the best estimate by our staff for the entering fall class of 2008. Especially young counselors tell us this section is a quick ready reference—a marker for them. And if you're looking for schools that do not require SAT's, please see "www.fairtest.org" for the latest list.

As in the past, when a state university is noted like Wisconsin, we mean the flagship at Madison, if no other city follows in parenthesis.

Finally, in the middle of the book, you will find every college's website. You know to add the "www." up front.

Frederick E. Rugg

San Diego County, California
January, 2008 (25th Edition)

ACKNOWLEDGMENTS

I would like to thank the following for their help in the preparation of this guidebook: Phi Beta Kappa Office, Bureau of Educational Statistics, our Research Aides, Officers of Institutional Research who returned our requests, and especially the great number of secondary counselors who've filled out questionnaires and tip me off on quality departments to look at. I am independent of the colleges and these people are, too.

A "Thank You" also goes to the counselors and students I've worked with who have contributed each in their own way. At last count, I've worked 25,000 hours in five secondary school guidance cubicles with 30 counselors, and conducted over 600 workshops with over 8000 counselors. Of course I've learned from them. Together we've probably done the college admissions process a million times. Also I thank the counselors and students and university officials in the United States and abroad for their help, suggestions, and, yes, their complaints. I appreciate, too, those departments who have sent us vitae on their professors. College PR officers who write always get a reading. And the same goes for anyone who e-mails me. Eighty percent of college personnel who write me and tip me off on a great major at their school find it in the next year's book!

I am also grateful to George Gibbs, Ed Wall, Reg Alexander, Arvin R. Anderson, Howard Ahlskog, Hy Kleinman, Michele M. Charles, Gary Metras, Edward Field, Betty Rossie, Horacio Rodrigues, A.P. Stevens, Madeline Field, Cyrus Benson, John Barker, Fred Ames, Matthew Jagielski, Gilbert Field, Jeff Sheehan, Charles Doebler, Joan Girard, Mrs. Fran Fisher, Ralph Strycharz, Dennis Gurn, John DeBonville, Sammy Edwards, Eric Goodhart, Kevin L. Miller, Gloria Broecker, Hoover Sutton, Francona, J.R., Rebecca Lou, Cousin Leonard, Dave Congalton, Steve Stassen, Dwayne Copeland, Dianne Pelletier, Art Northrop, Roger Dexter, Carl Schulkin, Peter Frederick Stassen, and to all the secretaries I've worked with over the years.

And finally, a special thanks to my wife, Barbara, for her patience and industry, and daughters, Betsie and Susan.

Inquiries and comments about this guide should be addressed to:

Rugg's Recommendations
P.O. Box 417
Fallbrook, CA 92088

SECTION ONE
RECOMMENDED UNDERGRADUATE PROGRAMS

AGRICULTURE

Author's Note: *Students in the schools of Agriculture, in general, tend to have median college test scores below the University's overall median.*

GROUP I
Most Selective

Cornell (NY)	L	Maryland, U. of	XL
Florida, U. of	XL	Pennsylvania State	XL
Illinois, U. of (Urbana-Champaign)	XL	Rutgers (NJ)	L
Iowa State	XL		

GROUP II
Very Selective

Auburn (AL)	L	Minnesota, U. of	XL
California, U. of (Davis)	XL	Missouri, U. of	XL
California, U. of (Riverside)	L	New Hampshire, U. of	L
Cal. Poly. State U. (San Luis Obispo)	L	North Carolina State	L
Clemson (SC)	L	Puerto Rico, U. of (Mayaguez)	L
Connecticut, U. of	XL	Purdue (IN)	XL
Hawaii, U. of	L	Texas A&M	XL
Kansas State	L	Vermont, U. of	M
Maine, U. of	L	Virginia Tech	L
Michigan State	XL	Wisconsin, U. of	XL

GROUP III
Selective

Arizona, U. of	XL	Northwest Missouri State (MO)	M
Arkansas, U. of	L	Ohio State	XL
Berea (KY)	R	Oklahoma State	L
Cal. Poly. State U. (Pomona)	L	Oregon State	L
California State U. (Chico)	L	Ozarks, College of the (MO)	R
California State U. (Fresno)	L	Tarleton State (TX)	M
Colorado State	L	Tennessee, U. of	XL
Delaware Valley (PA)	R	Tennessee, U. of (Martin)	M
Dordt (IA)	R	Texas State U. (San Marcos)	L
Georgia, U. of	XL	Texas Tech U.	L
Idaho, U. of	L	Tuskegee University (AL)	M
Kentucky, U. of	L	Utah State	L
Louisiana State	XL	Washington State	L
Mississippi State	L	Western Illinois	L
Montana State	L	Western Kentucky	L
Murray State (KY)	M	Wilmington (OH)	S
Nebraska, U. of	L	Wisconsin, U. of (Platteville)	M
Nevada, U. of (Reno)	L	Wisconsin, U. of (River Falls)	M
New Mexico State U.	L	Wyoming, U. of	L
North Dakota State	L		

AMERICAN STUDIES

GROUP I
Most Selective

American U. (DC) .... M
Amherst (MA) .... R
Brandeis (MA) .... M
Brown (RI) .... M
Buffalo (SUNY) (NY) L
California, U. of (San Diego) L
Carleton (MN) .... R
Case Western Reserve (OH) .... M
Chicago, U. of (IL) .... M
Emory (GA) .... M
Franklin & Marshall (PA) .... R
George Washington (DC) .... M
Georgetown (DC) .... M
Harvard (MA) .... M
Johns Hopkins (MD) .... M
Kalamazoo (MI) .... R
Lehigh (PA) .... M
Maryland, U. of XL
Maryland, U. of (Baltimore County) ...... M
Michigan, U. of XL

Minnesota, U. of XL
Muhlenberg (PA) .... R
North Carolina, U. of L
Northwestern (IL) .... M
Pennsylvania, U. of L
Pomona (CA) .... R
Sarah Lawrence (NY) .... R
▲ Smith (MA) .... R
St. Olaf (MN) .... R
South, U. of the (TN) .... R
Stanford (CA) .... M
Trinity (CT) .... R
Tulane (LA) .... M
Virginia, U. of L
Wake Forest (NC) .... M
Wesleyan (CT) .... R
William & Mary (VA) .... R
Williams (MA) .... R
Yale (CT) .... M

GROUP II
Very Selective

Alabama, U. of L
Arizona, U. of XL
Bowling Green (OH) L
California State U. (Fresno) L
California State U. (Fullerton) L
California, U. of (Santa Cruz) .... M
DePaul (IL) L
Eastern Connecticut .... M
Florida State L
Fredonia (SUNY)(NY) .... M
George Mason (VA) L
Hawaii, U. of L
Hillsdale (MI) .... R
Hobart & Wm. Smith (NY) .... R
Iowa, U. of XL
Kansas, U. of L
Knox (IL) .... R
La Salle (PA) .... M
Lebanon Valley (PA) .... R
Loyola Marymount (CA) .... M

Manhattanville (NY) .... R
Mary Washington (VA) .... M
Massachusetts, U. of (Boston) .... M
New Mexico, U. of L
▲ Pine Manor (MA) .... S
Queens (CUNY)(NY) L
Queens (NC) .... R
Ramapo (NJ) .... M
Randolph College (VA) .... S
Rider (NJ) .... R
Skidmore (NY) .... R
South Florida, U. of L
Texas, U. of XL
Wagner (NY) .... R
Washington College (MD) .... S
Washington State XL
Wells (NY) .... S
▲ Wesleyan College (GA) .... S
Western Connecticut .... M
Wyoming, U. of L

Enrollment Code

■ *Men Only*
▲ *Women Only*

S = Small (less than 1000 students)   R = Moderate (1000-3000 students)   M = Medium (3000-8000 students)
L = Large (8000-20,000 students)   XL = Extra Large (over 20,000 students)

ANTHROPOLOGY

GROUP I
Most Selective

American (DC) .... M	Kenyon (OH) .... R
Albany (SUNY) (NY) L	Lafayette (PA) .... R
▲ Barnard (NY) .... R	Lawrence (WI) .... R
Binghamton (SUNY)(NY) L	Macalester (MN) .... R
Boston U. (MA) L	MIT (MA) .... M
Bowdoin (ME) .... R	Michigan, U. of XL
Brandeis (MA) .... R	New College (FL) .... S
▲ Bryn Mawr (PA) .... S	New York U. L
Buffalo (SUNY) (NY) L	North Carolina, U. of L
California, U. of (Berkeley) XL	Northwestern (IL) .... M
California, U. of (Los Angeles) XL	Notre Dame (IN) .... M
Case Western Reserve (OH) .... M	Pennsylvania, U. of L
Chicago, U. of (IL) .... M	Pitzer (CA) .... S
Colorado College .... R	Pomona (CA) .... R
Columbia (NY) .... M	Princeton (NJ) .... M
Connecticut College .... R	Reed (OR) .... R
Dartmouth (NH) .... M	Rice (TX) .... M
Duke (NC) .... M	Rutgers (NJ) L
Emory (GA) .... M	Skidmore (NY) .... R
Florida, U. of XL	▲ Smith (MA) .... R
Georgetown (DC) .... M	Southern Methodist (TX) .... M
Grinnell (IA) .... R	South, U. of the (TN) .... R
Harvard (MA) .... M	Stanford (CA) .... M
Illinois, U. of (Urbana-Champaign) XL	Tulane (LA) .... M
Johns Hopkins (MD) .... M	Vanderbilt (TN) .... M
Kalamazoo (MI) .... R	Washington U. (MO) .... M
Kansas State L	Yale (CT) .... M

GROUP II
Very Selective

Alabama, U. of L	Hunter (CUNY)(NY) L
Arizona, U. of XL	Indiana (PA) L
Arizona State XL	Iowa, U. of XL
Beloit (WI) .... R	Ithaca (NY) .... M
Brown (RI) .... M	James Madision (VA) L
California State U. (Chico) L	Kansas, U. of L
California, U. of (Irvine) L	Knox (IL) .... R
California, U. of (Santa Cruz) .... M	Loyola (IL) .... M
California, U. of (Davis) XL	Luther (IA) .... R
City College (CUNY)(NY) L	Maine, U. of L
Colorado State L	Maryland, U. of XL
Colorado, U. of L	Massachusetts, U. of L
Earlham (IN) .... R	Michigan State XL
George Mason (VA) L	Nevada, U. of (Las Vegas) L
George Washington (DC) .... M	Oklahoma, U. of XL
Grand Valley (MI) L	Oregon, U. of L
Hamline (MN) .... R	Pacific Lutheran (WA) .... R
Hofstra (NY) .... M	

GROUP II continues next page

ANTHROPOLOGY, continued

GROUP II, continued

Pittsburgh, U. of (PA)........................ L
Rhode Island, U. of L
Ripon (WI) .... R
St. Mary's College of Maryland .... R
Sonoma State (CA) .... M
South Florida, U. of L
Stony Brook (SUNY)(NY) L
▲ Sweet Briar (VA) .... S
Syracuse (NY) L

Texas A&M XL
Towson (MD) L
Tulsa, U. of (OK) .... M
Washington State L
Washington, U. of XL
Western Washington U. .... R
William Paterson (NJ) .... M
Wisconsin, U. of XL
Wisconsin, U. of (Milwaukee) L

GROUP III
Selective

Alaska, U. of (Fairbanks) .... M
Arkansas, U. of L
Ball State (IN) L
California State U. (Fullerton) L
California State U. (Long Beach) L
California State U. (Sacramento) ...... M
Central Washington L
Colorado, U. of (Colorado Springs) . M
Fort Lewis (CO) .... M
Hawaii, U. of L
Humboldt State (CA) .... M
Louisiana State Xl
Massachusetts, U. of (Boston) .... M

Mercyhurst (PA) .... R
Minnesota State U. (Moorhead) .... M
New Mexico State U. L
New Mexico, U. of L
Pittsburgh, U. of (Greensburg) .... R
Plattsburgh (SUNY)(NY) .... M
Potsdam (SUNY)(NY) .... M
Queens (CUNY) (NY) L
Tennessee, U. of XL
Texas State U. (San Marcos) L
Western Connecticut .... M
Wyoming, U. of L

Enrollment Code

■ *Men Only*
▲ *Women Only*

S = Small (less than 1000 students)   R = Moderate (1000-3000 students)   M = Medium (3000-8000 students)
L = Large (8000-20,000 students)   XL = Extra Large (over 20,000 students)

ARCHITECTURE

GROUP I
Most Selective

▲ Barnard (NY) .... R
Buffalo (SUNY) (NY) L
California, U. of (Berkeley) XL
Carnegie Mellon (PA) .... M
Columbia (NY)................................ M
Cooper Union (NY) .... S
Cornell (NY) L
Florida, U. of XL
Georgia Inst. of Tech. L
Illinois Inst. of Tech. .... R
Illinois, U. of (Urbana-Champaign) XL
Lehigh (PA) .... M
Maryland, U. of XL
Miami, U. of (FL)............................ L

Miami U. (OH) L
Michigan, U. of XL
Minnesota, U. of XL
MIT (MA) .... M
New Jersey Inst. of Tech .... M
Notre Dame (IN) .... M
Princeton (NJ) .... M
Rensselaer (NY) .... M
Rice (TX) .... M
Temple (PA) XL
Tulane (LA) .... M
Virginia, U. of L
Washington U. (MO) .... M
Yale (CT) .... M

GROUP II
Very Selective

Arizona State XL
Arizona, U. of................................ XL
Auburn (AL) L
Boston Arch. Center (MA) .... S
California College of Art & Crafts .... S
Cal. Poly. State U. (San Luis Obispo) L
Catholic U. (DC) .... M
Cincinnati, U. of (OH)...................... L
Clemson (SC) L
Detroit Mercy, U. of (MI) .... M
Drexel (PA) .... M
Drury (MO) .... R
Florida International L
Kentucky, U. of L
Houston, U. of (TX)......................... L
Illinois, U. of (Chicago) L
Iowa State XL
Kansas State L
Kansas, U. of L
Kentucky, U. of L
Milwaukee Sch. of Engineering (WI) .... R
Montana State L
Nebraska, U. of.............................. L

North Carolina State L
Northeastern (MA) L
Ohio State XL
Oklahoma, U. of XL
Oklahoma State L
Oregon, U. of L
Parsons (NY) .... R
Pennsylvania State XL
Puerto Rico, U. of L
Rhode Island School of Design (RI) .... R
Southern California, U. of................. L
Syracuse (NY) L
Tennessee, U. of XL
Texas A&M XL
Texas Tech U. L
Texas, U. of (Austin) XL
Utah, U. of................................... L
Virginia Tech................................. L
Washington State L
Washington, U. of........................... XL
West Virginia U. L

Landscape Architecture

Enrollment Code		
■ *Men Only*	S = **Small** (less than 1000 students)	R = **Moderate** (1000-3000 students) M = **Medium** (3000-8000 students)
▲ *Women Only*	L = **Large** (8000-20,000 students)	XL = **Extra Large** (over 20,000 students)

ARCHITECTURE, continued

GROUP III
Selective

Andrews (MI)	R	New York Institute of Tech	M
Arkansas, U. of	L	North Carolina (Charlotte)	L
Cal. Poly. State U. (Pomona)	L	North Dakota State	L
City College (CUNY) (NY)	L	Norwich (VT)	R
Florida A&M	M	Philadelphia U. (PA)	R
Howard (DC)	M	Pratt Inst. (NY)	R
Idaho, U. of	L	Roger Williams (RI)	M
Kent State (OH)	L	Southern Polytechnic (GA)	R
Louisiana-Lafayette	L	Texas, U. of (Arlington)	L
Louisiana State	XL	Texas, U. of (San Antonio)	L
Mississippi State	L	Tuskegee University (AL)	M
Morgan State (MD)	M	Wisconsin, U. of (Milwaukee)	L
Nevada, U. of (Las Vegas)	L	π Woodbury (CA)	S

π *Also, Interior Architecture*

Enrollment Code			
■ *Men Only*	S = Small (less than 1000 students)	R = Moderate (1000-3000 students)	M = Medium (3000-8000 students)
▲ *Women Only*	L = Large (8000-20,000 students)	XL = Extra Large (over 20,000 students)	

ART (STUDIO)

GROUP I
Most Selective

Albany (SUNY)(NY)	L	Macalester (MN)	R
American U. (DC)	M	Michigan, U. of	XL
Bard (NY)	R	Middlebury (VT)	R
Bates (ME)	R	New Jersey, College of	M
Binghamton (SUNY)(NY)	L	New York U.	L
Boston College (MA)	L	Pennsylvania, U. of	L
Boston U. (MA)	L	Pepperdine (CA)	R
Brown (RI)	M	R.I. School of Design	R
▲ Bryn Mawr (PA)	S	Rhodes (TN)	R
Buffalo (SUNY)(NY)	L	Rochester, U. of (NY)	M
Carnegie Mellon (PA)	M	Sarah Lawrence (NY)	R
Centre (KY)	R	▲ Scripps (CA)	S
Chicago, U. of (IL)	M	Skidmore (NY)	R
Colby (ME)	R	▲ Smith (MA)	R
Colgate (NY)	R	Southwestern (TX)	R
Colorado College	R	Stanford (CA)	M
Connecticut College	R	St. Olaf (MN)	R
Cooper Union (NY)	S	Trinity (TX)	R
Cornell (NY)	L	Tulane (LA)	M
Cornish (WA)	S	Vassar (NY)	R
Dallas, U. of (TX)	R	Virginia, U. of	L
Dartmouth (NH)	M	Washington & Lee (VA)	R
DePauw (IN)	R	Washington U. (MO)	M
Drew (NJ)	R	▲ Wellesley (MA)	R
Florida, U. of	XL	Wesleyan (CT)	R
Furman (SC)	R	Wheaton (IL)	R
Harvard (MA)	M	Whitman (WA)	R
Haverford (PA)	S	Williams (MA)	R
Kenyon (OH)	R	Wisconsin, U. of (Madison)	XL
Lafayette (PA)	R	Yale (CT)	M
Lawrence (WI)	R		

Enrollment Code

■ *Men Only* ▲ *Women Only*   S = Small (less than 1000 students)   R = Moderate (1000-3000 students)   M = Medium (3000-8000 students)
L = Large (8000-20,000 students)   XL = Extra Large (over 20,000 students)

ART (STUDIO), continued

GROUP II
Very Selective

▲Agnes Scott (GA)	S	Gordon (MA)	R
Alabama, U. of	L	Guilford (NC)	R
Alaska, U. of (Anchorage)	M	Hamline (MN)	R
Albright (PA)	R	Hobart & William Smith (NY)	R
Alfred (NY)	R	Hofstra (NY)	M
Alma (MI)	R	▲Hollins (VA)	S
Arizona, U. of	XL	Hood (MD)	S
Art Center College of Design (CA)	R	Houghton (NY)	S
Art Institute of Chicago (IL)	R	Houston, U. of (TX)	L
Asbury (KY)	R	Hunter (CUNY) (NY)	L
Auburn (AL)	L	Illinois, U. of (Chicago)	L
Augustana (IL)	R	Indiana (PA)	L
Belmont (TN)	R	Iowa State	XL
Birmingham-Southern (AL)	R	Iowa, U. of	XL
Bowling Green (OH)	L	James Madison (VA)	L
Bradley (IL)	M	Juniata (PA)	R
Brigham Young (UT)	XL	Kansas, U. of	L
Butler (IN)	R	Kansas State	L
California College of Arts & Crafts	S	Knox (IL)	R
California Institute of the Arts	S	Lake Forest (IL)	R
California, U. of (Davis)	XL	Lebanon Valley (PA)	R
California, U. of (Irvine)	L	Lindenwood (MO)	M
California, U. of (Santa Barbara)	L	Longwood (VA)	R
Carroll (WI)	R	Loras (IA)	R
Centenary (LA)	S	Louisville (KY)	L
Cincinnati, U. of (OH)	L	Loyola (IL)	M
Clarke (IA)	S	Loyola (LA)	R
Cleveland Institute of Art (OH)	S	Loyola Marymount (CA)	M
Coastal Carolina (SC)	M	Manhattanville (NY)	S
Coe (IA)	R	Marietta (OH)	R
Colorado State	L	Maryland Institute–College of Art	S
Connecticut, U. of	XL	Maryland, U. of (Baltimore County)	M
▲Converse (SC)	S	Mass. College of Art	R
Cornell (IA)	R	Messiah (PA)	R
Creighton (NE)	M	▲Mills (CA)	S
Dana (NE)	S	Minnesota, U. of (Morris)	R
Delaware, U. of	L	Mississippi State	L
Denison (OH)	R	Missouri, U. of (Kansas City)	M
Denver, U. of (CO)	M	Montana State	L
Drake (IA)	M	Moore College of Art (PA)	S
East Carolina (NC)	L	Moravian (PA)	R
Elmira (NY)	R	Morningside (IA)	S
Florida International	L	Mount Mercy (IA)	S
Florida State	L	Muhlenberg (PA)	R
Fredonia (SUNY)(NY)	M		

GROUP II continues next page

ART (STUDIO), continued

GROUP II, continued

Nazareth (NY)	R	San Diego State (CA)	XL
North Dakota, U. of	M	San Francisco Art Institute (CA)	S
North Texas	L	Sch. of the Art Institute of Chicago	S
Ohio State	XL	Shepherd (WV)	M
Ohio U.	L	Southern Methodist (TX)	M
Oregon, U. of	L	Syracuse (NY)	L
Otis Art Institute (CA)	R	Temple (PA)	L
Pacific, U. of the (CA)	M	Tennessee, U. of	XL
Pacific U. (OR)	R	Tulsa, U. of (OK)	R
Parsons School of Design (NY)	R	Utah, U. of	L
Portland State (OR)	M	Washington & Jefferson (PA)	R
Pratt Institute (NY)	R	Washington, U. of	XL
Principia (IL)	S	▲Wesleyan Col. (GA)	S
Purchase (SUNY)(NY)	R	Western Washington U.	L
Randolph College (VA)	S	Westminster (UT)	R
Redlands, U. of (CA)	R	West Virginia, U. of	L
▲Rosemont (PA)	R	Wheaton (MA)	R
Rowan (NJ)	M	Whitworth (WA)	R
▲St. Mary's College (IN)	R	Wisconsin Lutheran	S
St. Rose (NY)	R	Wisconsin, U. of (Steven's Point)	L
Salisbury State (MD)	M	Wittenberg (OH)	R

Enrollment Code

■ *Men Only* | S = Small (less than 1000 students)   R = Moderate (1000-3000 students)   M = Medium (3000-8000 students)
▲ *Women Only* | L = Large (8000-20,000 students)   XL = Extra Large (over 20,000 students)

ART (STUDIO), continued

GROUP III
Selective

Abilene Christian (TX) .... M	George Fox (OR) .... R
Adrian (MI) .... R	Georgia Southern L
Anna Maria (MA)............................... S	Goucher (MD) .... R
Aquinas (MI) .... R	Grand Valley (MI) L
Arcadia (PA) .... R	Greensboro College (NC) .... S
Arizona State XL	Hastings (NE) .... R
Arts, U. of the (PA)............................. R	Hawaii, U. of L
Ball State (IN) L	Henderson State (AR)........................ M
Belhaven (MS) .... R	Humboldt State (CA) .... M
Berea (WV) .... R	Huntington (IN) .... S
Bloomsburg (PA) .... M	Indiana State L
Boise State (ID) L	Jacksonville (FL) .... R
Brescia (KY) .... S	Johnson State (VT) .... R
Briar Cliff (IA) .... R	Judson (AL) .... S
California College of Arts & Crafts .... S	Kansas City Art institute (MO) .... S
California State U. (Channel Islands) .... R	Kean (NJ) .... M
California State U. (East Bay) .... M	Keene State (NH) .... R
California State U. (Fresno) L	Kent State (OH) L
California State U. (Long Beach) L	Kutztown (PA) .... M
California State U. (Los Angeles) L	Lambuth (TN) .... S
California State U. (Monterey Bay) .... R	Lesley (MA) .... S
California State U. (Northridge) L	Lewis-Clark State (ID) .... R
California State U. (San Bernardino) ...... M	Lock Haven (PA) .... M
California State U. (San Jose) L	Long Island U. (C.W.Post)(NY) .... M
Case Western Reserve (OH)............... M	Louisiana-Lafayette L
Castleton State (VT) .... R	Louisiana State XL
▲Cedar Crest (PA) .... S	Lycoming (PA) .... R
▲Chatham (PA)................................... S	▲Mary Baldwin (VA) .... S
Chowan (NC) .... S	Marymount Manhattan (NY) .... R
Coker (SC) .... S	Maryville (St. Louis) (MO) .... R
Colorado, U. of (Denver) .... M	Marywood (PA)................................. R
Columbia (MO) .... R	Massachusetts, U. of (Dartmouth) .... M
Culver-Stockton (MO)........................ S	Massachusetts, U. of (Lowell) .... M
Dordt (IA) .... R	McPherson (KS) .... S
East Tennessee................................. L	Memphis College of Art (TN)............. S
Eastern Illinois L	Memphis, U. of (TN) L
Edgewood (WI) .... S	▲Meredith (NC)................................. R
Edinboro (PA) .... M	Mercyhurst (PA) .... R
Emmanuel (MA) .... S	Midwestern State U. (TX) .... M
Emporia State (KS) .... M	Millersville (PA) .... M
Endicott (MA) .... R	Millikin (IL) .... R
Fairleigh Dickinson (NJ) .... M	Minnesota, U. of (Duluth) .... M
Fontbonne (MO) .... R	Minnesota State U. (Moorhead)........ M
Fort Hays (KS) .... M	Mississippi College .... R
Fort Lewis (CO) .... M	
Frostburg (MD) .... M	

GROUP III continues next page

ART (STUDIO), continued

••• ———————————— GROUP III, continued ———————————— •••

Missouri Southern State	M
Monmouth (NJ)	R
Montana State (Billings)	R
Montclair State (NJ)	M
Montevallo (AL)	R
Montserrat (MA)	S
Mount St. Joseph (OH)	R
Mount St. Mary's (CA)	R
Murray State (KY)	M
Museum of Fine Arts, School of (MA)	R
Nebraska, U. of (Kearney)	M
Nevada, U. of (Las Vegas)	L
New Mexico, U. of	L
Nicholls State (LA)	M
North Carolina (Asheville)	R
North Carolina (Greensboro)	M
North Carolina, U. of (Pembroke)	R
Northern Illinois U.	L
Northern Iowa	L
Northern Michigan	M
Northwestern (MN)	R
Old Dominion (VA)	L
Otterbein (OH)	R
Ozarks, College of the (MO)	R
Pennsylvania Acad. of the Fine Arts	S
▲ Pine Manor (MA)	S
Plattsburgh (SUNY)(NY)	M
Plymouth State (NH)	M
Potsdam (SUNY)(NY)	M
Roanoke (VA)	R
Rockford (IL)	S
Rocky Mountain (MT)	S
St. Edward's (TX)	M
St. Francis (IN)	R
▲ Salem College (NC)	S
Salem State (MA)	M
Santa Fe, College of (NM)	S
▲ Seton Hill (PA)	S
Shawnee State (OH)	R
Siena Heights (MI)	S
South Dakota, U. of	M
Southern Maine	M
Southern Oregon State U.	M
Texas A&M (Corpus Christi)	M
Texas Tech. U.	L
Texas, U. of (El Paso)	L
Texas, U. of (San Antonio)	L
Towson (MD)	L
Union University (TN)	R
Virginia Commonwealth U.	L
Visual Arts, School of (NY)	R
Wayne State (MI)	L
Weber State (UT)	L
West Chester (PA)	M
West Virginia Wesleyan	R
Western Connecticut	M
Western Michigan	L
Wingate (NC)	R
Winthrop (SC)	M
Wisconsin, U. of (Green Bay)	M
Wisconsin, U. of (Superior)	M
Youngstown State (OH)	L

ART HISTORY

GROUP I
Most Selective

Albany (SUNY)(NY) L	Northwestern (IL) .... M
▲Barnard (NY) .... R	Oberlin (OH) .... R
Binghamton (SUNY)(NY) L	Pennsylvania, U. of L
Boston U. (MA) L	Pittsburgh, U. of (PA) L
Bowdoin (ME) .... R	Pomona (CA) .... R
Brown (RI) .... M	Princeton (NJ) .... M
▲Bryn Mawr (PA) .... S	Reed (OR) .... R
California, U. of (Los Angeles) XL	Rochester, U. of (NY) .... M
Case Western Reserve U. (OH) .... M	Rutgers (NJ) L
Chicago, U. of (IL) .... M	Sarah Lawrence (NY) .... R
Colgate (NY) .... R	▲Scripps (CA) .... S
Colorado College .... R	Skidmore (NY) .... R
Columbia (NY) .... M	▲Smith (MA) .... R
Connecticut College .... R	Stanford (CA) .... M
Cornell (NY) L	Swarthmore (PA) .... R
Emory (GA) .... M	Syracuse (NY) L
Georgetown (DC) .... M	Trinity (CT) .... R
George Washington (DC) .... M	Trinity (TX) .... R
Harvard (MA) .... M	Vanderbilt (TN) .... M
Johns Hopkins (MD) .... M	Vassar (NY) .... R
Lawrence (WI) .... R	Washington U. (MO) .... M
Michigan, U. of XL	▲Wellesley (MA) .... R
Middlebury (VT) .... R	Willamette (OR) .... R
▲Mount Holyoke (MA) .... R	Williams (MA) .... R
New York U. L	Wisconsin, U. of XL
North Carolina, U. of L	Yale (CT) .... M

GROUP II
Very Selective

California State U. (Northridge) L	Lebanon Valley (PA) .... R
California, U. of (Riverside) L	Manhattanville (NY) .... S
California, U. of (Santa Barbara) L	Massachusetts, U. of (Lowell) .... M
California, U. of (Santa Cruz) .... M	McDaniel (MD) .... R
City College (CUNY)(NY) L	▲Mills (CA) .... S
Clarke (IA) .... S	Moore College of Art (PA) .... S
College of Charleston (SC) L	Minnesota, U. of XL
Colorado State L	Missouri, U. of XL
Columbia College (IL) .... M	Missouri, U. of (Kansas City) .... M
Delaware, U. of L	New Paltz (SUNY)(NY) .... M
Denison (OH) .... R	Oakland (MI) .... M
Denver, U. of (CO) .... M	Oregon, U. of L
East Carolina L	Queens (CUNY)(NY) L
Eastern Connecticut .... M	▲Rosemont (PA) .... S
Edinboro (PA) .... M	▲Salem College (NC) .... S
Florida State L	San Diego State U. (CA) XL
George Mason (VA) L	Sonoma State (CA) .... M
Georgia, U. of XL	Southern Methodist (TX) .... M
▲Hollins (VA) .... S	Stony Brook (SUNY)(NY) L
Hunter (CUNY) (NY) L	▲Sweet Briar (VA) .... S
Illinois, U. of (Chicago) L	Utah, U. of L
Indiana (PA) L	Washington, U. of XL
Juniata (PA) .... R	Wayne State (MI) L
Kansas, U. of L	Wheaton (MA) .... R
Lake Forest (IL) .... R	Wooster (OH) .... R

ASTRONOMY

GROUP I
Most Selective

Amherst (MA) .... R	▲ Mount Holyoke (MA) .... R
Boston U. L	Northwestern (IL) .... M
Brigham Young (UT) XL	Pennsylvania, U. of L
▲ Bryn Mawr (PA) .... S	Pennsylvania State XL
California Inst. of Tech. .... S	Union (NY) .... R
Case Western Reserve U. (OH) .... M	Vassar (NY) .... R
Cornell (NY) L	Villanova (PA) .... M
# Franklin & Marshall (PA) .... R	Virginia, U. of L
Harvard (MA) .... M	▲ Wellesley (MA) .... R
Haverford (PA) .... S	Wesleyan (CT) .... R
Illinois, U. of (Urbana-Champaign) XL	Whitman (WA) .... R
Michigan, U. of XL	Williams (MA) .... R
MIT (MA) .... M	Wisconsin, U. of XL

GROUP II
Very Selective

Arizona, U. of XL	Minnesota, U. of XL
Colorado, U. of L	Minnesota State U. (Mankato) L
Drake (IA) .... M	North Carolina State L
Earlham (IN) .... R	Ohio State U. XL
Florida Inst. of Tech. .... R	Oklahoma, U. of XL
Florida, U. of XL	Pittsburgh, U. of (PA) L
Georgia, U. of XL	San Diego State XL
Hawaii, U. of L	San Francisco State U. L
Indiana U. XL	Southern California L
Iowa, U. of XL	Stony Brook (SUNY) (NY) L
Kansas, U. of L	Texas, U. of (Austin) XL
Maryland, U. of XL	Washington, U. of XL
Massachusetts, U. of L	Wheaton (MA) .... R

GROUP III
Selective

Benedictine (KS) .... R	Nebraska, U. of L
Georgia State L	Northern Arizona XL
Louisiana State XL	Western Connecticut .... M
Lycoming (PA) .... R	Wisconsin, U. of (La Crosse) L
Montana, U. of .... M	Wyoming, U. of L

 # Also Astrophysics

Enrollment Code		
■ *Men Only*	S = **Small** (less than 1000 students)	R = **Moderate** (1000-3000 students)	M = **Medium** (3000-8000 students)
▲ *Women Only*	L = **Large** (8000-20,000 students)	XL = **Extra Large** (over 20,000 students)

BIOCHEMISTRY (Molecular Biology)

GROUP I
Most Selective

▲Barnard (NY)	R	Harvard (MA)	M
Binghamton (SUNY) (NY)	L	Iowa, U. of	XL
Bowdoin (ME)	R	Kenyon (OH)	M
Brandeis (MA)	R	Lehigh (PA)	M
Brown (RI)	M	Miami, U. of (FL)	L
California, U. of (Berkeley)	XL	Minnesota, U. of	XL
California, U. of (Los Angeles)	XL	MIT (MA)	M
California, U. of (San Diego)	L	▲Mount Holyoke (MA)	R
Case Western Reserve (OH)	M	Pennsylvania, U. of	L
Chicago, U. of (IL)	M	Princeton (NJ)	M
Clarkson (NY)	M	Rice (TX)	M
Columbia (NY)	M	Rutgers (NJ)	L
Connecticut College	R	Rochester, U. of (NY)	M
Cornell (NY)	L	Swarthmore (PA)	R
Dallas, U. of (TX)	R	Tulane (LA)	M
DePauw (IL)	R	Union (NY)	R
Geneseo (SUNY) (NY)	M	Virginia, U. of	L
Georgetown (DC)	M	Worcester Poly Inst. (MA)	R
Georgia, U. of	XL	Yale (CT)	M

GROUP II
Very Selective

Albright (PA)	R	Missouri, U. of	XL
Arizona State	XL	Monmouth (IL)	S
Austin (TX)	R	Moravian (PA)	R
Beloit (WI)	R	Muhlenberg (PA)	R
Bethel (MN)	M	Nebraska, U. of	L
California Poly State U. (San Luis Obispo)	L	Ohio State	XL
California, U. of (Davis)	XL	Oklahoma State	L
California, U. of (Riverside)	L	Pennsylvania State	XL
Centre (KY)	R	Pittsburgh, U. of (PA)	L
Clark (MA)	R	Purdue (IN)	XL
Colorado, U. of	L	Ramapo (NJ)	M
Connecticut, U. of	XL	Regis (CO)	R
Denison (OH)	R	Ripon (WI)	R
Florida Inst. of Tech.	R	Sciences, U. of the (PA)	S
Ithaca (NY)	M	Siena (NY)	R
Kansas State	L	Skidmore (NY)	R
Knox (IL)	R	St. Andrews Presbyterian (NC)	S
Lewis & Clark (OR)	R	Stony Brook (SUNY) (NY)	L
Louisiana State	XL	Susquehanna (PA)	R
Maine, U. of	L	Virginia Tech.	L
McDaniel (MD)	R	Washington State	L
Michigan State	XL	Washington, U. of	XL
Mississippi State	L	Wisconsin, U. of	XL

GROUP III
Selective

California State U. (Fullerton)	L	Ohio Northern	R
Framingham (MA)	M	Oregon State	L
Indiana (PA)	L	Regis (MA)	S
Misericordia, College (PA)	S	Sacred Heart (CT)	R
Nevada, U. of (Reno)	L	Temple (PA)	L
Northern Illinois U.	L		

BIOLOGY

GROUP I
Most Selective

Albany (SUNY) (NY)	L	Haverford (PA)	S
Amherst (MA)	R	Holy Cross (MA)	R
Austin (TX)	R	Illinois Wesleyan	R
▲ Barnard (NY)	R	Iowa State	XL
Bates (ME)	R	Johns Hopkins (MD)	M
Binghampton (SUNY)(NY)	L	Kalamazoo (MI)	R
Boston College (MA)	L	Kenyon (OH)	R
Boston University (MA)	L	Lafayette (PA)	R
Bowdoin (ME)	R	Lawrence (WI)	R
Brandeis (MA)	R	Lehigh (PA)	M
Brown (RI)	M	Macalester (MN)	R
▲ Bryn Mawr (PA)	S	Miami, U. of (FL)	L
Bucknell (PA)	R	Middlebury (VT)	R
Buffalo (SUNY)(NY)	L	Minnesota, U. of (Morris)	R
California Inst. of Tech.	S	Missouri, U. of (Rolla)	M
California, U. of (Berkeley)	XL	MIT (MA)	M
California, U. of (Los Angeles)	XL	▲ Mount Holyoke (MA)	R
California, U. of (San Diego)	L	New College (FL)	S
Carleton (MN)	R	North Carolina, U. of	L
Case Western Reserve (OH)	M	Notre Dame (IN)	M
Centre (KY)	R	Oberlin (OH)	R
Chicago, U. of (IL)	M	Occidental (CA)	R
Claremont McKenna (CA)	R	Pepperdine (CA)	R
Clarkson (NY)	M	Pitzer (CA)	S
Colby (ME)	R	Pomona (CA)	R
Colgate (NY)	R	Princeton (NJ)	M
Colorado Col.	R	Providence (RI)	M
Columbia (NY)	M	Reed (OR)	R
Connecticut College	R	Rennselaer (NY)	M
Cornell (NY)	L	Rhodes (TN)	R
Dallas, U. of (TX)	R	Rice (TX)	R
Dartmouth (NH)	M	Richmond, U. of (VA)	R
Davidson (NC)	R	Rochester, U. of (NY)	M
DePauw (IN)	R	Rutgers (NJ)	L
Dickinson (PA)	R	Skidmore (NY)	R
Duke (NC)	M	▲ Smith (MA)	R
Emory (GA)	M	South, U. of the (TN)	R
Franklin & Marshall (PA)	R	Southwestern (TX)	R
Furman (SC)	R	Stanford (CA)	M
Geneseo (SUNY) (NY)	M	St. Mary's Col. of Maryland	R
Georgetown (DC)	M	St. Olaf (MN)	R
Gettysburg (PA)	R	Swarthmore (PA)	R
Grinnell (IA)	R	Trinity (CT)	R
Hamilton (NY)	R	Trinity (TX)	R
Harvard (MA)	M		
Harvey Mudd (CA)	S		

GROUP I continues next page

BIOLOGY, continued

● GROUP I, continued ●

Tufts (MA)	M
Tulane (LA)	M
Union (NY)	R
Ursinus (PA)	R
Vanderbilt (TN)	M
Vassar (NY)	R
Vermont, U. of	L
Villanova (PA)	M
Virginia, U. of	L
■ Wabash (IN)	S
Wake Forest (NC)	M
Washington & Lee (VA)	M

Washington U. (MO)	M
▲ Wellesley (MA)	R
Wesleyan (CT)	R
Wheaton (IL)	R
Whitman (WA)	R
Willamette (OR)	R
William & Mary (VA)	M
Williams (MA)	R
Worcester Poly Inst. (MA)	R
Yale (CT)	M
Yeshiva (NY)	R

●● GROUP II ●●
Very Selective

▲ Agnes Scott (GA)	S
Albertson (ID)	S
Albright (PA)	R
Allegheny (PA)	R
Alfred (NY)	R
Alma (MI)	R
Arizona State	XL
Arizona, U. of	XL
Augustana (IL)	R
Augustana (SD)	R
Belmont (TN)	R
Beloit (WI)	R
Benedictine (IL)	R
Berry (GA)	R
# Bethel (IN)	R
Bethel (MN)	M
Birmingham-Southern (AL)	R
Cal. Poly. State U. (San Luis Obispo)	L
California State U. (Chico)	L
California, U. of (Davis)	XL
California, U. of (Irvine)	L
California, U. of (Merced)	R
California, U. of (Riverside)	L
California, U. of (Santa Barbara)	L
California, U. of (Santa Cruz)	M
Canisius (NY)	M
Centenary (LA)	S

Central (IA)	R
Clark (MA)	R
Clarke (IA)	S
Clemson (SC)	L
Coe (IA)	R
Colorado, U. of	L
Columbia College (SC)	R
Concordia (MN)	R
Connecticut, U. of	XL
Cornell Col. (IA)	R
Creighton (NE)	M
Delaware, U. of	L
Denison (OH)	R
Denver, U. of (CO)	M
Drake (IA)	M
Drury (MO)	R
Duquesne (PA)	M
Earlham (IN)	R
Eckerd (FL)	R
Elizabethtown (PA)	R
Elon (NC)	R
Erskine (SC)	S
Evansville (IN)	R
Fairfield (CT)	M
Florida Inst. of Tech	R

*Also Environmental Biology*

GROUP II continues next page

Enrollment Code

■ *Men Only*	S = Small (less than 1000 students) R = Moderate (1000-3000 students) M = Medium (3000-8000 students)
▲ *Women Only*	L = Large (8000-20,000 students) XL = Extra Large (over 20,000 students)

BIOLOGY, continued

GROUP II, continued

Florida International	L
Florida Southern	R
Gannon (PA)	M
Georgetown (KY)	R
Georgia State	L
Georgia, U. of	XL
Gonzaga (WA)	R
Gordon (MA)	R
Grand Valley (MI)	L
Grove City (PA)	R
Guilford (NC)	R
Gustavus Adolphus (MN)	R
Hamline (MN)	R
■ Hampden-Sydney (VA)	S
Hampton (VA)	M
π Harrisburg U. (PA)	S
Hendrix (AR)	R
Hillsdale (MI)	R
Hiram (OH)	R
Hobart & William Smith (NY)	R
Hood (MD)	S
Hope (MI)	R
Houghton (NY)	S
Houston, U. of (TX)	L
Hunter (CUNY)(NY)	L
Illinois College	S
Illinois, U. of (Chicago)	L
Indiana (PA)	L
Indiana U.	XL
Ithaca (NY)	M
Juniata (PA)	R
Kansas State	L
Kansas, U. of	L
Kentucky, U.of	L
King's (PA)	R
Knox (IL)	R
Lake Forest (IL)	S
LeMoyne (NY)	R
Lewis & Clark (OR)	R
Lipscomb (TN)	R
Linfield (OR)	R
Loras (IA)	R

Loyola (IL)	M
Loyola (LA)	R
Loyola (MD)	R
Luther (IA)	R
Marist (NY)	M
Marquette (WI)	M
Mary Washington (VA)	M
Maryville U. - St. Louis (MO)	R
McDaniel (MD)	R
McKendree (IL)	R
Merrimack (MA)	R
Messiah (PA)	R
Michigan State	XL
Millersville (PA)	M
Millsaps (MS)	S
Minnesota, U. of (Duluth)	M
Minnesota State U. (Moorhead)	M
Missouri, U. of (Kansas City)	M
Mobile, U. of (AL)	R
Monmouth (IL)	S
Montana Tech.	R
Morningside (IA)	S
Mount Mercy (IA)	S
Muhlenberg (PA)	R
Murray State (KY)	M
Nazareth (NY)	R
Nebraska Wesleyan	R
New Hampshire, U. of	L
New Mexico State	L
New Mexico, U. of	L
North Carolina, U. of (Wilmington)	L
North Central (IL)	R
North Dakota, U. of	M
Oglethorpe (GA)	R
Ohio Northern	R
Ohio Wesleyan	R
Oklahoma Christian	R
Oklahoma City U.	R
Oklahoma, U. of	L
Oregon, U. of	L

π *Biotechnology and Biosciences*

GROUP II continues next page

BIOLOGY, continued

GROUP II, continued

Oswego (SUNY)(NY)	M
Pacific Lutheran (WA)	R
Pacific University (OR)	R
Presbyterian (SC)	R
Puget Sound (WA)	R
Randolph College (VA)	S
Randolph-Macon (VA)	R
Rhode Island, U. of	L
Ripon (WI)	R
Roanoke (VA)	R
Rochester Inst. of Tech. (NY)	L
Rowan (NJ)	M
Salisbury State (MD)	M
Sciences in Philadelphia (PA)	R
Scranton, U. of (PA)	M
▲ Scripps (CA)	S
Seattle Pacific (WA)	R
Siena (NY)	R
Spring Hill (AL)	R
St. John's (MN)	R
St. Louis (MO)	M
St. Michael's (VT)	R
St. Norbert (WI)	R
St. Scholastica (MN)	R
Stonehill (MA)	R
Stony Brook (SUNY) (NY)	L
Susquehanna (PA)	R
Texas, U. of (Austin)	XL

Texas Christian	M
Transylvania (KY)	S
Truman State (MO)	M
Tulsa, U. of (OK)	R
Utah, U. of	L
Valparaiso U. (TN)	M
Virginia Tech.	L
Washington, U. of	XL
Washington & Jefferson (PA)	R
Washington College (MD)	S
Wells (NY)	S
West Chester (PA)	M
West Florida, U. of	M
Westminster (MO)	S
Westminster (PA)	R
Westminster (UT)	R
Westmont (CA)	R
West Virginia U.	L
Wheaton (MA)	R
William Jewell (MO)	R
Winona State U. (MN)	M
Winthrop (SC)	M
Wisconsin, U. of (Milwaukee)	L
Wisconsin, U. of (Stevens Point)	M
Wittenberg (OH)	R
Wofford (SC)	R
Wooster (OH)	R
Xavier (OH)	R

BIOLOGY continues next page

Enrollment Code		
■ *Men Only*	S = Small (less than 1000 students)	R = Moderate (1000-3000 students)	M = Medium (3000-8000 students)
▲ *Women Only*	L = Large (8000-20,000 students)	XL = Extra Large (over 20,000 students)	

BIOLOGY, continued

GROUP III
Selective

Alaska, U. of (Fairbanks)	M
▲Alverno (WI)	R
Arcadia (PA)	R
Aquinas (MI)	R
Azusa Pacific (CA)	R
Baker (KS)	R
Ball State (IN)	L
Barry (FL)	R
Berea (KY)	R
Bethany (WV)	S
Blackburn (IL)	S
Briar Cliff (IA)	R
Brooklyn (CUNY)(NY)	L
California Poly State U. (Pomona)	L
California State U. (Channel Islands)	R
California State U. (Monterey Bay)	R
Carroll (MT)	R
▲Cedar Crest (PA)	S
Central Michigan	L
Colby-Sawyer (NH)	S
College of Charleston (SC)	L
Colorado, U. of (Denver)	M
Daemen (NY)	R
Delaware Valley (PA)	R
DeSales (PA)	S
Dillard (LA)	R
Doane (NE)	S
D'Youville (NY)	R
East Stroudsburg (PA)	M
East Tennessee	L
Eastern Connecticut	M
Eastern Oregon	R
Elmhurst (IL)	R
Emmanuel (MA)	S
Findlay (OH)	M
Fitchburg (MA)	R
Fort Lewis (CO)	M
Framingham (MA)	M
George Fox (OR)	R
Gwynedd-Mercy (PA)	S
Hardin-Simmons (TX)	R
Heidelberg (OH)	S
Holy Names (CA)	S
Houston Baptist (TX)	R
# Humboldt State (CA)	M
Immaculata (PA)	S
Jacksonville (FL)	R
Jacksonville State (AL)	M
Kentucky Wesleyan	S
Lambuth (TN)	S
Lewis-Clark State (ID)	R
Lock Haven (PA)	M
Long Island U. (C.W. Post)(NY)	R
Louisiana - Lafayette	L
Lycoming (PA)	R
Lynchburg (VA)	R
Lyndon State (VT)	R
Maryville (TN)	S
Memphis, U. of (TN)	L
▲Meredith (NC)	R
Middle Tennessee	L
Millersville (PA)	M
Milligan (TN)	S
Misericordia, College (PA)	S
Missouri Southern State	M
Morgan State (MD)	M
Mount St. Joseph (OH)	R
Mount St. Mary's (CA)	R
Nicholls State (LA)	M
North Carolina (Pembroke)	R
North Georgia	M
Northern Illinois U.	L
Northern Michigan	M
Northland (WI)	S
Northwestern (IA)	R
▲Pine Manor (MA)	S
Pittsburgh, U. of (Bradford)	S
Point Park (PA)	R
Puerto Rico (Cayey), U. of	M
Reinhardt (GA)	R
Rhode Island College	M
Rider (NJ)	R
Rockford (IL)	S
Rocky Mountain (MT)	S
Roger Williams (RI)	M
St. Francis (PA)	R

*Especially Fisheries Biology*

GROUP III continues next page

BIOLOGY, continued

GROUP III, continued

Shippensburg (PA)	M	Utah State	L
South Alabama	M	Virginia Wesleyan	R
South Dakota, U. of	M	Wartburg (IA)	R
Southern Oregon State U.	M	Wayne State (MI)	L
▲Spelman (GA)	R	Western Colorado	R
Saint Scholastica (MN)	R	Western Kentucky	L
St. Vincent (PA)	R	West Chester (PA)	M
Temple (PA)	L	West Virginia Wesleyan	R
Texas A&M (Corpus Christi)	M	Wheeling Jesuit (WV)	R
Texas Lutheran	R	Wilkes (PA)	R
Texas, U. of (Arlington)	L	Wisconsin, U. of (Eau Claire)	L
Texas, U. of (San Antonio)	L	Wisconsin, U. of (Platteville)	M
Texas State U. (San Marcos)	L	Wyoming, U. of	L
Thomas More (KY)	R	Xavier University of Louisiana	R
Tougaloo (MS)	S		

BOTANY / PLANT SCIENCE

GROUP I
Most Selective

California, U. of (Berkeley)	XL	Florida, U. of	XL
Connecticut College	R	Miami U. (OH)	L
Cornell (NY)	L	Michigan, U. of	XL
Duke (NC)	M	North Carolina, U. of	L

GROUP II
Very Selective

California, U. of (Davis)	XL	Ohio Wesleyan	R
California, U. of (Riverside)	L	Oklahoma, U. of	XL
Connecticut, U. of	XL	Oklahoma State	L
Delaware, U. of	L	Pennsylvania State	XL
Maine, U. of	L	Purdue (IN)	XL
Maryland, U. of	L	Tennessee, U. of	L
Michigan State	XL	Texas, U. of (Austin)	XL
Montana, U. of	M	Vermont, U. of	L
North Carolina State	L	Washington, U. of	XL
Ohio U.	L	Wisconsin, U. of	XL

GROUP III
Selective

Alabama, U. of	L	Louisiana State	XL
Ball State (IN)	L	Northern Arizona	XL
Colorado State	L	Oregon State	L
Eastern Connecticut	M	Southeastern Oklahoma State	M
Eastern Illinois	L	Southern Illinois U. (Carbondale)	L
Hawaii, U. of	L	Wyoming, U. of	L
Humboldt State (CA)	M		

Enrollment Code	
■ *Men Only*	S = Small (less than 1000 students) R = Moderate (1000-3000 students) M = Medium (3000-8000 students)
▲ *Women Only*	L = Large (8000-20,000 students) XL = Extra Large (over 20,000 students)

BUSINESS ADMINISTRATION

GROUP I
Most Selective

Albany (SUNY) (NY)	L	Michigan, U. of	XL
American (DC)	M	Missouri, U. of	XL
Babson (MA)	R	MIT (MA)	M
Binghamton (SUNY) (NY)	L	Muhlenberg (PA)	R
Boston College (MA)	L	New Jersey, College of	M
Boston U. (MA)	L	New York U.	L
Bucknell (PA)	R	North Carolina, U. of	L
Buffalo (SUNY) (NY)	L	Notre Dame (IN)	M
California, U. of (Berkeley)	XL	Ohio State	XL
California, U. of (Los Angeles)	XL	Pennsylvania, U. of	L
Carnegie Mellon (PA)	M	Rensselaer (NY)	M
Case Western Reserve U. (OH)	M	Rhodes (TN)	R
Claremont McKenna (CA)	R	Richmond, U. of (VA)	R
Clarkson (NY)	M	Rutgers (NJ)	L
Cornell (NY)	L	Santa Clara U. (CA)	M
Emory (GA)	M	Southern California, U. of	L
Fairfield (CT)	R	Southwestern (TX)	R
Florida, U. of	XL	Syracuse (NY)	L
Florida State	L	Trinity (TX)	R
Franklin & Marshall (PA)	R	Tulane (LA)	M
Furman (SC)	R	U.S. Air Force Academy (CO)	M
Geneseo (SUNY) (NY)	M	Vermont, U. of	L
Georgetown (DC)	M	Villanova (PA)	M
George Washington (DC)	M	Virginia Poly. Institute	L
Georgia Inst. of Tech	L	Virginia, U. of	L
Gettysburg (PA)	R	Wake Forest (NC)	M
Gustavus Adolphus (MN)	R	Washington U. (MO)	M
Illinois, U. of (Urbana-Champaign)	XL	Washington & Lee (VA)	M
Indiana U.	XL	William & Mary (VA)	M
Lafayette (PA)	R	Wisconsin, U. of	XL
Lehigh (PA)	M	Worcester Poly Inst. (MA)	R
Miami, U. of (FL)	L	Yeshiva (NY)	R
Miami U. (OH)	L		

GROUP II
Very Selective

Adrian (MI)	R	Arizona, U. of	XL
▲ Agnes Scott (GA)	S	Arizona State	XL
Alabama, U. of	L	Asbury (KY)	R
Alabama, U. of (Huntsville)	M	Auburn (AL)	L
Alaska Pacific	S	Augsburg (MN)	R
Albertson (ID)	S	Augustana (IL)	R
Albright (PA)	R	Austin (TX)	R
Alfred (NY)	R		
Alma (MI)	R		

GROUP II continues next page

BUSINESS ADMINISTRATION, continued

GROUP II, continued

Baylor (TX)	M	Evansville (IN)	R
Belmont (TN)	R	Flagler (FL)	R
Bentley (MA)	M	Florida Atlantic	L
Berry (GA)	R	Florida Gulf Coast U.	M
Birmingham Southern (AL)	R	Florida Inst. of Tech.	R
Bowling Green (OH)	L	Florida International	M
Bradley (IL)	M	Fordham (NY)	L
Brigham Young (UT)	XL	Fredonia (SUNY) (NY)	M
Bryant (RI)	R	George Mason (VA)	L
Buena Vista (IA)	R	Georgetown College (KY)	R
Butler (IN)	R	Gonzaga (WA)	R
Cal. Poly. State U. (San Luis Obispo)	L	Goucher (MD)	S
California State (Fullerton)	L	Grove City (PA)	R
California, U. of (Riverside)	L	Guilford (NC)	R
California, U. of (Santa Barbara)	L	Hampton (VA)	M
Capital U. (OH)	R	Hanover (IN)	R
Centenary (LA)	S	Harding (AR)	M
Central Florida, U. of	XL	Hendrix (AR)	R
Charleston, College of (SC)	L	Hillsdale (MI)	R
Christian Brothers (TN)	R	Hofstra (NY)	M
Cincinnati, U. of (OH)	L	Hood (MD)	S
Clark (MA)	R	Houston, U. of (TX)	L
Clemson (SC)	L	Howard (DC)	M
Coe (IA)	R	Idaho, U. of	L
Colorado, U. of	L	Illinois College	S
Colorado, U. of (Col. Springs)	M	Illinois, U. of (Chicago)	L
Columbia College (SC)	R	Illinois, U. of (Springfield)	R
Concordia (MN)	R	Indiana U. of Pennsylvania	L
Connecticut, U. of	XL	Indiana Wesleyan	M
Creighton (NE)	M	Iowa State	XL
Dayton, U. of (OH)	M	Iowa, U. of	XL
Delaware, U. of	L	Ithaca (NY)	M
Denver, U. of (CO)	M	James Madison (VA)	M
DePaul (IL)	L	John Carroll (OH)	M
Dominican (IL)	S	▲ Judson (AL)	S
Drake (IA)	M	Juniata (PA)	R
Dubuque, U. of (IA)	S	Kansas, U. of	L
Duquesne (PA)	M	Kansas State	L
Eastern Michigan	L	Kansas Wesleyan	S
Eckerd (FL)	R	Kentucky, U. of	L
Elizabethtown (PA)	R	LaSalle (PA)	M
Elon (NC)	R		
Erskine (SC)	S		

GROUP II continues next page

BUSINESS ADMINISTRATION, continued

GROUP II, continued

Lebanon Valley (PA) .... R	North Carolina, U. of (Greensboro) ...... M
LeMoyne (NY) .... R	North Carolina, U. of (Wilmington L
LeTourneau (TX) .... R	North Dakota, U. of .... M
Lewis & Clark (OR) .... R	Northeastern (MA) L
Lindenwood (MO) .... M	Northwestern (MN) .... R
Lipscomb (TN) .... R	Northern Arizona XL
Longwood (VA) .... R	North Florida .... M
Loras (IA) .... R	Oglethorpe (GA) .... R
Loyola (MD) .... R	Ohio U. L
Loyola (LA) .... R	Oklahoma City U. (OK) .... R
Loyola Marymount (CA) .... M	Oklahoma State L
Luther (IA) .... R	Oklahoma, U. of XL
Manhattan (NY) .... M	Old Dominion (VA) L
Manhattanville (NY) .... R	Oregon, U. of L
Marietta (OH) .... R	Oswego (SUNY) (NY) .... M
Marist (NY) .... M	Pacific Lutheran (WA) .... R
Marquette (WI) .... M	Pacific, U. of the (CA) .... M
Maryland, U. of XL	Pacific University (OR) .... R
Mary Washington (VA) .... M	Palm Beach Atlantic (FL) .... R
Massachusetts, U. of L	Pennsylvania State XL
Massachusetts, U. of (Lowell) .... M	Pepperdine (CA) .... R
Master's (CA) .... R	Pittsburgh, U. of (PA) L
McDaniel (MD) .... R	Plattsburgh (SUNY) (NY) .... M
Messiah (PA) .... R	Portland State (OR) L
Michigan, U. of (Dearborn) .... M	Portland, U. of (OR) .... R
Michigan State XL	Presbyterian (SC) .... R
Michigan Tech .... M	Principia (IL) .... S
Millersville (PA) .... M	Providence (RI) .... M
Millsaps (MS) .... S	Puerto Rico, U. of L
Milwaukee School of Engineering (WI) ... R	Puget Sound (WA) .... R
Minnesota, U. of XL	Purdue (IN) XL
Mississippi College .... R	Queens (NC) .... R
Mississippi, U. of L	Ramapo (NJ) .... M
Mississippi U. for Women .... R	Randolph-Macon (VA) .... R
Missouri, U. of (Kansas City) .... M	Redlands, U. of (CA) .... R
Missouri, U. of (St. Louis) .... M	Richard Stockton (NJ) .... M
Mobile, U. of (AL) .... R	Ripon (WI) .... R
Monmouth (IL) .... S	Roanoke (VA) .... R
Moravian (PA) .... R	Rochester Inst. of Tech (NY) L
Morningside (IA) .... S	Rockhurst (MO) .... R
Nazareth (NY) .... R	Rowan (NJ) .... M
New Hampshire, U. of L	Rutgers-Newark (NJ) .... M
Newman University (KS) .... S	Salem College (NC) .... S
New Mexico, U. of L	Samford (AL) .... R
New Mexico State L	
New Paltz (SUNY)(NY) .... M	

GROUP II continues next page

BUSINESS ADMINISTRATION, continued

GROUP II, continued

San Diego State U. (CA)	XL
San Diego, U. of (CA)	M
San Francisco, U. of (CA)	M
Sciences, U. of the (PA)	S
Scranton, U. of (PA)	M
Seton Hall (NJ)	M
Shaw (NC)	R
Shepherd (WV)	M
Siena (NY)	R
▲Simmons (MA)	R
Skidmore (NY)	R
Southern Methodist (TX)	M
Spring Hill (AL)	R
St. Bonaventure (NY)	R
▲St. Catherine (MN)	R
St. John's (MN)	R
St. Joseph's U. (PA)	R
St. Louis U. (MO)	M
St. Mary's Col. of CA	R
▲St. Mary's Col. (IN)	R
St. Mary's Col. (MN)	R
St. Michael's Col. (VT)	R
St. Norbert (WI)	R
# St. Scholastica (MN)	R
Southern Oregon State U.	M
Stetson (FL)	R
Stonehill (MA)	R
Susquehanna U. (PA)	R
Temple (PA)	L
Texas A&M	XL
Texas A&M at Galveston	S
Texas Christian	M

Texas Tech U.	L
Texas, U. of (Austin)	XL
Texas, U. of (Dallas)	M
Transylvania (KY)	S
▲Trinity (DC)	S
Truman State (MO)	M
Tulsa, U. of (OK)	R
Ursinus (PA)	R
Utah, U. of	L
Valparaiso (IN)	M
Virginia Tech.	R
Wartburg (IA)	R
Washington College (MD)	S
Washington State	L
Washington, U. of	XL
Wells (NY)	S
▲Wesleyan College (GA)	S
Western Michigan	L
Westminster (MO)	S
Westminster (UT)	R
West Virginia U.	L
Whitworth (WA)	R
Wilberforce (OH)	S
William Jewell Col. (MO)	R
Winona State U. (MN)	M
Wisconsin, U. of (Milwaukee)	L
Wisconsin, U. of (Stevens Point)	M
Wittenberg (OH)	R
Wofford (SC)	R
Wyoming, U. of	L
Xavier (OH)	R

 # Also, Organizational Behavior and Marketing

Enrollment Code

■ *Men Only*   S = Small (less than 1000 students)   R = Moderate (1000-3000 students)   M = Medium (3000-8000 students)
▲ *Women Only*   L = Large (8000-20,000 students)   XL = Extra Large (over 20,000 students)

BUSINESS ADMINISTRATION, continued

GROUP III
Selective

Abilene Christian (TX)	M
Akron, U. of (OH)	L
Alabama, U. of (Birmingham)	M
Alaska, U. of (Anchorage)	M
Alaska, U. of (Fairbanks)	M
Alderson-Broaddus (WV)	S
▲ Alverno (WI)	R
American International (MA)	R
Anna Maria (MA)	S
Appalachian State (NC)	L
Aquinas (MI)	R
Arkansas, U. of	L
Ashland (OH)	R
Assumption (MA)	R
Averett (VA)	S
Avila (MO)	S
Azusa Pacific (CA)	R
Baker (KS)	R
Baldwin-Wallace (OH)	R
Barry (FL)	R
▲ Bay Path (MA)	R
Baruch (CUNY) (NY)	L
Belhaven (MS)	R
Bellarmine (KY)	R
Belmont Abbey (NC)	S
Benedictine (KS)	R
Benedictine (IL)	R
▲ Bennett (NC)	S
Berea (KY)	R
Bethel (MN)	R
Blackburn (IL)	S
Bloomsburg (PA)	M
Bluffton (OH)	S
Boise State (ID)	L
Brescia (KY)	S
Briar Cliff (IA)	R
Bridgewater (VA)	R
Brockport (SUNY) (NY)	M
Caldwell (NJ)	S
California Lutheran	R
California Maritime Academy	S
Cal. Poly. State U. (Pomona)	L
California State U. (Bakersfield)	M
California State U. (Channel Islands)	R
California State U. (Dominguez Hills)	M
California State U. (East Bay)	M

California State U. (Fresno)	L
California State U. (Fullerton)	L
California State U. (Los Angeles)	L
California State U. (Northridge)	L
California State U. (Sacramento)	M
California State U. (San Bernardino)	M
California State U. (San Marcos)	M
California State U. (Stanislaus)	M
Campbell (NC)	R
Canisius (NY)	M
Carthage (WI)	R
Castleton (VT)	R
Catawba (NC)	S
Cedarville (OH)	R
Central Arkansas	M
Central Connecticut	M
Central Oklahoma	L
Central Washington	L
Chaminade (HI)	R
π Champlain (VT)	R
Chapman (CA)	R
▲ Chatham (PA)	S
Chowan (NC)	S
Christopher Newport (VA)	M
Cincinnati, U. of (OH)	L
Citadel, The (SC)	R
Clark Atlanta (GA)	M
Coastal Carolina (SC)	M
Coker (SC)	S
Colorado State	L
Colorado, U. of (Denver)	M
Columbia College (MO)	R
Concordia (CA)	R
Concordia (NE)	R
Culver-Stockton (MO)	S
Daemen (NY)	R
Delaware Valley (PA)	R
Dillard (LA)	R
Doane (NE)	S
East Tennessee	L
Eastern (PA)	R
Eastern Connecticut	M
Eastern Illinois	L

π *Also, Electronic Games &*
Interactive Development

GROUP III continues next page

BUSINESS ADMINISTRATION, continued

• • • —— GROUP III, continued ——— • • •

Eastern Nazarene (MA)	R
Eastern Oregon	R
Edgewood (WI)	S
Elmhurst (IL)	R
Elmira (NY)	R
Emory & Henry (VA)	S
Endicott (MA)	R
Eureka (IL)	S
Fairleigh Dickinson (NJ)	M
Fairmont State (WV)	M
Faulkner (AL)	R
Ferris State (MI)	L
Findlay (OH)	M
Fisk (TN)	S
Florida A&M	M
Fontbonne (MO)	R
Framingham (MA)	M
Freed-Hardeman (TN)	R
Frostburg (MD)	M
Gannon (PA)	M
Gardner-Webb (NC)	S
George Fox (OR)	R
Georgia Southern	L
Georgia State	L
Graceland (IA)	R
Grambling (LA)	M
Green Mountain (VT)	S
Hartford, U. of (CT)	M
Hartwick (NY)	R
Hastings (NE)	R
Hawaii Pacific	M
Heidelberg (OH)	S
Henderson State (AR)	M
Hillsdale (MI)	R
Husson (ME)	S
Immaculata (PA)	S
Indiana Institute of Tech.	S
Indiana State U.	L
Iona (NY)	M
Jacksonville (FL)	R
Jamestown (ND)	R
Kennesaw State (GA)	R
Kentucky Wesleyan (KY)	S
King's (PA)	R
LaSell (MA)	S
LaVerne, U. of (CA)	R

Lenoir-Rhyne (NC)	R
Lesley (MA)	S
Linfield (OR)	R
Long Island U. (C.W. Post) (NY)	R
Louisiana-Lafayette	L
Louisiana Tech.	M
Louisville (KY)	L
Lyndon State (VT)	R
Maine (Farmington)	R
Maine, U. of	L
Malone (OH)	R
Manchester (IN)	R
Marshall (WV)	L
▲ Mary Baldwin (VA)	S
Marygrove (MI)	R
Mass. Col. of Lib. Arts (N. Adams)	R
Massachusetts, U. of (Boston)	M
Massachusetts, U. of (Dartmouth)	M
McMurray (TX)	R
Mercer (GA)	R
Mercyhurst (PA)	R
▲ Meredith (NC)	R
Merrimack (MA)	R
Middle Tennessee	L
Milligan (TN)	S
Mississippi State	L
Missouri Southern State	M
Monmouth (NJ)	R
Montana, U. of	M
Montana State (Billings)	R
Montana State	L
Montclair State (NJ)	M
Montreat (NC)	S
■ Morehouse (GA)	R
Mount Mercy (IA)	S
Mount St. Joseph (OH)	R
Mount St. Mary's (CA)	R
Mount St. Mary's (MD)	R
Mount Union (OH)	R
Murray State (KY)	M
Muskingum (OH)	R
Nebraska, U. of	L
Nebraska, U. of (Kearney)	M
Nebraska, U. of (Omaha)	L

GROUP III continues next page

BUSINESS ADMINISTRATION, continued

••• ━━━━━ GROUP III, continued ━━━━━ •••

Nevada, U. of (Las Vegas) L	Robert Morris (PA) .... M
Nevada, U. of (Reno) L	Rockford (IL) .... S
New Orleans, U. of L	Roger Williams (RI) .... M
Niagara (NY) .... R	Roosevelt (IL) .... R
Nicholls State (LA) .... M	Sacred Heart (CT) .... R
North Carolina, U. of (Charlotte) L	San Jose State (CA) L
North Carolina, U. of (Pembroke) ...... R	Schreiner (TX) .... S
North Georgia .... M	Seattle U. (WA) .... R
North Texas L	Shippensburg (PA) .... M
Northern Arizona L	Silver Lake (WI) .... S
Northern Colorado L	Simpson (IA) .... R
Northern Illinois L	Sonoma State (CA) .... M
Northern Iowa, U. of L	South Alabama .... M
Northern Kentucky L	South Carolina, U. of L
Northwestern U. of Louisiana L	South Dakota, U. of .... M
Northwood University (MI) .... R	Southeastern Missouri State L
Nova Southeastern (FL) .... R	Southeastern Oklahoma State .... M
Nyack (NY) .... R	Southern Illinois L
Oakland U. (MI) .... M	Southern Maine .... M
Oakland City U. (IN) .... R	Southern Mississippi L
Ohio Northern .... R	Southern Oregon State U. .... M
Oral Roberts (OK) .... M	South Florida, U. of XL
Oregon Inst. of Tech. .... R	Southwestern Oklahoma .... M
Ozarks, College of the (MO) .... R	▲Stephens (MO) .... S
Pace (NY) .... R	St. Ambrose (IA) .... R
Penn State (Erie)(PA) .... M	St. Andrews Presbyterian (NC) .... S
Peru State (NE) .... R	St. Edward's (TX) .... M
Philadelphia U. (PA) .... R	St. Francis (NY) .... R
▲Pine Manor (MA) .... S	St. John Fisher (NY) L
Pittsburg State (KS) .... M	St. John's (NY) L
Pittsburgh, U. of (Greensburg) .... R	St. Joseph's (IN) .... S
Pittsburgh, U. of (Johnstown) .... R	St. Joseph's (NY) .... R
Point Loma (CA) .... R	St. Martin's (WA) .... S
Potsdam (SUNY) (NY) .... M	St. Mary's (TX) .... R
Presentation (SD) .... S	St. Peter's (NJ) .... R
Puerto Rico (CAYEY), U. of .... M	St. Rose (NY) .... R
Quincy (IL) .... R	St. Thomas (MN) .... M
Quinnipiac (CT) .... R	St. Vincent's (PA) .... R
Phillips (OK) .... R	Suffolk (MA) .... R
Radford (VA) .... M	Tampa, U. of (FL) .... R
Regis (CO) .... R	Taylor (IN) .... R
Reinhardt (GA) .... R	
Rider (NJ) .... M	*GROUP III continues next page*

Enrollment Code

■ *Men Only*	S = Small (less than 1000 students) R = Moderate (1000-3000 students) M = Medium (3000-8000 students)
▲ *Women Only*	L = Large (8000-20,000 students) XL = Extra Large (over 20,000 students)

BUSINESS ADMINISTRATION, continued

GROUP III, continued

Tennessee, U. of	L
Texas A&M (Commerce)	M
Texas A&M (Corpus Christi)	M
Texas Lutheran	R
Texas State U. (San Marcos)	L
Texas Wesleyan	R
Texas, U. of (El Paso)	L
Texas, U. of (San Antonio)	L
Texas, U. of (Tyler)	R
Thomas More (KY)	R
Toledo, U. of	L
Towson (MD)	L
Troy State (AL)	M
Utica College (NY)	R
Virginia Commonwealth	L
Virginia Wesleyan	R
Visual Arts, School of (NY)	R
Wagner (NY)	R
Washington & Jefferson (PA)	R
Wayne State (MI)	L
Weber State (UT)	L

West Chester (PA)	M
West Florida, U. of	M
Western Carolina (NC)	M
Western Connecticut State	M
Western New England (MA)	R
Western State (CO)	R
Whittier (CA)	R
Wichita State (KS)	M
Widener (PA)	R
William Paterson (NJ)	M
Winthrop (SC)	M
Wisconsin, U. of (Eau Claire)	L
Wisconsin, U. of (Green Bay)	M
Wisconsin, U. of (LaCrosse)	L
Wisconsin, U. of (Stout)	M
# Wisconsin, U. of (Whitewater)	L
Woodbury (CA)	S
Worcester State (MA)	M
Xavier U. of Louisiana	R
York (PA)	M
Youngstown State (OH)	L

*Especially Accounting*

CHEMISTRY

GROUP I
Most Selective

Albany (SUNY)(NY)	L	Harvey Mudd (CA)	S
Allegheny (PA)	R	Haverford (PA)	S
Amherst (MA)	R	Holy Cross (MA)	R
▲Barnard (NY)	R	Illinois Wesleyan	R
Bates (ME)	R	Illinois, U. of (Urbana-Champaign)	XL
Binghamton (SUNY)(NY)	L	Iowa State	XL
Boston College (MA)	L	Johns Hopkins (MD)	M
Boston U. (MA)	L	Kalamazoo (MI)	R
Bowdoin (ME)	R	Kenyon (OH)	R
Brandeis (MA)	M	Lafayette (PA)	R
Brown (RI)	M	Lawrence (WI)	R
▲Bryn Mawr (PA)	S	Loyola (MD)	M
Bucknell (PA)	M	Macalester (MN)	R
Buffalo (SUNY)(NY)	L	MIT (MA)	M
California Inst. of Tech.	S	Miami, U. of (FL)	L
California, U. of (Berkeley)	XL	Michigan, U. of	XL
California, U. of (Los Angeles)	XL	Middlebury (VT)	R
California, U. of (San Diego)	L	Missouri, U. of (Rolla)	M
Carleton (MN)	R	▲Mount Holyoke (MA)	R
Carnegie Mellon (PA)	M	New College (FL)	S
Case Western Reserve U. (OH)	M	New Jersey, College of	M
Centre (KY)	R	New Jersey Inst. of Tech	M
Chicago, U. of (IL)	M	New Mexico Inst. of Tech.	R
Claremont McKenna (CA)	R	North Carolina, U. of	L
Clarkson (NY)	M	Northeastern (MA)	L
Colby (ME)	R	Northwestern (IL)	M
Colgate (NY)	R	Notre Dame (IN)	M
Colorado College	R	Oberlin (OH)	R
Columbia (NY)	M	Occidental (CA)	R
Connecticut College	R	Pennsylvania State	XL
Cornell (NY)	L	Pomona (CA)	R
Dartmouth (NH)	M	Princeton (NJ)	M
Davidson (NC)	R	Puget Sound (WA)	R
DePauw (IN)	R	Reed (OR)	R
Drew (NJ)	R	Rennselaer (NY)	M
Duke (NC)	M	Rhodes (TN)	R
Emory (GA)	M	Rice (TX)	M
Franklin & Marshall (PA)	R	Richmond (VA)	M
Furman (SC)	R	Rochester, U. of (NY)	M
Georgetown (DC)	M	Rose-Hulman (IN)	R
Georgia Inst. of Tech	L	Rutgers (NJ)	L
Gonzaga (WA)	M	Siena (NY)	R
Grinnell (IA)	R	Skidmore (NY)	R
Gustavus Adolphus (MN)	R		
Hamilton (NY)	R		
Harvard (MA)	M		

GROUP I continues next page

CHEMISTRY, continued

================= **GROUP I, continued** =================

South, U. of the (TN) .... R	Wake Forest (NC) .... M
Southwestern (TX) .... R	Washington & Lee (VA) .... R
St. Olaf (MN) .... R	Washington U. (MO) .... M
Stanford (CA) .... M	▲ Wellesley (MA) .... R
Trinity (CT) .... R	Wesleyan (CT) .... R
Trinity (TX) .... R	Wheaton (IL) .... R
Tufts (MA) .... M	Whitman (WA) .... R
Union (NY) .... R	Willamette (OR) .... R
United States Naval Academy (MD) .... M	Williams (MA) .... R
Virginia, U. of L	Wisconsin, U. of XL
■ Wabash (IN) .... S	Worcester Poly Inst.(MA) .... R

================= **GROUP II** =================
Very Selective

Adelphi (NY) .... M	Clemson (SC) L
Alabama, U. of (Huntsville) .... M	Coe (IA) .... R
Albertson (ID) .... S	Colorado, U. of L
Alfred (NY) .... R	Concordia (MN) .... R
Alma (MI) .... R	Converse (SC) .... S
Arcadia (PA) .... R	Creighton (NE) .... R
Arizona, U. of XL	Delaware, U. of L
Augustana (SD) .... R	Denver, U. of (CO) .... M
Austin (TX) .... R	DePaul (IL) L
Baylor (TX) .... M	Drake (IA) .... M
Bemidji State (MN) .... M	Duquesne (PA) .... M
Berea (KY) .... R	Earlham (IN) .... R
Berry (GA) .... R	Eastern Michigan L
Bethany (WV) .... S	Elizabethtown (PA) .... R
Birmingham-Southern (AL) .... R	Elmhurst (IL) .... R
Bradley (IL) .... M	Evansville (IN) .... R
Brigham Young (UT) L	Florida Inst. of Tech........................ R
Brooklyn College (CUNY)(NY) L	Florida Southern .... R
Butler (IN) .... R	Florida State L
California, U. of (Davis) XL	Geneva (PA) .... R
California, U. of (Irvine) L	Georgetown (KY) .... R
California, U. of (Santa Barbara) L	George Washington (DC) .... M
California, U. of (Santa Cruz) .... M	Georgia, U. of XL
Capital (OH) .... R	Goucher (MD) .... S
Carroll (WI) .... R	Hamline (MN)................................. R
Centenary (LA)................................ S	■ Hampden-Sydney (VA) .... S
Central (IA) .... R	Hampton (VA)................................. M
Citadel, The (SC) .... R	Hanover (IN)................................... R
City College (CUNY)(NY) L	π Harrisburg U. (PA) .... S
Clark (MA) .... R	
Clarke (IA)..................................... S	

π *Environmental Chemistry*
GROUP II continues next page

CHEMISTRY, continued

GROUP II, continued

Hendrix (AR)	R
Hiram (OH)	R
Hobart & William Smith (NY)	R
▲ Hollins (VA)	S
Hope (MI)	R
Houghton (NY)	S
Houston, U. of (TX)	L
Howard (DC)	M
Hunter (CUNY)(NY)	L
Huntingdon (AL)	S
Indiana U.	XL
Iowa, U. of	XL
Ithaca Col.	M
John Carroll (OH)	R
Juniata (PA)	R
Kansas, U. of	L
Kansas Wesleyan	S
Kent State (OH)	L
Knox (IL)	R
Lake Forest (IL)	R
LaSalle (PA)	M
Lebanon Valley (PA)	R
Lehigh (PA)	M
LeMoyne (NY)	R
Lewis & Clark (OR)	R
Linfield (OR)	R
Lipscomb (TN)	R
Loras (IA)	R
Louisiana State	XL
Louisiana-Lafayette	L
Louisville (KY)	L
Loyola (LA)	R
Lycoming (PA)	R
Lyon (AR)	M
Maine, U. of	L
Manhattan (NY)	M
Mansfield (PA)	R
Marist (NY)	M
Marquette (WI)	M
Maryland, U. of (Baltimore County)	M
Mary Washington (VA)	M
Massachusetts, U. of	L
Massachusetts, U. of (Boston)	M
Massachusetts, U. of (Lowell)	M
McKendree (IL)	R
McMurry (TX)	R
Mercer (GA)	M
Merrimack (MA)	R
Michigan State	XL
Michigan, U. of (Dearborn)	M
Millsaps (MS)	S
Minnesota, U. of (Morris)	R
Missouri, U. of (Kansas City)	M
Missouri, U. of (St. Louis)	M
Monmouth (IL)	S
Montana Tech	R
Montana State	L
Morningside (IA)	S
Muhlenberg (PA)	R
Murray State (KY)	M
Nebraska Wesleyan	R
New Hampshire, U. of	L
New Mexico State	L
North Carolina, U. of (Charlotte)	L
North Carolina, U. of (Wilmington)	L
North Carolina State	L
North Central (IL)	R
North Dakota, U. of	M
Ohio Northern	R
Ohio State	XL
Ohio University	L
Ohio Wesleyan	R
Oklahoma, U. of	XL
Oregon, U. of	L
Otterbein (OH)	R
Ouachita Baptist (AR)	R
Pacific, U. of the (CA)	R
Pittsburgh, U. of (PA)	L
Portland, U. of (OR)	R
Providence (RI)	M
Puerto Rico, U of (Mayaguez)	L
Purdue (IN)	XL
Richard Stockton (NJ)	M
Ripon (WI)	S

GROUP II continues next page

CHEMISTRY, continued

GROUP II, continued

Roanoke (VA)	R
Rochester Institute of Tech. (NY)	L
Rockhurst (MO)	R
Rollins (FL)	R
St. John's (MN)	R
St. Louis (MO)	M
St. Michael's (VT)	R
St. Thomas (MN)	R
St. Thomas (TX)	R
St. Vincent (PA)	R
San Diego State U. (CA)	XL
Sciences in Philadelphia (PA)	R
Seattle Pacific (WA)	R
Seattle U. (WA)	R
Shepherd (WV)	M
South Dakota School of Mines	R
South Florida, U. of	L
▲Spelman (GA)	R
Spring Hill (AL)	R
Stetson (FL)	R
Stonehill (MA)	R
Stony Brook (SUNY) (NY)	L
Susquehanna (PA)	R
▲Sweet Briar (VA)	S
Syracuse (NY)	L
Temple (PA)	L
Tennessee, U. of (Chattanooga)	M
Texas A&M	XL
Transylvania (KY)	S
Truman State (MO)	M
Ursinus (PA)	R
Utah State	L
Utah, U. of	L
Vermont, U. of	L
Virginia Military Inst.	R
Virginia Tech.	L
Viterbo (WI)	R
Washington & Jefferson (PA)	R
Washington, U. of	XL
Wayne State (MI)	L
Wells (NY)	S
West Florida, U. of	M
West Virginia U.	L
Westminster (UT)	R
Westmont (CA)	R
Whitworth (WA)	R
Wiliam Jewell (MO)	R
Winthrop (SC)	M
Wisconsin Lutheran	S
Wisconsin, U. of (Milwaukee)	L
Wittenberg (OH)	R
Wofford (SC)	R
Wooster (OH)	R

CHEMISTRY continues next page

Enrollment Code

■ *Men Only*
▲ *Women Only*

S = Small (less than 1000 students)   R = Moderate (1000-3000 students)   M = Medium (3000-8000 students)
L = Large (8000-20,000 students)   XL = Extra Large (over 20,000 students)

CHEMISTRY, continued

GROUP III
Selective

Abilene Christian (TX)	M	Mercyhurst (PA)	R
Akron, U. of (OH)	L	Middle Tennessee	L
Alabama, U. of (Birmingham)	M	Millersville (PA)	M
Andrews (MI)	R	Milligan (TN)	S
Aquinas (MI)	R	Montana, U. of	M
Ashland (OH)	R	Mount St. Joseph (OH)	R
Baldwin-Wallace (OH)	R	Muskingum (OH)	R
Benedictine (KS)	R	Nicholls State (LA)	M
Bethany (KS)	S	North Dakota State	L
Bluffton (OH)	S	Northern Illinois U.	L
Brockport (SUNY)(NY)	M	Northern Kentucky	L
California (PA)	M	Northern Michigan	M
California State U. (Chico)	L	Northwestern (IA)	R
California State U. (Dominguez Hills)	M	Oakland U. (MI)	M
California State U. (Fresno)	L	Pittsburgh, U. of (Johnstown)	R
California State U. (Fullerton)	L	Pitzer (CA)	S
California State U. (Long Beach)	L	Puerto Rico, U. of (Cayey)	L
California State U. (San Jose)	L	Queens (CUNY)(NY)	L
California State U. (San Marcos)	M	Rider (NJ)	R
Carroll (MT)	R	St. Francis (PA)	R
Carson-Newman (TN)	R	St. John's (NY)	L
Central Washington	L	St. Mary's (MN)	R
College of Charleston (SC)	L	St. Scholastica (MN)	R
Colorado, U. of (Colorado Springs)	M	Salem State (MA)	M
Cumberland (KY)	R	Shippensburg (PA)	M
Delaware Valley (PA)	R	Shorter (GA)	R
DeSales (PA)	S	Sonoma State (CA)	M
East Stroudsburg (PA)	M	Southern Connecticut	M
Eastern Illinois	L	Southern Illinois U. (Carbondale)	L
Eastern Washington	L	Southern Maine	M
Emporia State (KS)	M	Southern Oregon State U.	M
Framingham (MA)	M	Southwestern Oklahoma	M
Gannon (PA)	M	▲ Sweet Briar (VA)	S
Georgia State	L	Tennessee, U. of	XL
Henderson State (AR)	M	Texas A&M (Corpus Christi)	M
High Point (NC)	R	Texas Lutheran	R
Houston Baptist (TX)	R	Thomas More (KY)	R
Humboldt State (CA)	M	Towson (MD)	L
Illinois State	L	Union (TN)	R
Kennesaw State (GA)	R	Wayne State (NE)	R
Kentucky Wesleyan	R	West Chester (PA)	M
King (TN)	S	Western Carolina (NC)	M
King's (PA)	R	Western Illinois	L
Lamar (TX)	M	Wheeling Jesuit (WV)	R
Lambuth (TN)	S	Whittier (CA)	R
Lewis-Clark State (ID)	R	Winona State (MN)	M
Lock Haven (PA)	M	Wisconsin, U. of (Eau Claire)	L
Long Island U. (Brooklyn)(NY)	M	Wisconsin, U. of (LaCrosse)	L
Long Island U. (C.W. Post)(NY)	R	Wisconsin, U. of (Platteville)	M
Marietta (OH)	R	Wisconsin, U. of (Stevens Point)	M
Marshall (WV)	L	Worcester State (MA)	M
▲ Mary Baldwin (VA)	S	Wyoming, U. of	L
Maryville (TN)	R	Xavier (OH)	R
Massachusetts, U. of (Dartmouth)	M	Xavier U. of Louisiana	R
Memphis, U. of (TN)	L		

CLASSICS

─────────────── **GROUP I** ───────────────
Most Selective

Agnes Scott (GA) .... S	Maryland, U. of (Baltimore County) ... M
Amherst (MA) .... R	Michigan, U. of XL
▲ Barnard (NY) .... R	Middlebury (VT) .... R
Bowdoin (ME) .... R	Minnesota, U. of XL
Brown (RI) .... M	New York U. .... M
▲ Bryn Mawr (PA) .... S	North Carolina, U. of L
Buffalo (SUNY)(NY) L	Northwestern (IL) .... M
California, U. of (Berkeley) XL	Notre Dame (IN) .... R
Carleton (MN) .... R	Oberlin (OH) .... R
Case Western Reserve (OH) .... M	Pennsylvania, U. of............................ L
Centre (KY) .... R	Pittsburgh, U. of (PA) L
Chicago, U. of (IL) .... M	Princeton (NJ) .... M
Colgate (NY) .... R	Reed (OR) .... R
Columbia (NY)..................................... M	Rhodes (TN) .... R
Connecticut College .... R	St. Olaf (MN) .... R
Dallas, U. of (TX) .... R	▲ Scripps (CA) .... S
Dartmouth (NH) .... M	Skidmore (NY) .... R
Drew (NJ) .... R	Stanford (CA) .... M
Duke (NC) .... M	Swarthmore (PA) .... R
Emory (GA) .... M	Texas, U. of (Austin) XL
Franklin & Marshall (PA) .... R	Trinity (TX) .... R
Georgetown (DC) .... M	Tufts (MA) .... M
Grinnell (IA).. R	Vanderbilt (TN) .... M
Gustavus Adolphus (MN) .... R	Virginia, U. of L
Harvard (MA) .... M	■ Wabash (IN) .... S
Haverford (PA)..................................... S	Whitman (WA)..................................... R
Holy Cross (MA) .... R	Willamette (OR) .... R
Johns Hopkins (MD) .... M	William & Mary (VA) .... R
Kalamazoo (MI) .... R	Williams (MA) .... R
Kenyon (OH) .... R	Wisconsin, U. of XL
Macalester (MN)................................. R	Yale (CT) .... M

Enrollment Code	
■ *Men Only* S = Small (less than 1000 students) R = Moderate (1000-3000 students) M = Medium (3000-8000 students)	
▲ *Women Only* L = Large (8000-20,000 students) XL = Extra Large (over 20,000 students)	

CLASSICS, continued

GROUP II
Very Selective

Baylor (TX) .... M

Beloit (WI) .... R

Brooklyn College (CUNY)(NY) L

California State U. (Long Beach) L

California, U. of (Santa Barbara) L

Catholic U. (DC) .... M

Cincinnati, U. of L

Creighton (NE) .... M

Duquesne (PA) .... M

Florida State L

Florida, U. of XL

Fordham (NY) L

Georgia, U. of L

■ Hampden-Sydney (VA) .... S

Hanover (IN) .... R

▲ Hollins (VA) .... S

Hope (MI) .... R

Howard (DC) .... M

Hunter (CUNY)(NY) L

Illinois, U. of (Chicago) L

Kentucky, U. of L

Loyola (IL) .... M

Loyola (MD) .... M

Loyola Marymount (CA) .... M

π Mary Washington (VA) .... M

Massachusetts, U. of (Boston) .... M

Millsaps (MS) .... S

Misericordia, College (PA) .... S

Missippi, U. of L

Missouri, U. of XL

Missouri State L

Montana, U. of L

Montclair State (NJ) .... M

Nebraska, U. of L

North Carolina (Asheville) .... R

North Carolina (Greensboro) .... M

Ohio State XL

Ohio U. L

Oklahoma, U. of XL

Puget Sound (WA) .... R

Randolph College (VA) .... S

Randolph-Macon (VA) .... R

Rollins (FL) .... R

St. Anselm (NH) .... R

St. John's/St. Benedict (MN) .... R

Tennessee, U. of XL

Virginia Tech. L

Washington, U. of XL

Wooster, College of the (OH) .... R

Xavier (OH) .... R

π *Also, Classical Archeology*

COMPUTER SCIENCE

GROUP I
Most Selective

Albany, (SUNY)(NY) L	Macalester (MN) .... R
Binghamton (SUNY)(NY) L	Maryland, U. of (Baltimore County) .... M
Boston College (MA) L	Maryland, U. of XL
Brandeis (MA) .... R	Michigan, U. of XL
Brown (RI) .... M	MIT (MA) .... M
Bucknell (PA) .... R	Miami U. (OH) L
Buffalo (SUNY)(NY) L	Miami, U. of (FL) L
California, U. of (Berkeley) XL	Middlebury (VT) .... R
California, U. of (Los Angeles) XL	Missouri, U. of (Rolla) .... M
Carleton (MN) .... R	▲ Mount Holyoke (MA) .... R
Carnegie Mellon (PA) .... M	New Jersey, College of .... M
Case Western Reserve U. (OH) .... M	New Mexico Inst. of Tech. .... R
Chicago, U. of (IL) .... M	New York U. L
Clarkson (NY) .... M	North Carolina, U. of L
Colgate (NY) .... R	North Carolina State L
Colorado School of Mines .... R	Pennsylvania State XL
Cornell (NY) L	Pittsburgh, U. of (PA) L
Dallas, U. of (TX) .... R	Princeton (NJ) .... M
Dartmouth (NH) .... M	Rensselaer (NY) .... M
Denison (OH) .... R	Rice (TX) .... M
DePauw (IN) .... R	Richmond, U. of (VA) .... R
Dickinson (PA) .... R	Rochester, U. of (NY) .... M
Furman (SC) .... R	Rose-Hulman (IN) .... R
George Washington (DC) .... M	St. Louis (MO) .... M
Georgia Institute of Tech. .... M	Stanford (CA) .... M
Grinnell (IA) .... R	Stevens Inst. of Tech (NJ) .... R
Hamilton (NY) .... R	Union (NY) .... R
Harvard (MA) .... M	United States Air Force Academy (CO) ..... M
Harvey Mudd (CA) .... S	Vassar (NY) .... R
Illinois, U. of XL	Washington, U. of XL
Illinois Institute of Technology .... R	Washington U. (MO) .... M
Iowa State XL	William & Mary (VA) .... M
Johns Hopkins (MD) .... M	Williams (MA) .... R
Lafayette (PA) .... R	Wisconsin, U. of XL
Lehigh (PA) .... M	Worcester Poly. Tech. (MA) .... R
Loyola (MD) .... M	Yeshiva (NY) .... R

COMPUTER SCIENCE, continued

GROUP II
Very Selective

Adelphi (NY)	M	Hunter (CUNY) (NY)	L
Alabama, U. of (Huntsville)	M	Idaho, U. of	L
Allegheny (PA)	R	Illinois College	S
Alma (MI)	R	Illinois, U. of (Springfield)	R
Arcadia (PA)	R	Iowa, U. of	XL
Auburn (AL)	L	James Madison (VA)	M
Augsburg (MN)	R	Juniata (PA)	R
Bemidji State (MN)	M	Kansas State	L
Benedictine (IL)	R	Kennesaw State (GA)	R
▲ Bennett (NC)	S	Kent State (OH)	L
Bradley (IL)	M	Kentucky, U. of	L
Brooklyn College (CUNY)(NY)	L	LaSalle (PA)	M
Bryant (RI)	R	LeTourneau (TX)	R
Buena Vista (IA)	R	Linfield (OR)	R
Butler (IN)	R	Louisiana State	XL
Cal. Poly. State U. (San Luis Obispo)	L	Maine, U. of	M
California, U. of (Irvine)	L	Manhattan (NY)	M
California, U. of (Merced)	R	Marist (NY)	M
California, U. of (San Diego)	L	Marquette (WI)	M
California, U. of (Santa Barbara)	L	Mary Washington (VA)	M
California, U. of (Santa Cruz)	M	Massachusetts, U. of	L
Capital (OH)	R	Massachusetts, U. of (Lowell)	M
Carroll (MT)	R	McKendree (IL)	R
Carroll (WI)	R	Mercer (GA)	R
Central (IA)	R	Michigan, U. of (Dearborn)	M
Central Florida, U. of	XL	Michigan Tech	M
Clarke (IA)	S	Millsaps (MS)	S
Clemson (SC)	L	Minnesota, U. of (Morris)	R
Cogswell (CA)	S	Missouri, U. of (Kansas City)	M
Colorado State	L	Mobile, U. of (AL)	R
Denver, U. of (CO)	M	Montana State	L
DePaul (IL)	L	Montana Tech.	R
Drexel (PA)	M	Montana, U. of	M
Eckerd (FL)	R	Moravian (PA)	R
Embry-Riddle (FL)	M	Murray State (KY)	M
Florida Atlantic	L	New Hampshire, U. of	L
Florida Inst. of Tech	M	New Jersey Inst. of Tech	M
Florida State	L	New Mexico State	L
Gannon (PA)	M	New York Inst. of Tech	M
George Mason (VA)	L	North Central (IL)	R
Goucher (MD)	R	North Dakota, U. of	M
Harrisburg U. (PA)	S	Northeastern (MA)	L
Hawaii, U. of	L	Ohio State	XL
Hendrix (AR)	R	Ohio U.	L
Hiram (OH)	R		
Hofstra (NY)	M		

GROUP II continues next page

COMPUTER SCIENCE, continued

GROUP II, continued

Oklahoma, U. of	XL
Oklahoma City U.	R
Oregon, U. of	L
Pace (NY)	M
Pacific Lutheran (WA)	R
Pacific University (OR)	R
Pepperdine (CA)	R
Pittsburgh, U. of (Johnstown)	R
Polytechnic Univ. of New York	R
Portland State (OR)	L
Potsdam (SUNY) (NY)	M
Puerto Rico, U. of (Mayaguez)	L
Purdue (IN)	XL
Queens (CUNY)(NY)	L
Ramapo (NJ)	M
Regis (CO)	R
Rhode Island, U. of	L
Roanoke (VA)	R
Rochester Inst. of Tech (NY)	L
Rowan (NJ)	M
Rutgers (Camden) (NJ)	M
Santa Clara U. (CA)	M
St. Ambrose (IA)	R
St. Cloud (MN)	L
St. Edward's (TX)	M
St. John's (MN)	R
St. Norbert (WI)	R
St. Scholastica (MN)	R
Sciences, U. of the (PA)	S
Shippensburg (PA)	M
South Carolina, U. of	L
South Dakota School of Mines	R
Stetson (FL)	R
Stonehill (MA)	R
Stony Brook (SUNY) (NY)	L
Syracuse (NY)	L
Taylor (IN)	R
Texas, U. of	XL
Texas, U. of (Dallas)	M
Transylvania (KY)	S
Tulsa, U of (OK)	R
Utah, U. of	L
Virginia Tech.	L
Wayne State (MI)	L
Webster (MO)	R
Westminster (PA)	R
Westminster (UT)	R
West Virginia U.	L
William Jewell (MO)	R
Winona State U. (MN)	M
Wofford (SC)	R

COMPUTER SCIENCE continues next page

Enrollment Code

■ *Men Only*
▲ *Women Only*

S = Small (less than 1000 students)   R = Moderate (1000-3000 students)   M = Medium (3000-8000 students)
L = Large (8000-20,000 students)   XL = Extra Large (over 20,000 students)

COMPUTER SCIENCE, continued

GROUP III
Selective

Adrian (MI)	R
Alabama, U. of (Birmingham)	M
Arkansas, U. of	L
Arizona State	XL
Baker (KS)	R
Baldwin-Wallace (OH)	R
Ball State (IN)	L
Baruch (CUNY)(NY)	L
Belhaven (MS)	R
Benedictine (KS)	R
Bloomsburg (PA)	M
Brockport (SUNY) (NY)	M
Cal. Poly. State U. (Pomona)	L
California State U. (Chico)	L
California State U. (East Bay)	M
California State U. (Monterey Bay)	R
California State U. (Northridge)	L
California State U. (Sacramento)	M
California State U. (San Bernardino)	M
California State U. (San Jose)	L
California State U. (San Marcos)	M
California State U. (Stanislaus)	M
Canisius (NY)	M
Catawba (NC)	S
π Champlain (VT)	R
Charleston Southern (SC)	R
Christopher Newport (VA)	M
Chowan (NC)	S
Clark Atlanta (GA)	M
Coastal Carolina (SC)	M
Colorado, U. of (Col. Springs)	M
Colorado, U. of (Denver)	M
East Stroudsburg (PA)	M
Eastern Connecticut	M
Eastern Michigan	L
Eureka (IL)	S
Evansville (IN)	R
Ferris State (MI)	L
Fitchburg (MA)	R
Florida Gulf Coast U.	M
Frostburg (MD)	M
Gardner-Webb (NC)	R
Georgia State	L
Great Falls (MT)	S
Hawaii Pacific	M
Heidelberg (OH)	S
High Point (NC)	R
Husson (ME)	S
Indiana Inst. of Tech.	S
Iona (NY)	M
Jacksonville (FL)	R
Jacksonville State (AL)	M
Jamestown (ND)	R
Johnson C. Smith (NC)	R
Kansas Wesleyan	S
Lamar (TX)	M
Laverne (CA)	R
Lenoir-Rhyne (NC)	R
Liberty (VA)	R
Long Island U. (Brooklyn)(NY)	M
Long Island U. (C.W. Post)(NY)	M
Loras (IA)	R
Louisiana-Lafayette	L
Loyola U. (LA)	M
Lynchburg (VA)	R
Marygrove (MI)	R
Memphis, U. of (TN)	L
Midwestern State U. (TX)	M
Millersville (PA)	M
Minnesota State U. (Mankato)	L
Minnesota, U. of (Duluth)	L
Mississippi College	R
Mississippi State	L
Missouri State	L
Monmouth (NJ)	M
■ Morehouse (GA)	R
Mount St. Joseph (OH)	R
Mount St. Mary's (NY)	S
Mount Union (OH)	R
Muskingum (OH)	R
Nebraska, U. of (Omaha)	L
Nevada, U. of (Reno)	L
New Mexico, U. of	L
Northeastern Illinois	M
Northern Michigan	M
Northwestern Louisiana	L
North Carolina (Greensboro)	M
North Florida	M

π *Electronic Games &*
Interactive Development

GROUP III continues next page

COMPUTER SCIENCE, continued

••• ———————————— GROUP III, continued ———————————— •••

Oakland U. (MI)	M	Southern Maine	M
Oklahoma Christian	R	Southern Polytechnic (GA)	R
Old Dominion (VA)	L	▲ Spelman (GA)	R
Oswego (SUNY)(NY)	M	Temple (PA)	L
Ozarks, College of the (MO)	R	Texas, U. of (Arlington)	L
Penn State (Harrisburg)(PA)	R	Texas, U. of (Tyler)	R
Pittsburgh, U. of (Bradford)	R	Texas State U. (San Marcos)	L
Quinnipiac (CT)	R	Thomas More (KY)	R
Rider (NJ)	M	Weber State (UT)	L
Robert Morris (PA)	R	West Chester (PA)	M
Roosevelt (IL)	R	West Florida, U. of	M
St. Joseph's (NY)	R	West Virginia Wesleyan	R
St. Mary (KS)	S	Western Carolina (NC)	M
▲ St. Mary (NE)	S	Western Kentucky	L
St. Mary's (MN)	R	Western Michigan	L
Salem State (MA)	M	Western New England (MA)	R
San Jose State U. (CA)	L	Wilkes (PA)	R
Southeastern Louisiana	L	William Paterson (NJ)	M
Southern Connecticut	M	Wisconsin (LaCrosse)	L

Enrollment Code

■ *Men Only*
▲ *Women Only*

S = Small (less than 1000 students)   R = Moderate (1000-3000 students)   M = Medium (3000-8000 students)
L = Large (8000-20,000 students)   XL = Extra Large (over 20,000 students)

DANCE/DRAMA/THEATER

GROUP I
Most Selective

Allegheny (PA).. R	Kenyon (OH) .... R
American Acad. of Dramatic Arts (NY) ... S	Knox (IL).. R
American U. (DC) .... M	Lawrence (WI) .... R
Amherst (MA)... R	Macalester (MN) .... R
▲Barnard (NY)... R	Maryland, U. of (Baltimore County)...... M
Binghamton (SUNY)(NY) L	Miami, U. of (FL) L
Boston College (MA) L	Michigan, U. of XL
Boston U. (MA)...................................... L	Middlebury (VT) .... R
Brandeis (MA) .... R	▲Mount Holyoke (MA) .... R
Bucknell (PA) .... M	New School U. (Eugene Lang)(NY) .... S
Buffalo (SUNY)(NY) L	New York U... L
California, U. of (Los Angeles) XL	North Carolina, U. of L
California, U. of (San Diego) L	Northwestern (IL) .... M
Carleton (MN)....................................... R	Oberlin (OH) .... R
Carnegie Mellon (PA) .... M	Pomona (CA) .... R
Case Western Reserve (OH).............. M	Princeton (NJ) .... M
Colgate (NY) .... R	Rutgers (NJ) L
Colorado College .... R	St. Olaf (MN) .... R
Columbia (NY)..................................... M	Sarah Lawrence (NY) .... R
Connecticut College .... R	Skidmore (NY) .... R
Cornell (NY)... L	South, U. of the (TN) .... R
Dallas, U. of (TX) .... R	Southwestern (TX) .... R
Dartmouth (NH) .... M	Tufts (MA) .... M
Davidson (NC)....................................... R	Tulane (LA) .... M
Denison (OH) .... R	Vassar (NY) .... R
Drew (NJ) .... R	Wake Forest (NC) .... M
George Washington (DC) .... M	Wesleyan (CT) .... R
Gettysburg (PA) .... R	Whitman (WA)....................................... R
Hamilton (NY) .... R	William & Mary (VA) .... R
Illinois, U. of XL	Williams (MA) .... R
Illinois Wesleyan .... R	Yale (CT) .... M
Juilliard (NY)... S	

DANCE / DRAMA / THEATER continues next page

■ *Men Only*	**Enrollment Code**
▲ *Women Only*	S = Small (less than 1000 students) R = Moderate (1000-3000 students) M = Medium (3000-8000 students)
	L = Large (8000-20,000 students) XL = Extra Large (over 20,000 students)

DANCE/DRAMA/THEATER, continued

GROUP II
Very Selective

Adelphi (NY)	M
Alabama, U. of	L
Arizona, U. of	XL
Arizona State	XL
Bard (NY)	R
Baylor (TX)	M
Beloit (WI)	R
Bennington (VT)	S
Birmingham-Southern (AL)	R
Brooklyn College (CUNY)(NY)	L
Butler (IN)	R
California Institute of the Arts	S
California, U. of (Irvine)	L
California, U. of (Riverside)	L
Cal. Poly State U. (San Luis Obispo)	L
Catholic U. (DC)	M
Central Florida, U. of	XL
Charleston, College of (SC)	L
Clarke (IA)	S
Coe (IA)	R
Columbia College (IL)	M
Columbia College (SC)	R
Cornish (WA)	S
Creighton (NE)	M
DePaul (IL)	L
Drake (IA)	M
π Elon (NC)	R
Emerson (MA)	M
Florida, U. of	XL
Florida State	L
Florida Southern	R
Fordham (NY)	L
Fredonia (SUNY)(NY)	M
George Mason (VA)	L
Georgia, U. of	L
Goucher (MD)	S
Grand Valley (MI)	L
Hanover (IN)	R
Hartwick (NY)	R
Hawaii, U. of	L
Hofstra (NY)	M
▲ Hollins (VA)	S
Hope (WI)	R
Houston, U. of (TX)	L
Hunter (CUNY)(NY)	L
Indiana U.	XL
Iowa, U. of	XL
Ithaca (NY)	M
James Madison (VA)	M
Kansas, U. of	L
Kansas State	L
LeMoyne (NY)	R
Lindenwood (MO)	M
Linfield (OR)	R
Long Island U.(C.W. Post)(NY)	R
Loyola (IL)	M
Luther (IA)	R
Lycoming (PA)	R
Lyon (AR)	S
Maine, U. of	L
Manhattanville (NY)	R
McDaniel (MD)	R
Millsaps (MS)	S
Minnesota State U. (Mankato)	L
Minnesota, U. of	XL
Missouri, U. of (Kansas City)	M
Muhlenberg (PA)	R
Nebraska Wesleyan	R
Nevada, U. of (Las Vegas)	M
New Hampshire, U. of	R
New Mexico, U. of	L
No. Carolina School of the Arts	S
Occidental (CA)	R
Ohio U.	L
Oklahoma City U.	R
Oklahoma, U. of	XL
Oklahoma State	L
Pace (NY)	M
Purchase (SUNY) (NY)	M
Rollins (FL)	R
Santa Clara (CA)	M
▲ Scripps (CA)	S
Seattle Pacific (WA)	R
Shepherd (WV)	R
South Carolina, U. of	L
Southern California	L
Southern Methodist (TX)	M
Stanford (CA)	M
Susquehanna (PA)	R
▲ Sweet Briar (VA)	S
Syracuse (NY)	L
Texas Christian	M
Texas, U. of	XL
Ursinus (PA)	R
Utah State	L
Utah, U. of	L
Virginia Commonwealth U.	L
Viterbo (WI)	R
Wartburg (IA)	R
Washington, U. of	XL
Wells (NY)	S
Western Maryland	R
West Virginia U.	L
Wheaton (MA)	R
Wisconsin, U. of	XL
Wisconsin, U. of (Milwaukee)	L
Wisconsin, U. of (Stevens Point)	M
Wooster (OH)	R

π *Music Theatre*

DANCE/DRAMA/THEATER, continued

GROUP III
Selective

+ + Akron, U. of (OH)	L
Alabama, U. of (Birmingham)	M
Alaska, U. of (Fairbanks)	M
Aquinas (MI)	R
Arcadia (PA)	R
Arts, U. of the (PA)	R
Barry (FL)	R
Bethany (WV)	S
Belhaven (MS)	R
** Benedictine (KS)	R
Boise State (ID)	L
Brenau (GA)	R
Brockport (SUNY)(NY)	M
California State U. (Long Beach)	L
California State U. (Northridge)	L
California State U. (Sacramento)	M
Catawba (NC)	S
Central Michigan	L
Coker (SC)	S
Converse College (SC)	S
Dana (NE)	S
DeSales (PA)	S
Evansville (IN)	R
Fontbonne (MO)	R
Franklin (IN)	S
Greensboro College (NC)	S
Hartford, U. of (CT)	M
Illinois State	L
Indiana State	L
Jacksonville (FL)	R
Johnson State (VT)	R
Keene State (NH)	R
Long Island U. (Brooklyn)(NY)	M
Longwood (VA)	R
Marymount Manhattan (NY)	R
▲ Mary Baldwin (VA)	S
McPherson (KS)	S
▲ Meredith (NC)	R
Milliken (IL)	R
Missouri State	L
Montana, U. of	M
Niagara (NY)	R
Northwestern College (IA)	R
Ohio State	XL
Otterbein (OH)	R
# Point Park (PA)	R
Rockford (IL)	S
Rocky Mountain (MT)	S
Salem State (MA)	M
San Francisco State (CA)	L
Santa Fe, College of (NM)	S
Seattle U. (WA)	R
▲ Seton Hill (PA)	S
++ Slippery Rock (PA)	M
Southern Maine	M
Southern Missippi	L
Southern Utah	M
South Florida, U. of	L
Springfield (MA)	M
St. Edward's (TX)	M
St. Mary's (MN)	R
Sterling (KS)	S
Stephens (MO)	S
Tarleton State (TX)	M
Temple (PA)	L
Texas, U. of (El Paso)	L
Texas State U. (San Marcos)	L
Towson (MD)	L
Wagner (NY)	R
Wayne State (MI)	L
Weber State (UT)	L
Webster (MO)	R
Western Michigan	L
* Western St. Coll. of Colorado	R
π West Virginia Wesleyan	R
++Winthrop(SC)	M

π *Music Theater*
++ *Especially Dance*
# *Musical Theater and Dance*
** *Also, Theater Management*
* *Communication and Theater - One Major*

	Enrollment Code	
■ *Men Only*	S = Small (less than 1000 students)	R = Moderate (1000-3000 students)	M = Medium (3000-8000 students)
▲ *Women Only*	L = Large (8000-20,000 students)	XL = Extra Large (over 20,000 students)

ECONOMICS

GROUP I
Most Selective

Albany (SUNY)(NY)	L	Lehigh (PA)	M
American U. (DC)	M	Macalester (MN)	R
Amherst (MA)	R	Miami, U. of (OH)	L
Babson (MA)	R	Michigan, U. of	XL
▲ Barnard (NY)	R	MIT (MA)	M
Bates (ME)	R	Middlebury (VT)	R
Binghamton (SUNY)(NY)	L	Minnesota, U. of	XL
Boston College (MA)	L	▲ Mount Holyoke (MA)	R
Boston University (MA)	L	New York U.	L
Bowdoin (ME)	R	Northwestern (IL)	M
Brandeis (MA)	R	Oberlin (OH)	R
Brown (RI)	M	Occidental (CA)	R
▲ Bryn Mawr (PA)	S	Pennsylvania, U. of	L
Bucknell (PA)	M	Pomona (CA)	R
California, U. of (Los Angeles)	XL	Princeton (NJ)	M
California, U. of (San Diego)	L	Reed (OR)	R
Carleton (MN)	R	Rensselaer (NY)	M
Carnegie Mellon (PA)	M	Rhodes (TN)	R
Case Western Reserve (OH)	M	Rice (TX)	M
Chicago, U. of (IL)	M	Richmond (VA)	R
Claremont McKenna (CA)	R	Rochester, U. of (NY)	M
Colby (ME)	R	Rose-Hulman (IN)	R
Colgate (NY)	R	Rutgers (NJ)	L
Colorado College	R	▲ Smith (MA)	R
Colorado School of Mines	R	St. Mary's Col. of Maryland	R
Columbia (NY)	M	St. Olaf (MN)	R
Connecticut College	R	South, U. of the (TN)	R
Cornell (NY)	L	Southwestern (TX)	R
Dallas, U. of (TX)	R	Stanford (CA)	M
Dartmouth (NH)	M	Swarthmore (PA)	R
Davidson (NC)	R	Trinity (CT)	R
DePauw (IN)	R	Trinity (TX)	R
Drew (NJ)	R	Tufts (MA)	M
Duke (NC)	M	U.S. Military Academy (NY)	M
Emory (GA)	M	Union (NY)	R
Franklin & Marshall (PA)	R	Vanderbilt (TN)	M
Furman (SC)	R	Vassar (NY)	R
George Washington (DC)	M	Villanova (PA)	M
Georgetown (DC)	M	Virginia, U. of	L
Georgia Inst. of Tech.	M	■ Wabash (IN)	S
Gettysburg (PA)	R	Wake Forest (NC)	M
Grinnell (IA)	R	Washington & Lee (VA)	R
Hamilton (NY)	R	▲ Wellesley (MA)	R
Harvard (MA)	M	Wesleyan (CT)	R
Haverford (PA)	S	Whitman (WA)	R
Holy Cross (MA)	R	Willamette (OR)	R
Illinois Wesleyan	R	William & Mary (VA)	R
Kalamazoo (MI)	R	Williams (MA)	R
Kenyon (OH)	R	Worcester Poly. Inst. (MA)	R
Lafayette (PA)	R	Yale (CT)	M
Lawrence (WI)	R		

ECONOMICS, continued

GROUP II
Very Selective

▲Agnes Scott (GA) .... S
Alaska, U. of (Anchorage) .... M
\# Albion (MI) .... R
Allegheny (PA) .... R
Assumption (MA) .... R
Auburn (AL) .... M
Baruch (CUNY)(NY) L
Beloit (WI) .... R
Bentley (MA) .... M
Bethany (WV) .... S
Bradley (IL) .... M
Brigham Young (UT) L
California, U. of (Davis) XL
California, U. of (Merced) .... R
California, U. of (Santa Cruz) .... M
California State U. (Bakersfield) .... M
California State U. (Long Beach) L
California State U. (Santa Barbara) L
Centre (KY) .... R
City College (CUNY)(NY) L
Clark (MA) .... R
Clemson (SC) L
Colorado, U. of L
Connecticut, U. of XL
Cornell College (IA) .... R
Delaware, U. of L
Denison (OH) .... R
Drake (IA) .... M
Florida Atlantic L
Florida State L
George Mason (VA) L
Georgia State L
Georgia, U. of XL
Grove City (PA) .... R
Guilford (NC) .... R
■ Hampden-Sydney (VA) .... S
Hanover (IN) .... R
Hendrix (AR) .... R
Hillsdale (MI) .... R
Hobart & William Smith (NY) .... R
▲Hollins (VA) .... S
Illinois Col. .... S
Illinois, U. of (Chicago) L
Iowa State XL
John Carroll (OH) .... R
Kansas, U. of L
Knox (IL) .... R

Lake Forest (IL) .... R
Linfield (OR) .... R
Loras (IA) .... R
Loyola (LA) .... R
Loyola Marymount (CA) .... M
Lyon (AR) .... S
Maine, U. of L
Manhattanville (NY) .... R
Maryland, U. of XL
Maryland, U. of (Baltimore County) ..... M
Mary Washington (VA) .... M
Massachusetts, U. of L
Mercer (GA) .... R
Michigan State XL
Michigan, U. of (Dearborn) .... M
Missouri, U. of XL
Missouri, U. of (Kansas City) .... M
Moravian (PA) .... R
Muhlenberg (PA) .... R
Nebraska, U. of L
New Mexico, U. of L
North Carolina State L
Oglethorpe (GA) .... R
Ohio State XL
Ohio Wesleyan (OH) .... R
Oklahoma, U. of XL
Oregon State L
Pittsburgh, U. of (PA) L
Puget Sound (WA) .... R
Oneonta (SUNY) (NY) .... M
Randolph-Macon (VA) .... R
Rhode Island, U. of L
Richard Stockton (NJ) .... M
Ripon (WI) .... S
Rochester Inst. of Tech. (NY) L
Rollins (FL) .... R
▲Salem Col. (NC) .... S
San Francisco, U. of .... M
St. John's (MN) .... R
St. Lawrence (NY) .... R
St. Thomas (MN) .... R
Seattle U. (WA) .... R
Southern Methodist (TX) L
▲Spelman (GA) .... R

\# *Also, Economics & Business*

GROUP II continues next page

Enrollment Code

■ *Men Only* ▲ *Women Only* S = Small (less than 1000 students) R = Moderate (1000-3000 students) M = Medium (3000-8000 students) L = Large (8000-20,000 students) XL = Extra Large (over 20,000 students)

ECONOMICS, continued

GROUP II, continued

Susquehanna (PA)	R
Texas A&M	XL
Texas, U. of (Dallas)	M
Truman State (MO)	M
Ursinus (PA)	R
Vermont, U. of	L
Virginia Military Inst.	R
Washington & Jefferson (PA)	R

Washington, U. of	XL
Westminster Col. (MO)	S
Westmont Col. (CA)	R
Wheaton (MA)	R
Wofford (SC)	R
Wooster (OH)	R
Xavier (OH)	R

GROUP III
Selective

Arkansas, U. of	L
Baldwin-Wallace (OH)	R
Bellarmine (KY)	R
Berea (WV)	R
California State U. (Bakersfield)	M
California State U. (Channel Islands)	R
California State U. (Chico)	L
California State U. (East Bay)	M
California State U. (Northridge)	L
Central Missouri	L
Central Oklahoma	L
East Carolina	L
East Tennessee	L
Eastern Connecticut	M
Eastern Washington	L
Framingham (MA)	M
Hardin-Simmons (TX)	R
Hawaii Pacific	M
Heidelberg (OH)	S
Indiana U.-Purdue U.-Indianapolis (IN)	L
Louisiana-Lafayette	L
Louisiana State	XL
Marshall (WV)	L
Memphis, U. of (TN)	L
Millersville (PA)	M
Mississippi, U. of	L

Monmouth (IL)	S
Montana State	L
Nebraska, U. of (Kearney)	M
Nebraska, U. of (Omaha)	L
Northern Iowa	L
Northern Michigan	M
Northwood University (MI)	R
Oakland U. (MI)	M
Old Dominion (VA)	L
Northern Colorado	L
Queens (CUNY)(NY)	L
Rhode Island College	M
Robert Morris (PA)	M
St. Anselm (NH)	R
Shippensberg (PA)	M
South Dakota State U.	M
Southern Connecticut	M
Southern Utah	M
Toledo, U. of (OH)	L
Washington State	L
Weber State (UT)	L
Whittier (CA)	R
Wilson (PA)	S
Wisconsin, U. of (Milwaukee)	L
Wright State (OH)	L
Wyoming, U. of	L

Enrollment Code

■ *Men Only* S = Small (less than 1000 students) R = Moderate (1000-3000 students) M = Medium (3000-8000 students)
▲ *Women Only* L = Large (8000-20,000 students) XL = Extra Large (over 20,000 students)

EDUCATION

GROUP I
Most Selective

Albany (SUNY)(NY)	L
Boston College (MA)	L
Boston U. (MA)	L
Bucknell (PA)	R
Buffalo (SUNY) (NY)	L
Connecticut Col.	R
Dallas, U. of (TX)	R
Dickinson (PA)	R
Earlham (IN)	R
Geneseo (SUNY) (NY)	M
Illinois, U. of	XL
Iowa, U. of	XL
Miami, U. of (FL)	M
Miami U. (OH)	L
Michigan, U. of	XL
New Jersey, College of	M
New School U. (Lang)(NY)	S
North Carolina, U. of	L
Pittsburgh, U. of (PA)	L
Occidental (CA)	R
Rutgers (NJ)	L
Skidmore (NY)	R
Southern California	L
Stanford (CA)	M
Swarthmore (PA)	S
Trinity (TX)	R
➤ Tufts (MA)	M
Vanderbilt (TN)	M
▲ Wellesley (MA)	R
Wheaton (IL)	R
William & Mary (VA)	M

➤ *Child Study*

GROUP II
Very Selective

Adelphi (NY)	M
Adrian (MI)	R
Alaska Pacific	S
Albertson (ID)	S
Alfred (NY)	R
Alma (MI)	R
Arizona, U. of	XL
Asbury (KY)	R
Auburn (AL)	L
Augustana (IL)	R
Augustana (SD)	R
Austin (TX)	R
Baylor (TX)	L
Benedictine (IL)	R
Berry (GA)	R
π Bethel (IN)	R
Biola (CA)	R
Birmingham Southern (AL)	R
Bradley (IL)	M
Bridgewater (MA)	M
Brigham Young (UT)	XL
Bryan (TN)	S
Buena Vista (IA)	R
Butler (IN)	R
California, U. of (Riverside)	L
California, U. of (Santa Barbara)	L
Calvin (MI)	M
Capital U. (OH)	R
Carroll (WI)	R
Centenary (LA)	S
Central (IA)	R
Central Florida, U. of	XL
Centre (KY)	R
Chestnut Hill (PA)	S
Christian Brothers (TN)	R
Cincinnati, U. of (OH)	L
Clarke (IA)	S
Clemson (SC)	L
Coe (IA)	R
Columbia College (SC)	R
Concordia (MN)	R
Connecticut, U. of	XL
Cornell College (IA)	R
Creighton (NE)	M
Dayton, U. of (OH)	M
Delaware, U. of	L
DePaul (IL)	L
Drake (IA)	M
Drury (MO)	R
Duquesne (PA)	M
Eastern Michigan	L
Elizabethtown (PA)	R
Elon (NC)	R
Erskine (SC)	S
Evansville (IN)	R
π Flagler (FL)	R
Florida International	L
Florida Southern	R
Florida State	L

π *Also American Sign Language / Deaf Interpretation*

GROUP II continues next page

EDUCATION, continued

GROUP II, continued

Fredonia (SUNY) (NY) ...... M	Minnesota, U. of XL
Georgetown College (KY) ...... R	Minnesota, U. of (Duluth) ...... M
Georgia, U. of XL	Minnesota, U. of (Morris) ...... R
Gonzaga (WA) ...... R	Mississippi, U. of L
Goucher (MD) ...... R	Mississippi U. for Women ...... R
Grand Valley (MI) L	Missouri State L
Grove City (PA) ...... R	Missouri, U. of (Kansas City) ...... M
Guilford (NC) ...... R	Missouri, U. of (St. Louis) ...... M
Gustavus Adolphus (MN) ...... R	Moravian (PA) ...... R
Hamline (MN) ...... R	Morningside (IA) ...... S
Hanover (IN) ...... R	Mount St. Mary's (MD) ...... R
Harding (AR) ...... M	Nazareth (NY) ...... R
Hillsdale (MI) ...... R	Nebraska, U. of L
Hiram (OH) ...... R	New Hampshire, U. of L
Hofstra (NY) ...... M	New Mexico State L
Hood (MD) ...... S	New Orleans (LA) L
Houghton (NY) ...... S	New Paltz (SUNY) (NY) ...... M
Hunter (CUNY) (NY) L	North Carolina State L
Illinois College ...... S	North Carolina, U. of (Asheville) ...... R
Indiana, U. XL	North Carolina, U. of (Greensboro) ...... M
Indiana, U. of (PA) L	North Dakota, U. of ...... M
Iowa State XL	North Florida ...... M
James Madison (VA) ...... M	Ohio Northern ...... R
Juniata (PA) ...... R	Ohio U. L
Kansas, U. of L	Oklahoma, U. of XL
Kansas State L	Oklahoma State L
Kentucky, U. of L	Oneonta (SUNY)(NY) ...... M
Lake Forest (IL) ...... R	Oregon, U. of L
La Salle (PA) ...... M	Oswego (SUNY)(NY) ...... M
LeMoyne (NY) ...... R	Pacific Lutheran (WA) ...... R
LeTourneau (TX) ...... R	Pacific, U. of the (CA) ...... M
Lindenwood (MO) ...... M	Palm Beach Atlantic (FL) ...... R
Lipscomb (TN) ...... R	Pennsylvania State XL
Loras (IA) ...... R	Portland, U. of (OR) ...... R
Loyola (MD) ...... M	Potsdam (SUNY) (NY) ...... M
Luther (IA) ...... R	Principia (IL) ...... S
Lyon (AR) ...... S	Providence (RI) ...... M
Maine, U. of L	Puerto Rico, U. of L
Manhattan (NY) ...... M	Queens (CUNY) (NY) L
Manhattanville (NY) ...... R	Redlands, U. of (CA) ...... R
Marquette (WI) ...... M	Regis (CO) ...... R
Maryland, U. of XL	Rockhurst (MO) ...... R
Maryland, U. of (Baltimore County) ... M	Rowan (NJ) ...... M
McDaniel (MD) ...... R	St. Bonaventure (NY) ...... R
Mercer (GA) ...... R	St. Catherine (MN) ...... R
Messiah (PA) ...... R	St. John's/ St. Benedict (MN) ...... R
Michigan State XL	St. Louis (MO) ...... M
Millersville (PA) ...... M	St. Martin's (WA) ...... S
▲Mills (CA) ...... S	St. Mary's Col. (CA) ...... R
Millsaps (MS) ...... S	▲St. Mary's Col. (IN) ...... R
Minnesota State U. (Moorhead) ...... M	

GROUP II continues next page

EDUCATION, continued

·· ━━━━━━━━━━━━ GROUP II, continued ━━━━━━━━━━━━ ··

St. Mary's Col. (MN)	R	Ursinus (PA)	R
St. Michael's (VT)	R	Valparaiso (IN)	R
St. Norbert (WI)	R	Washington & Jefferson (PA)	R
St. Thomas (MN)	R	Washington State	L
Salisbury State (MD)	M	Washington, U. of	XL
San Diego State U. (CA)	XL	Wayne State (MI)	L
Seattle Pacific (WA)	R	Wells (NY)	S
Shepherd (WV)	M	Western Michigan	L
Shippensburg (PA)	M	Western Washington U.	L
South Florida, U. of	L	Westminster (UT)	R
Stetson (FL)	R	Whitworth (WA)	R
Susquehanna (PA)	R	William Jewell Col. (MO)	R
Tennessee, U. of	XL	Winona State U. (MN)	M
Tennessee Tech	M	Wisconsin Lutheran	S
Texas A&M	XL	Wisconsin, U. of	XL
Texas Christian	M	Wisconsin, U. of (Milwaukee)	L
Texas, U. of (Austin)	XL	Wisconsin, U. of (Stevens Point)	M
Towson (MD)	L	Wittenberg (OH)	R
Transylvania (KY)	R	Wofford (SC)	R
Truman State (MO)	M	York (PA)	M

··· ━━━━━━━━━━━━ GROUP III ━━━━━━━━━━━━ ···
Selective

Akron, U. of (OH)	L	▲Bennett (NC)	S
Alaska, U. of (Anchorage)	M	Berea (KY)	R
Alderson-Broaddus (WV)	S	Bethany (KS)	S
▲Alverno (WI)	R	Bethany (WV)	S
Anderson (IN)	R	Bethel (KS)	S
Appalachian State (NC)	L	Bethel (MN)	R
Arcadia (PA)	R	Blackburn (IL)	S
Arkansas, U. of	L	Bluffton (OH)	S
Arizona State	XL	Boise State (ID)	L
Ashland (OH)	R	Bowling Green (OH)	L
Assumption (MA)	R	Bloomsburg (PA)	M
Augsburg (MN)	R	Brescia (KY)	S
Averett (VA)	S	Brockport (SUNY) (NY)	M
Avila (MO)	S	Brooklyn College (CUNY)(NY)	L
Baker (KS)	R	Caldwell (NJ)	S
Baldwin-Wallace (OH)	R	California Lutheran	R
Ball State (IN)	L	California State U. (Bakersfield)	M
Barry (FL)	R	California State U. (Channel Islands)	R
Belhaven (MS)	R	California State U. (Fresno)	L
Bellarmine (KY)	R	California State U. (Monterey Bay)	R
Belmont (TN)	R	California State U. (Los Angeles)	L
Bemidji State (MN)	M	California State U. (Sacramento)	M
Benedictine (KS)	R		

GROUP III continues next page

Enrollment Code

■ *Men Only* | S = Small (less than 1000 students) | R = Moderate (1000-3000 students) | M = Medium (3000-8000 students)
▲ *Women Only* | L = Large (8000-20,000 students) | XL = Extra Large (over 20,000 students)

EDUCATION, continued

California State U. (San Bernardino)	M
California State U. (San Marcos)	M
California State U. (Stanislaus)	M
California (PA)	M
Canisius (NY)	M
Carson-Newman (TN)	R
Castleton State (VT)	R
Catawba (NC)	S
Cedarville (OH)	R
Central Connecticut	M
Central Michigan U.	L
Central Oklahoma	L
Chaminade (HI)	R
Charleston Southern (SC)	R
Citadel, The (SC)	R
City College (CUNY) (NY)	L
Claflin (SC)	R
Clark Atlanta (GA)	M
Coastal Carolina (SC)	M
Coker (SC)	S
Colby-Sawyer (NH)	S
College of Charleston (SC)	M
Colorado, U. of (Colorado Springs)	M
Concordia (NE)	R
▲ Converse (SC)	S
Cumberland (KY)	R
Daemen (NY)	R
Dana (NB)	S
Dillard (LA)	R
Doane (NE)	S
Dominican (CA)	S
Dordt (IA)	R
Dubuque, U. of (IA)	S
D'Youville (NY)	R
East Carolina (NC)	L
East Central (OK)	M
East Stroudsburg (PA)	M
Eastern Connecticut	M
Eastern Illinois	L
Eastern Kentucky	L
Eastern Mennonite (VA)	R
Eastern Oregon	R
Edgewood (WI)	S
Edinboro (PA)	M
Elmhurst (IL)	R
Elmira (NY)	R
Elms (MA)	S
Emporia State (KS)	M
Eureka (IL)	S
Fairmont (WV)	M

Findlay (OH)	M
Fitchburg State (MA)	R
Florida A&M	M
Florida Atlantic	L
Florida Gulf Coast U.	M
Fontbonne (MO)	R
Fort Hays (KS)	M
Framingham State (MA)	M
Franklin (IN)	S
Freed-Hardeman (TN)	R
Friends (KS)	R
Frostburg (MD)	M
Gannon (PA)	M
Geneva (PA)	R
George Fox (OR)	R
Georgia Southern	L
Georgia Southwestern	R
Georgia State	L
Gordon (MA)	R
Graceland (IA)	R
Grambling (LA)	M
Great Falls (MT)	S
Greensboro College (NC)	S
Hannibal-La Grange (MO)	R
Hardin-Simmons (TX)	R
Hartford, U. of (CT)	M
Hastings (NE)	R
Heidelberg (OH)	S
Henderson State (AR)	M
Herbert Lehman (CUNY) (NY)	L
High Point (NC)	R
Holy Names (CA)	S
Houston, U. of (TX)	L
Huntingdon (AL)	S
Huntington (IN)	S
Husson (ME)	S
Illinois State	L
Immaculata (PA)	S
Indiana State U.	L
Indiana U.-Purdue U.-Indianapolis (IN)	L
Iona (NY)	M
Jacksonville (FL)	R
Jacksonville State (AL)	M
Jamestown (ND)	R
Johnson State (VT)	R
▲ Judson (AL)	S
Kansas Wesleyan	S
Kean (NJ)	M

GROUP III continues next page

EDUCATION, continued

Keene State (NH)	R	Missouri Baptist	M
Kennesaw State (GA)	R	Missouri Southern State	M
Kent State (OH)	L	Mobile, U. of (AL)	R
Kentucky Wesleyan	S	Monmouth (IL)	S
King (TN)	S	Montana, U. of	M
King's (PA)	R	Montana State (Billings)	R
Kutztown (PA)	M	Montclair State (NJ)	M
Lamar (TX)	M	Montevallo (AL)	R
Lambuth (TN)	S	Mount St. Joseph (OH)	R
Lasell (MA)	S	Mount Mercy (IA)	S
Laverne, U. of (CA)	R	Mount St. Mary's (NY)	S
Lesley (MA)	S	Mount Union (OH)	R
Lewis-Clark State (ID)	R	Murray State (KY)	M
Liberty (VA)	R	Muskingum (OH)	R
Linfield (OR)	R	Nebraska, U. of (Kearney)	M
Lock Haven (PA)	M	Nebraska, U. of (Omaha)	L
Long Island U. (Brooklyn)(NY)	M	Nevada, U. of (Las Vegas)	L
Long Island U. (C.W.Post)(NY)	M	Nevada, U. of (Reno)	L
Longwood (VA)	R	New Mexico, U. of	L
Louisiana College	R	Niagara (NY)	R
Louisiana-Lafayette	L	Nicholls State (LA)	M
Louisiana-Monroe	M	North Dakota State	L
Louisiana Tech.	M	North Georgia	M
Lynchburg (VA)	R	Northeastern Illinois	M
MacMurray (IL)	S	Northeastern State (OK)	L
Maine (Farmington)	R	Northern Arizona	L
Manchester (IN)	R	Northern Colorado	L
Mansfield (PA)	R	Northern Illinois U.	L
Marietta (OH)	R	Northern Iowa	L
Marshall (WV)	L	Northern Kentucky	L
Marygrove (MI)	R	Northern Michigan	M
Maryville (St. Louis) (MO)	R	Northwestern (IA)	R
Marywood (PA)	R	Northwestern (MN)	R
Mass. Coll. of Lib. Arts (N. Adams)	R	Northwestern Louisiana	L
Mass. St. Col. System	M	Nyack (NY)	R
McKendree (IL)	R	Oakland (MI)	M
McPherson (KS)	S	Oakland City U. (IN)	R
Memphis, U. of (TN)	L	Ohio State	L
Mercy (NY)	M	Ohio Wesleyan	R
Mercyhurst (PA)	R	Oklahoma Baptist	R
Middle Tennessee	L	Oklahoma Christian	R
Millikin (IL)	R	Old Dominion (VA)	L
Misericordia, College (PA)	S	Olivet Nazarene (IL)	R
Mississippi College	R		
Mississippi State	L		

GROUP III continues next page

EDUCATION, continued

GROUP III, continued

Oral Roberts (OK) .... M	Southern Mississippi L
Ouachita Baptist (AR) .... R	Southern Nazarene (OK) .... R
Ozarks, College of the (MO) .... R	Southern Oregon State U. .... M
Peru State (NE) .... R	Southern Utah .... M
Philadelphia Biblical (PA) .... S	Southwest Baptist (MO) .... R
Piedmont (GA) .... S	Southwestern Oklahoma .... M
Pittsburg State (KS) .... M	Springfield (MA) .... M
Pittsburgh, U. of (Johnstown) .... R	▲Stephens (MO) .... S
Plymouth State (NH) .... M	Sterling (KS) .... S
Point Loma (CA) .... R	Tabor (KS) .... S
Point Park (PA) .... R	Texas A&M (Corpus Christi) .... M
Puerto Rico (Cayey), U. of L	Texas Lutheran .... R
Radford (VA) .... M	Texas State U. (San Marcos) L
Reinhardt (GA) .... R	Texas Tech. U. L
Robert Morris (PA) .... R	Texas, U. of (El Paso) L
Rhode Island College .... M	Texas Wesleyan .... R
Rider (NJ) .... R	Thomas More (KY) .... R
Rocky Mountain (MT) .... S	Tougaloo (MS) .... S
Roger Williams (RI) .... R	Troy State (AL) .... M
Saginaw Valley (MI) .... M	Utah State L
St. Ambrose (IA) .... R	Wagner (NY) .... R
St. Andrews Presbyterian (NC) .... S	Walsh (OH) .... R
St. Cloud (MN) L	Wartburg (IA) .... R
St. Edward's (TX) .... M	Washburn (KS) .... M
St. Francis (IN) .... R	Weber State (UT) L
St. Joseph's (IN) .... S	Western Carolina (NC) .... M
St. Joseph's (ME) .... S	Western Connecticut .... M
St. Joseph's (NY) .... R	Western Illinois L
▲St. Joseph Col. (CT) .... S	Western Kentucky L
St. Mary (KS) .... S	Western New England (MA) .... R
St. Mary (NE) .... S	Westfield State (MA) .... M
St. Rose (NY) .... R	West Florida, U. of .... M
St. Scholastica (MN) .... R	West Virginia Wesleyan .... R
St. Thomas Aquinas (NY) .... R	▲Wheelock (MA) .... S
Salem State (MA) .... M	Whittier (CA) .... R
Santa Fe, College of (NM) .... S	Widener (PA) .... R
Seton Hall (NJ) .... M	Wilmington (OH) .... S
Shawnee State (OH) .... R	Winthrop (SC) .... M
Shorter (GA) .... R	Wisconsin, U. of (Platteville) .... M
Silver Lake (WI) .... S	Wisconsin, U. of (River Falls) .... M
Simpson (IA) .... S	Wisconsin, U. of (Superior) .... M
Slippery Rock (PA) .... M	Worcester State (MA) .... M
Southeast Missouri State L	Wyoming, U. of................................ L
Southeastern Louisiana.................... L	Xavier U. of Louisiana .... R
Southern Connecticut .... M	York (NE).. S
Southern Illinois U. (Edwardsville) L	

ENGINEERING

GROUP I
Most Selective

Binghamton (SUNY)(NY)	L	Minnesota, U. of	XL
Boston U. (MA)	L	Missouri, U. of (Rolla)	M
Brown (RI)	M	New Mexico Inst. of Mining & Tech.	R
Bucknell (PA)	M	New Jersey, College of	M
Buffalo (SUNY) (NY)	L	Northwestern (IL)	M
California Inst. of Tech.	S	Notre Dame (IN)	M
California, U. of (Berkeley)	XL	Olin (MA)	S
California, U. of (Davis)	XL	Pennsylvania State	XL
California, U. of (Los Angeles)	XL	Pennsylvania, U. of	L
California, U. of (San Diego)	L	Princeton (NJ)	M
California, U. of (Santa Barbara)	L	Rensselaer (NY)	M
Carnegie Mellon (PA)	M	Rice (TX)	M
Case Western Reserve U. (OH)	M	Rochester, U. of	M
Clarkson (NY)	M	Rose-Hulman (IN)	R
Colorado School of Mines	R	Rutgers (NJ)	L
Columbia (NY)	M	▲ Smith (MA)	R
Cooper Union (NY)	S	Southern California, U. of	L
Cornell (NY)	L	Stanford (CA)	M
Dartmouth (NH)	M	Stevens Inst. of Tech. (NJ)	R
Duke (NC)	M	Swarthmore (PA)	R
Florida, U. of	XL	Texas, U. of (Austin)	XL
George Washington (DC)	M	Trinity (CT)	R
Georgia Inst. of Tech.	M	Tufts (MA)	M
Harvey Mudd (CA)	S	Tulane (LA)	M
Illinois Inst. of Tech.	R	Union (NY)	R
Illinois, U. of (Urbana-Champaign)	XL	U.S. Air Force Academy (CO)	M
Iowa State	XL	U.S. Coast Guard Academy (CT)	S
Iowa, U. of	XL	U.S. Military Academy (NY)	M
Johns Hopkins (MD)	M	U.S. Naval Academy (MD)	M
Kettering (MI)	R	Vanderbilt (TN)	M
Lafayette (PA)	R	Villanova (PA)	M
Lehigh (PA)	M	Virginia, U. of	L
Maryland, U. of	XL	Washington U. (MO)	M
MIT (MA)	M	Washington, U. of	L
Miami U. (OH)	L	Worcester Poly. Tech. (MA)	R
Michigan, U. of	XL		

ENGINEERING continues next page

Enrollment Code

■ *Men Only* ▲ *Women Only* | S = Small (less than 1000 students) R = Moderate (1000-3000 students) M = Medium (3000-8000 students)
L = Large (8000-20,000 students) XL = Extra Large (over 20,000 students)

ENGINEERING, continued

GROUP II
Very Selective

Akron, U. of (OH)	L	Florida Inst. of Tech. .... R
Alabama, U. of	L	Florida International L
Alabama, U. of (Birmingham)	M	Gannon (PA) .... R
Alabama, U. of (Huntsville)	M	Geneva (PA) .... R
Alaska, U. of (Fairbanks)	M	Gonzaga (WA) .... R
Alfred (NY)	R	Grand Valley (MI) L
Arizona, U. of	XL	Grove City (PA) .... R
Arizona State	XL	Hartford, U. of (CT) .... M
Arkansas, U. of	L	Houston, U. of (TX) L
Auburn (AL)	L	Howard (DC) .... M
Baylor (TX)	M	Idaho, U. of L
Boise State (ID)	L	Illinois, U. of (Chicago) L
Bradley (IL)	M	Indiana U./Purdue U./Indianapolis L
Brigham Young (UT)	L	Kansas, U. of L
Butler (IN)	R	Kansas State L
California State U. (Fresno)	L	Kentucky, U. of L
California State U. (Fullerton)	L	Lamar (TX) .... M
California State U. (Los Angeles)	L	LeTourneau College (TX) .... R
California State U. (Northridge)	L	Lipscomb (TN) .... R
California State U. (Sacramento)	M	Louisiana-Lafayette L
California, U. of (Irvine)	L	Louisiana State XL
California, U. of (Merced)	R	Louisville (KY) L
California, U. of (Riverside)	L	Lowell, U. of (MA) L
California, U. of (Santa Cruz)	M	Loyola (MD) .... R
California Maritime Academy	S	Loyola Marymount (CA) .... M
Cal. Poly State U. (Pomona)	L	Maine, U. of L
Cal. Poly. State U. (San Luis Obispo)	L	Manhattan (NY) .... M
Calvin (MI)	M	π Marietta (OH) .... R
Carroll (MT)	R	Maritime College (SUNY)(NY) .... S
Catholic U. (DC)	M	Marquette (WI) .... M
Central Connecticut	M	Massachusetts, U. of L
Central Florida, U. of	XL	# Massachusetts, U. of (Dartmouth) .... M
Christian Brothers (TN)	R	Massachusetts, U. of (Lowell) .... M
Cincinnati, U. of (OH)	L	Mass. Maritime Academy .... S
Citadel, The (SC)	R	Memphis, U. of (TN) L
City College (CUNY)(NY)	L	Mercer (GA) .... R
Clemson (SC)	L	Messiah (PA) .... R
Cogswell (CA)	S	Michigan State XL
Colorado State	L	Michigan Tech. .... M
Colorado, U. of	L	Michigan, U. of XL
Colorado, U. of (Col. Springs)	R	Michigan, U. of (Dearborn) .... M
Connecticut, U. of	XL	Milwaukee Sch. of Engine (WI) .... R
Dayton, U. of (OH)	M	Minnesota State U. (Mankato) L
Delaware, U. of	L	Minnesota, U. of (Duluth) .... M
Denver, U. of (CA)	M	Mississippi State L
Detroit Mercy (MI)	M	Mississippi, U. of L
Dordt (IA)	R	Missouri, U. of XL
Drexel (PA)	M	
Embry-Riddle (FL)	M	π Petroleum Engineering
Florida A&M	M	# Also, Textile Science / Industry
Florida Atlantic	L	GROUP II continues next page

ENGINEERING, continued

GROUP II, continued

Montana Tech.	R
Montana State	L
Morgan State (MD)	M
Nebraska, U. of	L
Nevada, U. of (Las Vegas)	L
Nevada, U. of (Reno)	L
New Hampshire, U. of	L
New Jersey Inst. of Tech.	M
New Mexico, U. of	L
New Mexico State U.	L
New Orleans, U. of	L
New Paltz (SUNY)(NY)	M
New York Institute of Tech	M
North Carolina, U. of (Charlotte)	L
North Carolina State	L
North Dakota State	L
North Dakota, U. of	M
Northeastern (MA)	L
Northern Illinois U.	L
Norwich (VT)	R
Oakland U. (MI)	M
Ohio Northern	R
Ohio State	XL
Ohio U.	L
Oklahoma, U. of	XL
Old Dominion (VA)	L
Oregon Inst. of Tech.	R
Oregon State	L
Pacific, U. of the (CA)	R
Penn State (Harrisburg)(PA)	R
Pittsburgh, U. of	L
Pittsburgh, U. of (Johnstown)	R
Polytechnic Univ. of NY	R
Portland, U. of (OR)	R
Portland State (OR)	M
Puerto Rico, U. of (Mayaguez)	L
Purdue (IN)	XL
+ Rhode Island, U. of	L
Rochester Inst. of Tech. (NY)	L
Roger Williams (RI)	M
Rowan (NJ)	M
St. Louis U. (MO)	M
St. Martin's (WA)	S
San Diego State (CA)	XL
San Jose State (CA)	L
Santa Clara U. (CA)	M
Seattle Pacific (WA)	R
Seattle U. (WA)	R
South Carolina, U. of	L
So. Dakota School of Mines	R
South Dakota State U.	M
Southern Illinois U. (Carbondale)	L
Southern Illinois U. (Edwardsville)	L
Southern Maine, U. of	M
Southern Methodist (TX)	L
Southern Polytechnic (GA)	R
South Florida, U. of	L
Stony Brook (SUNY) (NY)	L
▲ Sweet Briar (VA)	S
Syracuse (NY)	L
Tennessee Tech	M
Tennessee, U. of	XL
Texas A&M	XL
Texas A&M (Kingsville)	M
Texas Tech U.	L
Texas, U. of (Arlington)	L
Texas, U. of (Dallas)	M
Texas, U. of (San Antonio)	L
Texas, U. of (El Paso)	L
Texas, U. of (Tyler)	R
Toledo, U. of (OH)	L
Tri-State (IN)	R
Tulsa, U. of (OK)	R
Tuskegee University (AL)	M
Utah, U. of	L
Utah State	L
Valparaiso (IN)	M
Virginia Commonwealth	L
Virginia Military Inst.	R
Virginia Tech.	L
Walla Walla (WA)	R
Washington State	L
Wayne State (MI)	L
West Virginia U.	L
* Western Michigan	L
Western New England (MA)	R
Westminster (UT)	R
Widener (PA)	R
Wilkes (PA)	R
Wisconsin, U. of	XL
Wisconsin, U. of (Platteville)	M
Wright State (OH)	L
Wyoming, U. of	L

+ *And International Engineering*
* *Also, Engineering Management Technology*

Enrollment Code

■ Men Only ▲ Women Only

S = Small (less than 1000 students)   R = Moderate (1000-3000 students)   M = Medium (3000-8000 students)

L = Large (8000-20,000 students)   XL = Extra Large (over 20,000 students)

ENGLISH

•━━━━━━━━━━ **GROUP I** ━━━━━━━━•
Most Selective

Albany (SUNY)(NY)	L	Macalester (MN)	R
Allegheny (PA)	R	Maryland, U. of	XL
Amherst (MA)	R	Miami, U. of (FL)	L
Bard (NY)	R	Miami U. (OH)	L
▲ Barnard (NY)	R	Michigan, U. of	XL
Bates (ME)	R	Middlebury (VT)	R
Binghamton (SUNY)(NY)	L	Minnesota, U. of	XL
Boston Col. (MA)	L	▲ Mount Holyoke (MA)	R
Bowdoin (ME)	R	New (FL)	S
Brandeis (MA)	R	North Carolina, U. of	L
Brown (RI)	M	New Jersey, College of	M
▲ Bryn Mawr (PA)	S	New School U. (Lang)(NY)	S
Bucknell (PA)	M	Northwestern (IL)	M
Buffalo (SUNY) (NY)	L	Notre Dame (IN)	M
California, U. of (Berkeley)	XL	Oberlin (OH)	R
California, U. of (Los Angeles)	XL	Occidental (CA)	R
Carleton (MN)	R	Pennsylvania, U. of	L
Carnegie Mellon (PA)	M	Pitzer (CA)	S
Centre (KY)	R	Pomona (CA)	R
Chicago, U. of (IL)	M	Princeton (NJ)	M
Claremont McKenna (CA)	R	Puget Sound, U. of (WA)	R
Colby (ME)	R	Reed (OR)	R
Colgate (NY)	R	Rhodes (TN)	R
Colorado College	R	Rice (TX)	M
Columbia (NY)	M	Richmond, U. of (VA)	R
Connecticut Col.	R	Rochester, U. of (NY)	M
Cornell (NY)	L	Rutgers (NJ)	L
Dallas, U. of (TX)	R	Sarah Lawrence (NY)	R
Dartmouth (NH)	M	Skidmore (NY)	R
Davidson (NC)	R	▲ Smith (MA)	R
DePauw (IN)	R	South, U. of the (TN)	R
Dickinson (PA)	R	Southwestern (TX)	R
Drew (NJ)	R	Stanford (CA)	M
Duke (NC)	M	St. Olaf (MN)	R
Emory (GA)	M	Swarthmore (PA)	R
Florida, U. of	XL	Trinity (CT)	R
Franklin & Marshall (PA)	R	Trinity (TX)	R
Geneseo (SUNY)(NY)	M	Tufts (MA)	M
Georgetown (DC)	M	Union (NY)	R
Gettysburg (PA)	R	Vanderbilt (TN)	M
Grinnell (IA)	R	Vassar (NY)	R
Gustavus Adolphus (MN)	R	Virginia, U. of	L
Hamilton (NY)	R	■ Wabash (IN)	S
Harvard (MA)	M	Wake Forest (NC)	M
Haverford (PA)	S	Washington & Lee (VA)	R
Holy Cross (MA)	R	Washington U. (MO)	M
Illinois, U. of	XL	▲ Wellesley (MA)	R
Illinois Wesleyan	R	Wesleyan (CT)	R
Iowa, U. of	XL	Wheaton (IL)	R
Kalamazoo (MI)	R	Whitman (WA)	R
Kenyon (OH)	R	Willamette (OR)	R
Knox (IL)	R	William & Mary (VA)	R
Lafayette (PA)	R	Williams (MA)	R
Lawrence (WI)	R	Wisconsin, U. of	XL
Lehigh (PA)	M	Yale (CT)	M

ENGLISH, continued

GROUP II
Very Selective

▲ Agnes Scott (GA)	S	Creighton (NE)	M
Alabama, U. of	L	Delaware, U. of	L
Albertson (ID)	S	Denison (OH)	R
Albion (MI)	R	DePaul (IL)	L
Alfred (NY)	R	Denver, U. of (CO)	M
Alma (MI)	R	Drake (IA)	M
Arizona, U. of	XL	Drury (MO)	R
Arizona State	XL	Earlham (IN)	R
Auburn (AL)	L	Eckerd (FL)	R
Augustana (IL)	R	Elizabethtown (PA)	R
Augustana (SD)	R	Emerson (MA)	M
Baylor (TX)	M	Evansville (IN)	R
Belmont (TN)	R	Flagler (FL)	R
Beloit (WI)	R	Florida State	L
Bemidji State (MN)	M	Fordham (NY)	L
Bennington (VT)	S	Franciscan U. of Steubenville (OH)	R
Bentley (MA)	M	Fredonia (SUNY)(NY)	M
Berea (KY)	R	George Mason (VA)	L
Berry (GA)	R	Georgetown College (KY)	R
Bethany (WV)	S	Georgia, U. of	XL
Birmingham-Southern (AL)	R	Gonzaga (WA)	R
Bradley (IL)	M	Gordon (MA)	R
Brigham Young (UT)	XL	Goucher (MD)	R
Bryn Athyn (PA)	S	Grand Valley (MI)	L
California, U. of (Davis)	XL	Grove City (PA)	R
California, U. of (Irvine)	L	Guilford (NC)	R
Cal Poly State U. (San Luis Obispo)	L	Hamline (MN)	R
Calvin (MI)	M	■ Hampton-Sydney (VA)	S
Canisius (NY)	M	Hampton (VA)	M
Catholic (DC)	M	Hanover (IN)	R
Centenary (LA)	S	Hawaii, U. of	L
Central (IA)	R	Hawaii Pacific	R
Central Florida	XL	Hendrix (AR)	R
Central Michigan	L	Herbert Lehman (CUNY)(NY)	M
Chapman (CA)	R	Hillsdale (MI)	R
Cincinnati, U. of (OH)	L	Hiram (OH)	R
Clark (MA)	R	Hobart & Wm. Smith (NY)	R
Clemson (SC)	L	Hofstra (NY)	M
Coe (IA)	R	▲ Hollins (VA)	S
Colorado, U. of	L	Hood (MD)	S
Concordia (MN)	R	Hope (MI)	R
Cornell Col. (IA)	R		

GROUP II continues next page

Enrollment Code

■ *Men Only*	S = Small (less than 1000 students) R = Moderate (1000-3000 students) M = Medium (3000-8000 students)
▲ *Women Only*	L = Large (8000-20,000 students) XL = Extra Large (over 20,000 students)

ENGLISH, continued

GROUP II, continued

College	Code
Houghton (NY)	R
Houston, U. of (TX)	L
Howard (DC)	M
Hunter (CUNY) (NY)	L
Illinois, U. of (Chicago)	L
Iowa State	XL
John Carroll (OH)	M
▲ Judson (AL)	S
Juniata (PA)	R
Kansas State	L
Kent State (OH)	L
Kentucky, U. of	L
Kentucky Wesleyan	S
Lake Forest (IL)	R
LaSalle (PA)	M
LeMoyne (NY)	R
Lewis & Clark (OR)	R
Lipscomb (TN)	R
Loras (IA)	R
Loyola (LA)	R
Loyola Marymount (CA)	M
Luther (IA)	R
Lycoming (PA)	R
Lyon (AR)	S
Manhattanville (NY)	R
Marietta (OH)	R
Marquette (WI)	M
Mary Washington (VA)	M
Massachusetts, U. of	L
Master's (CA)	R
McDaniel (MD)	R
McKendree (IL)	R
Messiah (PA)	R
Michigan State	XL
▲ Mills (CA)	S
Millsaps (MS)	S
Minnesota, U. of (Morris)	R
Mississippi, U. of	L
Mississippi U. for Women	R
Missouri, U. of	XL
Missouri, U. of (Kansas City)	M
Montana, U. of	M

College	Code
■ Morehouse (GA)	R
Morgan State (MD)	M
Mount Mercy (IA)	S
Muhlenberg (PA)	R
Murray State (KY)	M
Nazareth (NY)	R
Nevada, U. of (Las Vegas)	L
Nevada, U. of (Reno)	L
New Hampshire, U. of	L
New Mexico State U.	L
New Orleans (LA)	L
New Paltz (SUNY)(NY)	M
North Carolina, U. of (Wilmington)	L
North Carolina State	L
North Central (IL)	R
North Dakota, U. of	M
Northeastern (MA)	L
Oglethorpe (GA)	R
Ohio State	XL
Ohio U.	L
Ohio Wesleyan	R
Oklahoma Baptist	R
Oklahoma City U.	R
Oklahoma, U. of	XL
Oklahoma State	L
Oneonta (SUNY)(NY)	M
Oregon, U. of	L
Oswego (SUNY)(NY)	M
Otterbein (OH)	R
Pace (NY)	R
Pacific University (OR)	R
Pittsburgh, U. of (PA)	L
Portland State (OR)	L
Presbyterian (SC)	R
Principia (IL)	S
Providence (RI)	M
Purchase (SUNY) (NY)	M
Queens (NC)	R
Queens (CUNY)(NY)	L
Randolph College (VA)	S
Randolph-Macon (VA)	R

GROUP II continues next page

Enrollment Code

■ *Men Only*
▲ *Women Only*

S = Small (less than 1000 students)   R = Moderate (1000-3000 students)   M = Medium (3000-8000 students)
L = Large (8000-20,000 students)   XL = Extra Large (over 20,000 students)

ENGLISH, continued

─── **GROUP II, continued** ───

Redlands, U. of (CA) .... R	Texas A&M XL
Ripon (WI) .... S	Truman State (MO) .... M
Roanoke (VA) .... R	Tulsa, U. of (OK) .... R
Rollins (FL) .... R	Utah State L
Rutgers (Camden) NJ .... M	Virginia Poly. Institute L
St. Anselm (NH) .... R	Warren Wilson (NC) .... S
St. Bonaventure (NY) .... R	Wartburg (IA) .... R
▲ St. Catherine (MN) .... R	Washington & Jefferson (PA) .... R
St. Joseph's U. (PA) .... R	Washington, U. of XL
St. Lawrence (NY) .... R	Washington State L
St. Louis U. (MO) .... M	Wells (NY) .... S
▲ St. Mary's Col. (IN) .... R	West Chester (PA) .... M
St. Mary's College of Maryland .... R	Western Michigan L
St. Norbert (WI) .... R	Western Washington U. L
St. Scholastica (MN) .... R	Westminster (MO) .... S
San Diego State (CA) XL	Westminster (UT) .... R
Santa Clara U. (CA) .... M	Wheaton (MA) .... R
▲ Scripps (CA) .... S	Whitworth (WA) .... R
Seattle Pacific (WA) .... R	William Jewell (MO) .... R
Shepherd (WV) .... M	Winona State U. (MN) .... M
South Carolina, U. of L	Winthrop (SC) .... M
Spring Hill (AL) .... R	Wittenberg (OH) .... R
Stetson (FL) .... R	Wofford (SC) .... S
Stony Brook (SUNY) (NY) L	Wooster (OH) .... R
Susquehanna (PA) .... R	Wyoming, U. of L

ENGLISH, continued

GROUP III
Selective

Adrian (MI) .... R	East Central (OK) .... R
Alabama, U. of (Birmingham) .... M	East Tennessee L
Alabama, U. of (Huntsville) .... M	Eastern Illinois L
▲ Alverno (WI) .... R	Eastern Michigan L
Appalachian State (NC) L	Eastern Nazarene (MA) .... R
Aquinas (MI) .... R	Eastern Oregon .... R
Arkansas, U. of L	Eastern Washington L
Arcadia (PA) .... R	Edinboro (PA) .... M
Assumption (MA) .... R	Eureka (IL) .... S
Augsburg (MN) .... R	Fairleigh Dickinson (NJ) .... M
Augusta (GA) .... M	Florida A&M .... M
Azusa Pacific (CA) .... R	Florida Gulf Coast U. .... M
Baldwin-Wallace (OH) .... R	Fort Hays (KS) .... M
Baruch (CUNY)(NY) L	Fort Lewis (CO) .... M
Bellarmine (KY) .... R	Friends (KS) .... R
Bethel (IN) .... R	Georgia Southwestern .... R
Brescia (KY) .... S	Goshen (IN) .... R
Briar Cliff (IA) .... R	Gwynedd-Mercy (PA) .... S
Brockport (SUNY)(NY) .... M	Illinois College .... S
California (PA) .... M	Illinois State L
California State U. (Bakersfield) .... M	I.U. P.U.I. (IN) L
California State U. (Channel Islands) .... R	Jamestown (ND) .... R
California State U. (East Bay) .... M	Johnson State (VT) .... R
California State U. (Fresno) L	Kean (NJ) .... M
California State U. (Fullerton) L	Keene State (NH) .... R
California State U. (Monterey Bay) .... R	Kennesaw State (GA) .... R
California State U. (Northridge) L	King (TN) .... S
California State U. (Sacramento) .... M	King's (PA) .... R
Campbell (NC) .... R	Kutztown (PA) .... M
Carson-Newman (TN) .... R	Lewis-Clark State (ID) .... R
Central Washington L	Lindenwood (MO) .... M
Charleston Southern (SC) .... R	Long Island U. (Brooklyn)(NY) .... R
Chestnut Hill (PA) .... S	Long Island U. (C.W. Post)(NY) .... R
Chowan (NC) .... S	Longwood (VA) .... R
Christopher Newport (VA) .... M	Louisiana College .... R
Citadel, The (SC) .... R	Louisiana-Lafayette L
City College (CUNY)(NY) L	Louisiana State XL
Colby-Sawyer (NH) .... S	Lynchburg (VA) .... R
Daemen (NY) .... R	Lyndon State (VT) .... R
Dana (NB) .... S	Maine (Farmington) .... R
Delaware Valley (PA) .... R	Mansfield (PA) .... R
DeSales (PA) .... S	▲ Mary Baldwin (VA) .... S
Doane (NE) .... S	Marygrove (MI) .... R
Dordt (IA) .... R	Mass. Coll. of Lib. Arts (N. Adams) .... R
D'Youville (NY) .... R	Massachusetts, U. of (Boston) .... M
East Carolina L	

GROUP III continues next page

ENGLISH, continued

••• ━━━━━━━━━━━━━━━━ **GROUP III, continued** ━━━━━━━━━━━━━━━ •••

Memphis, U. of (TN)	L
Mercyhurst (PA)	R
▲ Meredith (NC)	R
Merrimack (MA)	R
Middle Tennessee	L
Millersville (PA)	M
Millikin (IL)	R
Misericordia (PA)	S
Missouri Southern State	M
Montclair State (NJ)	M
Montevallo (AL)	R
Mount St. Joseph (OH)	R
Mount Union (OH)	R
Muskingum (OH)	R
Niagara (NY)	R
Nicholls State (LA)	M
Northeastern Illinois	M
Northeastern State (OK)	L
Northern Colorado	L
Northern Iowa	L
Northern Kentucky	L
Northern Michigan	M
Northwestern (IA)	R
Oklahoma Christian	R
Penn State (Erie)(PA)	M
Pittsburgh, U. of (Greensburg)	R
Point Park (PA)	R
Plymouth State (NH)	M
Regis (MA)	S
Rhode Island, U. of	L
Robert Morris (PA)	R
Rockford (IL)	S
Rocky Mountain (MT)	S
▲ Rosemont (PA)	S
St. Edward's (TX)	M
St. Mary (KS)	S
St. Mary's U. of San Antonio (TX)	R
St. Peter's (NJ)	R
▲ Salem Col. (NC)	S
San Francisco State (CA)	L
Schreiner (TX)	S

Seattle U. (WA)	R
Shippensburg (PA)	M
Slippery Rock (PA)	M
South Alabama	M
South Dakota, U. of	M
Southeastern Louisiana	L
Southern Connecticut	M
Southern Nazarene (OK)	R
Southern Utah	M
Southwestern (KS)	S
▲ Spelman (GA)	R
Springfield (MA)	M
Tarleton State (TX)	M
Temple (PA)	L
Tennessee, U. of	XL
Tennessee, U. of (Chattanooga)	M
Tennessee, U. of (Martin)	M
Texas, U. of (San Antonio)	L
Texas, U. of (Tyler)	R
Texas A&M (Corpus Christi)	M
Texas Tech. U.	L
Troy State (AL)	M
Utah, U. of	L
Walla Walla (WA)	R
Walsh (OH)	R
Western Carolina (NC)	M
Western Connecticut	M
Western Illinois	L
Western St. Coll. of Colorado	R
Westfield (MA)	M
West Virginia Wesleyan	R
Wheeling Jesuit (WV)	R
Wichita State (KS)	M
Whittier (CA)	R
Wilkes (PA)	R
William Paterson (NJ)	M
Wilmington (OH)	S
Wisconsin, U. of (Eau Claire)	L
Wisconsin, U. of (Milwaukee)	R
Wisconsin, U. of (Platteville)	M

FOREIGN LANGUAGES

GROUP I
Most Selective

Albany (SUNY)(NY)	L
Allegheny (PA)	R
Bard (NY)	R
▲ Barnard (NY)	R
Bates (ME)	R
Binghamton (SUNY)(NY)	L
Boston College (MA)	L
Boston U. (MA)	L
Bowdoin (ME)	R
Brown (RI)	M
▲ Bryn Mawr (PA)	S
California, U. of (Berkeley)	XL
California, U. of (Los Angeles)	XL
Carleton (MN)	R
Chicago, U. of (IL)	M
Colby (ME)	R
Colgate (NY)	R
Columbia (NY)	M
Connecticut College	R
Dallas, U. of (TX)	R
Dartmouth (NH)	M
DePauw (IN)	R
Dickinson (PA)	R
Drew (NJ)	R
Emory (GA)	M
Florida, U. of	XL
Franklin & Marshall (PA)	R
Georgetown (DC)	M
Grinnell (IA)	R
Gustavus Adolphus (MN)	R
Harvard (MA)	M
Haverford (PA)	S
Holy Cross (MA)	R
Illinois, U. of (Urbana-Champaign)	XL
Kalamazoo (MI)	R

Lawrence (WI)	R
Loyola (MD)	M
Macalester (MN)	R
Maryland, U. of	XL
Michigan, U. of	XL
Middlebury (VT)	R
Minnesota, U. of	XL
▲ Mt. Holyoke (MA)	R
New York U.	M
North Carolina, U. of	L
Northwestern (IL)	M
Notre Dame (IN)	M
Pennsylvania, U. of	L
Pomona (CA)	R
Princeton (NJ)	M
Reed (OR)	R
Rhodes (TN)	R
Rochester, U. of (NY)	M
Rutgers (NJ)	L
▲ Scripps (CA)	S
Skidmore (NY)	R
▲ Smith (MA)	R
South, U. of the (TN)	R
Southwestern (TX)	R
Stanford (CA)	M
Trinity (TX)	R
Tulane (LA)	M
Virginia, U. of	L
Wake Forest (NC)	M
Washington & Lee (VA)	R
Washington U. (MO)	M
▲ Wellesley (MA)	R
Whitman (WA)	R
William & Mary (VA)	M
Yale (CT)	M

FOREIGN LANGUAGES continues next page

Enrollment Code

■ *Men Only*　　S = Small (less than 1000 students)　　R = Moderate (1000-3000 students)　　M = Medium (3000-8000 students)
▲ *Women Only*　　　L = Large (8000-20,000 students)　　XL = Extra Large (over 20,000 students)

FOREIGN LANGUAGES, continued

GROUP II
Very Selective

▲Agnes Scott (GA) .... S
Alabama, U. of L
Arizona, U. of........................ XL
Arizona State XL
Beloit (WI) .... R
Brigham Young (UT) XL
California, U. of (Santa Barbara) L
Calvin (MI) .... M
Catholic (DC)......................... M
Central (IA) .... R
Centre (KY) .... R
Charleston, College of (SC)............... L
Clark (MA) .... R
Clemson (SC) L
Concordia (MN) .... R
Drake (IA) .... M
Earlham (IN).......................... R
Eckerd (FL) .... R
Georgia, U. of XL
Grand Valley (MI) L
Gustavus Adolphus (MN) .... R
Hawaii, U. of L
Herbert Lehman (CUNY)(NY) .... M
Hillsdale (MI)......................... R
▲Hollins (VA) .... S
Hope (MI) .... R
Hunter (CUNY)(NY) L
Ilinois College .... S
Illinois, U. of (Chicago)................... L
Indiana U. XL
Iowa, U. of............................ XL
James Madison (VA) L
Kansas, U. of L
Kansas State L
Lake Forest (IL) .... R
Lewis & Clark (OR) .... R

Linfield (OR) .... R
Lyon (AR) .... S
▲Mills (CA) .... S
Minnesota, U. of (Morris)................. R
Moravian (PA) .... R
Nazareth (NY) .... R
Nebraska, U. of L
New Hampshire, U. of L
New Paltz (SUNY)(NY) .... M
North Carolina (Charlotte) L
Ohio State XL
Oregon, U. of L
Pacific University (OR) .... R
Pepperdine (CA) .... R
Pittsburgh, U. of (PA) L
Portland State (OR) L
Puerto Rico, U. of (Mayaguez) L
Randolph-Macon (VA) .... R
▲Rosemont (PA) .... S
St. Anselm (NH) .... R
South Carolina, U. of L
Stony Brook (SUNY)(NY) L
▲Sweet Briar (VA) .... S
Temple (PA) L
Texas, U. of (Austin) XL
▲Trinity (DC) .... S
Truman State (MO) .... M
Utah, U. of L
Valparaiso U. (IN) .... M
Vermont, U. of L
Virginia Commonwealth L
Wells (NY) .... S
West Chester (PA) .... M
Wheaton (MA) .... R
Wisconsin, U. of XL
Wofford (SC) .... R

GROUP III
Selective

Bethany (WV) .... S
California State U. (Sacramento) ...... M
Carthage (WI) .... R
Eastern Washington .... M
Emory & Henry (VA) .... S
Mansfield (PA) .... R
Montana State........................ L
New Mexico, U. of L
Northwestern (IA).................... R

Slippery Rock (PA) .... M
South Alabama .... M
South Florida, U. of L
Southern Oregon State U. .... M
Wayne State (MI)..................... L
Western Michigan L
Wisconsin, U. of (Milwaukee) L

FOREIGN LANGUAGES continues next page

FOREIGN LANGUAGES, continued

Some Recommendations by Specific Departments
Compiled initially with the help of Minnesota's Jeff Sheehan, Secondary School Counselor

FRENCH

Arizona, U. of	XL
California, U. of (Berkeley)	XL
Central (IA)	R
Colby (ME)	R
Columbia (NY)	M
Dartmouth (NH)	M
Emory (GA)	R
Georgetown (DC)	M
Harvard (MA)	M
Holy Cross (MA)	M
Indiana U.	XL
Indiana (PA)	L
▲Mills (CA)	S
▲Mount Holyoke (MA)	R
North Carolina, U. of	L
Northwestern (IL)	M
Princeton (NJ)	M
Rhodes (TN)	R
San Diego State U. (CA)	L
▲Scripps (CA)	S
Tufts (MA)	M
Tulane (LA)	M
Vassar (NY)	R
Washington U. (MO)	M
▲Wellesley (MA)	R
Wittenberg (OH)	R

GERMAN

Boston College (MA)	L
Brown (RI)	M
California, U. of (Berkeley)	XL
California, U. of (Santa Barbara)	L
Colorado, U. of	L
Hunter (CUNY)(NY)	L
Illinois, U. of (Urbana-Champaign)	XL
Indiana U.	XL
Indiana (PA)	L
Michigan State	XL
Penn State	XL
Pennsylvania, U. of	L
Princeton (NJ)	M
Rhode Island., U. of	L
Stanford (CA)	M
Texas, U. of (Austin)	XL
Williams (MA)	R
Wisconsin, U. of	XL
Wofford (SC)	R

JAPANESE

Brigham Young (UT)	XL
Connecticut College	R
Harvard (MA)	M
Hawaii, U. of (Manoa)	L
Ohio State	L
Oregon, U. of	L
Pacific University (OR)	R
Pennsylvania, U. of	L
Pittsburgh, U. of (PA)	L
Washington, U. of	XL
Wisconsin, U. of	XL

SPANISH

Bradley (IL)	M
Brigham Young (UT)	XL
Buffalo (SUNY) (NY)	L
California State U. (San Marcos)	M
California, U. of (Irvine)	M
California, U. of (San Diego)	L
California, U. of (Santa Barbara)	L
Central (IA)	R
Colby (ME)	R
George Washington (DC)	M
Greensboro College (NC)	S
Indiana U.	XL
Kansas, U. of	L
Lawrence (WI)	R
Lyon (AR)	S
Maryland, U. of	XL
Massachusetts, U. of (Dartmouth)	M
Messiah (PA)	R
Northwestern (IA)	R
Pittsburgh, U. of	L
Puerto Rico, U. of (Mayaguez)	L
Rutgers (NJ)	L
San Diego State U. (CA)	L
▲Scripps (CA)	S
Southern Connecticut	M
Texas, U. of	XL
Utah, U. of	L
Vanderbilt (TN)	M
Wisconsin, U. of	XL
Worcester State (MA)	M

FORESTRY

GROUP I
Most Selective

Florida, U. of XL

Illinois, U. of XL

North Carolina State L

South, U. of the (TN) .... R

SUNY Coll. of Env. Sci. & Forestry .... R

GROUP II
Very Selective

Arizona, U. of XL

Auburn (AL) L

Berry (GA) .... R

Clemson (SC) L

Colorado State L

Connecticut, U. of XL

Georgia, U. of L

Iowa State XL

Kentucky, U. of L

Maine, U. of L

Massachusetts, U. of L

Michigan State XL

Michigan Tech .... M

Minnesota, U. of XL

Mississippi State L

Missouri, U. of XL

New Hampshire, U. of L

Oklahoma State L

Pennsylvania State XL

Purdue (IN) XL

Syracuse (NY) L

Tennessee, U. of XL

Texas A&M XL

Virginia Tech L

Washington, U. of XL

West Virginia U. L

Wisconsin, U. of XL

GROUP III
Selective

Humboldt State (CA) .... M

Idaho, U. of L

Montana, U. of .... M

Northern Arizona XL

Oregon State L

Paul Smith's (NY) .... S

Southern Illinois (Carbondale) L

Stephen F. Austin (TX) L

Utah State L

GEOGRAPHY

GROUP I
Most Selective

Boston U. (MA)	L	Johns Hopkins (MD)	M
Buffalo (SUNY)(NY)	L	Macalester (MN)	R
California, U. of (Berkeley)	XL	Maryland, U. of	XL
Chicago, U. of (IL)	M	Miami U. (OH)	L
Clark (MA)	R	Michigan, U. of	XL
Colgate (NY)	R	Middlebury (VT)	R
Dartmouth (NH)	M	Minnesota, U. of	XL
Florida, U. of	XL	Sarah Lawrence (NY)	R
George Washington (DC)	M		

GROUP II
Very Selective

Arizona State	XL	Ohio State	XL
Bemidji State (MN)	M	Oklahoma, U. of	XL
California, U. of (Santa Barbara)	L	Oklahoma State	L
Colorado, U. of	L	Oregon, U. of	L
Colorado, U. of (Colorado Springs)	M	Oneonta (SUNY)(NY)	M
Denver, U. of (CO)	M	Pennsylvania State	XL
DePaul (IL)	L	Radford (VA)	M
Florida International	L	San Diego State U. (CA)	L
Georgia, U. of	L	South Carolina, U. of	L
# Harrisburg U. (PA)	S	Syracuse (NY)	L
Hunter (CUNY)(NY)	L	Texas, U. of (Austin)	XL
Indiana U.	XL	Vermont, U. of	L
Kansas State	L	Virginia Poly. Institute	L
Kansas, U. of	L	Washington, U. of	XL
Louisiana State	XL	Western Washington U.	L
Mary Washington (VA)	M	Wisconsin, U. of (Madison)	XL
Michigan State	XL	Wittenberg (OH)	R
New Paltz (SUNY)(NY)	M		

GROUP III
Selective

Aquinas (MI)	R	Louisiana Tech.	M
Ball State (IN)	M	Maine (Farmington)	R
Bloomsburg (PA)	M	Mansfield (PA)	R
Bridgewater (MA)	M	Massachusetts, U. of (Boston)	M
California State U. (Chico)	L	New Orleans (LA)	L
California State U. (Long Beach)	L	North Carolina (Charlotte)	L
California State U. (Northridge)	L	Salem State (MA)	M
California State U. (Stanislaus)	M	Sonoma State (CA)	M
Carthage (WI)	R	Southern Connecticut	M
Central Connecticut	M	Southern Illinois U. (Carbondale)	L
Central Michigan	L	Texas A&M (Corpus Christi)	M
Central Washington	L	Texas State U. (San Marcos)	L
Edinboro (PA)	M	Western Illinois	L
π Elmhurst (IL)	R	Wisconsin, U. of (LaCrosse)	L
Frostburg (MD)	M	Wyoming, U. of	L
++Indiana (PA)	L		
Indiana State	L		
Keene State (NH)	R		

++ *Especially Regional Planning*
\# *Geography and Geospatial Imaging*
π *Geography and Environmental Planning*

GEOLOGY

GROUP I
Most Selective

Amherst (MA)	R		Lehigh (PA)	M
Bates (ME)	R		Massachusetts, U. of	L
Binghamton (SUNY)(NY)	L		MIT (MA)	M
Bowdoin (ME)	R		Michigan, U. of	XL
Brown (RI)	M		Minnesota, U. of	XL
▲ Bryn Mawr (PA)	R		▲ Mount Holyoke (MA)	R
California Inst. of Tech.	S		Oberlin (OH)	R
California, U. of (Berkeley)	XL		Pennsylvania, U. of	L
Carleton (MN)	R		Pennsylvania State	XL
Chicago, U. of (IL)	M		Pomona (CA)	R
Colgate (NY)	R		Princeton (NJ)	M
Colorado Col.	R		Rennselaer (NY)	M
Colorado School of Mines	R		Rochester, U. of (NY)	M
Columbia (NY)	M		Skidmore (NY)	R
Dartmouth (NH)	M		▲ Smith (MA)	R
Franklin & Marshall (PA)	R		South, U. of the (TN)	R
Furman (SC)	R		Union (NY)	R
Geneseo (SUNY) (NY)	M		Vanderbilt (TN)	M
Gustavus Adolphus (MN)	R		Washington & Lee (VA)	R
Hamilton (NY)	R		Washington U. (MO)	M
Harvard (MA)	M		Whitman (WA)	R
Lafayette (PA)	R		William & Mary (VA)	M

GROUP II
Very Selective

Alaska, U. of (Fairbanks)	M		Earlham (IN)	R
Albany (SUNY) (NY)	L		Eastern Washington	L
Alabama, U. of	L		Guilford (NC)	R
Allegheny (PA)	R		Hanover (IN)	R
Arizona State	XL		Hope (MI)	R
Arizona, U. of	XL		Houston, U. of	XL
Beloit (WI)	R		Idaho, U. of	L
Bowling Green (OH)	L		Indiana U.	XL
Brigham Young (UT)	XL		Juniata (PA)	R
California, U. of (Davis)	XL		Mary Washington (VA)	M
California, U. of (Santa Barbara)	L		Michigan State	XL
Centenary College (LA)	S		Michigan Tech	M
College of Charleston (SC)	L		Millsaps (MS)	S
Colorado State	L		Minnesota, U. of (Duluth)	M
Colorado, U. of	L		Minnesota, U. of (Morris)	R
Cornell Col. (IA)	R		New Hampshire, U. of	L
Dayton, U. of (OH)	M		New Mexico Inst. of Mining & Tech.	R
Denison (OH)	R			
Denver, U. of (CO)	M			

GROUP II continues next page

GEOLOGY, continued

GROUP II, continued

New Mexico, U. of	L
North Carolina, U. of (Wilmington)	L
Ohio State	XL
Oklahoma, U. of	XL
Oklahoma State	L
Oregon State	L
Purdue (IN)	XL
Rhode Island, U. of	L
St. Lawrence (NY)	R
St. Thomas (MN)	M
San Diego State (CA)	L
π South Carolina, U. of	L
South Dakota School of Mines	R
Stony Brook (SUNY) (NY)	L
Texas A&M	XL
Texas Christian	M
Texas, U. of (Austin)	XL
Tulsa, U. of (OK)	M
Utah, U. of	L
Vermont, U. of	M
Washington, U. of	XL
West Virginia U.	L
Wisconsin, U. of	XL
Wooster, College of (OH)	R

π *Also Geophysics*

GROUP III
Selective

Bloomsburg (PA)	M
Boise State (ID)	L
Brockport (SUNY)(NY)	M
Brooklyn College (CUNY) (NY)	L
California State U. (Bakersfield)	M
California State U. (Chico)	L
California State U. (East Bay)	M
California State U. (Sacramento)	M
Edinboro (PA)	M
Emporia State (KS)	M
Fort Lewis (CO)	M
Hartwick (NY)	R
Lamar (TX)	M
Louisiana-Lafayette	L
Louisiana State	XL
Montana, U. of	M
Muskingum (OH)	R
Nevada, U. of (Reno)	L
Nevada, U. of (Las Vegas)	L
New Mexico State U.	L
North Carolina (Wilmington)	M
Northland (WI)	S
Northern Arizona	XL
Northern Illinois U.	L
Oneonta (SUNY)(NY)	M
Plattsburgh (SUNY)(NY)	M
Salem State (MA)	M
Texas A&M (Corpus Christi)	M
West Chester (PA)	M
Western State Coll. of Colorado	R
Wright State (OH)	L
Wyoming, U. of	L

HISTORY

GROUP I
Most Selective

Albany (SUNY)(NY)	L		Haverford (PA)	S
Albertson (ID)	S		Holy Cross (MA)	R
Albion (MI)	R		Illinois, U. of (Urbana-Champaign)	XL
American (DC)	M		James Madison (VA)	L
Amherst (MA)	R		Johns Hopkins (MD)	M
▲ Barnard (NY)	R		Kalamazoo (MI)	R
Bates (ME)	R		Kenyon (OH)	R
Binghamton (SUNY)(NY)	L		Lafayette (PA)	R
Boston Col. (MA)	L		Lawrence (WI)	R
Boston U. (MA)	L		Lehigh (PA)	M
Bowdoin (ME)	R		Macalester (MN)	R
Brandeis (MA)	R		Maryland, U. of (Baltimore County)	M
Brown (RI)	M		MIT (MA)	M
▲ Bryn Mawr (PA)	S		Miami, U. of	L
Bucknell (PA)	M		Michigan, U. of	XL
Buffalo (SUNY)(NY)	L		Middlebury (VT)	R
California, U. of (Berkeley)	XL		Minnesota, U. of	XL
California, U. of (Los Angeles)	XL		Missouri, U. of (Rolla)	M
Carleton (MN)	R		▲ Mount Holyoke (MA)	R
Carnegie Mellon (PA)	M		New College (FL)	S
Case Western Reserve (OH)	M		New Jersey, College of	M
Centre (KY)	R		New York U.	L
Chicago, U. of (IL)	M		North Carolina, U. of	L
Claremont McKenna (CA)	R		Northwestern (IL)	M
Colgate (NY)	R		Notre Dame (IN)	M
Colorado Col.	R		Oberlin (OH)	R
Columbia (NY)	M		Pennsylvania, U. of	L
Connecticut Col.	R		Pitzer (CA)	S
Cornell (NY)	L		Pomona (CA)	R
Dallas, U. of (TX)	R		Princeton (NJ)	M
Dartmouth (NH)	M		Reed (OR)	R
Davidson (NC)	R		Rhodes (TN)	R
DePauw (IN)	R		Rice (TX)	M
Dickinson (PA)	R		Richmond, U. of (VA)	R
Drew (NJ)	R		Rochester, U. of (NY)	M
Duke (NC)	M		Rutgers (NJ)	L
Emory (GA)	M		St. Olaf (MN)	R
Florida, U. of	XL		Sarah Lawrence (NY)	R
Furman (SC)	R		▲ Smith (MA)	R
Geneseo (SUNY)(NY)	M		South, U. of the (TN)	R
George Washington (DC)	M		Southwestern (TX)	R
Georgetown (DC)	M		Swarthmore (PA)	R
Georgia Institute of Tech.	L		Texas Christian U. (TX)	M
Gettysburg (PA)	R		Trinity (TX)	R
Grinnell (IA)	R		Tufts (MA)	M
Hamilton (NY)	R			
Harvard (MA)	M			

GROUP I continues next page

HISTORY, continued

GROUP I, continued

Tulane (LA)	M
Union (NY)	R
U.S. Military Academy (NY)	M
Vanderbilt (TN)	R
Vassar (NY)	R
Virginia, U. of	L
■ Wabash (IN)	S
Wake Forest (NC)	M
Washington & Lee (VA)	R
▲ Wellesley (MA)	R
Wesleyan U. (CT)	R
Wheaton (IL)	R
Whitman (WA)	R
William & Mary (VA)	M
Williams (MA)	R
Yale (CT)	M
Yeshiva (NY)	R

GROUP II
Very Selective

▲ Agnes Scott (GA)	S
Albion (MI)	R
Alfred (NY)	R
Allegheny (PA)	R
Alma (MI)	R
Arizona State	XL
Arizona, U. of	XL
Auburn (AL)	L
Austin (TX)	R
Bard (NY)	R
Baylor (TX)	M
Beloit (WI)	R
Birmingham-Southern (AL)	R
Bryan (TN)	S
Bryn Athyn (PA)	S
California, U. of (Davis)	XL
California, U. of (Merced)	R
California, U. of (Riverside)	L
California, U. of (Santa Cruz)	M
Cal. Poly State U. (San Luis Obispo)	L
Calvin (MI)	M
Canisius (NY)	M
Christendom (VA)	S
Cincinnati, U. of (OH)	L
City College (CUNY)(NY)	L
Coe (IA)	R
Colorado U. of	L
Connecticut U. of	XL
Cornell College (IA)	R
Covenant (GA)	S
Delaware, U. of	L
Denison (OH)	R
DePaul (IL)	L
Denver, U. of (CO)	M
Drake (IA)	M
East Carolina	L
Eastern Michigan	L
Elmira (NY)	R
Erskine (SC)	S
Florida Atlantic	L
Florida State	L
Georgetown College (KY)	R
Georgia, U. of	L
Gonzaga (WA)	R
Goucher (MD)	S
Guilford (NC)	R
Gustavus Adolphus (MN)	R
■ Hampden-Sydney (VA)	S
Hamline (MN)	R
Hanover (IN)	R
Hawaii, U. of	L
Hillsdale (MI)	R
Hiram (OH)	R
Hobart & William Smith (NY)	R
▲ Hollins (VA)	S
Hood (MD)	S
Houghton (NY)	S
Illinois College	S
Illinois, U. of (Chicago)	L
Indiana U.	XL
Iowa, U. of	XL
John Carroll (OH)	R
Juniata (PA)	R
Kansas, U. of	L
Kansas State	L
Kentucky, U. of	L
Kentucky Wesleyan	S

GROUP II continues next paga

HISTORY, continued

━━ GROUP II, continued ━━

Knox (IL) .... R	▲Rosemont (PA) .... S
Lake Forest (IL) .... R	Rowan (NJ) .... M
LeMoyne (NY) .... R	Rutgers (Camden) (NJ) .... M
Lewis & Clark (OR) .... R	St. Joseph's (PA) .... R
Linfield (OR) .... R	St. John's/ St. Benedict (MN) .... R
Loras (IA) .... R	St. Mary's College of Maryland .... R
Loyola (LA) .... R	St. Norbert (WI) .... R
Loyola Marymount (CA) .... M	San Diego State U. (CA) XL
Luther (IA) .... R	Santa Clara U. (CA) .... M
Manhattanville (NY) .... R	Seattle U. (WA) .... R
Mansfield (PA) .... R	Shepherd (WV) .... M
Marquette (WI) .... M	South Carolina, U. of L
Maryland, U. of XL	Southern Methodist (TX) L
+ Mary Washington (VA) .... M	Spring Hill (AL) .... R
Massachusetts, U. of L	Stetson (FL) .... R
Mass. College of Liberal Arts (N. Adams). R	Stony Brook (SUNY)(NY) L
McMurry (TX) .... R	Tennessee, U. of XL
Miami, U. of (FL) .... M	Texas A&M XL
Michigan State XL	Texas Tech U. L
Millersville (PA) .... M	Texas, U. of (Austin) XL
Millsaps (MS) .... S	Texas, U. of (Dallas) .... M
Minnesota, U. of (Morris) .... R	Trinity (CT) .... R
Missouri, U. of XL	Tulsa, U. of (OK) .... M
Missouri, U. of (Kansas City) .... M	Utah, U. of L
Monmouth (IL) .... S	Vermont, U. of L
■ Morehouse (GA) .... R	Virginia Tech. L
Muhlenberg (PA) .... R	Virginia Military Institute .... R
Nebraska, U. of L	Warren Wilson (NC) .... S
New Mexico State U. L	Wartburg (IA) .... R
New Orleans, U. of (LA) L	Washington College (MD) .... S
North Carolina (Asheville) .... R	Washington State L
Northeastern (MA) L	Washington, U. of XL
Oglethorpe (GA) .... S	Washington & Jefferson (PA) .... R
Ohio State XL	Webster (MO) .... R
Ohio U. L	Wells (NY) .... S
Oklahoma, U. of XL	Western Michigan L
Oklahoma City U. .... R	Westminster (MO) .... S
Oklahoma State L	Westminster (UT) .... S
Oregon State L	Wheaton (MA) .... R
Ozarks, College of the (MO) .... R	Whitworth (WA) .... R
Pittsburgh, U. of (PA) L	Willamette (OR) .... R
Plattsburgh (SUNY)(NY) .... M	William Paterson (NJ) .... M
Portland, U. of (OR) .... R	Winona State U. (MN) .... M
Presbyterian (SC) .... R	Winthrop (SC) .... M
Providence (RI) .... M	Wisconsin, U. of XL
Purchase (SUNY)(NY) .... M	Wittenberg (OH) .... R
Queens (NC) .... R	Wofford (SC) .... R
Ramapo (NJ) .... M	Wooster (OH) .... R
Richard Stockton (NJ) .... M	Xavier (OH) .... R
Ripon (WI) .... S	
Roanoke (VA) .... R	*+ And Historic Preservation Major*

HISTORY, continued

GROUP III
Selective

Akron, U. of (OH)	L	McPherson (KS)	S
Alabama, U. of	L	Middle Tennessee	L
Appalachian State (NC)	L	Michigan, U. of	XL
Arkansas, U. of	L	Milligan (TN)	S
Assumption (MA)	R	Misericordia (PA)	S
Baldwin-Wallace (OH)	R	Mississippi, U. of	L
Baruch (CUNY)(NY)	L	Montevallo (AL)	R
Bellarmine (KY)	R	Morgan State (MD)	M
Boise State (ID)	L	Mount St. Mary's (MD)	R
Briar Cliff (IA)	R	Murray State (KY)	M
Bridgewater (MA)	M	Muskingum (OH)	R
Bridgewater (VA)	R	Nevada, U. of (Las Vegas)	L
Brockport (SUNY)(NY)	M	New Mexico, U. of	L
California State U. (Channel Islands)	R	North Carolina (Greensboro)	M
California State U. (East Bay)	M	Northern Colorado	L
California State U. (Fullerton)	L	Northern Iowa	L
California State U. (Long Beach)	L	Northwestern (IA)	S
California State U. (San Marcos)	M	Northwestern Louisiana	L
Campbell (NC)	R	Oklahoma Baptist	R
Capital U. (OH)	R	Old Dominion (VA)	L
Carroll (MT)	R	Oneonta (SUNY)(NY)	M
Carson-Newman (TN)	R	Oswego (SUNY)(NY)	M
Central Connecticut	M	Pittsburgh, U. of (Greenburg)	R
Charleston, U. of (WV)	S	Quincy (IL)	R
Cumberland (KY)	R	Regis (CO)	R
Delaware State	R	Rhode Island College	M
East Tennessee	L	St. Ambrose (IA)	R
Eastern Connecticut	M	St. Joseph's (NY)	R
Fairmont State (WV)	M	St. Mary's (MN)	R
Fitchburg (MA)	R	Salem State (MA)	M
Fredonia (SUNY)(NY)	M	Shippensburg (PA)	M
Georgia Southern	L	South Dakota, U. of	M
Graceland (IA)	R	Southern Illinois U. (Carbondale)	L
Hastings (NE)	R	Southern Mississippi	L
Heidelberg (OH)	S	Tarleton State (TX)	M
Holy Names (CA)	S	Texas A&M (Corpus Christi)	M
Houston, U. of (TX)	L	Texas Lutheran	R
Indiana (PA)	L	Texas State U. (San Marcos)	L
I.U. P.U.I. (IN)	L	Texas, U. of (San Antonio)	L
Kennesaw State (GA)	R	Toledo, U. of	L
Kutztown (PA)	M	Western St. Col. of Colorado	R
Lambuth (TN)	S	West Kentucky	L
Liberty (VA)	R	West Virginia Wesleyan	R
Lock Haven (PA)	M	Wheeling Jesuit (WV)	R
Louisiana College	R	Wilkes (PA)	R
Louisiana State	XL	Wilmington (OH)	S
Manchester (IN)	R	Wingate (NC)	R
▲ Mary Baldwin (VA)	S	Wisconsin, U. of (Green Bay)	M
Maryville (TN)	S	Wisconsin, U. of (Milwaukee)	L
Massachusetts U. of (Boston)	M		

HOME ECONOMICS/FAMILY STUDIES

GROUP I
Most Selective

Florida State	L	Penn State	XL
Iowa State	XL	Wisconsin, U. of	XL

GROUP II
Very Selective

# Bradley (IL)	M	Oklahoma State	L
Brigham Young (UT)	XL	Oneonta (SUNY) (NY)	M
Connecticut, U. of	XL	Purdue (IN)	XL
Georgia, U. of	XL	Rhode Island, U. of	L
➤ Kansas State	L	π Seattle Pacific (WA)	M
Masters (CA)	R	Utah, U. of	L
Michigan State	XL	Utah State	L
Nebraska, U. of	L	Western Michigan	L
New Hampshire, U. of	L	Wisconsin, U. of (Stout)	M
Northern Illinois U.	L		

Family & Consumer Science
π *Apparel Design, also Clothing*
➤ *Nutritional & Exercise Sciences*

GROUP III
Selective

Akron, U. of (OH)	L	Montevallo (AL)	R
Berea (KY)	R	Nevada, U. of (Reno)	L
California State U. (Fresno)	L	New Mexico State U.	L
California State U. (Sacramento)	M	Nicholls State (LA)	M
Central Michigan	L	North Carolina (Greensboro)	M
Eastern Illinois	L	North Dakota State	L
Framingham State (MA)	M	Oregon State	L
Georgia Southern	L	Point Loma (CA)	R
Marywood (PA)	R	Texas Tech. U.	L
Montclair State (NJ)	M	Washington State	L

Enrollment Code

■ *Men Only*   S = Small (less than 1000 students)   R = Moderate (1000-3000 students)   M = Medium (3000-8000 students)
▲ *Women Only*   L = Large (8000-20,000 students)   XL = Extra Large (over 20,000 students)

JOURNALISM/COMMUNICATIONS

━━ GROUP I ━━
Most Selective

American U. (DC)	M	New York U	L
Boston College (MA)	L	North Carolina, U. of	L
Boston U. (MA)	L	Northeastern (MA)	L
California, U. of (Los Angeles)	XL	Northwestern (IL)	M
California, U. of (San Diego)	L	Ohio U.	L
Creighton (NE)	M	# Pomona (CA)	R
DePauw (IN)	R	Southern California	L
Florida, U. of	XL	Southwestern (TX)	R
Gettysburg (PA)	R	Stanford (CA)	M
Illinois, U. of (Urbana-Champaign)	XL	Syracuse (NY)	L
Macalester (MN)	R	Trinity (TX)	R
Miami, U. of (FL)	L	Villanova (PA)	M
Michigan, U. of	XL	Washington & Lee (VA)	R
Minnesota, U. of	XL	Wheaton (IL)	R
Missouri, U. of	XL	Wisconsin, U. of	XL

━━ GROUP II ━━
Very Selective

Adelphi (NY)	M	Fairfield (CT)	M
Alabama, U. of	L	Flagler (FL)	R
Alabama, U. of (Huntsville)	M	Florida Inst. of Tech.	R
Alfred (NY)	R	Fordham (NY)	M
Alma (MI)	R	Fredonia (SUNY) (NY)	M
Arizona State	XL	Geneva (PA)	R
Arizona, U. of	XL	George Mason (VA)	L
Asbury (KY)	R	Georgetown College (KY)	R
Auburn (AL)	L	Georgia State	L
Bryan (TN)	S	Georgia, U. of	XL
California Poly. State U. (SLO)	L	Gonzaga (WA)	R
Canisius (NY)	M	Hampton (VA)	M
Capital (OH)	R	Hanover (IN)	R
Central Florida, U. of	XL	Hastings (NE)	R
Chapman (CA)	R	Houston, U. of (TX)	L
Charleston, College of (SC)	L	Illinois College	S
Clark (MA)	R	Indiana State	L
Clarke (IA)	S	Indiana U.	XL
Colorado, U. of	L	Indiana U. of Pennsylvania	L
Colorado, U. of (Colorado Springs)	M	Iowa, U. of	XL
Columbia College (IL)	M	Ithaca (NY)	M
Connecticut, U. of	XL	James Madison (VA)	M
Dayton, U. of (OH)	M	John Carroll (OH)	M
Delaware, U. of	L	Juniata (PA)	R
Denver, U. of (CO)	M	Kansas, U. of	L
DePaul (IL)	L	Kansas State	L
Drake (IA)	M	Kentucky, U. of	L
Dubuque, U. of (IA)	S		
Duquesne (PA)	M		
Emerson (MA)	M		

*Media Studies*
GROUP II continues next page

JOURNALISM/COMMUNICATIONS, continued

GROUP II, continued

La Salle (PA)	M
LeMoyne (NY)	R
Linfield (OR)	R
Loras (IA)	R
Louisiana State	XL
Loyola (MD)	R
Loyola Marymount (CA)	M
Maine, U. of	L
Mansfield (PA)	M
Marist (NY)	M
π Marquette (WI)	M
Marshall (WV)	L
Mary Baldwin (VA)	S
Maryland, U. of	XL
Massachusetts, U. of	L
Master's (CA)	R
Memphis, U. of (TN)	L
Michigan State	L
Milligan (TN)	S
▲ Mills College (CA)	S
Minnesota, U. of (Duluth)	M
Mississippi, U. of	L
Mississippi U. for Women	R
Missouri, U. of (Kansas City)	M
Montana, U. of	M
Moravian (PA)	R
Muhlenberg (PA)	R
Nevada, U. of (Reno)	L
New Hampshire, U. of	L
North Central (IL)	R
North Florida	M
North Texas	L
Ohio State	XL
Ohio Wesleyan	R
Oklahoma, U. of	XL
Oregon, U. of	L
Oswego (SUNY)(NY)	M
Pennsylvania State	XL
Pepperdine (CA)	R
Pittsburgh, U. of (PA)	L
Plattsburgh (SUNY)(NY)	M
Purchase (SUNY)(NY)	M
Quinnipiac (CT)	R
Ramapo (NJ)	M
Randolph College (VA)	S

Rhode Island, U. of	L
Rowan (NJ)	M
St. Ambrose (IA)	R
St. Bonaventure (NY)	R
St. Cloud (MN)	L
St. Louis (MO)	M
St. Mary's (IN)	R
St. Michael's (VT)	R
St. Norbert (WI)	R
St. Thomas (MN)	M
San Diego State U. (CA)	XL
Santa Clara U. (CA)	M
Scranton, U. of (PA)	M
▲ Simmons (MA)	R
South Alabama	M
South Carolina, U. of	L
Southern Illinois U. (Carbondale)	L
Southern Methodist (TX)	M
Spring Hill (AL)	R
▲ Stephens (MO)	S
Suffolk (MA)	R
Susquehanna U. (PA)	R
Temple (PA)	L
Texas A&M	S
Texas Christian U.	M
Texas, U. of (Arlington)	L
Texas, U. of (Austin)	XL
Tulsa, U. of (OK)	R
Virginia Tech.	L
Wartburg (IA)	R
Washington State	L
West Florida, U. of	M
West Virginia U.	L
Western Michigan	L
Western Washington U.	L
Westminster (UT)	R
Whitworth (WA)	R
Winona State U. (MN)	L
Wisconsin Lutheran	S
Wisconsin, U. of (Stevens Point)	M
Xavier (OH)	R
York (PA)	R

π *Especially Broadcasting*

JOURNALISM/COMMUNICATIONS continues next page

Enrollment Code

■ *Men Only*　　S = Small (less than 1000 students)　　R = Moderate (1000-3000 students)　　M = Medium (3000-8000 students)

▲ *Women Only*　　L = Large (8000-20,000 students)　　XL = Extra Large (over 20,000 students)

JOURNALISM/COMMUNICATIONS, continued

••• ———————————————— **GROUP III** ———————————————— •••
Selective

▲Alverno (WI) .... R
Appalachian State (NC) L
Arkansas, U. of................................... L
Augsburg (MN) .... R
+ Azusa Pacific (CA) .... R
Ball State (IN) L
Bemidji State (MN) .... M
Bethany (WV) .... S
Bridgewater State (WA) .... M
Brockport (SUNY) (NY)..................... M
Buena Vista (IA) .... R
Butler (IN) .... R
California Lutheran .... R
California State U. (Fullerton) L
California State U. (Long Beach) L
California State U. (Northridge) L
California State U. (Sacramento) .... M
California State U. (San Bernardino) ...... M
Castleton State (VT) .... R
Central Missouri L
▲Chatham (PA)..................................... S
Dana (NE) .... S
East Tennessee................................... L
Eastern Connecticut .... M
Eastern Illinois L
Eastern Kentucky L
Elon (NC) .... R
Endicott (MA)..................................... R
Fitchburg (MA) .... R
Florida A&M .... M
Florida Southern................................. R
Fontbonne (MO) .... R
Franklin (IN) .... S
Gwynedd-Mercy (PA) .... S
Hardin-Simmons (TX) .... R
Hartford, U. of (CT) .... M
Hawaii Pacific .... M
Hofstra (NY)....................................... M
Howard (DC) .... M
Hunter (CUNY) (NY) L
Idaho, U. of L
I.U. P.U.I. (IN) L
Iona (NY)... M
Jacksonville (FL) .... R
Johnson C. Smith (NC)....................... R

▲Judson (AL) .... S
Keene State (NH)................................ R
Kent State (OH) L
Kentucky Wesleyan .... S
Lewis-Clark State (ID) .... R
Liberty (VA)... R
Lindenwood (MO) .... M
Louisiana-Monroe .... M
Loyola (IL) .... M
Loyola U. (LA) .... M
Lynchburg (VA) .... R
• Lyndon State (VT)............................... R
Marietta (OH) .... R
Marymount Manhattan (NY) .... R
Mass. College of Lib. Arts (N. Adams) .... R
Minnesota, U. of (Duluth) .... M
Misericordia, College (PA) .... S
Missouri Southern State..................... M
Missouri, U. of (St. Louis) .... M
Monmouth (NJ) .... R
Montana, U. of .... M
Morningside (IA) .... S
Montevallo (AL)................................... R
Muskingum (OH)................................. R
Murray State (KY) .... M
Nebraska, U. of L
North Carolina, U. of (Greensboro) ...... M
North Carolina, U. of (Pembroke) .... R
North Dakota, U. of............................ M
Northern Illinois U. L
Northern Iowa L
Northern Kentucky............................. L
Northwest Missouri State .... M
Oakland U. (MI) .... M
Oklahoma City U................................ R
Otterbein (OH) .... R
Palm Beach Atlantic (FL) .... R
▲Pine Manor (MA)............................... S
Regis (CO) .... R
Regis (MA) .... S
Reinhardt (GA) .... R

+ *Media Studies*
● *Also Broadcasting, also Television Studies*

GROUP III continues next page

JOURNALISM/COMMUNICATIONS, continued

GROUP III, continued

Rider (NJ)	R	Texas Wesleyan	R
Robert Morris (PA)	R	Texas, U. of (El Paso)	L
Roger Williams (RI)	M	Towson (MD)	L
Roosevelt (IL)	R	Virginia Wesleyan	R
St. Edward's (TX)	M	Walla Walla (WA)	R
St. John Fisher (NY)	R	Weber State (UT)	L
St. Mary's College (MN)	R	West Chester (PA)	M
Samford (AL)	R	Western Illinois	L
San Jose State (CA)	L	Western New England (MA)	R
Seton Hall (NJ)	M	Wichita State (KS)	M
Southeastern Louisiana	L	Wingate (NC)	R
Southern Connecticut	M	Wisconsin, U. of (LaCrosse)	L
Southern Maine	M	Wisconsin, U. of (Whitewater)	L
Southern Utah	M	Worcester State (MA)	M
Tampa, U. of (FL)	R		

MATHEMATICS

GROUP I
Most Selective

▲Agnes Scott (GA) .... M
Albany (SUNY)(NY) L
American U. (DC) .... M
▲Barnard (NY) .... R
Bates (ME) .... R
Binghamton (SUNY) (NY) L
Boston U. (MA) L
Bowdoin (ME) .... R
Brandeis (MA) .... R
▲Bryn Mawr (PA) .... R
Bucknell (PA) .... M
Buffalo (SUNY)(NY) L
California Inst. of Tech. .... S
California, U. of (Berkeley) XL
California, U. of (Los Angeles) XL
California, U. of (San Diego) L
Carnegie Mellon (PA) .... M
Carleton (MN) .... R
Case Western Reserve U. (OH) .... M
Chicago, U. of (IL) .... M
Clarkson (NY) .... M
Colby (ME) .... R
Colgate (NY) .... R
Colorado College .... R
Colorado School of Mines .... R
Columbia (NY) .... M
Connecticut College .... R
Dartmouth (NH) .... M
Davidson (NC) .... R
Dickinson (PA) .... R
Duke (NC) .... M
Florida, U. of XL
Geneseo (SUNY)(NY) .... M
Georgia Inst. of Tech. L
Grinnell (IA) .... R
Harvard (MA) .... M
Harvey Mudd (CA) .... S
Haverford (PA) .... S
Holy Cross (MA) .... R
Illinois Inst. of Tech. .... R
Illinois, U. of (Urbana-Champaign) XL
Kenyon (OH) .... R
Lehigh (PA) .... M
Macalester (MN) .... R
Maryland, U. of (Baltimore County) ... M
Miami U. (OH) L

Michigan, U. of XL
MIT (MA) .... M
Middlebury (VT) .... R
▲Mount Holyoke (MA) .... R
New College (FL) .... S
New Jersey, College of .... M
New Jersey Inst. of Tech. .... M
New Mexico Inst. of Mining & Tech. ..... R
New York U. L
Northwestern (IL) .... M
Notre Dame (IN) .... M
Oberlin (OH) .... R
Occidental (CA) .... R
Pennsylvania, U. of L
Pittsburgh, U. of (PA) L
Pomona (CA) .... R
Princeton (NJ) .... M
Providence (RI) .... M
Reed (OR) .... R
Rensselaer (NY) .... M
Rice (TX) .... M
Rhodes (TN) .... R
Rochester, U. of (NY) .... M
Rose-Hulman (IN) .... R
Stanford (CA) .... M
St. Louis (MO) .... M
St. Mary's Col. of Maryland .... R
St. Olaf (MN) .... R
Trinity (CT) .... R
Tulane (LA) .... M
Union (NY) .... R
United States Air Force Academy (CO) .... M
Vassar (NY) .... R
Villanova (PA) .... M
■Wabash (IN) .... S
Wake Forest (NC) .... M
Washington & Lee (VA) .... R
Washington U. (MO) .... M
▲Wellesley (MA) .... R
Wesleyan (CT) .... R
Wheaton (IL) .... R
Whitman (WA) .... R
Willamette (OR) .... R
Wisconsin, U. of XL
Worcester Poly Inst. (MA) .... R
Yale (CT) .... M

Enrollment Code		
■ *Men Only*	S = Small (less than 1000 students)	R = Moderate (1000-3000 students) M = Medium (3000-8000 students)
▲ *Women Only*	L = Large (8000-20,000 students)	XL = Extra Large (over 20,000 students)

MATHEMATICS, continued

GROUP II
Very Selective

Adrian (MI)	R	Loyola (IL)	M
Alabama, U. of (Huntsville)	M	Loyola Marymount (CA)	M
Albertson (ID)	S	Luther (IA)	R
Albion (MI)	R	Lyon (AR)	S
Arcadia (PA)	R	Manhattan (NY)	M
Arizona State	XL	Marist (NY)	M
Auburn (AL)	L	Marquette (WI)	M
Baylor (TX)	M	Mary Washington (VA)	M
Bellarmine (KY)	R	Massachusetts, U. of (Lowell)	M
Belmont (TN)	R	Michigan State	XL
Benedictine (IL)	R	Michigan Tech	M
Bentley (MA)	M	Michigan, U. of (Dearborn)	M
Birmingham-Southern (AL)	R	Millsaps (MS)	S
Bowling Green (OH)	L	Mississippi State	L
Bryant (RI)	R	Missouri State	L
California Poly. State U. (SLO)	L	Montana State	L
California, U. of (Davis)	XL	Montana Tech.	R
California, U. of (Irvine)	L	Moravian (PA)	R
California, U. of (Riverside)	L	■ Morehouse (GA)	R
California, U. of (Santa Cruz)	M	Muhlenberg (PA)	R
Carroll (MT)	R	Nazareth (NY)	R
Cincinnati, U. of (OH)	L	New Mexico State	L
College of Charleston (SC)	L	Newman U. (KS)	S
Colorado, U. of	L	North Carolina State	L
Concordia (MN)	R	North Dakota, U. of	M
DePaul (IL)	L	North Florida	M
Earlham (IN)	R	Ohio Northern	R
Evansville (IN)	R	Ohio State	XL
Fairfield (CT)	M	Ohio U.	L
Florida Atlantic	L	Oklahoma, U. of	Xl
George Mason (VA)	L	Oklahoma State	L
Grand Valley (MI)	L	Oregon, U. of	L
Hendrix (AR)	R	Otterbein (OH)	R
Herbert Lehman (CUNY)(NY)	M	Portland, U. of (OR)	R
Hiram (OH)	R	Potsdam (SUNY) (NY)	M
Illinois College	S	Puerto Rico, U. of (Mayaguez)	L
Illinois, U. of (Chicago)	L	Ramapo (NJ)	M
James Madison (VA)	L	Richard Stockton (NJ)	M
John Carroll (OH)	R	Roanoke (VA)	R
Juniata (PA)	R	Rochester Inst. of Tech.	L
Kansas State	L	Rockhurst (MO)	R
Kennesaw State (GA)	R	San Diego, U. of (CA)	M
Knox (IL)	R	Seattle U. (WA)	R
Lafayette (PA)	R	▲ Simmons (MA)	R
LaSalle (PA)	M	South Dakota School of Mines	R
Lebanon Valley (PA)	R		
Linfield (OR)	R		

GROUP II continues next page

MATHEMATICS, continued

•• ━━━━━━━━━━━━━ **GROUP II, continued** ━━━━━━━━━━━━━ ••

Southern California, U. of	L	Valparaiso (IN)	M
Stetson (FL)	R	Virginia Tech.	L
Stony Brook (SUNY)(NY)	L	Washington, U. of	XL
▲ Sweet Briar (VA)	S	Wheaton (MA)	R
Texas, U. of (Austin)	XL	Winthrop (SC)	M
Towson (MD)	L	Wisconsin Lutheran	S
▲ Trinity (DC)	S	Wofford (SC)	R
Truman State (MO)	M	Wooster (OH)	R

•• ━━━━━━━━━━━━━ **GROUP III** ━━━━━━━━━━━━━ •••
Selective

Averett (VA)	S	Messiah (PA)	R
Baldwin-Wallace (OH)	R	Middle Tennessee	L
Ball State (IN)	L	Midwestern State U. (TX)	M
▲ Bennett (NC)	S	Millersville (PA)	M
Bloomsburg (PA)	M	Minnesota State U. (Moorhead)	M
Bluffton (OH)	S	Monmouth (NJ)	R
Boise State (ID)	L	Montana, U. of	M
Briar Cliff (IA)	R	Montana State (Billings)	R
California State U. (Channel Islands)	R	Montclair State (NJ)	M
California State U. (Dominguez Hills)	M	Montevallo (AL)	R
California State U. (Monterey Bay)	R	Mount St. Joseph (OH)	R
California State U. (San Jose)	L	Murray State (KY)	M
Christopher Newport (VA)	M	North Dakota State	L
City College (CUNY)(NY)	L	Northeastern State (OK)	L
Clark Atlanta (GA)	M	Northern Illinois U.	L
Colorado, U. of (Denver)	M	Northern State (OK)	L
East Carolina	L	Northern Michigan	M
East Tennessee	L	Northwestern Louisiana	L
Eastern Connecticut	M	Oakland (MI)	M
Eastern Illinois	L	Ozarks, College of the (MO)	R
Eastern Washington	L	Penn State (Erie)(PA)	M
Findlay (OH)	M	Pittsburgh, U. of (Johnstown)	R
Fisk (TN)	S	Rhode Island College	M
Fitchburg (MA)	R	St. Joseph's (NY)	R
Fontbonne (MO)	R	Simpson (IA)	R
Georgia State	L	South Dakota State U.	M
High Point (NC)	R	Southern Polytechnic (GA)	R
Humboldt State (CA)	M	Tennessee, U. of (Chattanooga)	M
Indiana (PA)	L	Tennessee, U. of (Martin)	M
Indiana State	L	Texas A&M (Corpus Christi)	M
I.U. P.U.I. (IN)	L	Texas State U. (San Marcos)	L
Lewis-Clark State (ID)	R	Texas Tech. U.	L
Long Island U. (C.W. Post)(NY)	M	Texas, U. of (Tyler)	R
Louisiana-Lafayette	L	Weber State (UT)	L
Louisiana State	XL	Western Carolina (NC)	M
Lynchburg (VA)	R	Wheeling Jesuit (WV)	R
Malone (OH)	R	Wilkes (PA)	R
Marshall (WV)	L	Wisconsin, U. of (Eau Claire)	L
▲ Meredith (NC)	R	Wisconsin, U. of (Stevens Point)	M

MUSIC

GROUP I
Most Selective

▲ Barnard (NY) .... R	Lawrence (WI) .... R
Beloit (WI) .... R	Manhattan School of Music (NY) ...... S
Binghamton (SUNY)(NY) L	Mannes School of Music (NY) .... S
Boston College (MA) L	Miami, U. of (FL) L
Boston U. (MA) L	Miami U. (OH) L
Bowdoin (ME) .... R	Michigan, U. of XL
Brandeis (MA) .... R	Minnesota, U. of XL
Bucknell (PA) .... R	▲ Mount Holyoke (MA) .... R
Buffalo (SUNY)(NY) L	New York U. L
California, U. of (Berkeley) XL	Northwestern (IL) .... M
California, U. of (Los Angeles) XL	Oberlin (OH) .... R
California, U. of (San Diego) L	Pomona (CA) .... R
Carleton (MN)...................................... R	Princeton (NJ) .... M
Carnegie-Mellon (PA) .... M	Rhodes (TN) .... R
Case Western Reserve U. (OH) .... M	Rice (TX) .... M
Chicago, U. of (IL) .... M	Rochester, U. of (NY) .... M
Cleveland Inst. of Music (OH) .... S	Rutgers (NJ) L
Colby (ME) .... R	Sarah Lawrence (NY) .... R
Columbia (NY)..................................... M	▲ Scripps (CA) .... S
Connecticut College .... R	Skidmore (NY) .... R
π DePauw (IN) .... R	▲ Smith (MA) .... R
Florida, U. of XL	Southern California, U. of L
Furman (SC) .... R	Southwestern (TX) .... R
Geneseo (SUNY) (NY)......................... M	Stanford (CA) .... M
Gustavus Adolphus (MN) .... R	St. Mary's College of Maryland .... R
Harvard (MA) .... M	St. Olaf (MN) .... R
Illinois, U. of (Urbana-Champaign) XL	Texas, U. of (Austin) XL
Illinois Wesleyan .... R	Vanderbilt (TN) .... M
Indiana U. XL	Vassar (NY) .... R
Iowa, U. of.. XL	Virginia, U. of L
Johns Hopkins (MD) .... M	Wheaton (IL) .... R
Juilliard (NY).. S	Whitman (WA)...................................... R
Kalamazoo (MI) .... R	Willamette (OR) .... R
Kenyon (OH) .... R	Wisconsin, U. of XL
Knox (IL) .... R	Yale (CT) .... M

π *Music and Music Business*

MUSIC continues next page

Enrollment Code		
■ *Men Only*	S = Small (less than 1000 students)	R = Moderate (1000-3000 students)	M = Medium (3000-8000 students)
▲ *Women Only*	L = Large (8000-20,000 students)	XL = Extra Large (over 20,000 students)

MUSIC, continued

GROUP II
Very Selective

Alabama, U. of	L	
Alaska Pacific	S	
Albertson (ID)	S	
Arizona State	XL	
Asbury (KY)	R	
Augustana (IL)	R	
Augustana (SD)	M	
Bard (NY)	R	
Baylor (TX)	M	
Bemidji State (MN)	M	
Bennington (VT)	S	
Berklee College of Music (MA)	R	
Birmingham-Southern (AL)	R	
Boston Conservatory	S	
Brigham Young (UT)	L	
Bryan (TN)	S	
Butler (IN)	R	
Cal. Inst. of the Arts	S	
California, U. of (Riverside)	L	
California, U. of (Santa Barbara)	L	
California, U. of (Santa Cruz)	M	
Cal. Poly. State U. (San Luis Obispo)	L	
Capital (OH)	R	
Catholic U. (DC)	M	
Centenary (LA)	S	
Central (IA)	R	
Central Florida	XL	
Chapman (CA)	R	
Cincinnati, U. of	L	
Clark (MA)	R	
Clarke (IA)	S	
Coe (IA)	R	
Colorado, U. of	L	
Concordia (CA)	R	
Concordia (MN)	R	
▲Converse (SC)	S	
Cornish (WA)	S	
Covenant (GA)	S	
Creighton (NE)	M	
Curtis Institute of Music (PA)	S	
Dayton, U. of (OH)	M	
Denison (OH)	R	
π Denver, U. of	R	
DePaul (IL)	L	
Drake (IA)	M	

Drury (MO)	R	
Elizabethtown (PA)	R	
Evansville (IN)	R	
Florida State	L	
π Florida Southern	R	
π Fredonia (SUNY) (NY)	M	
Georgia State	L	
Georgia, U. of	L	
Gordon (MA)	R	
Harding (AR)	M	
Hiram (OH)	R	
Hofstra (NY)	M	
Hope (MI)	R	
Houghton (NY)	S	
Houston Baptist (TX)	R	
Houston, U. of (TX)	L	
Idaho, U. of	L	
Illinois, U. of (Chicago)	L	
Iowa State	XL	
Ithaca (NY)	M	
James Madison (VA)	L	
▲Judson (AL)	S	
Kansas State	L	
Kansas, U. of	L	
Kentucky, U. of	L	
Lake Forest (IL)	R	
π Lebanon Valley (PA)	R	
Lewis & Clark (OR)	R	
Linfield (OR)	R	
Louisiana State	XL	
Loyola (IL)	M	
Luther (IA)	R	
Maine, U. of	M	
Manhattanville (NY)	R	
Maryland, U. of	XL	
Maryville (TN)	S	
Massachusetts, U. of	L	
Masters (CA)	R	
McDaniel (MD)	R	
Mercer (GA)	R	
Michigan State	XL	
Milliken (IL)	R	

π　Music and Music Business

GROUP II continues next page

MUSIC, continued

•• —————————— GROUP II, continued —————————— ••

▲ Mills (CA) .... S
Millsaps (MS) .... S
Missouri, U. of XL
Missouri, U. of (Kansas City) .... M
Mobile, U. of (AL) .... R
Moravian (PA) .... R
Morningside (IA) .... S
Murray State (KY) .... M
Nazareth (NY) .... R
Nebraska, U. of L
New England Conservatory (MA) .... S
New Hampshire, U. of L
North Carolina School of the Arts .... S
North Florida .... M
North Texas L
Northwestern (MN) .... R
Ohio State XL
Ohio U. L
π Oklahoma City U. .... R
Oklahoma State L
π Oneonta (SUNY)(NY) .... M
Oregon, U. of L
Pacific Lutheran (WA) .... R
Pacific, U. of the (CA) .... R
Point Loma (CA) .... R
Portland State (OR) L
π Potsdam (SUNY) (NY) .... M
Purchase (SUNY) (NY) .... M
π Puget Sound (WA) .... R
Queens (NC) .... R

Queens (CUNY)(NY) L
Redlands, U. of (CA) .... R
Rhode Island, U. of L
Roanoke (VA) .... R
Rowan (NJ) .... M
San Francisco Conservatory (CA) .... S
Santa Clara U. (CA) .... M
Shepherd (WV) .... M
▲ St. Catherine (MN) .... R
Stetson (FL) .... R
Stony Brook (SUNY)(NY) L
Susquehanna (PA) .... R
Syracuse (NY) L
Temple (PA) .... M
Texas Christian .... M
Tulsa, U. of (OK) .... M
Utah State L
Valparaiso (IN) .... R
Wartburg (IA) .... R
Washington, U. of XL
Webster (MO) .... R
Wells (NY) .... S
West Chester (PA) .... M
West Virginia, U. of L
Western Michigan L
Whitworth (WA) .... R
William Jewell Col. (MO) .... R
Wisconsin Lutheran .... S
Wittenberg (OH) .... R
Wooster, College of (OH) .... R

π *Music and Music Business*

MUSIC continues next page

Enrollment Code		
■ *Men Only*	S = Small (less than 1000 students)	R = Moderate (1000-3000 students)	M = Medium (3000-8000 students)
▲ *Women Only*	L = Large (8000-20,000 students)	XL = Extra Large (over 20,000 students)	

MUSIC, continued

━━━━━━━━━━━━━━ **GROUP III** ━━━━━━━━━━━━
Selective

Alderson-Broaddus (WV) .... S	Duquesne (PA) .... M
Anderson (IN) .... R	East Carolina L
Andrews (MI) .... R	Eastern Michigan L
Anna Maria (MA) .... S	Edgewood (WI) .... S
Aquinas (MI) .... R	π Elmhurst (IL) .... R
Arkansas, U. of L	➤ Five Towns College (NY) .... S
Arts, U. of the (PA) .... R	Fort Hays (KS) .... M
➤ Azusa Pacific (CA) .... R	Friends (KS) .... R
Baker (KS) .... R	Goshen (IN) .... R
π Baldwin-Wallace (OH) .... R	Hannibal-La Grange (MO) .... R
Belhaven (MS) .... S	Hardin-Simmons (TX) .... R
➤ Belmont (TN) .... R	Hartford, U. of (CT) .... M
Benedictine (KS) .... R	Hartwick (NY) .... R
Berea (WV) .... R	Hastings (NE) .... S
Bethany (KS) .... S	Heidelberg (OH) .... R
Bethany (WV) .... R	Holy Names (CA) .... S
Bethel (IN) .... R	Huntingdon (AL) .... S
Bethel (KS) .... S	Huntington (IN) .... S
Bowling Green (OH) L	Illinois State L
Bluffton (OH) .... S	Immaculata (PA) .... S
Brenau (GA) .... R	Indiana (PA) L
Briar Cliff (IA) .... R	Indiana State L
Bridgewater (VA) .... R	Jacksonville (FL) .... R
Brooklyn (CUNY)(NY) L	Jacksonville State (AL) .... M
California State U. (East Bay) .... M	John Brown (AR) .... R
California State U. (Fresno) L	Johnson State (VT) .... R
California State U. (Fullerton) L	Keene State (NH) .... R
California State U. (Long Beach) L	Kent State (OH) L
California State U. (Northridge) L	Kentucky Wesleyan .... R
California State U. (Sacramento) ...... M	Kutztown (PA) .... M
California State U. (San Jose) L	Lenoir-Rhyne (NC) .... R
Carson-Newman (TN) .... R	Lock Haven (PA) .... M
Carthage (WI) .... R	Long Island U. (C.W. Post)(NY) .... M
Cedarville (OH) .... R	Longwood (VA) .... R
Central Connecticut .... M	Louisiana College .... R
Central Michigan L	Louisiana-Lafayette L
Central Oklahoma L	Louisiana- Monroe .... M
Central Washington L	Louisville (KY) L
Charleston Southern (SC) .... R	π Loyola (LA) .... M
Christopher Newport (VA) .... M	Lynchburg (VA) .... R
Coker (SC) .... S	Malone (OH) .... R
Columbia College (SC) .... R	
Cumberland (KY) .... R	
Dana (NE) .... S	
Doane (NE) .... S	

➤ *Music Business*

π *Music and Music Business*

GROUP III continues next page

MUSIC, continued

▬ GROUP III, continued ▬

Mansfield (PA)	R
Marywood (PA)	R
Massachusetts, U. of (Boston)	M
Massachusetts, U. of (Lowell)	M
McPherson (KS)	S
Memphis, U. of (TN)	L
▲ Meredith (NC)	R
π Middle Tennessee	L
Milligan (TN)	S
π Minnesota State U. (Moorhead)	M
Minnesota, U. of (Duluth)	M
Mississippi College	R
Missouri Baptist	M
π Monmouth (NJ)	R
Montana, U. of	M
Montclair State (NJ)	M
Montevallo (AL)	R
π Montreat (NC)	S
Mount St. Joseph (OH)	R
Mount St. Mary's (CA)	R
Mount Union (OH)	R
Muskingum (OH)	R
Nevada, U. of (Las Vegas)	L
Nevada, U. of (Reno)	L
New Mexico State U.	L
Northern Colorado	L
Northwestern College (IA)	R
Northwestern Louisiana	L
Nyack (NY)	R
Oakland City U. (IN)	R
Oklahoma Baptist	R
Oral Roberts (OK)	M
π Otterbein (OH)	R
Ouachita (AR)	R
Peru State (NE)	R
Philadelphia Biblical (PA)	S
Pittsburg State (KS)	M
Rhode Island College	M
Rider (NJ)	M
Rocky Mountain (MT)	S
Roosevelt (IL)	R
Samford (AL)	R
▲ Seton Hill (PA)	S
Shenandoah (VA)	R
Shorter (GA)	R
Simpson (IA)	R
Slippery Rock (PA)	M
Sonoma State (CA)	M
South Dakota, U. of	M
South Florida, U. of	L
π Southern Illinois U. (Carbondale)	L
Southern Maine	M
Southern Mississippi	L
Southwest Baptist (MO)	R
Southwestern (KS)	S
Sterling (KS)	S
Tampa, U. of (FL)	R
Tarleton State (TX)	M
Texas Lutheran	R
Texas, U. of (El Paso)	L
Texas, U. of (San Antonio)	L
Towson (MD)	L
Union University (TN)	R
Virginia Commonwealth	L
Viterbo (WI)	R
Wayne State (MI)	L
Weber State (UT)	L
Western Carolina (NC)	M
Western Connecticut	M
π Western Illlinois	L
Western St. Coll. of Colorado	R
Westfield (MA)	M
π William Paterson (NJ)	M
Wingate (NC)	R
π Wisconsin, U. of (Stevens Point)	M
Wisconsin, U. of (Superior)	M
Xavier U. of Louisiana	R

π *Music and Music Business*

Enrollment Code			
■ *Men Only*	S = Small (less than 1000 students)	R = Moderate (1000-3000 students)	M = Medium (3000-8000 students)
▲ *Women Only*	L = Large (8000-20,000 students)	XL = Extra Large (over 20,000 students)	

NURSING

GROUP I
Most Selective

Binghamton (SUNY) (NY)	L	Miami, U. of (FL)	L
Boston Col. (MA)	L	Missouri, U. of	XL
Buffalo (SUNY)(NY)	L	New York U.	L
Case Western Reserve U. (OH)	M	North Carolina, U. of	L
Colorado, U. of	L	Northern Michigan	M
Columbia (NY)	M	Pennsylvania, U. of	L
Duke (NC)	M	Rochester, U. of (NY)	M
Emory (GA)	M	St. Olaf (MN)	R
Florida, U. of	XL	Vanderbilt (TN)	M
Georgetown (DC)	M	Villanova (PA)	M
Gustavus Adolphus (MN)	R	Virginia, U. of	L
Illinois, U. of	XL	Washington, U. of	XL
Illinois Wesleyan	R	Wisconsin, U. of	L
Johns Hopkins (MD)	M		

GROUP II
Very Selective

Adelphi (NY)	M	Franciscan U. of Steubenville (OH)	R
Alabama, U. of (Huntsville)	M	George Mason (VA)	M
Arizona, U. of	XL	Gwynedd-Mercy (PA)	S
Barry (FL)	R	Harding (AR)	M
Baylor (TX)	M	Hope (MI)	R
Belmont (TN)	R	Houston Baptist (TX)	R
Bethel (MN)	R	Hunter (CUNY) (NY)	L
Bradley (IL)	M	Illinois, U. of (Chicago)	L
Calvin (MI)	R	Indiana U.	XL
Capital (OH)	R	Indiana U. of Pennsylvania	L
Carroll (WI)	R	Iowa, U. of	XL
Catholic U. (DC)	M	Kansas, U. of	L
Cincinnati, U. of (OH)	L	Kentucky, U. of	L
Clarke (IA)	S	LaSalle (PA)	M
Coe (IA)	R	Lebanon Valley (PA)	R
Connecticut, U. of	XL	Lipscomb (TN)	R
Creighton (NE)	M	Louisiana-Lafayette	L
Daemen (NY)	R	Louisville (KY)	L
Delaware, U. of	L	Loyola (IL)	M
Detroit Mercy (MI)	M	Luther (IA)	R
Duquesne (PA)	M	Maine, U. of	L
Elmira (NY)	R	Marquette (WI)	M
Evansville (IN)	R	➤ Maryland, U. of (Baltimore County)	M
Fairfield (CT)	M		
Florida Atlantic	L		
Florida Gulf Coast U.	M		
Florida International	L		

➤ *Health Policy, also*

GROUP II continues next page

NURSING, continued

GROUP II, continued

Massachusetts, U. of	L
McKendree (IL)	R
McMurry (TX)	R
Mercer (GA)	R
Michigan State	XL
Michigan, U. of	XL
Milwaukee Sch. of Engine (WI)	R
Minnesota, U. of	XL
Mississippi U. for Women	R
Missouri, U. of (St. Louis)	M
Mobile, U. of (AL)	R
Montana Tech.	R
Moravian (PA)	R
Morningside (IA)	S
Mount Mercy (IA)	S
Nazareth (NY)	R
New Hampshire, U. of	L
New Jersey, College of	M
New Mexico, U. of	L
North Dakota, U. of	M
North Florida	M
Northeastern (MA)	L
Ohio Northern	R
Ohio State	XL
Pace (NY)	M
Pacific Lutheran (WA)	R
Pennsylvania State	XL
Pittsburgh, U. of (PA)	L
Portland, U. of (OR)	R
Purdue (IN)	XL
Quinnipiac (CT)	R

Rockhurst (MO)	R
Rutgers-Newark (NJ)	M
Samford (AL)	R
San Diego, U. of (CA)	M
San Francisco, U. of (CA)	M
Seattle Pacific (WA)	R
Seton Hall (NJ)	M
▲ Simmons (MA)	R
South Carolina, U. of	L
South Dakota State U.	M
St. Anselm (NH)	R
▲ St. Catherine (MN)	R
St John's/St. Benedict (MN)	R
St. Louis (MO)	M
▲ St. Mary's College (IN)	R
Texas Christian U.	M
Texas, U. of (Health Sci. Ctr.-S. Antonio)	R
Truman State (MO)	M
Union University (TN)	R
Valparaiso U. (IN)	M
Vermont, U. of	M
Viterbo (WI)	R
Virginia Commonwealth	L
Webster (MD)	R
West Virginia U.	L
Western Michigan	L
Westminster (UT)	R
William Jewell (MO)	R
Wisconsin, U. of (Milwaukee)	XL
Wyoming, U. of	M
York (PA)	M

NURSING continues next page

Enrollment Code

■ *Men Only*   S = Small (less than 1000 students)   R = Moderate (1000-3000 students)   M = Medium (3000-8000 students)
▲ *Women Only*   L = Large (8000-20,000 students)   XL = Extra Large (over 20,000 students)

NURSING, continued

GROUP III
Selective

Abilene Christian (TX)	M	Eastern Oregon	R
Akron, U. of (OH)	L	Eastern Washington	L
Alabama, U. of (Birmingham)	M	Edgewood (WI)	S
Alabama, U. of (Huntsville)	M	Elmhurst (IL)	R
Alaska, U. of (Fairbanks)	M	Elms (MA)	S
Alderson-Broaddus (WV)	S	Emporia State (KS)	M
▲Alverno (WI)	R	Fairmont State (WV)	M
Andrews (MI)	R	Ferris State (MI)	L
Arizona State	XL	Fitchburg (MA)	R
Avila (MO)	S	Fort Hays (KS)	M
Azusa Pacific (CA)	R	Gannon (PA)	M
Baker (KS)	R	Georgia Southern	L
Ball State (IN)	L	Georgia Southwestern	R
Bellarmine (KY)	R	Georgia State	L
Berea (KY)	R	Goshen (IN)	R
Bethel (IN)	R	Graceland (IA)	R
Bethel (KS)	S	Grambling (LA)	M
Bloomsburg (PA)	M	Hardin-Simmons (TX)	R
Boise State (ID)	L	Hartwick (NY)	R
Briar Cliff (IA)	R	Hawaii Pacific	M
Brockport (SUNY)(NY)	M	Henderson State (AR)	M
California (PA)	M	Herbert Lehman (CUNY)(NY)	M
California State U. (Bakersfield)	M	Holy Names (CA)	S
California State U. (Chico)	L	Howard (DC)	M
California State U. (Dominguez Hills)	M	Husson (ME)	S
California State U. (Fresno)	L	Idaho State	L
California State U. (Fullerton)	L	Immaculata (PA)	S
California State U. (Los Angeles)	L	Ind.U.-Purdue U.-Indianapolis (IN)	L
California State U. (San Jose)	L	Jacksonville (FL)	R
Carroll (MT)	R	Jacksonville State (AL)	M
Carson-Newman (TN)	R	Jamestown (ND)	R
▲Cedar Crest (PA)	S	Kansas Wesleyan	S
Cedarville (OH)	R	Kean (NJ)	M
Central Arkansas	M	Kennesaw State (GA)	R
Central Missouri	L	Kent State (OH)	L
Charleston, U. of (WV)	S	King (TN)	S
Colby-Sawyer (NH)	S	Lamar (TX)	M
Colorado, U. of (Colorado Springs)	M	Lenoir-Rhyne (NC)	R
DeSales (PA)	R	Lewis-Clark State (ID)	R
Dillard (LA)	R	Liberty (VA)	R
Dixie State (UT)	M	Long Island U. (Brooklyn)(NY)	M
Dominican (CA)	S	Louisiana College	R
D'Youville (NY)	R	MacMurray (IL)	S
East Carolina (NC)	L	Malone (OH)	R
East Stroudsburg (PA)	M	Marshall (WV)	L
East Tennessee	L	Marymount (VA)	R
Eastern (PA)	R	Maryville (St. Louis) (MO)	R
Eastern Kentucky	L	Massachusetts, U. of (Boston)	M
Eastern Mennonite (VA)	R	Massachusetts, U. of (Dartmouth)	M
Eastern Michigan	L		

GROUP III continues next page

NURSING, continued

•••——————————— **GROUP III**, continued ——————————•••

Massachusetts, U. of (Lowell)	M	St. Francis (IN)	R
Memphis, U. of (TN)	L	St. Francis (PA)	R
Mercy (NY)	M	St. Joseph's (ME)	S
Middle Tennessee	L	St, Mary, College of (NE)	S
Midwestern State U. (TX)	M	# St. Scholastica (MN)	R
Milligan (TN)	R	Salem State (MA)	M
Millikin (IL)	R	San Diego State (CA)	L
Misericordia, College (PA)	S	Seattle U. (WA)	R
Mississippi College	R	Shenandoah (VA)	R
Missouri Southern State	M	Sonoma State (CA)	M
Molloy (NY)	R	South Alabama	M
Montana State	L	South Dakota, U. of	M
Mount St. Joseph (OH)	R	South Florida, U. of	L
Mount St. Mary's (CA)	R	Southern Illinois U. (Edwardsville)	L
Mount St. Mary's (NY)	S	Southern Maine, U. of	M
Murray State (KY)	M	Southern Mississippi	L
Nevada, U. of (Las Vegas)	L	Southern Nazarene (OK)	R
Nevada, U. of (Reno)	L	Southwestern (KS)	S
Newman U. (KS)	S	Texas A&M (Corpus Christi)	M
New Mexico State U.	L	Texas, U.of (Arlington)	L
Nicholls State (LA)	M	Texas, U. of (El Paso)	L
North Carolina, U. of (Charlotte)	L	Texas, U.of (Tyler)	R
North Carolina, U. of (Greensboro)	M	Thomas More (KY)	R
North Carolina, U. of (Wilmington)	L	Towson (MD)	L
Northern Colorado	L	Troy State (AL)	M
Northern Illinois U.	L	Tuskegee University (AL)	M
Northwestern Louisiana	L	Union (NE)	R
Oakland (MI)	M	Union University (TN)	R
Oklahoma Baptist	R	Villa Julie (MD)	R
Oklahoma City U.	R	Walla Walla (WA)	R
Old Dominion (VA)	L	Walsh (OH)	R
Olivet Nazarene (IL)	R	Washburn (KS)	M
Oral Roberts (OK)	M	Wayne State (MI)	L
Pittsburgh, U. of (Bradford)	R	Weber State (UT)	L
Pittsburg State (KS)	M	Western Carolina (NC)	M
Plattsburgh (SUNY) (NY)	M	Western Connecticut State	M
Point Loma (CA)	R	Western Kentucky	L
Presentation (SD)	S	Wheeling Jesuit (WV)	R
Quincy (IL)	R	Widener (PA)	R
Regis (CO)	R	Wilkes (PA)	R
Regis (MA)	S	William Paterson (NJ)	M
Rhode Island, U. of	L	Wisconsin, U. of (Eau Claire)	L
Rhode Island College	M	Worcester State (MA)	M
Rockford (IL)	S	Wright State (OH)	L
Russell Sage (The Sage Colleges)(NY)	R		
Saginaw Valley (MI)	M		
St. Ambrose (IA)	R		

 # Also, Health Informatics and
Information Systems

Enrollment Code		
■ *Men Only*	S = Small (less than 1000 students)	M = Medium (3000-8000 students)
▲ *Women Only*	R = Moderate (1000-3000 students)	
	L = Large (8000-20,000 students)	XL = Extra Large (over 20,000 students)

PHARMACY

GROUP I
Most Selective

Buffalo (SUNY) (NY)	L	Michigan, U. of	XL
Butler (IN)	R	Minnesota, U. of	XL
Creighton (NE)	M	North Carolina, U. of	L
Florida, U. of	XL	Purdue (IN)	XL
Illinois, U. of	XL	Rutgers (NJ)	L
Iowa, U. of	XL	Wisconsin, U. of	L

GROUP II
Very Selective

Albany Col. of Pharmacy (NY)	S	Northwestern Louisiana	L
Arizona, U. of	XL	North Dakota State	L
Auburn (AL)	L	Nova Southeastern (FL)	R
Campbell (NC)	R	Ohio Northern U.	R
Cincinnati, U. of (OH)	L	Ohio State	XL
Connecticut, U. of	XL	Oklahoma, U. of	XL
Drake (IA)	M	Pacific, U. of the (CA)	R
Duquesne (PA)	M	Palm Beach Atlantic (FL)	R
Ferris State (MI)	L	Pittsburgh, U. of	L
Florida A&M	L	Rhode Island, U. of	L
Georgia, U. of	L	Samford (AL)	R
Hawaii, U. of (Hilo)	R	+ Sciences in Philadelphia, U. of (PA)	R
Houston, U. of (TX)	L	South Carolina, U. of	L
Howard (DC)	M	South Dakota State U.	M
Idaho State	L	Southern California, U. of	L
Illinois, U. of (Chicago)	L	Southwestern Oklahoma	M
Kansas, U. of	L	St. John's (NY)	L
Kentucky, U. of	L	St. Louis Col. of Pharmacy (MO)	S
Long Island U. (Brooklyn)(NY)	M	Temple (PA)	L
Louisiana-Monroe	M	Texas, U. of (Austin)	XL
Maryland, U. of	XL	Toledo, U. of	L
Mass. College of Pharmacy	R	Utah, U. of	L
Mercer (GA)	R	Virginia Commonwealth U.	L
Minnesota, U. of (Duluth)	M	Washington State	L
Mississippi, U. of	L	Wayne State (MI)	L
Missouri, U. of (Kansas City)	M	West Virginia U.	L
Montana, U. of	M	Wyoming, U. of	L
New Mexico, U. of	L	Xavier (LA)	R
Northeastern (MA)	L		

+ *Also Pharmaceutical Marketing*

PHILOSOPHY

GROUP I
Most Selective

Albany (SUNY)(NY)	L		Lawrence (WI)	R
American (DC)	M		Macalester (MN)	R
Austin (TX)	R		Michigan, U. of	XL
▲ Barnard (NY)	R		Minnesota, U. of	XL
Bates (ME)	R	▲	Mount Holyoke (MA)	R
Binghamton (SUNY) (NY)	L		New College (FL)	S
Boston Col. (MA)	L		New York U.	L
Boston U. (MA)	L		North Carolina, U. of	L
Bowdoin (ME)	R		Notre Dame (IN)	M
Brown (RI)	M		Oberlin (OH)	R
Bucknell (PA)	M		Ohio State	XL
California, U. of (Berkeley)	XL		Pennsylvania, U. of	L
California, U. of (Los Angeles)	XL		Pittsburgh, U. of (PA)	L
Carleton (MN)	R		Pomona (CA)	R
Carnegie Mellon (PA)	M		Princeton (NJ)	M
Centre (KY)	R		Reed (OR)	R
Chicago, U. of (IL)	M		Rhodes (TN)	R
Claremont McKenna (CA)	R		Rochester, U. of (NY)	M
Colby (ME)	R		Rutgers (NJ)	L
Colgate (NY)	R	▲	Smith (MA)	R
Colorado Col.	R		Southwestern (TX)	R
Columbia (NY)	M		St. Olaf (MN)	R
Connecticut Col.	R		Swarthmore (PA)	R
Cornell (NY)	L		Texas, U. of (Austin)	XL
Creighton (NE)	M		Trinity (CT)	R
Dallas, U. of (TX)	R		Trinity (TX)	R
Davidson (NC)	R		Tufts (MA)	M
DePauw (IN)	R		Tulane (LA)	M
Duke (NC)	M		Vanderbilt (TN)	M
Florida State	L		Vassar (NY)	R
Florida, U. of	XL		Villanova (PA)	M
Geneseo (SUNY)(NY)	M	■	Wabash (IN)	S
George Washington (DC)	M		Washington U. (MO)	M
Georgetown (DC)	M		Washington, U. of	XL
Gettysburg (PA)	R		Wheaton (IL)	R
Hamilton (NY)	R		Whitman (WA)	R
Harvard (MA)	M		Willamette (OR)	R
Haverford (PA)	S		Willaim & Mary (VA)	R
Holy Cross (MA)	R		Wisconsin, U. of	XL
Illinois Wesleyan	R		Yale (CT)	M
Johns Hopkins (MD)	M			
Kenyon (OH)	R			

PHILOSOPHY continues next page

Enrollment Code		
■ *Men Only*	S = Small (less than 1000 students)	R = Moderate (1000-3000 students) M = Medium (3000-8000 students)
▲ *Women Only*	L = Large (8000-20,000 students)	XL = Extra Large (over 20,000 students)

PHILOSOPHY, continued

―――――――――――― **GROUP II** ――――――――――――
Very Selective

Alabama, U. of L	Elon (NC) .... R
Alabama, U. of (Birmingham) .... M	Frostburg (MD) .... M
Alabama, U. of (Huntsville) .... M	Fordham (NY) L
Allegheny (PA) .... R	Fort Hays (KS) .... M
Albion (MI) .... R	Franciscan U. of Steubenville (OH) ...... R
Arizona, U. of XL	George Mason (VA) L
Asbury (KY) .... R	Georgia State L
Assumption (MA) .... R	Georgia, U. of L
Bellarmine (KY) .... R	Gonzaga (WA) .... E
Belmont (TN) .... R	Gordon (MA) .... R
Benedictine (KS) .... R	Hamline (MN) .... R
Bethel (IN) .... R	Hanover (IN) .... R
Bethel (MN) .... M	Herbert Lehman (CUNY)(NY) L
Biola (CA) .... R	Hobart & Wm. Smith (NY) .... R
Bowling Green (OH) L	Hood (MD) .... S
Brooklyn (CUNY)(NY) L	Illinois, U. of (Chicago) L
California, U. of (Santa Barbara) L	Indiana (PA) L
California, U. of (Santa Cruz) .... M	Indiana U. XL
California State U. (Dominguez Hills) ..... M	Iowa State XL
California State U. (Fresno) L	John Carroll (OH) .... R
California State U. (Hayward) .... M	Kansas State L
California State U. (Long Beach) L	Kent State (OH) L
California State U. (Northridge) L	Kutztown (PA) .... M
California State U. (Stanislaus) .... M	Lake Forest (IL) .... R
Calvin (MI) .... R	La Salle (PA) .... M
Carroll (MT) .... R	Lewis & Clark (OR) .... R
Catholic (DC) .... R	Loras (IA) .... R
Central (IA) .... R	Louisiana State XL
Central Florida XL	Loyola (IL) .... M
Christendom (VA) .... S	Loyola (LA) .... M
Christopher Newport (VA) .... M	Loyola (MD) .... M
City College (CUNY)(NY) L	Lycoming (PA) .... R
Clarke (IA) .... S	Maine, U. of L
Coastal Carolina (SC) .... M	Mansfield (PA) .... R
Cornell Col. (IA) .... R	Marquette (WI) .... M
Dayton, U. of (OH) .... M	Maryland, U. of XL
Denison (OH) .... R	Mass. College of Lib. Arts (N.Adams) ...... R
DePaul (IL) L	Massachusetts, U. of (Boston) .... M
DeSales (PA) .... S	Merrimack (MA) .... R
Detroit Mercy (MI) .... M	Messiah (PA) .... R
Doane (NB) .... S	Michigan, U. of (Dearborn) .... M
Earlham (IN) .... R	Michigan State XL
East Tennessee L	Milligan (TN) .... S
Edinboro (PA) .... M	

GROUP II continues next page

PHILOSOPHY, continued

●●━━━━━━ GROUP II, continued ━━━━━━●●

Minnesota, U. of (Morris) .... R	St. Andrews Presbyterian (NC) .... S
Missouri, U. of XL	St. Bonaventure (NY) .... R
Missouri, U. of (St. Louis) .... M	▲ St. Catherine (MN) .... R
Molloy (NY) .... R	St. Cloud (MN) L
Mount Mercy (IA) .... S	St. Francis (PA) .... R
Mount St. Mary's (MD) .... R	St. John's (NY) L
Muhlenberg (PA) .... R	St. John's/St. Benedict (MN) .... R
Nazareth (NY) .... R	St. Louis (MO) .... M
New Hampshire, U. of L	▲ St. Mary's College (IN) .... R
New Paltz (SUNY)(NY) .... M	St. Mary's (MN) .... R
North Carolina, U. of (Charlotte) L	St. Thomas (MN) .... M
Northeastern (MA) L	St. Thomas, U. of (TX) .... R
Northeastern Illinois .... M	Salisbury State (MD) .... M
Northern Illinois L	Santa Clara U. (CA) .... M
Northwestern (IA) .... R	Seattle U. (WA) .... R
Oklahoma Baptist .... R	Seton Hall (NJ) .... M
Oneonta (SUNY)(NY) .... M	Skidmore (NY) .... R
Oregon State L	South Alabama .... M
Ozarks, College of the (MO) .... R	South Florida, U. of L
Portland, U. of (OR) .... R	Stony Brook (SUNY) (NY) L
Providence (RI) .... M	Texas A&M XL
Purchase (SUNY)(NY) .... M	Transylvania (KY) .... R
Queens (CUNY)(NY) L	Utah, U. of L
Redlands (CA) .... R	Webster (MO) .... R
Regis (CO) .... R	West Chester (PA) .... M
Rhode Island College .... M	Westminster (UT) .... R
Richard Stockton (NJ) .... M	Wheeling Jesuit (WV) .... R
Rockhurst (MO) .... R	Wofford (SC) .... R
Rowan (NJ) .... M	Worcester State (MA) .... M
St. Ambrose (IA) .... R	Xavier (OH) .... R

PHYSICS

GROUP I
Most Selective

Albany (SUNY)(NY) L	Lawrence (WI) .... R
Allegheny (PA)................................. R	Lehigh (PA) .... M
Amherst (MA)................................... R	Macalester (MN)............................... R
▲ Barnard (NY) .... R	Maryland, U. of XL
Bates (ME) .... R	MIT (MA) .... M
Binghamton (SUNY) (NY) L	Miami U. (OH) L
Boston U. (MA) L	Michigan, U. of XL
Brandeis (MA) .... M	Michigan, U. of (Dearborn) .... M
Brown (RI) .... M	Middlebury (VT) .... R
▲ Bryn Mawr (PA) .... S	Missouri, U. of (Rolla) .... M
Buffalo (SUNY)(NY) L	▲ Mount Holyoke (MA) .... R
California Inst. of Tech. .... S	New College (FL) .... S
California, U. of (Berkeley)............. XL	New Jersey, College of .... M
California, U. of (San Diego) L	New Mexico Inst. of Mining & Tech. .... R
Carleton (MN)................................... R	New York U. L
Carnegie Mellon (PA) .... M	North Carolina, U. of L
Case Western Reserve U. (OH) .... M	Notre Dame (IN) .... M
Centre (KY) .... R	Oberlin (OH) .... R
Chicago, U. of (IL) .... M	Occidental (CA) .... R
Clarkson (NY) .... M	Pennsylvania, U. of L
Colorado School of Mines .... R	Pomona (CA) .... R
Columbia (NY)................................... M	Princeton (NJ) .... M
Connecticut College .... R	Reed (OR) .... R
Cornell (NY)..................................... L	Rensselaer (NY) .... M
Dartmouth (NH) .... M	Rhodes (TN) .... R
Denison (OH) .... R	Rice (TX) .... M
DePauw (IN) .... R	Rochester, U. of (NY) .... M
Dickinson (PA) .... R	Rose-Hulman (IN) .... R
Florida, U. of XL	Rutgers (NJ)..................................... L
Franklin & Marshall (PA) .... R	St. Olaf (MN) .... R
Furman (SC) .... R	▲ Smith (MA) .... R
Geneseo (SUNY) (NY)....................... M	South, U. of the (TN) .... R
Georgetown (DC) .... M	Stanford (CA) .... M
Georgia Inst. of Tech. .... M	Swarthmore (PA) .... R
Gettysburg (PA) .... R	Texas, U. of (Dallas) .... M
Grinnell (IA)..................................... R	Trinity (TX)...................................... R
Gustavus Adolphus (MN) .... R	United States Air Force Academy (CO) .... M
Hamilton (NY) .... R	Vanderbilt (TN) .... M
Harvard (MA) .... M	Wake Forest (NC) .... M
Harvey Mudd (CA) .... S	Washington & Lee (VA) .... R
Haverford (PA) .... S	Washington, U. of............................ XL
Holy Cross (MA) .... R	Washington U. (MO) .... M
Illinois, U. of (Urbana-Champaign) XL	▲ Wellesley (MA) .... R
Illinois Institute of Tech .... R	Wheaton (IL) .... R
Illinois Wesleyan .... R	Whitman (WA)................................... R
Iowa State XL	William & Mary (VA) .... M
Iowa, U. of..................................... XL	Worcester Poly. Inst. (MA) .... R
Johns Hopkins (MD) .... M	Yale (CT) .... M
Kenyon (OH) .... R	Yeshiva (NY) .... R
Kalamazoo (MI) .... R	
# Kettering (MI)................................. R	

 # Applied Physics
PHYSICS continues next page

PHYSICS, continued

GROUP II
Very Selective

Adelphi (NY) .... M
▲ Agnes Scott (GA) .... S
Alabama, U. of (Huntsville) .... M
Arizona State XL
Auburn (AL) L
Augsburg (MN) .... R
Beloit (WI) .... R
Bethany (WV) .... S
Bradley (IL) .... M
Cal. Poly. State U. (San Luis Obispo) L
California, U. of (Davis) XL
California, U. of (Irvine) L
California, U. of (Santa Barbara) L
California, U. of (Santa Cruz) .... M
Calvin (MI) .... R
Catholic (DC) .... R
Central Florida XL
Clark (MA) .... R
Clemson (SC) L
Coe (IA) .... R
Colorado, U. of L
Colorado, U. of (Colorado Springs) .... M
Creighton (NE) .... M
Denver, U. of (CO) .... M
Elmhurst (IL) .... R
Evansville, U. of (IN) .... R
Fairfield (CT) .... M
Florida Inst. of Tech .... R
Florida State L
George Mason (VA) L
Guilford (NC) .... R
Hamline (MN) .... R
Hanover (IN) .... R
Hendrix (AR) .... R
Hope (MI) .... M
Houston, U. of (TX) L
Humboldt State (CA) .... M
Idaho, U. of L
Kansas State L
Kansas, U. of L
Kent State (OH) L
Knox (IL) .... R
Lewis & Clark (OR) .... R
Linfield (OR) .... R
Loras (IA) .... R
Loyola (IL) .... M
Maine, U. of L

Mansfield (PA) .... R
Marietta (OH) .... R
Maryland, U. of (Baltimore County) ...... M
Massachusetts, U. of (Lowell) .... M
McDaniel (MD) .... R
Michigan State XL
Michigan Tech .... M
Mississippi, U. of L
Mississippi State L
Montana State L
Nebraska, U. of L
New Hampshire, U. of L
New Orleans (LA) L
North Carolina State L
Oakland (MI) .... M
Ohio State XL
Ohio U. L
Oklahoma State L
Oregon State L
Pacific University (OR) .... R
Pittsburgh, U. of (PA) L
Presbyterian (SC) .... R
Ramapo (NJ) .... M
Rochester Inst. of Tech. (NY) L
Rollins (FL) .... R
Rowan (NJ) .... M
St. John's (MN) .... R
Santa Clara U. (CA) .... M
Shippensburg (PA) .... M
Sonoma State (CA) .... M
South Carolina, U. of L
South Dakota School of Mines .... R
Stockton State (NJ) .... M
Stony Brook (SUNY) (NY) L
Syracuse (NY) L
Tennessee, U. of XL
Texas, U. of (Austin) XL
Tulsa, U. of (OK) .... M
Ursinus (PA) .... R
Vermont, U. of .... M
Washington State L
West Virginia L
Westminster (UT) .... R
Whitworth (WA) .... R
William Jewell (MO) .... R
Wisconsin, U. of XL
Xavier (OH) .... R

PHYSICS continues next page

Enrollment Code

■ *Men Only* | S = Small (less than 1000 students) | R = Moderate (1000-3000 students) | M = Medium (3000-8000 students)
▲ *Women Only* | L = Large (8000-20,000 students) | XL = Extra Large (over 20,000 students)

PHYSICS, continued

GROUP III
Selective

Arkansas, U. of	L	Louisiana State	XL
Ball State (IN)	L	▲ Mary Baldwin (VA)	S
Brooklyn Col. (CUNY) (NY)	L	Mass. College of Lib. Arts (N. Adams)	R
California Poly. State U. (Pomona)	L	Massachusetts, U. of (Boston)	M
California State U. (Dominguez Hills)	M	Millersville (PA)	M
California State U. (Northridge)	L	Minnesota State U. (Moorhead)	M
California State U. (San Jose)	L	Muskingum (OH)	R
Carthage (WI)	R	Nevada, U. of (Reno)	L
Christopher Newport (VA)	M	Northern Illinois U.	L
City Col. (CUNY) (NY)	L	Northern Michigan	M
Clark Atlanta (GA)	M	Northwestern (IA)	R
Doane (NE)	S	Old Dominion (VA)	L
East Stroudsburg (PA)	M	Oneonta (SUNY)(NY)	M
Eastern Michigan	L	Ozarks, College of the (MO)	R
Edinboro (PA)	M	Penn State (Erie)(PA)	M
Fisk (TN)	S	Southern Connecticut	M
Florida A&M	M	Thomas More (KY)	R
Fort Lewis (CO)	M	Tuskegee (AL)	M
Georgia State	L	Union (TN)	R
Goshen (IN)	R	Washburn (KS)	M
Hastings (NE)	R	Weber State (UT)	L
Indiana (PA)	L	π West Virginia Wesleyan	R
Indiana State	L	Western Kentucky	L
Jacksonville (FL)	R	Western Michigan	L
Louisiana-Lafayette	L	Wisconsin, U. of (Milwaukee)	L

π *Engineering Physics*

Enrollment Code

■ *Men Only* S = Small (less than 1000 students) R = Moderate (1000-3000 students) M = Medium (3000-8000 students)
▲ *Women Only* L = Large (8000-20,000 students) XL = Extra Large (over 20,000 students)

POLITICAL SCIENCE

GROUP I
Most Selective

American U. (DC) .... M	Miami, U. of (OH) L
Amherst (MA) .... R	Michigan, U. of XL
Binghamton (SUNY)(NY) L	Middlebury (VT) .... R
▲ Barnard (NY) .... R	Minnesota, U. of XL
Bates (ME) .... R	▲ Mount Holyoke (MA) .... R
Boston College (MA) L	Muhlenberg (PA) .... R
Boston U. (MA) L	North Carolina, U. of L
Bowdoin (ME) .... R	Northwestern (IL) .... M
Brandeis (MA) .... R	Notre Dame (IN) .... M
Brown (RI) .... M	Oberlin (OH) .... R
California, U. of (Berkeley) XL	Occidental (CA) .... R
California, U. of (Los Angeles) XL	Pennsylvania, U. of L
California, U. of (San Diego) L	Pomona (CA) .... R
Carleton (MN) .... R	Princeton (NJ) .... M
Centre (KY) .... R	Rhodes (TN) .... R
Chicago, U. of (IL) .... M	Rice (TX) .... M
Claremont McKenna (CA) .... R	Richmond, U. of (VA) .... M
Colby (ME) .... R	Rochester, U. of (NY) .... M
Colgate (NY) .... R	Rutgers (NJ) L
Colorado Col. .... R	▲ Scripps (CA) .... S
Columbia (NY) .... M	▲ Smith (MA) .... R
Connecticut Col. .... R	South, U. of the (TN) .... R
Connecticut, U. of XL	Southwestern (TX) .... R
Dallas, U. of (TX) .... R	Stanford (CA) .... M
Dartmouth (NH) .... M	Swarthmore (PA) .... R
Davidson (NC) .... M	Texas A&M XL
DePauw (IN) .... R	Texas, U. of (Austin) XL
Dickinson (PA) .... R	Trinity (TX) .... R
Drew (NJ) .... R	Tufts (MA) .... M
Duke (NC) .... M	Tulane (LA) .... M
Emory (GA) .... M	Union (NY) .... R
Florida, U. of XL	U.S. Air Force Academy (CO) .... M
Franklin & Marshall (PA) .... R	U.S. Military Academy (NY) .... M
Furman (SC) .... R	U.S. Naval Academy (MD) .... M
Georgetown (DC) .... M	Ursinus (PA) .... R
George Washington (DC) .... M	Vanderbilt (TN) .... M
Gettysburg (PA) .... R	Villanova (PA) .... M
Grinnell (IA) .... R	Virginia, U. of L
Hamilton (NY) .... R	■ Wabash (IN) .... S
Harvard (MA) .... M	Wake Forest (NC) .... M
Haverford (PA) .... S	Washington & Lee (VA) .... R
Holy Cross (MA) .... R	▲ Wellesley (MA) .... R
Illinois, U. of XL	Wesleyan (CT) .... R
Johns Hopkins (MD) .... M	Whitman (WA) .... R
Kalamazoo (MI) .... R	Willamette (OR) .... R
Kenyon (OH) .... R	William & Mary (VA) .... M
Lafayette (PA) .... R	Williams (MA) .... R
Lehigh (PA) .... M	Yale (CT) .... M
Macalester (MN) .... R	Yeshiva (NY) .... R
MIT (MA) .... M	

POLITICAL SCIENCE continues next page

POLITICAL SCIENCE, continued

GROUP II
Very Selective

▲Agnes Scott (GA) .... S
Albany (SUNY)(NY) L
Albertson (ID) .... S
Albion (MI) .... R
Alma (MI) .... R
Arcadia (PA) .... R
Auburn (AL) L
Austin (TX) .... R
Belmont (TN) .... R
Bethany (WV) .... S
Bradley (IL) .... M
California, U. of (Davis) XL
California, U. of (Riverside) L
California, U. of (Santa Barbara) L
Catholic U. (DC) .... M
Clark (MA) .... R
Clemson (SC) L
Colorado State L
College of Charleston (SC) L
Cornell College (IA) .... R
Creighton (NE) .... M
Dayton, U. of (OH) .... M
Delaware, U. of L
Denison (OH) .... R
DePaul (IL) L
Drake (IA) .... M
Elon (NC) .... R
Emerson (MA) .... M
Florida International L
George Mason (VA) L
Georgia, U. of Xl
Gonzaga (WA) .... R
Goucher (MD) .... R
Grove City (PA) .... R
Guilford (NC) .... R
Hampden-Sydney (VA) .... S
Hawaii, U. of L
Hendrix (AR) .... R
Hillsdale (MI) .... R
Hobart & William Smith (NY) .... R
Hofstra (NY) .... M

▲Hollins (VA) .... S
Hood (MD) .... S
Hope (MI) .... R
Howard (DC) .... M
Hunter (CUNY)(NY) L
Illinois College .... S
Illinois, U. of (Chicago) L
Iowa, U. of XL
James Madison (VA) .... M
John Carroll (OH) .... R
Kansas, U. of L
Kennesaw State (GA) .... R
Kent State (OH) L
Knox (IL) .... R
Lake Forest (IL) .... R
Lipscomb (TN) .... R
Lyon (AR) .... S
Manhattan (NY) .... M
Manhattanville (NY) .... R
Marist (NY) .... M
Marquette (WI) .... M
Maryland, U. of XL
Maryland, U. of (Baltimore County) .... M
Mary Washington (VA) .... M
Massachusetts, U. of L
McDaniel (MD) .... R
Merrimack (MA) .... R
Millersville (PA) .... M
Millsaps (MS) .... S
Minnesota, U. of (Morris) .... R
Missouri, U. of XL
Missouri, U. of (St. Louis) .... M
▲Morehouse (GA) .... R
North Carolina (Charlotte) L
North Central (IL) .... R
North Texas L
Oglethorpe (GA) .... S
Ohio State XL
Ohio U. L
Ohio Wesleyan .... R

GROUP II continues next page

Enrollment Code

■ **Men Only**   S = Small (less than 1000 students)   R = Moderate (1000-3000 students)   M = Medium (3000-8000 students)
▲ **Women Only**   L = Large (8000-20,000 students)   XL = Extra Large (over 20,000 students)

POLITICAL SCIENCE, continued

GROUP II, continued

Oklahoma City U.	R
Oklahoma, U. of	XL
Oklahoma State	L
Oregon, U. of	L
Oswego (SUNY)(NY)	M
Pittsburgh, U. of (PA)	L
Portland, U. of (OR)	R
Presbyterian (SC)	R
Providence (RI)	M
Puget Sound (WA)	R
Purchase (SUNY)(NY)	M
Ramapo (NJ)	M
Randolph Macon (VA)	R
Redlands, U. of (CA)	R
Regis (CO)	R
Richard Stockton (NJ)	M
Ripon (WI)	S
Roanoke (VA)	R
St. Bonaventure (NY)	R
St. Cloud (MN)	L
St. John's (MN)	R
St. John's (NY)	L
St. Joseph's (PA)	R
St. Lawrence (NY)	R
St. Mary's College of Maryland	R
San Diego, U. of (CA)	M
Santa Clara U. (CA)	M
Siena (NY)	R

Skidmore (NY)	R
South Carolina	L
Spring Hill (AL)	R
Stonehill (MA)	R
Stony Brook (SUNY)(NY)	L
Susquehanna (PA)	R
▲Sweet Briar (VA)	S
Syracuse (NY)	L
Tennessee, U. of	XL
▲Trinity (DC)	S
Utah, U. of	L
Vermont, U. of	L
Washington, U. of	XL
Washington & Jefferson (PA)	R
Webster (MO)	R
Westchester (PA)	M
Western Washington U.	R
Westminster (MO)	S
Westminster (UT)	R
West Virginia U.	L
Wheaton (MA)	R
Wilberforce (OH)	S
Winthrop (SC)	M
Wisconsin, U. of	XL
Wittenberg (OH)	R
Wofford (SC)	R
Wooster, College of the (OH)	R
Wyoming, U. of	L

Enrollment Code

■ *Men Only*   S = Small (less than 1000 students)   R = Moderate (1000-3000 students)   M = Medium (3000-8000 students)
▲ *Women Only*   L = Large (8000-20,000 students)   XL = Extra Large (over 20,000 students)

POLITICAL SCIENCE, continued

GROUP III
Selective

Adrian (MI)	R	Lock Haven (PA)	M
Albright (PA)	R	Louisiana State	XL
Appalachian State (NC)	L	Louisville (KY)	L
Arizona State	XL	Manchester (IN)	R
Azusa Pacific (CA)	R	▲ Mary Baldwin (VA)	S
Baker (KS)	R	Massachusetts, U. of (Boston)	M
Baldwin-Wallace (OH)	R	Mercyhurst (PA)	R
Ball State (IN)	L	Michigan State	XL
Belmont Abbey (NC)	S	Missouri State	L
▲ Bennett (NC)	S	Monmouth (NJ)	R
Bridgewater (MA)	M	Montana , U. of	M
Brockport (SUNY)(NY)	M	Montana State	L
California State U. (Chico)	L	Mount St. Mary's (MD)	R
California State U. (Fullerton)	L	Mount Union (OH)	R
California State U. (Long Beach)	L	Muskingum (OH)	R
California State U. (Northridge)	L	Nebraska, U. of (Omaha)	L
California State U. (Sacramento)	M	Nevada, U. of (Las Vegas)	L
California State U. (San Marcos)	M	Nevada, U. of (Reno)	L
California State U. (Stanislaus)	M	New Mexico State U.	L
Campbell (NC)	R	New Orleans, U. of (LA)	L
Carthage (WI)	R	▲ Pine Manor (MA)	S
▲ Chatham (PA)	S	Pittsburgh, U. of (Greensburg)	R
Christopher Newport (VA)	M	Queens (CUNY)(NY)	L
City College (CUNY)(NY)	L	Radford (VA)	M
▲ Converse (SC)	S	Regis (MA)	R
Eastern Connecticut	M	Rhode Island, U. of	L
Eastern Illinois	L	St. Mary's (TX)	R
Eastern Kentucky	L	South Dakota, U. of	M
Eastern Michigan	L	Southern Connecticut	M
Fairleigh Dickinson (NJ)	M	Southern Illinois U. (Carbondale)	L
Gardner-Webb (NC)	S	Southern Illinois U. (Edwardsville)	L
Grambling (LA)	M	▲ Spelman (GA)	R
Hartwick (NY)	R	Suffolk (MA)	R
Heidelburg (OH)	S	Texas, U. of (Arlington)	L
Iona (NY)	M	Utah State	L
Illinois State	L	Virginia Wesleyan	R
John Jay (CUNY)(NY)	M	Westfield (MA)	M
Kutztown (PA)	M	Whittier (CA)	R
Laverne (CA)	R	Wisconsin, U. of (Milwaukee)	L

Enrollment Code

■ *Men Only*
▲ *Women Only*

S = Small (less than 1000 students)   R = Moderate (1000-3000 students)   M = Medium (3000-8000 students)

L = Large (8000-20,000 students)   XL = Extra Large (over 20,000 students)

PRE-LAW

Author's Note: Law School Associations usually recommend that a student choose a major dependent upon one's own individual intellectual interests and upon "the quality of undergraduate education" provided by various departments and colleges. The following recommended colleges have been taken primarily from our recommended departments in English, Economics, and Political Science.

GROUP I
Most Selective

Albany (SUNY) (NY)	L	Franklin & Marshall (PA)	R
Allegheny (PA)	R	Furman (SC)	R
American U. (DC)	M	Georgetown (DC)	M
Amherst (MA)	R	George Washington (DC)	M
Bard (NY)	R	Gettysburg (PA)	R
▲ Barnard (NY)	R	Grinnell (IA)	R
Bates (ME)	R	Hamilton (NY)	R
Binghamton (SUNY) (NY)	L	Harvard (MA)	M
Boston Col. (MA)	L	Haverford (PA)	S
Boston U. (MA)	L	Holy Cross (MA)	R
Bowdoin (ME)	R	Illinois, U. of (Chicago)	L
Brandeis (MA)	R	Illinois, U. of (Urbana-Champaign)	XL
Brown (RI)	M	Illinois Wesleyan	R
▲ Bryn Mawr (PA)	S	Iowa, U. of	XL
Bucknell (PA)	M	Johns Hopkins (MD)	M
Buffalo (SUNY) (NY)	L	Kalamazoo (MI)	R
California, U. of (Berkeley)	XL	Kenyon (OH)	R
California, U. of (Los Angeles)	XL	Lafayette (PA)	R
California, U. of (San Diego)	L	Macalester (MN)	R
Carleton (MN)	R	Maryland, U. of (Baltimore County)	M
Carnegie Mellon (PA)	M	MIT (MA)	M
Case Western Reserve (OH)	M	Miami, U. of (FL)	L
Centre (KY)	R	Miami U. (OH)	L
Chicago, U. of (IL)	M	Michigan, U. of	XL
Claremont McKenna (CA)	R	Middlebury (VT)	R
Clark (MA)	R	Minnesota, U. of	XL
Clarkson (NY)	M	▲ Mount Holyoke (MA)	R
Colby (ME)	R	Muhlenberg (PA)	R
Colgate (NY)	R	New College (FL)	S
Colorado Col.	R	New Jersey, College of	M
Columbia (NY)	M	North Carolina, U. of	L
Connecticut Col.	R	Northwestern (IL)	M
Cornell (NY)	L	Notre Dame (IN)	M
Dallas, U. of (TX)	R	Oberlin (OH)	R
Dartmouth (NH)	M	Occidental (CA)	R
Davidson (NC)	R	Pennsylvania, U. of	L
DePauw (IN)	R	Pitzer (CA)	S
Dickinson (PA)	R	Pomona (CA)	R
Drew (NJ)	R	Princeton (NJ)	M
Duke (NC)	M	Providence (RI)	M
Emory (GA)	M		
Florida, U. of	XL		

GROUP I continues next page

PRE-LAW, continued

GROUP I, Continued

Reed (OR)	R
Rhodes (TN)	R
Richmond, U. of (VA)	M
Rice (TX)	M
Richmond, U. of (VA)	M
Rochester, U. of (NY)	M
Rutgers (NJ)	L
Sarah Lawrence (NY)	R
Skidmore (NY)	R
▲ Smith (MA)	R
South, U. of the (TN)	R
Southwestern (TX)	R
Stanford (CA)	M
St. Louis (MO)	M
St. Olaf (MN)	R
Swarthmore (PA)	R
Trinity (CT)	R
Trinity (TX)	R
Tufts (MA)	M
Tulane (LA)	M
Union (NY)	R
Vanderbilt (TN)	M
Vassar (NY)	R
Villanova (PA)	M
Virginia, U. of	L
■ Wabash (IN)	S
Wake Forest (NC)	M
Washington & Lee (VA)	R
Washington U. (MO)	M
▲ Wellesley (MA)	R
Wesleyan U. (CT)	R
Wheaton (IL)	R
Whitman (WA)	R
Williams (MA)	R
Wisconsin, U. of	XL
Worcester Poly. Inst. (MA)	R
Yale (CT)	M

GROUP II
Very Selective

▲ Agnes Scott (GA)	S
Alabama, U. of	L
Albertson (ID)	S
Albion (MI)	R
Alfred (NY)	R
Alma (MI)	R
Arcadia (PA)	R
Arizona, U. of	XL
Augsburg (MN)	R
Augustana (IL)	R
Baylor (TX)	R
Belmont (TN)	R
Bennington (VT)	S
Birmingham-Southern (AL)	R
Bradley (IL)	M
Brigham Young (UT)	XL
Butler (IN)	R
California, U. of (Davis)	XL
California, U. of (Irvine)	L
California, U. of (Riverside)	L
California, U. of (Santa Barbara)	L
Calvin (MI)	M
Catholic (DC)	R
Chapman (CA)	R
City College (CUNY)(NY)	L
Clark (MA)	R
Columbia Col. (SC)	R
Connecticut, U. of	XL
Cornell Col. (IA)	R
Creighton (NE)	M
Dayton, U. of (OH)	M
Delaware, U. of	L
Denison (OH)	R
Denver, U. of (CO)	M
DePaul (IL)	L
Drake (IA)	M
Drury (MO)	R
Evansville (IN)	R
Elizabethtown (PA)	R
Flagler (FL)	R
Fordham (NY)	L
George Mason (VA)	L
Georgetown College (KY)	R
Georgia, U. of	XL
Gonzaga (WA)	R
Goucher (MD)	R

GROUP II continues next page

Enrollment Code

■ *Men Only*
▲ *Women Only*

S = Small (less than 1000 students)   R = Moderate (1000-3000 students)   M = Medium (3000-8000 students)
L = Large (8000-20,000 students)   XL = Extra Large (over 20,000 students)

| **PRE-LAW,** continued |

━━━━━━━━━━━ **GROUP II,** continued ━━━━━━━━━━━

Grand Valley (MI)	L	North Carolina, U. of (Wilmington)	L
Guilford (NC)	R	North Carolina State	L
Hamline (MN)	R	North Central (IL)	R
■ Hampden-Sydney (VA)	S	Oglethorpe (GA)	S
Hampton (VA)	M	Ohio State	XL
Hartwick (NY)	R	Ohio U.	L
Hendrix (AR)	R	Ohio Wesleyan	R
Hiram (OH)	R	Oklahoma City U.	R
Hobart & Wm. Smith (NY)	R	Oklahoma, U. of	XL
Hofstra (NY)	M	Oneonta (SUNY) (NY)	M
Hood (MD)	S	Oregon, U. of	L
Hope (MI)	R	Oswego (SUNY)(NY)	M
Howard (DC)	M	Pittsburgh, U. of (PA)	L
Hunter (CUNY) (NY)	L	Portland State (OR)	L
Illinois College	S	Presbyterian (SC)	R
Illinois, U. of (Chicago)	L	Principia (IL)	S
Indiana (PA)	L	Puget Sound (WA)	R
Iowa State	XL	Purchase (SUNY) (NY)	M
James Madison (VA)	L	Queens (NC)	R
Juniata (PA)	R	Randolph College (VA)	S
Kansas State	L	Randolph-Macon (VA)	R
Knox (IL)	R	Redlands, U. of (CA)	R
Lake Forest (IL)	R	Ripon (WI)	S
LaSalle (PA)	M	Rowan (NJ)	M
Lawrence (WI)	R	Rutgers (Camden) (NJ)	M
Lebanon Valley (PA)	R	▲Salem College (NC)	S
Loras (IA)	R	Salisbury State (MD)	M
Loyola (LA)	R	San Diego, U. of	M
Loyola (MD)	M	San Francisco, U. of (CA)	M
Manhattan (NY)	M	Santa Clara U. (CA)	R
Marietta (OH)	R	▲Scripps (CA)	S
Marquette (WI)	M	Seton Hall (AL)	M
Maryland, U. of	XL	Siena (NY)	R
Massachusetts, U. of	L	South Carolina, U. of	L
Mercyhurst (PA)	R	South Dakota, U. of	M
Michigan State	XL	Spring Hill (AL)	R
Michigan, U. of (Dearborn)	M	St. Bonaventure (NY)	R
Millersville (PA)	M	St. Cloud (MN)	L
Millsaps (MS)	S	St. John's (MN)	R
Minnesota, U. of (Morris)	R	St. Lawrence (NY)	R
Mississippi, U. of	L	▲St. Mary's Col. (IN)	R
Missouri, U. of	XL	Stetson (FL)	R
Nebraska, U. of	L	Stonehill (MA)	R
New Hampshire, U. of	L	
North Carolina, U. of (Charlotte)	L	

GROUP II continues next page

PRE-LAW, continued

GROUP II, continued

Stony Brook (SUNY) (NY)	L
▲ Sweet Briar (VA)	S
Syracuse (NY)	L
▲ Trinity (DC)	S
Tuskegee (AL)	M
Ursinus (PA)	R
Vermont, U. of	L
Virginia Commonwealth U.	L
Virginia Military Inst.	R
Warren Wilson (NC)	S
Washington & Jefferson (PA)	R
Washington, U. of	XL
Wells (NY)	S
West Chester (PA)	M
West Virginia U.	L
Western New England (MA)	R
Western Washington U.	L
Westminster Col. (MO)	S
Westmont (CA)	R
Wheaton (MA)	R
Wilberforce (OH)	S
Wittenberg (OH)	R
Wofford (SC)	R
Wooster (OH)	R

GROUP III
Selective

Adrian (MI)	R
Albright (PA)	R
Arkansas, U. of	L
Baldwin-Wallace (OH)	R
Belmont Abbey (NC)	S
▲ Bennett (NC)	S
Bethany (WV)	S
Brockport (SUNY)(NY)	M
California State U. (Channel Islands)	R
California State U. (Long Beach)	L
California State U. (Monterey Bay)	R
California State U. (Northridge)	L
Campbell (NC)	R
▲ Chatham (PA)	S
Chestnut Hill (PA)	S
Citidel, The (SC)	R
Emerson (MA)	M
Fairleigh Dickinson (NJ)	M
Fisk (TN)	S
Florida A&M	M
Fort Lewis (CO)	M
Gwynedd-Mercy (PA)	S
Hawaii, U. of	L
Heidelberg (OH)	S
▲ Hollins (VA)	S
Illinois State	L
Laverne (CA)	R
Longwood (VA)	R
Louisiana College	R
Louisiana-Lafayette	L
Louisiana State	XL
Lynchburg (VA)	R
Massachusetts, U. of (Boston)	M
Missouri State	L
Molloy (NY)	R
Mount St. Joseph (OH)	R
Mount St. Mary's (MD)	R
Niagara (NY)	R
Northland (WI)	S
Radford (VA)	M
Rhode Island, U. of	L
Roanoke (VA)	R
Rockford (IL)	S
▲ Rosemont (PA)	S
San Francisco State (CA)	L
Seattle U. (WA)	R
▲ Spelman (GA)	R
St. Anselm (NH)	R
St. Francis (PA)	R
St. Mary's (TX)	R
▲ Stephens (MO)	S
Temple (PA)	L
Tennessee, U. of	XL
Utah, U. of	L
Virginia Wesleyan	R
Whittier (CA)	R
Wilson (PA)	S
Wisconsin, U. of (Milwaukee)	L
Wyoming, U. of	L

Enrollment Code

■ *Men Only* S = Small (less than 1000 students)   R = Moderate (1000-3000 students)   M = Medium (3000-8000 students)
▲ *Women Only* L = Large (8000-20,000 students)   XL = Extra Large (over 20,000 students)

PRE-MED/PRE-DENTAL

Author's Note: In addition to general college requirements and requirements of their major department, premedical and predental students must usually pass with a good grade the following: general chemistry, zoology, organic chemistry, general biology, English composition or literature, and general physics.

Other required or highly recommended courses are: advanced biology, psychology or sociology, physical chemistry, calculus, and quantitative chemistry. Of course, the wise path to follow is to consult the exact course requirements of the school you expect to apply to. The recommended colleges below are taken primarily from our recommended departments in biology and chemistry.

GROUP I
Most Selective

Albany (SUNY) (NY)	L	Furman (SC)	R
Allegheny (PA)	R	Geneseo (SUNY) (NY)	M
American U. (DC)	M	Georgetown (DC)	M
Amherst (MA)	R	Gettysburg (PA)	R
Bates (ME)	R	Grinnell (IA)	R
Binghamton (SUNY) (NY)	L	Hamilton (NY)	R
Boston Col. (MA)	L	Harvard (MA)	M
Boston U. (MA)	L	Harvey Mudd (CA)	S
Bowdoin (ME)	R	Haverford (PA)	S
Brandeis (MA)	R	Holy Cross (MA)	R
Brown (RI)	M	Illinois, U. of (Urbana-Champaign)	XL
▲ Bryn Mawr (PA)	S	Illinois Wesleyan	R
Bucknell (PA)	M	Iowa State	XL
Buffalo (SUNY) (NY)	L	Iowa, U. of	XL
California Inst. of Tech.	S	Johns Hopkins (MD)	M
California, U. of (Berkeley)	XL	Kalamazoo (MI)	R
California, U. of (Los Angeles)	XL	Kenyon (OH)	R
California, U. of (San Diego)	L	Knox (IL)	R
Carleton (MN)	R	Lafayette (PA)	R
Carnegie-Mellon (PA)	M	Lawrence (WI)	R
Case Western Reserve U. (OH)	M	Macalester (MN)	R
Centre (KY)	R	Miami, U. of (FL)	L
Chicago, U. of (IL)	M	Miami, U. of (OH)	L
Claremont McKenna (CA)	R	MIT (MA)	M
Clark (MA)	R	Michigan, U. of	XL
Colby (ME)	R	Middlebury (VT)	R
Colgate (NY)	R	▲ Mount Holyoke (MA)	R
Colorado Col.	R	New College (FL)	S
Colorado School of Mines	R	New Jersey, College of	M
Columbia (NY)	M	North Carolina, U. of	L
Cornell (NY)	L	Northwestern (IL)	M
Dallas, U. of (TX)	R	Notre Dame (IN)	M
Dartmouth (NH)	M	Oberlin (OH)	R
Davidson (NC)	R	Occidental (CA)	R
DePauw (IN)	R	Pitzer (CA)	S
Dickinson (PA)	M	Pomona (CA)	R
Drew (NJ)	R	Princeton (NJ)	M
Duke (NC)	R	Puget Sound (WA)	R
Emory (GA)	M	Reed (OR)	R
Fairfield (CT)	M	Rhodes (TN)	R
Florida, U. of	XL	Rice (TX)	M
Franklin & Marshall (PA)	R		

GROUP I continues next page

PRE-MED/PRE-DENTAL, continued

GROUP I, continued

Richmond, U. of (VA)	R
Rochester, U. of (NY)	M
Rutgers (NJ)	L
Skidmore (NY)	R
▲ Smith (MA)	R
South, U. of the (TN)	R
Southwestern (TX)	R
Stanford (CA)	M
Stetson (FL)	R
St. Mary's College of Maryland	R
St. Olaf (MN)	R
Swarthmore (PA)	S
Texas, U. of (Austin)	XL
Trinity (CT)	R
Trinity (TX)	R
Tufts (MA)	M
Tulane (LA)	M
Union (NY)	R
Ursinus (PA)	R
Vanderbilt (TN)	M
Vassar (NY)	R
Villanova (PA)	M
Virginia, U. of	L
■ Wabash (IN)	S
Wake Forest (NC)	M
Washington & Lee (VA)	M
Washington U. (MO)	M
▲ Wellesley (MA)	R
Wesleyan (CT)	R
Wheaton (IL)	R
Whitman (WA)	R
Willamette (OR)	R
William & Mary (VA)	M
Williams (MA)	R
Yale (CT)	M
Yeshiva (NY)	R

GROUP II
Very Selective

▲ Agnes Scott (GA)	S
Alabama, U. of	l
Albertson (ID)	S
Albion (MI)	R
Albright (PA)	R
Alfred (NY)	R
Alma (MI)	R
Arizona State	XL
Arizona, U. of	XL
Augustana (SD)	M
Austin (TX)	R
Baylor (TX)	M
Berry (GA)	R
Bethany (WV)	S
Birmingham-Southern (AL)	R
Brigham Young (UT)	XL
Butler (IN)	R
California, U. of (Davis)	XL
California, U. of (Irvine)	L
California, U. of (Riverside)	L
California, U. of (Santa Barbara)	L
California, U. of (Santa Cruz)	M
Canisius (NY)	M
Carroll (WI)	R
Chapman (CA)	R
City College (CUNY)(NY)	L
College of Charleston (SC)	L
Columbia Col. (SC)	R
Colorado, U. of	L
Concordia (MN)	R
Connecticut, U. of	XL
Cornell (IA)	R
Creighton (NE)	M
Dayton, U. of (OH)	M
Delaware, U. of	L
DePaul (IL)	L
Denison (OH)	R
Denver, U. of (CO)	M
DeSales (PA)	R
Duquesne (PA)	M
Earlham (IN)	R
Eckerd (FL)	R
Erskine (SC)	S
Evansville (IN)	R
Florida State	L
Fordham (NY)	M
Franklin (IN)	S

GROUP II continues next page

Enrollment Code		
■ **Men Only**	S = Small (less than 1000 students)	R = Moderate (1000-3000 students)	M = Medium (3000-8000 students)
▲ **Women Only**	L = Large (8000-20,000 students)	XL = Extra Large (over 20,000 students)

PRE-MED/PRE-DENTAL, continued

GROUP II, continued

Gannon (PA)	M	Michigan, U. of (Dearborn)	M
Georgia, U. of	XL	Millsaps (MS)	R
Gonzaga (WA)	R	Minnesota, U. of (Morris)	R
Goucher (MD)	R	Mississippi, U. of	L
Guilford (NC)	R	Mississippi State	L
Hamline (MN)	R	Missouri, U. of	XL
Harrisburg U. (PA)	S	Monmouth (IL)	S
Hawaii Pacific	R	Moravian (PA)	R
■ Hampden-Sydney (VA)	S	Morningside (IA)	S
Hendrix (AR)	R	Muhlenberg (PA)	R
Hiram (OH)	R	Nebraska Wesleyan	R
Hobart & Wm. Smith (NY)	R	Nevada, U. of (Reno)	L
Hofstra (NY)	M	New Hampshire, U. of	L
▲ Hollins (VA)	S	New York U.	L
Hood (MD)	S	North Carolina, U. of (Charlotte)	L
Hope (MI)	R	North Central (IL)	R
Houghton (NY)	S	Oglethorpe (GA)	S
Houston Baptist (TX)	R	Ohio State	XL
Houston, U. of (TX)	L	Ohio Wesleyan	R
Howard (DC)	M	Oregon, U. of	L
Huntingdon (AL)	S	Pacific Lutheran (OR)	R
Illinois, U. of (Chicago)	L	Pacific University (OR)	R
Indiana U.	XL	Pennsylvania State	XL
Indiana Wesleyan	M	Pittsburgh, U. of (PA)	L
Ithaca Col. (NY)	M	Presbyterian (SC)	R
James Madison (VA)	L	Purchase (SUNY)(NY)	M
Juniata (PA)	R	Randolph College (VA)	S
Kansas, U. of	L	Randolph-Macon (VA)	R
Kansas State	L	Redlands, U. of (CA)	R
Kentucky, U. of	L	Regis (CO)	R
Knox (IL)	R	Richard Stockton (NJ)	M
Lake Forest (IL)	R	Ripon (WI)	S
Lebanon Valley (PA)	R	Rowan (NJ)	M
Lewis & Clark (OR)	R	San Diego, U. of (CA)	M
Lipscomb (TN)	R	San Francisco, U. of (CA)	M
Loyola (IL)	M	Scranton, U. of (PA)	M
Loyola (LA)	R	▲ Scripps (CA)	S
Loyola (MD)	M	Seton Hall (NJ)	M
Lycoming (PA)	R	Siena (NY)	R
Manhattan (NY)	M	Spring Hill (AL)	R
Marquette (WI)	M	St. Francis (PA)	R
Mary Washington (VA)	M	St. John's (MN)	R
Massachusetts, U. of	L	St. Joseph's U. (PA)	R
McDaniel (MD)	R	St. Louis (MO)	M
Michigan State	XL		

GROUP II continues next page

PRE-MED/PRE-DENTAL, continued

GROUP II, continued

St. Louis Col. of Pharmacy (MO) .... S
St. Scholastica (MN) .... R
St. Thomas, U. of (MN) .... S
St. Thomas, U. of (TX) .... R
Stetson (FL) .... R
Stony Brook (SUNY) (NY) L
Susquehanna (PA) .... R
Tennessee, U. of XL
Texas A&M XL
Transylvania (KY) .... S
Truman State (MO) .... M
Tuskegee (AL) .... M
Utah, U. of L
Valparaiso U. (IN) .... M
Vermont, U. of L
Washington College (MD) .... S

Washington & Jefferson (PA)............. R
Washington, U. of XL
Wells (NY) .... S
West Florida, U. of .... M
West Virginia U L
Westminster (MO) .... S
Westminster (PA) .... R
Westmont (CA) .... R
Wheaton (MA) .... R
Winona State U. (MN) .... M
Wisconsin, U. of XL
Wittenberg (OH) .... R
Wofford (SC) .... R
Wooster (OH) .... R
Wyoming, U. of................................. L

GROUP III
Selective

American International (MA) .... R
Benedictine (IL) .... R
▲ Bennett (NC) .... S
Blackburn (IL) .... S
Brooklyn Col. (CUNY) (NY) L
California State U. (Channel Islands) .... R
California State U. (Fullerton) L
California State U. (Monterey Bay) .... R
California State U. (San Jose) L
Carroll (MT) .... R
Carson-Newman (TN) .... R
Delaware Valley (PA) .... R
Dillard (LA) .... R
East Carolina (NC) L
Elmhurst (IL)..................................... R
Findlay (OH) .... M
Florida A&M .... M
Florida Southern .... R
Freed-Hardeman (TN) .... R
Gardner-Webb (NC) .... R
Heidelberg (OH) .... S
Ind.U.-Purdue U.-Indianapolis (IN) .. L
Jacksonville (FL) .... R

Kentucky Wesleyan .... S
Louisiana College .... R
Louisiana-Lafayette L
Louisiana State XL
Lynchburg (VA) .... R
Mount St. Joseph (OH) .... R
Mount St. Mary's (MD) .... R
Nova Southeastern (FL) .... R
Rider (NJ) .... R
▲ Spelman (GA) .... R
St. Mary's (TX) .... R
St. Vincent (PA) .... R
South Dakota, U. of .... M
Temple (PA) L
Texas, U. of (San Antonio) L
Thomas More (KY) .... R
Virginia Commonwealth L
Virginia Wesleyan............................. R
Walla Walla (WA) .... R
Wartburg (IA) .... R
Wayne State (MI)............................... L
Wilkes (PA) .... R
Xavier U. of Louisiana .... R

Enrollment Code

■ *Men Only*
▲ *Women Only*

S = Small (less than 1000 students)   R = Moderate (1000-3000 students)   M = Medium (3000-8000 students)
L = Large (8000-20,000 students)   XL = Extra Large (over 20,000 students)

PSYCHOLOGY

GROUP I
Most Selective

Allegheny (PA)	R	Lafayette (PA)	R
Amherst (MA)	R	Lehigh (PA)	M
Bard (NY)	R	Macalester (MN)	R
▲Barnard (NY)	R	Miami, U. of (FL)	L
Bates (ME)	R	Miami U. (OH)	L
Binghamton (SUNY) (NY)	L	Michigan, U. of	XL
Boston U. (MA)	L	Minnesota, U. of	XL
Brandeis (MA)	R	▲Mount Holyoke (MA)	R
▲Bryn Mawr (PA)	S	New College (FL)	S
Bucknell (PA)	M	New Jersey, College of	M
Buffalo (SUNY)(NY)	L	New York U.	L
California, U. of (Berkeley)	XL	North Carolina, U. of	L
California, U. of (Los Angeles)	XL	Northwestern (IL)	M
California, U. of (San Diego)	L	Notre Dame, U of (IN)	M
Carleton (MN)	R	Occidental (CA)	R
Carnegie-Mellon (PA)	M	Pennsylvania, U. of	L
Case Western Reserve U. (OH)	M	Pitzer (CA)	S
Centre (KY)	R	Pomona (CA)	S
Chicago, U. of (IL)	M	Princeton (NJ)	M
Claremont McKenna (CA)	R	Reed (OR)	R
Clarkson (NY)	M	Richmond, U. of (VA)	R
Colby (ME)	R	Rhodes (TN)	R
Colgate (NY)	R	Rochester, U. of (NY)	M
Colorado College	R	Rutgers (NJ)	L
Columbia (NY)	M	▲Scripps (CA)	S
Connecticut Col.	R	▲Simmons (MA)	R
Dallas, U. of (TX)	R	Skidmore (NY)	R
Dartmouth (NH)	M	▲Smith (MA)	R
Davidson (NC)	R	Southwestern (TX)	R
DePauw (IN)	R	Stanford (CA)	M
Dickinson (PA)	R	St. Louis (MO)	M
Drew (NJ)	R	St. Mary's College of Maryland	R
Duke (NC)	M	St. Olaf (MN)	R
Emory (GA)	M	Swarthmore (PA)	R
Franklin & Marshall (PA)	R	Tufts (MA)	M
Furman (SC)	R	Tulane (LA)	M
Georgetown (DC)	M	Union (NY)	R
George Washington (DC)	M	Vanderbilt (TN)	M
Georgia Institute of Tech.	L	Vassar (NY)	R
Gettysburg (PA)	R	Virginia, U. of	L
Grinnell (IA)	R	■Wabash (IN)	S
Gustavus Adolphus (MN)	R	Wake Forest (NC)	M
Harvard (MA)	M	Washington U. (MO)	M
Haverford (PA)	S	Wesleyan (CT)	R
Holy Cross (MA)	R	Wheaton (IL)	R
Illinois, U. of (Urbana-Champaign)	XL	Whitman (WA)	R
Illinois Wesleyan	R	Willamette (OR)	R
James Madison (VA)	L	Williams (MA)	R
Johns Hopkins (MD)	M	Yale (CT)	M
Kalamazoo (MI)	R	Yeshiva (NY)	M
Kenyon (OH)	R		

PSYCHOLOGY continues next page

PSYCHOLOGY, continued

GROUP II
Very Selective

Adelphi (NY)	M
▲ Agnes Scott (GA)	S
Alabama, U. of	L
Alabama, U. of (Huntsville)	M
Albany (SUNY) (NY)	L
Albright (PA)	R
Alfred (NY)	R
Alma (MI)	R
Arizona State	XL
Arizona, U. of	XL
Belmont (TN)	R
Beloit (WI)	R
Berry (GA)	R
Bethany (WV)	S
Bowling Green (OH)	L
Birmingham-Southern (AL)	R
Brigham Young (UT)	XL
Cal. Poly State U. (SLO)	L
California, U. of (Irvine)	L
California, U. of (Merced)	R
California, U. of (Riverside)	L
California, U. of (Santa Barbara)	L
California, U. of (Santa Cruz)	M
Carroll (WI)	R
Catholic (DC)	R
Central Florida, U. of	XL
Chapman (CA)	R
Cincinnati, U. of	L
Clark (MA)	R
Coe (IA)	R
College of Charleston (SC)	L
Colorado State	L
Colorado, U. of	L
Concordia (MN)	R
Connecticut, U. of	XL
Cornell Col. (IA)	R
Creighton (NE)	M
Delaware, U. of	L
Denison (OH)	R
Denver, U. of (CO)	M
DePaul (IL)	L
Dubuque, U. of (IA)	S
Earlham (IN)	R
Eastern Michigan	L

Elmira (NY)	R
Elon (NC)	R
Fairfield (CT)	M
Fairmont (WV)	M
Flagler (FL)	R
Florida Atlantic	L
Florida Inst. of Tech.	R
Florida International	L
Florida State	L
George Mason (VA)	L
Georgia State	`L
Grand Valley (MI)	L
Guilford (NC)	R
Hamline (MN)	R
Hampton (VA)	M
Hanover (IN)	R
Hendrix (AR)	R
Herbert Lehman (CUNY) (NY)	L
Hobart & Wm. Smith (NY)	R
Hofstra (NY)	M
Hood (MD)	S
Hope (MI)	R
Houghton (NY)	S
Houston, U. of (TX)	L
Hunter (CUNY) (NY)	L
Illinois, U. of (Chicago)	L
Indiana U.	XL
Iowa, U. of	XL
John Carroll (OH)	R
Kansas State	L
Kansas, U. of	L
Kean (NJ)	M
Kentucky, U. of	L
Lake Forest (IL)	R
LaSalle (PA)	M
Lebanon Valley (PA)	R
LeMoyne (NY)	R
Loras (IA)	R
Louisiana State U.	L
Loyola (IL)	M
Loyola (MD)	M
Luther (IA)	R
Lycoming (PA)	R

GROUP II continues next page

Enrollment Code

■ *Men Only*
▲ *Women Only*

S = Small (less than 1000 students)   R = Moderate (1000-3000 students)   M = Medium (3000-8000 students)
L = Large (8000-20,000 students)   XL = Extra Large (over 20,000 students)

PSYCHOLOGY, continued

GROUP II, continued

Maine, U. of L
Manhattanville (NY) .... R
Marist (NY) .... M
Marquette (WI) .... R
Maryville (TN) .... S
Mary Washington (VA) .... M
Massachusetts, U. of L
Mercer (GA) .... R
Merrimack (MA) .... R
Michigan State XL
Millersville (PA) .... M
▲ Mills (CA) .... S
Minnesota, U. of (Morris) .... R
Missouri, U. of XL
Missouri, U. of (Kansas City) .... M
Missouri, U. of (St. Louis) .... M
Moravian (PA) .... R
Morningside (IA) .... S
Muhlenberg (PA) .... R
Nebraska Wesleyan .... R
Nevada, U. of (Las Vegas) L
New Paltz (SUNY) (NY) .... M
New Mexico, U. of L
New School U. (Eugene Lang)(NY) ...... S
Newman U. (KS) .... S
North Carolina (Asheville) .... R
North Carolina, U. of (Charlotte) L
North Carolina, U. of (Wilmington) L
North Carolina State L
Northeastern (MA) L
Ohio State XL
Ohio U. L
Ohio Wesleyan .... R
Oklahoma City U. .... R
Oklahoma, U. of XL
Oklahoma State L
Oregon, U. of L
Oswego (SUNY) (NY) .... M
Pace (NY) .... M
Pittsburgh, U. of (PA) L
Portland State (OR) L
Queens (CUNY) (NY) L
Quinnipiac (CT) .... R
Ramapo (NJ) .... M
Randolph College (VA) .... S
Randolph-Macon (VA) .... R
Rhode Island, U. of L
Roanoke (VA) .... R

Rockhurst (MO) .... R
Rollins (FL) .... R
Rutgers-Newark (NJ) .... M
Salisbury State (MD) .... M
San Diego State U. (CA) XL
San Francisco, U. of (CA) .... M
Santa Clara, U. of (CA) .... M
Shepherd (WV) .... M
Siena (NY) .... R
Southern California L
St. Lawrence (NY) .... R
St. Mary's College (CA) .... R
St. Thomas, U. of (TX) .... R
Stetson (FL) .... R
Stonehill (MA) .... R
Stony Brook (SUNY) (NY) L
Susquehanna (PA) .... R
▲ Sweet Briar (VA) .... S
Syracuse (NY) L
Texas, U. of (Austin) XL
Towson (MD) L
Transylvania (KY) .... R
Tulsa, U. of (OK) .... R
Valparaiso U. (IN) .... M
Vermont, U of L
Virginia Tech. L
Virginia, U. of L
Washington College (MD) .... S
Washington & Jefferson (PA) .... R
Washington, U. of XL
Webster (MO) .... R
Wells (NY) .... S
West Florida, U. of .... M
West Virginia U. L
Western Michigan L
Western Washington U. .... R
Westminster (MO) .... S
Westminster (UT) .... R
Westmont (CA) .... R
Wheaton (MA) .... R
Whitworth (WA) .... R
Winthrop (SC) .... M
Wisconsin, U. of XL
Wittenberg (OH) .... R
Wofford (SC) .... R
Xavier (OH) .... R

PSYCHOLOGY continues next page

PSYCHOLOGY, continued

GROUP III
Selective

Alabama, U. of (Birmingham) .... M	Coker (SC) .... S
Alaska Pacific .... S	Colby-Sawyer (NH) .... S
▲Alverno (WI) .... R	Colorado, U. of (Colorado Springs) .... M
American International (MA) .... R	Colorado, U. of (Denver) .... M
Aquinas (MI) .... R	Delaware State .... R
Arcadia (PA) .... R	Dominican (CA) .... S
Arkansas, U. of L	Dominican (IL) .... S
Averett (VA) .... S	D'Youville (NY) .... R
Baker (KS) .... R	East Carolina....................................... L
Baldwin-Wallace (OH) .... R	Eastern Connecticut .... M
Ball State (IN) L	Eastern Illinois L
▲Bay Path (MA)................................... R	Edgewood (WI) .... S
Bethel (MN) .... R	Elmhurst (IL).. R
Biola (CA) .... R	Findlay (OH) .... M
Blackburn (IL) .... S	Fitchburg (MA) .... R
Bridgewater (MA) .... M	Framingham (MA) .... M
Bridgewater (VA) .... R	Franciscan U. of Steubenville (OH) .... R
Brockport (SUNY)(NY) .... M	George Fox (OR) .... R
Brooklyn (CUNY)(NY) L	Hawaii, U. of (Hilo) .... R
Caldwell (NJ) .... S	▲Hollins (VA) .... S
California (PA) .... M	Holy Names (CA) .... S
California Lutheran .... R	John Jay College (CUNY)(NY) .... M
California State U. (Bakersfield) .... M	Johnson C. Smith (NC)....................... R
California State U. (Channel Islands) ..... R	▲Judson (AL) .... S
California State U. (Chico) L	Keene State (NH) .... R
California State U. (Dominguez Hills) ..... M	Kentucky Wesleyan .... S
California State U. (Long Beach) L	Kutztown (PA)..................................... M
California State U. (Los Angeles) L	Laverne (CA) .... R
California State U. (Northridge) L	Liberty (VA)... R
California State U. (Sacramento) .... M	Lindenwood (MO) .... M
California State U. (San Bernardino) ...... M	Lock Haven (PA) .... M
California State U. (San Marcos) .... M	Long Island U. (C.W.Post)(NY).............. M
California State U. (Stanislaus) .... M	Longwood (VA) .... R
Canisius (NY) .... M	Lyndon State(VT) .... R
Carson-Newman (TN) .... R	Lyon (AR) .... S
Carthage (WI) .... R	Maine, U. of (Farmington) .... R
Castleton State (VT) .... R	Manchester (IN).................................. R
▲Cedar Crest (PA) .... S	Marshall (WV) L
Central Connecticut........................... M	▲Mary Baldwin (VA) .... S
Central Michigan L	Marymount (VA).................................. R
Central Washington L	
Chaminade (HI) .... R	*GROUP III continues next page*

Enrollment Code			
■ *Men Only*	S = Small (less than 1000 students)	R = Moderate (1000-3000 students)	M = Medium (3000-8000 students)
▲ *Women Only*	L = Large (8000-20,000 students)	XL = Extra Large (over 20,000 students)	

PSYCHOLOGY, continued

GROUP III, continued

Marymount Manhattan (NY)	R	
Marywood (PA)	R	
Massachusetts, U. of (Dartmouth)	M	
Memphis, U. of (TN)	L	
Mercy (NY)	M	
▲ Meredith (NC)	R	
Middle Tennessee	L	
Millersville (PA)	M	
Minnesota State U. (Moorhead)	M	
Minnesota, U. of (Duluth)	L	
Molloy (NY)	R	
Montclair State (NJ)	M	
Mount St. Joseph (OH)	R	
Muskingum (OH)	R	
New Hampshire, U. of	L	
North Carolina (Greensboro)	M	
Northeastern State (OK)	L	
Northern Arizona	L	
Northern Iowa, U. of	L	
Northwestern (IA)	R	
Northwestern (MN)	R	
Nyack (NY)	R	
Oakland City U. (IN)	R	
Oklahoma Baptist	R	
Otterbein (OH)	R	
Ozarks, College of the (MO)	R	
Palm Beach Atlantic (FL)	R	
Penn State (Harrisburg)(PA)	R	
Peru State (NE)	R	
▲ Pine Manor (MA)	S	
Pittsburgh, U. of (Greensburg)	R	
Plattsburgh (SUNY)(NY)	M	
Point Park (PA)	R	
Potsdam (SUNY)(NY)	M	
Purchase (SUNY)(NY)	M	
Radford (VA)	M	
Regis (CO)	R	
Rhode Island College	M	
Rockford (IL)	S	
Roger Williams (RI)	M	
Roosevelt (IL)	R	
▲ Rosemont (PA)	S	
Russell Sage/The Sage Colleges (NY)	R	
Sacred Heart (CT)	R	
St. Ambrose (IA)	R	

St. Anselm (NH)	R
St. Edward's (TX)	M
St. Francis (NY)	R
St, John's (NY)	L
St. Joseph's (IN)	S
St. Joseph's (NY)	R
St. Martin's (WA)	S
St. Mary (KS)	S
St. Scholastica (MN)	R
St. Thomas Aquinas (NY)	R
St. Vincent (PA)	R
Salem State (MA)	M
Seton Hall (NJ)	M
Siena Heights (MI)	S
Shippensburg (PA)	M
Simpson (IA)	R
Sonoma State (CA)	M
South Dakota, U. of	M
Southern Connecticut	M
Southern Illinois U. (Carbondale)	L
Springfield (MA)	M
Staten Island (CUNY)(NY)	M
▲ Stephens (MO)	S
Taylor (IN)	R
Tennessee, U. of (Chattanooga)	M
Texas A&M (Corpus Christi)	M
Texas, U. of (El Paso)	L
Texas, U. of (San Antonio)	L
Texas, U. of (Tyler)	R
Texas Wesleyan	R
Virginia Commonwealth U.	L
Virginia Wesleyan	R
Wayne State (MI)	L
Western Kentucky	L
Western New England (MA)	R
Westfield (MA)	M
Wheeling Jesuit (WV)	R
Wilkes (PA)	R
Wilson (PA)	S
Wisconsin, U. of (Green Bay)	M
Wisconsin, U. of (Stout)	M
Worcester State (MA)	M
Wyoming, U. of	L
Xavier University of Louisiana	R
York (NE)	S

RELIGIOUS STUDIES

GROUP I
Most Selective

▲Barnard (NY) .... R
Bates (ME) .... R
Boston College (MA) L
Bowdoin (ME) .... R
Brown (RI) .... M
California, U. of (Berkeley) XL
Carleton (MN) .... R
Case Western Reserve (OH) .... M
Centre (KY) .... R
Chicago, U. of (IL) .... M
Claremont McKenna (CA) .... R
Colby (ME) .... R
Colgate (NY) .... R
Columbia (NY) .... M
Dartmouth (NH) .... M
Davidson (NC) .... R
DePauw (IN) .... R
Dickinson (PA) .... R
Drew (NJ) .... R
Duke (NC) .... M
Emory (GA) .... M
Furman (SC) .... R
Georgetown (DC) .... M
Grinnell (IA) .... R
Gustavus Adolphus (MN) .... R
Hamilton (NY) .... R
Haverford (PA) .... S
Holy Cross (MA) .... R
Kenyon (OH) .... R
Lawrence (WI) .... R
Macalester (MN) .... R
Middlebury (VT) .... R

▲Mount Holyoke (MA) .... R
New College (FL) .... S
North Carolina, U. of L
Northwestern (IL) .... M
Notre Dame (IN) .... M
Oberlin (OH) .... R
Occidental (CA) .... R
Pennsylvania, U. of L
Pittsburgh, U. of (PA) L
Pomona (CA) .... R
Princeton (NJ) .... M
Providence (RI) .... M
Rhodes (TN) .... R
Richmond, U. of (VA) .... R
Rutgers (NJ) L
St. Joseph's (PA) .... R
St. Olaf (MN) .... R
South, U. of the (TN) .... R
Southwestern (TX) .... R
Stanford (CA) .... M
Trinity (CT) .... R
Virginia, U. of L
■ Wabash (IN) .... S
Wake Forest (NC) .... M
▲Wellesley (MA) .... R
Wesleyan (CT) .... R
Wheaton (IL) .... R
Willamette (OR) .... R
William & Mary (VA) .... M
Wisconsin Lutheran .... S
Yale (CT) .... M

GROUP II
Very Selective

Alaska Pacific .... S
Arizona State XL
Asbury (KY) .... R
Augustana (SD) .... R
Austin (TX) .... R
Baylor (TX) .... M
Belmont (TN) .... R
Berea (KY) .... R
Bethany (WV) .... S
Bethel (IN) .... R
Bethel (MN) .... M
Birmingham-Southern (AL) .... R

Brigham Young (UT) XL
Bryan (TN) .... S
Bryn Athyn (PA) .... S
California, U. of (Santa Barbara) L
Capital (OH) .... R
Catholic U. (DC) .... M
Central (IA) .... R
Christendom (VA) .... S
Christian Brothers (TN) .... R
Concordia (CA) .... R

GROUP II continues next page

RELIGIOUS STUDIES, continued

•• ━━━━━━━━ GROUP II, continued ━━━━━━━━ ••

Creighton (NE)	M
Dana (NE)	S
Dayton, U. of (OH)	M
Denver, U. of (CO)	M
DePaul (IL)	L
Detroit Mercy (MI)	M
Drury (MO)	R
Duquesne (PA)	M
Earlham (IN)	R
Eckerd (FL)	R
Elizabethtown (PA)	R
Florida State	L
Fordham (NY)	M
Geneva (PA)	R
Gonzaga (WA)	R
Gordon (MA)	R
Guilford (NC)	R
Hamline (MN)	R
■ Hampden-Sydney (VA)	S
Hanover (IN)	R
Harding (AR)	M
Hendrix (AR)	R
Hiram (OH)	R
Hood (MD)	S
Hope (MI)	R
Houghton (NY)	S
Huntingdon (AL)	S
Indiana Wesleyan	M
Iowa, U. of	XL
John Carroll (OH)	R
LaSalle (PA)	M
LeMoyne (NY)	R
Lipscomb (TN)	R
Loras (IA)	R
Loyola (IL)	M
Loyola (LA)	R
Loyola Marymount (CA)	M
Luther (IA)	R
Lycoming (PA)	R
Manhattan (NY)	M
Manhattanville (NY)	R
Marquette)WI)	M
Master's (CA)	R
McMurry (TX)	R

Mercer (GA)	R
Merrimack (MA)	R
Messiah (PA)	R
Muhlenberg (PA)	R
Nazareth (NY)	R
Newman U. (KS)	S
North Carolina (Charlotte)	L
Oklahoma City U.	R
Pacific Lutheran (WA)	R
Portland, U. of (OR)	R
Presbyterian (SC)	R
Roanoke (VA)	R
Rockhurst (MO)	R
Rollins (FL)	R
Rowan (NJ)	M
St. Bonaventure (NY)	R
St. Edward's (TX)	M
St. John's (MN)	R
St. Louis U. (MO)	M
▲ St. Mary's College (IN)	R
St. Mary's (MN)	R
St. Scholastica (MN)	R
St. Thomas (MN)	R
St. Thomas, U. of (TX)	R
Sanford (AL)	R
San Diego, U. of (CA)	M
Santa Clara U. (CA)	M
Southern Methodist (TX)	L
Stetson (FL)	R
Stony Brook (SUNY) (NY)	L
Syracuse (NY)	L
Tennessee, U. of	XL
Texas Christian U.	M
Union (NE)	R
Valparaiso U. (IN)	M
Vermont, U. of	L
Wartburg (IA)	R
Westmont (CA)	R
Whitworth (WA)	R
Wittenberg (OH)	R
Wofford (SC)	R
Wooster (OH)	R
Xavier (OH)	R

RELIGIOUS STUDIES continues next page

Enrollment Code

■ *Men Only*	S = Small (less than 1000 students)	R = Moderate (1000-3000 students)	M = Medium (3000-8000 students)
▲ *Women Only*	L = Large (8000-20,000 students)	XL = Extra Large (over 20,000 students)

RELIGIOUS STUDIES, continued

GROUP III
Selective

Abilene Christain (TX)	M		Meredith (NC)	R
Andrews (MI)	R		Milligan (TN)	S
Aquinas (MI)	R		Mississippi College	R
Benedictine (KS)	R		Montreat (NC)	S
# Bethel (IN)	R	■	Morehouse (GA)	R
Brescia (KY)	S		Mount St. Joseph (OH)	R
California State U. (Chico)	L		Mount St. Mary's (CA)	R
California State U. (Fullerton)	L		Muskingum (OH)	R
California State U. (Long Beach)	L		Niagara (NY)	R
Carthage (WI)	R		Northwestern (IA)	S
Chaminade (HI)	R		Northwestern (MN)	R
Columbia College (SC)	R		Nyack (NY)	R
Concordia (NE)	R		Oakland City U. (IN)	R
Cumberland (KY)	R		Oklahoma Baptist	R
De Sales (PA)	S		Oklahoma Christian	R
Doane (NE)	S		Olivet Nazarene (IL)	R
Dordt (IA)	R		Oral Roberts (OK)	M
Eastern Mennonite (VA)	R		Ouachita Baptist (AR)	R
Fort Lewis (CO)	M		Philadelphia Biblical (PA)	S
Franciscan U. of Steubenville (OH)	R		Quincy (IL)	R
Freed-Hardeman (TN)	R		Regis (CO)	R
Gannon (PA)	M		St. Ambrose (IA)	R
George Fox (OR)	R	▲	St. Catherine (MN)	R
Greensboro College (NC)	S		St. Francis (IN)	R
Hardin-Simmons (TX)	R		St. John's (NY)	L
Hastings (NE)	R		St. Peter's (NJ)	R
High Point (NC)	R		St. Vincent (PA)	R
Holy Names (CA)	S		Seton Hall (NJ)	M
John Brown (AR)	R		Silver Lake (WI)	S
▲ Judson (AL)	S		Simpson (IA)	R
Kentucky Wesleyan	R		Southern Nazarene (OK)	R
King (TN)	S		Southwest Baptist (MO)	R
Lambuth (TN)	S		Taylor (IN)	R
Liberty (VA)	R		Texas Lutheran	R
Louisiana College	R		Union University (TN)	R
Louisiana State	XL		Virginia Commonwealth U.	L
Maryville (TN)	S		Virginia Wesleyan	R
Marywood (PA)	R		Wheeling Jesuit (WV)	R
Mercyhurst (PA)	R		York (NE)	S

 # Also, Youth Ministry,
Ministerial Studies

SOCIOLOGY

GROUP I
Most Selective

Amherst (MA)	R	Illinois, U. of (Urbana-Champaign)	XL
Bard (NY)	R	Johns Hopkins (MD)	M
▲ Barnard (NY)	R	Kalamazoo (MI)	R
Binghamton (SUNY)(NY)	M	Kenyon (OH)	R
Boston College (MA)	L	Lycoming (PA)	R
Bowdoin (ME)	R	Maryland, U. of	XL
▲ Bryn Mawr (PA)	S	Michigan, U. of	XL
Bucknell (PA)	M	Minnesota, U. of	XL
California, U. of (Berkeley)	XL	New Jersey, College of	M
California, U. of (Los Angeles)	XL	North Carolina, U. of	L
Chicago, U. of (IL)	M	Northwestern (IL)	M
Clarkson (NY)	M	Notre Dame (IN)	M
Colorado College	R	Oberlin (OH)	R
Columbia (NY)	M	Pennsylvania, U. of	L
Connecticut College	R	Pitzer (CA)	S
Dartmouth (NH)	M	Pomona (CA)	R
DePauw (IN)	R	Princeton (NJ)	M
Duke (NC)	M	Rutgers (NJ)	L
Emory (GA)	M	Southwestern (TX)	R
Florida, U. of	XL	Stanford (CA)	M
Franklin & Marshall (PA)	R	Trinity (TX)	R
Geneseo (SUNY)(NY)	M	Union (NY)	R
Georgetown (DC)	M	Virginia, U. of	L
George Washington (DC)	M	Wake Forest (NC)	M
Gettysburg (PA)	S	Wheaton (IL)	R
Grinnell (IA)	R	Willamette (OR)	R
Harvard (MA)	M	Yale (CT)	M
Holy Cross (MA)	R		

SOCIOLOGY continues next page

Enrollment Code

■ *Men Only*   S = Small (less than 1000 students)   R = Moderate (1000-3000 students)   M = Medium (3000-8000 students)

▲ *Women Only*   L = Large (8000-20,000 students)   XL = Extra Large (over 20,000 students)

SOCIOLOGY, continued

GROUP II
Very Selective

Albany (SUNY) (NY) L	Loyola Marymount (CA) .... M
Arizona, U. of............................ XL	Manhattanville (NY)............................ R
Asbury (KY) .... R	McDaniel (MD) .... R
Augsburg (MN) .... R	Merrimack (MA) .... R
Belmont (TN) .... R	Mississippi State L
Beloit (WI) .... R	Moravian (PA) .... R
Brigham Young (UT) XL	■ Morehouse (GA) .... R
Brown (RI) .... M	Mount Mercy (IA) .... S
California, U. of (Santa Barbara) L	New College (FL) .... S
Catholic (DC)................................ R	New Mexico, U. of L
Cincinnati, U. of (OH) L	North Carolina (Asheville) .... R
City College (CUNY)(NY) L	North Carolina, U. of (Wilmington) L
Clemson(SC) L	North Texas L
College of Charleston (SC) L	Ohio U. L
Colorado, U. of L	Oklahoma State L
Concordia (MN) .... R	Oregon, U. of L
Connecticut, U. of XL	Pace (NY) .... M
Cornell Col. (IA) .... R	Portland State (OR) L
Covenant (GA) .... S	Principia (IL) .... S
Dayton, U. of (OH) .... M	Puget Sound (WA) .... R
Denison (OH) .... R	Queens (CUNY)(NY) L
Denver, U. of (CO) .... M	Quinnipiac (CT) .... R
Drake (IA) .... M	Regis (CO)...................................... R
Earlham (IN)................................ R	Roanoke (VA) .... R
Florida International L	Rutgers (Camden) (NJ) .... M
Georgetown College (KY).................. R	▲ Salem Col. (NC) .... S
Gordon (MA) .... R	San Diego State U. (CA) XL
Hamline (MN)................................ R	▲ Simmons (MA) .... R
Hanover (IN) .... R	St. Lawrence (NY) .... R
Hawaii, U. of L	St. Mary's Col. (CA) .... R
Hendrix (AR) .... R	South Dakota School of Mines .... R
Herbert Lehman (CUNY)(NY) .... M	Stony Brook (SUNY)(NY) L
Hobart & Wm. Smith (NY) .... R	Syracuse (NY) L
Hofstra (NY)................................ M	Towson (MD) L
▲ Hollins (VA) .... S	▲ Trinity (DC) .... S
Howard (DC) .... M	Washington State L
Illinois College .... S	Washington, U. of............................ XL
Indiana U. XL	Wells (NY) .... S
Iowa, U. of.................................... XL	West Virginia U. L
Iowa State XL	Westminster (PA)............................ R
James Madison (VA)........................ M	Western Washington U. L
John Carroll (OH)............................ R	Wheaton (MA) .... R
Kansas State L	Winona State U. (MN) .... M
Knox (IL)...................................... R	Wisconsin, U. of XL
Lake Forest (IL) .... R	Wisconsin, U. of (Stevens Point)........ M
Lebanon Valley (PA) .... R	Wofford (SC).................................. R
Lewis & Clark (OR) .... R	Wooster (OH) .... R
Louisiana State XL	

SOCIOLOGY continues next page

SOCIOLOGY, continued

GROUP III
Selective

Adrian (MI) .... R
Akron, U. of (OH) L
Albright (PA) .... R
Augusta (GA) .... M
Belmont Abbey (NC) .... S
Benedictine (KS) .... R
Biola (CA) .... R
Bridgewater (VA) .... R
Bridgewater State (MA) .... M
California State U. (Fresno) L
California State U. (East Bay) .... M
California State U. (Fullerton) L
California State U. (Los Angeles) L
California State U. (Northridge) L
California State U. (Sacramento) .... M
California State U. (San Bernardino) ...... M
California State U. (San Marcos) .... M
Castleton State (VT) .... R
Central Connecticut .... M
Coker (SC) .... S
Colorado, U. of (Colorado Springs) .... M
Doane (NE) .... S
D'Youville (NY) .... R
Eastern (PA) .... R
Eastern Connecticut .... M
Eastern Michigan L
Fisk (TN) .... S
Fort Hays (KS) .... M
Framingham State (MA) .... M
Gardner-Webb (NC) .... S
George Fox (OR) .... R
Georgia State L
Grambling (LA) .... M
Hartford, U. of (CT) .... M
Hartwick (NY).. R
Hunter (CUNY)(NY) L
Johnson C. Smith (NC) .... R
Kean (NJ) .... M
Keene State (NH).................................... R
Illinois State L
Indiana (PA) L
Indiana U.-Purdue U.-Indianapolis (IN) L
Lamar (TX) .... M

Lenoir-Rhyne (NC) .... R
Longwood (VA)...................................... R
Louisville (KY) L
Lynchburg (VA) .... R
Manchester (IN) .... R
▲ Mary Baldwin (VA) .... S
Mass. Col. of Lib. Arts. (N. Adams) .... R
Massachusetts, U. of (Boston)........... M
Massachusetts, U. of (Dartmouth) .... M
Michigan State.................................. XL
Millersville (PA) .... M
Minnesota, U. of (Duluth) .... M
Missouri State L
Montana, U. of .... M
Montana State (Billings) .... R
π Mount St. Joseph (OH) .... R
Nevada, U. of (Las Vegas) L
Nevada, U. of (Reno) L
New Orleans (LA) L
North Carolina, U. of (Pembroke) ..... R
Northern Colorado............................. L
Northern Illinois L
Northern Michigan .... M
Old Dominion (VA) L
Piedmont (GA) .... S
Pittsburgh, U. of (Bradford)............... R
▲ Rosemont (PA) .... R
St. Anselm (NH) .... R
▲ St. Catherine (MN) .... R
St. Francis (PA) .... R
St. John's (NY) L
St. Mary's U. of San Antonio (TX) .... R
St. Rose (NY)...................................... R
Salem State (MA) .... M
San Francisco State (CA) L
Shaw (NC) .... R
Shippensburg (PA) .... M
Simpson (IA) .... R
Sonoma State (CA) .... M
South Alabama .... M
Southern Connecticut .... M

π *Criminology / Sociology*

GROUP III continues next page

Enrollment Code		
■ *Men Only* S = Small (less than 1000 students) R = Moderate (1000-3000 students) M = Medium (3000-8000 students)		
▲ *Women Only* L = Large (8000-20,000 students) XL = Extra Large (over 20,000 students)		

SOCIOLOGY, continued

GROUP III, continued

Southern Oregon State U.	M
▲ Spelman (GA)	R
Springfield (MA)	M
Suffolk (MA)	R
Tarleton State (TX)	M
Temple (PA)	L
Virginia Wesleyan	R
Wagner (NY)	R
West Chester (PA)	M
Western Connecticut State	M
Western Illinois	L
Western Kentucky	L
Western Michigan	L
Whitman (WA)	R
William Paterson (NJ)	M
Wilson (PA)	S
Wisconsin, U. of (LaCrosse)	L

ZOOLOGY

GROUP I
Most Selective

California, U. of (Berkeley) XL	Michigan, U. of XL
Cornell (NY) L	North Carolina, U. of L
Florida, U. of XL	Pennsylvania State XL
Miami, U. of (OH) L	Wisconsin, U. of XL

GROUP II
Very Selective

Albertson (ID) .... S	Michigan State XL
Arizona State XL	New Hampshire, U. of L
Brigham Young (UT) XL	North Carolina State L
California, U. of (Davis) XL	North Central (IL) .... R
California, U. of (Santa Barbara) L	Ohio Wesleyan .... R
Clemson (SC) L	Ohio U. L
Connecticut, U. of XL	Oklahoma, U. of XL
Georgia, U. of L	Oklahoma State L
Hawaii, U. of L	Oswego (SUNY)(NY) .... M
Indiana U. XL	Texas A&M XL
Iowa State XL	Texas, U. of (Austin) XL
Kansas, U. of L	Vermont, U. of L
Kentucky, U. of XL	Washington State L
Maryland, U. of XL	Washington, U. of XL
Massachusetts, U. of L	

GROUP III
Selective

Cal. Poly. State U. (Pomona) L	Oregon State L
California State U. (San Jose) L	San Jose State (CA) L
Colorado State L	Southeastern Oklahoma State .... M
Eastern Illinois L	Southern Illinois U. (Carbondale) L
Howard (DC) .... M	Tennessee, U. of XL
Louisiana-Lafayette L	Weber State (UT) L
Louisiana State XL	Wyoming, U. of L
Montana, U. of .... M	

Enrollment Code

■ *Men Only*   S = Small (less than 1000 students)   R = Moderate (1000-3000 students)   M = Medium (3000-8000 students)
▲ *Women Only*   L = Large (8000-20,000 students)   XL = Extra Large (over 20,000 students)

SECTION TWO

MISCELLANEOUS MAJORS

ACTUARIAL SCIENCE

Albany (SUNY) (NY)
Ball State (IN)
Bellarmine (KY)
Bradley (IL)
Brigham Young (UT)
Bryant (RI)
Butler (IN)
Carroll (MT)
Carroll (WI)
Central Florida
Central Michigan
Central Missouri
Central Oklahoma
Connecticut, U. of
Drake (IA)
Edinboro (PA)
Elizabethtown (PA)
Eastern Michigan
Florida State
Georgia State
Illinois, U. of
Iowa, U. of
Lebanon Valley (PA)
LeMoyne (NY)
Lycoming (PA)
Maryville (MO)

Minnesota State (Moorhead)
Minnesota, U. of
Nebraska, U. of
New York U.
North Central (IL)
Northern Iowa
Northwestern (IA)
Ohio State
Pennsylvania State
Pennsylvania, U. of
Purdue (IN)
Rider (NJ)
Robert Morris (PA)
Roosevelt (IL)
St. John's (NY)
▲ St. Mary's (IN)
St. Thomas (MN)
San Franciso State
▲ Seton Hill (PA)
Temple (PA)
Thiel (PA)
Texas, U. of (San Antonio)
Valparaiso (IN)
Wisconsin, U. of
Worcester Poly (MA)

AFRICANA STUDIES

Albany (SUNY) (NY)	Massachusetts, U. of
Bates (ME)	Mercer (GA)
Binghamton (SUNY)(NY)	Michigan State
Bowling Green (OH)	Minnesota, U. of
Brooklyn (CUNY) (NY)	■ Morehouse (GA)
California, U. of (Berkeley)	Nebraska, U. of (Omaha)
California, U. of (Santa Barbara)	New York U.
Chicago, U. of (IL)	North Carolina (Chapel Hill)
City (CUNY)(NY)	Northwestern (IL)
Coe (IA)	Oberlin (OH)
Columbia (NY)	Ohio State U.
Connecticut, U. of	Pennsylvania, U. of
Denison (OH)	Pittsburgh, U. of (PA)
Duke (NC)	Princeton (NJ)
Earlham (IN)	Portland State (OR)
Eastern Illinois	Rochester, U. of (NY)
Emory (GA)	Rutgers (NJ)
Florida, U. of	San Diego State (CA)
Franklin & Marshall (PA)	San Francisco State (CA)
Harvard (MA)	Stanford (CA)
Herbert Lehman (CUNY)(NY)	Stony Brook (SUNY)(NY)
Howard (DC)	Toledo, U. of (OH)
Illinois, U. of (Chicago)	Vassar (NY)
Kansas, U. of	Washington U. (MO)
Knox (IL)	▲ Wellesley (MA)
Louisiana State	Wesleyan (CT)
Louisville (KY)	Wooster (OH)
Loyola Marymount (CA)	Wisconsin, U. of
Luther (IA)	Yale (CT)

ALTERNATIVE COLLEGES (see page ix)

Atlantic, College of the (ME)	New School U.-Eugene Lang Coll. (NY)
Berea (WV)	Prescott (AZ)
Deep Springs (CA)	St. John's (MD) (NM)
Eugene Lang (NY)	Shimer (IL)
Evergreen (WA)	Simon's Rock (MA)
Goddard (VT)	Sterling (VT)
Hampshire (MA)	Thomas Aquinas (CA)
Marlboro (VT)	Unity (ME)
New College (FL)	Warren Wilson (NC)

■ *Men Only*
▲ *Women Only*

ANIMAL SCIENCE

Arizona, U. of
Arkansas, U. of
Auburn (AL)
Berry (GA)
Brigham Young (UT)
Cal Poly (Pomona)
Cal Poly (SLO)
Cal State U. (Fresno)
California, U. of (Davis)
Clemson (SC)
Colorado State
Connecticut, U. of
Cornell (NY)
Delaware Valley (PA)
Delaware, U. of
Florida, U. of
Georgia U. of
Hampshire (MA)
Hawaii, U. of
Idaho, U. of
Illinois, U. of
Iowa State
Kansas State
Kentucky, U. of
Louisiana State U.
Maine, U. of
Maryland, U. of
Massachusetts, U. of
Michigan State
Minnesota, U. of
Mississippi State
Missouri, U. of

Montana, U. of (Bozeman)
Nebraska, U. of
Nevada, U of (Reno)
New Hampshire, U. of
New Mexico State
North Carolina State
North Dakota State U.
Ohio State
Oklahoma State
Oregon State
Ozarks, College of the (MO)
Pennsylvania State
Purdue (IN)
Rhode Island, U. of
Rutgers (NJ)
South Dakota State
Southern Illinois (Carbondale)
Southwest Missouri
Tarleton State (TX)
Tennessee
Texas A&M
Texas A&M (Kingsville)
Texas Tech
Utah State
Vermont, U. of
Virginia Poly
Washington State
West Virginia U.
Wisconsin, U.of
Wisconsin, U.of (River Falls)
Wyoming, U. of

APPLIED MATHEMATICS

American (DC)
Auburn (AL)
▲ Barnard (NY)
Boston U. (MA)
Brown (RI)
Cal Tech
California, U. of (Berkeley)
California, U. of (Los Angeles)
California, U. of (San Diego)
Carnegie-Mellon (PA)
Case Western (OH)
Chicago, U. of (IL)
Clarkson (NY)
Colgate (NY)
Colorado, U. of
Columbia (NY)
Connecticut, U. of
Florida State
George Washington (DC)
Georgia Tech
Harvard (MA)
Houston, U. of (TX)
Idaho, U. of
Illinois Inst. of Tech
Kettering (MI)
Lehigh (PA)
Michigan, U. of
Missouri, U. of (Rolla)

Nevada, U. of (Reno)
New Jersey Inst of Tech.
North Carolina (Asheville)
Northwestern (IL)
Oregon Inst. of Tech.
Pittsburgh, U. of (PA)
Pittsburgh (Bradford)
Pitzer (CA)
Purdue (IN)
Queens (CUNY)(NY)
Rice (TX)
Rochester, U. of (NY)
Rochester Inst. of Tech (NY)
Rutgers (NJ)
San Jose State (CA)
Stony Brook (SUNY)(NY)
Tulane (LA)
Tulsa (OK)
Union (NY)
Virginia, U. of
Wake Forest (NC)
Washington U. (MO)
Western Michigan
Western Washington
Wisconsin
Worcester Poly (MA)
Yale (CT)

ARABIC

Binghamton (SUNY)(NY)
Brigham Young (UT)
California, U. of (Los Angeles)
Chicago, U. of (IL)
Georgetown (DC)
Harvard (MA)

Michigan, U. of
Notre Dame (IN)
Ohio State
Stevens Inst. of Tech. (NJ)
Texas, U. of
U.S. Military Academy (NY)

■ *Men Only*
▲ *Women Only*

ARCHAEOLOGY

Baylor (TX)
Boston U. (MA)
Bowdoin (ME)
Brown (RI)
▲ Bryn Mawr (PA)
Cornell (NY)
Dartmouth (NH)
Dickinson (PA)
Evansville (IN)
Florida State
George Washington (DC)
Hamilton (NY)
Harvard (MA)
Haverford (PA)
Hunter (CUNY) (NY)
Kent State (OH)
Maryland, U. of
π Mary Washington, U. of (VA)
Mercyhurst (PA)

Michigan, U. of
Missouri, U. of
New York U.
North Carolina, U. of (Greensboro)
North Carolina (Charlotte)
Oberlin (OH)
Potsdam (SUNY)(NY)
Rhode Island College
Texas, U. of
Virginia
Washington & Lee (VA)
Washington U. (MO)
▲ Wellesley (MA)
Wesleyan (CT)
West Florida
Wheaton (IL)
Wisconsin (La Crosse)
Wooster (OH)
Yale (CT)

π   *Classical Archeology*

ART THERAPY

Alverno (WI)
Anna Maria (MA)
Arcadia (PA)
Art Institute of Chicago (IL)
Avila (MO)
Barat (IL)
Bowling Green (OH)
Brescia (KY)
Capital U. (OH)
Carlow (PA)
▲ Cedar Crest
▲ Converse (SC)
▲ Edgewood (WI)
Emporia State (KS)
Harding (AR)
Indianapolis, U. of

Lesley (MA)
Long Island U. (CW Post)(NY)
Marygrove (MI)
Marian Col. of Fond du Lac (WI)
Mercyhurst (PA)
▲ Meredith (NC)
Millikin (IL)
Pittsburg (KS)
Russell Sage (NY)
Santa Fe, Col. of (NM)
▲ Seton Hill (PA)
Southern Illinois (Edwardsville)
Spring Hill (AL)
Springfield (MA)
St. Thomas Aquinas (NY)
Wisconsin (Superior)

■ *Men Only*
▲ *Women Only*

ATMOSPHERIC SCIENCES / METEOROLOGY

Albany (SUNY) (NY)
Arizona, U. of
Brockport (SUNY) (NY)
California (PA)
California, U. of (Davis)
Cornell (NY)
Creighton (NE)
Embry-Riddle (FL)
Florida Inst. of Tech.
Florida State
Hawaii
Iowa State
Kansas
Louisiana-Lafayette
Louisiana-Monroe
Lyndon State (VT)
Metropolitan State (CO)
Millersville (PA)
Nebraska
North Carolina, U. of (Asheville)
North Carolina State
North Dakota, U. of
Northern Illinois
Northland (WI)
Oklahoma, U. of
Oneonta (SUNY) (NY)
Pennsylvania State
Plymouth State (NH)
Purdue (IN)
St. Louis University (MO)
San Francisco State (CA)
San Jose State (CA)
South Alabama
Stony Brook (SUNY)(NY)
Texas A&M
Utah, U. of
Valparaiso (IN)
Washington, U. of
Western Illinois
Western Connecticut
Wilkes-Barre (PA)
Wisconsin, U. of
Wisconsin, U. of (Milwaukee)

■ *Men Only*
▲ *Women Only*

AUDIOLOGY/SPEECH/LANGUAGE THERAPY

Abilene Christian (TX)
Adelphi (NY)
Akron, U. of (OH)
Andrews (MI)
Arizona
Arizona State
Auburn (AL)
Ball State (IN)
Boston U.
Brooklyn (CUNY)(NY)
Buffalo (SUNY)(NY)
California State U. (East Bay)
California State U. (Fresno)
California State U. (San Marcos)
Clarion (PA)
Colorado
Columbia (SC)
East Tennessee
East Stroudsburg (PA)
Eastern Illinois
Eastern Washington
Elmhurst (IL)
Elmira (NY)
Florida
Florida State
Fontbonne (MO)
Fredonia (SUNY)(NY)
Geneseo (SUNY)(NY)
Geneva (PA)
George Washington (DC)
Hardin-Simmons (TX)
Hampton (VA)
Hawaii
Hofstra (NY)
Illinois, U. of
Iona (NY)
Iowa, U. of
Ithaca (NY)
James Madison (VA)
Kansas
Kean (NJ)
Lamar (TX)
LaSalle (PA)
Long Island U (Brooklyn)(NY)
Longwood (VA)
Louisiana-Lafayette
Loyola (MD)
Maine, U. of
Marquette (WI)
Marshall (WV)
Maryland, U. of
Marymount Manhattan (NY)
Maryville (TN)

Massachusetts, U. of
Mercy (NY)
Miami U. (OH)
Michigan State
Minnesota, U. of
Minnesota State U. (Moorhead)
Misericordia, College (PA)
Mississippi, U. of
Mississippi U. for Women
Montevallo (AL)
Moorhead (MN)
Nazareth (NY)
Nebraska
Nevada, U. of (Reno)
New Hampshire, U. of
New Mexico, U. of
New Paltz (SUNY) (NY)
New York U.
North Colorado
North Dakota, U. of
North Iowa
North Michigan
Ohio U.
Oklahoma
Pace (NY)
Plattsburg (SUNY) (NY)
Portland State (OR)
Purdue (IN)
Richard Stockton (NJ)
Rhode Island
St. John's (NY)
St. Louis U. (MO)
S. Alabama
S. Dakota, U. of
S. Florida
Science and Arts of Oklahoma
Southeastern Louisiana
Syracuse (NY)
Tennessee
Texas
Texas (Dallas)
Texas Christian
Towson (MD)
Tulsa (OK)
Utah State
Washington, U. of
Wayne State (MI)
West Virginia
Western Michigan
Western Washington
Worcester State (MA)
Wisconsin
Wyoming

■ *Men Only*
▲ *Women Only*

AVIATION MANAGEMENT

Aeronautics, College of (NY)
Alaska, U. of (Anchorage)
Auburn (AL)
Central Missouri
Daniel Webster (NH)
Dowling (NY)
Dubuque, U. of (IA)
Eastern Kentucky
Eastern Michigan
Embry-Riddle (FL)
Fairmont (WV)
Farmingdale (SUNY)(NY)
Florida Inst. of Tech.
Hampton (VA)
Henderson (AR)
Jacksonville (FL)

LeTourneau (TX)
Lewis (IL)
Louisiana-Monroe
Lynn (FL)
Metropolitan State (CO)
Middle Tennessee
Minnesota State U. (Mankato)
New Haven (CT)
North Dakota, U. of
Purdue (IN)
Robert Morris (PA)
Rocky Mountain (MT)
St. Francis (NY)
St. Louis (MO)
Southern Illinois U.
Tarleton State (TX)

AVIATION SCIENCE

Andrews (MI)
Averett (VA)
Baylor (TX)
Bowling Green (OH)
Daniel Webster (NH)
Dowling (NY)
Embry-Riddle (FL)
Fairmont (WV)
Florida Inst. of Tech.
Geneva (PA)
Georgia Institute of Technology
Grace (NE)
Hampton (VA)
Henderson State (AR)
Illinois, U. of
Kansas State
Kent State (OH)
Lewis (IL)
● Louisiana Tech.

Metropolitan State (CO)
Minnesota State U. (Mankato)
North Dakota, U. of
Northwestern (LA)
Ohio State
Ohio University
Oklahoma State
Purdue (IN)
Rocky Mountain (MT)
St. Cloud State (MN)
St. Louis U. (MO)
Salem State (MA)
Salem-Teikyo (WV)
San Jose State (CA)
Southern Illinois
Walla Walla (WA)
Western Michigan
Westminster (UT)

Aviation - Human Factors
● *Professional Aviation*

■ *Men Only*
▲ *Women Only*

BIOMEDICAL ENGINEERING

California, U. of (Berkeley)
California, U. of (Davis)
California, U. of (Santa Cruz)
City College (CUNY)(NY)
Cornell (NY)
Duke (NC)
Illinois Inst. of Tech.
Johns Hopkins (MD)
LeTourneau (TX)
Marquette (WI)
Michigan, U. of
Michigan Tech.
Milwaukee Sch. of Engine (WI)
North Carolina, U. of

North Carolina State
Northwestern (IL)
Pennsylvania, U. of
Purdue (IN)
Rensselaer (NY)
Rochester, U. of (NY)
Rose-Hulman (IN)
Rutgers (NJ)
Southern California
Stanford (CA)
Wisconsin, U. of
Wright State (OH)
Yale (CT)

BIOPHYSICS

Brown (RI)
Buffalo (SUNY)(NY)
California, U. of (Irvine)
California, U. of (San Diego)
Centenary (LA)
Chicago U. of (IL)
Columbia (NY)
Connecticut, U. of
Geneseo (SUNY)(NY)
■ Hampden-Sydney (VA)
Hampshire (MA)
Harvard (MA)
Houston, U. of (TX)
Illinois Institute of Tech.
Illinois, U. of
Iowa State

Johns Hopkins (MD)
Michigan, U. of
Minnesota, U. of
Oregon State
Oklahoma City U.
Pennsylvania, U. of
Pitzer (CA)
Rensselaer (NY)
Rice (TX)
St. Bonaventure (NY)
Scranton, U. of (PA)
Suffolk (MA)
Temple (PA)
Walla Walla (WA)
Washington U. (MO)

■ *Men Only*
▲ *Women Only*

CERAMICS

Alfred (NY)
Arcadia (PA)
Bennington (VT)
Bowling Green (OH)
Cleveland Institute of Art (OH)
Colorado State
East Carolina (NC)
Hartford, U. of (CT)
Kansas City Art Institute (MO)
Maryland Inst. College of Art
Massachusetts College of Art
Memphis College of Art (TN)
Miami (FL)

Montevallo (AL)
Moore (PA)
Museum of Fine Arts (MA)
New Paltz (SUNY)(NY)
North Texas
Oklahoma, U. of
Oneonta (SUNY)(NY)
Pratt (NY)
Rhode Island School of Design
San Jose State (CA)
Syracuse (NY)
Temple (PA)
Washington, U. of

CHINESE

Bard (NY)
Bates (ME)
California St U. (Long Beach)
California, U. of (Berkeley)
California, U. of (Davis)
California, U. of (Irvine)
California, U. of (Los Angeles)
California, U. of (Riverside)
California, U. of (Santa Barbara)
Colorado, U. of
Connecticut, U. of
Dartmouth (NH)
George Washington (DC)
Georgetown (DC)
Grinnell (IA)
Hamilton (NY)
Harvard (MA)
Hawaii, U. of
Hunter (CUNY)(NY)
Lawrence (WI)
Maryland, U. of
Massachusetts, U. of

Michigan, U. of
Middlebury (VT)
Minnesota, U. of
Montana, U. of
Notre Dame (IN)
Ohio State
Oregon, U. of
Pittsburgh, U. of
Pomona (CA)
Reed (OR)
Rutgers (NJ)
San Francisco State (CA)
San Jose (CA)
Scripps (CA)
Tufts (MA)
U.S. Military Academy (NY)
Vassar (NY)
Washington, U. of
▲Wellesley (MA)
Williams (MA)
Wisconsin, U. of
Yale (CT)

CINEMATOGRAPHY/FILM STUDIES/VIDEO PRODUCTION

* Arts, U. of the (PA)
Bard (NY)
Bennington (VT)
Bowling Green (OH)
Boston U. (MA)
Brooklyn (CUNY) (NY)
Brown (RI)
California College of theArts
California State U. (Long Beach)
California, U. of (Berkeley)
California, U. of (Irvine)
California, U. of (Los Angeles)
California, U. of (Santa Barbara)
California, U. of (Santa Cruz)
California Institute of the Arts
Central Florida
Chapman (CA)
Chicago, U. of (IL)
Claremont-McKenna (CA)
Clark (MA)
Cogswell (CA)
Colgate (NY)
Columbia (Hollywood)(CA)
Colorado State
Colorado, U. of
Columbia (IL)
Columbia (NY)
Columbus Coll. of Art & Design (OH)
Denison (OH)
DePauw (IN)
DeSales (PA)
Eastern Washington
Emerson (MA)
Emory (GA)
Evergreen (WA)
Florida
Florida State
Georgia State
Hampshire (MA)
Hofstra (NY)
▲Hollins
Howard (DC)
Hunter (CUNY) (NY)
Iowa
Ithaca (NY)
Kansas
Louisiana-Monroe
Loyola-Marymount (CA)

Massachusetts College of Art
Memphis (TN)
Michigan
Middlebury (VT)
New Orleans, U. of (LA)
New York U.
North Carolina, U. of (Greensboro)
North Carolina, U. of (Wilmington)
North Carolina School of the Arts
North Carolina State
North Texas
Northern Michigan
Northwestern (IL)
Oberlin (OH)
Oklahoma
Oklahoma City U.
Pennsylvania State
Pittsburgh, U. of (PA)
Pitzer (CA)
Point Park (PA)
Purchase (SUNY) (NY)
Purdue (IN)
Queens (CUNY) (NY)
Rhode Island College
Rhode Island School of Design
Rochester Inst. of Tech. (NY)
Rochester, U. of (NY)
San Francisco Art Institute (CA)
***San Francisco State (CA)
Santa Fe (NM)
Sarah Lawrence (NY)
Southern California
Southern Methodist (TX)
Syracuse (NY)
Temple (PA)
Texas Christian
Texas, U. of
Toledo (OH)
Towson (MD)
Visual Arts, School of (NY)
Wayne State (MI)
Webster (MO)
Wesleyan (CT)
Wisconsin (Milwaukee)
Woodbury (CA)

* and Writing for Media Performance
** Film and Photography
*** Especially Animation
# Also Animation

■ *Men Only*
▲ *Women Only*

COMPUTER ENGINEERING

Alabama, U. of (Huntsville)
Arkansas, U. of
Arizona, U. of
Arizona State
Auburn (AL)
Binghamton (SUNY)(NY)
California, U. of (Berkeley)
California, U. of (Davis)
California, U. of (Los Angeles)
California, U. of (San Diego)
California, U. of (Santa Cruz)
California Poly. (SLO)
California State U. (Long Beach)
Carnegie-Mellon (PA)
Case Western Reserve (OH)
Central Florida
Clarkson (NY)
Clemson (SC)
Colorado, U. of
Columbia (NY)
Cornell (NY)
Drexel (PA)
Florida Atlantic
Florida Inst. of Tech.
Florida State
Florida, U. of
George Mason (VA)
George Washington (DC)
Georgia Tech.
Gonzaga (WA)
Harvey Mudd (CA)
Illinois, U. of
Illinois, U. of (Chicago)
Illinois Inst. of Tech.
I.U.P.U.I. (IN)
Iowa
Iowa State
Johns Hopkins (MD)
Kansas, U. of
Kansas State
Kentucky, U. of
Kettering (MI)
Lehigh (PA)
Louisville, U. of (KY)
Marquette (WI)
Maryland, U. of
Maryland, U. of (Baltimore Co.)
Massachusetts, U. of (Dartmouth)

Massachusetts, U. of (Lowell)
MIT (MA)
Mercer (GA)
Michigan, U. of
Michigan State
Michigan Tech.
Milwaukee Sch. of Engin. (WI)
Missouri, U. of (Rolla)
Montana State
Nebraska, U. of
New Jersey Inst. of Tech.
New Mexico, U. of
New Mexico State U.
North Carolina (Charlotte)
North Carolina State
Northeastern (MA)
Northwestern (IL)
Notre Dame (IN)
Ohio State
Oklahoma, U. of
Oklahoma State
Old Dominion (VA)
Olin (MA)
Pennsylvania State
Pennsylvania, U. of
Pittsburgh, U. of (PA)
Princeton (NJ)
Puerto Rico (Mayaguez)
Purdue (IN)
Rensselaer (NY)
Rice (TX)
Rochester, U. of (NY)
Rochester Inst. of Tech. (NY)
Rose-Hulman (IN)
San Jose State (CA)
South Dakota School of Mines
South Florida
Stony Brook (SUNY)(NY)
Texas A&M
Texas, U. of (Arlington)
Union (NY)
Utah, U. of
Vanderbilt (TN)
Virginia Poly Tech.
Washington, U. of
Washington U. (MO)
Wright State (OH)

■ *Men Only*
▲ *Women Only*

COMPUTER GRAPHICS

Allegheny (PA)
American (DC)
Andrews (MI)
Arts, U. of the (PA)
Central Oklahoma
Champlain (VT)
Cogswell (CA)
Columbia (IL)
Columbus Coll. of Art & Design (OH)
Dominican (IL)
Dubuque (IA)
E. Michigan
Embry-Riddle (FL)
Fashion Institute of Tech. (NY)
Huntingdon (AL)
Jacksonville (FL)
\# John Brown (AR)
LaSalle (PA)
Lewis (IL)

Long Island U. (Brooklyn)(NY)
Loyola Marymount (CA)
Lyndon State (VT)
Memphis College of Art (TN)
Monmouth (NJ)
Montserrat (MA)
New York Institute of Tech.
Parsons (NY)
Pratt Institute (NY)
Purdue (IN)
Ringling (FL)
Robert Morris (PA)
Rochester Institute of Tech (NY)
Springfield (MA)
Syracuse (NY)
Taylor (IN)
Tampa (FL)
Woodbury (CA)

\# *Digital Media Arts*

■ *Men Only*
▲ *Women Only*

CREATIVE WRITING

▲ Agnes Scott (GA)
Alabama, U. of
Albertson (ID)
Allegheny (PA)
Arizona, U. of
Bard (NY)
Belhaven (MS)
Belmont (TN)
Beloit (WI)
Bennington (VT)
Bowling Green (OH)
* Briar Cliff (IA)
California Institute of the Arts
California, U. of (Riverside)
California, U. of (Santa Cruz)
Carlow (PA)
Carnegie Mellon (PA)
Chapman (CA)
Columbia (NY)
Creighton (NE)
Dana (NE)
Dominican (CA)
East Carolina (NC)
Eastern Kentucky
Eckerd (FL)
Emerson (MA)
Evansville (IN)
Florida State
Franklin & Marshall (PA)
Grand Valley (MI)
Hamilton (NY)
▲ Hollins (VA)
Houston, U. of (TX)

Iowa
Kenyon (OH)
Knox (IL)
* Lafayette (PA)
Lewis-Clark State (ID)
Linfield (OR)
Long Island U. (Southampton)(NY)
Loras (IA)
Lycoming (PA)
Maine (Farmington)
Memphis, U. of (TN)
Michigan, U. of
New Paltz (SUNY)(NY)
New School U. (Lang) (NY)
North Carolina (Wilmington)
Oberlin (OH)
Oregon, U. of
Pacific U. (OR)
Pittsburgh, U. of (PA)
Pittsburgh (Johnstown) (PA)
Princeton (NJ)
Purchase (SUNY) (NY)
Redlands (CA)
St. Andrews (NC)
San Francisco State (CA)
Santa Clara (CA)
Santa Fe, College of (NM)
Sarah Lawrence (NY)
▲ Stephens (MO)
Susquehanna (PA)
▲ Sweet Briar (VA)
Wheaton (MA)
Wichita State (KS)

* *Writing Major*
# *English & Creative Writing*

■ *Men Only*
▲ *Women Only*

CRIMINAL JUSTICE

Adelphi (NY)
Alaska, U. of (Anchorage)
Albany (SUNY) (NY)
Anna Maria (MA)
Arizona, U. of
Bloomsburg (PA)
Bowling Green (OH)
Brockport (SUNY) (NY)
Buena Vista (IA)
California State U. (Bakersfield)
California State U. (Fresno)
California State U. (Fullerton)
California State U. (Long Beach)
California State U. (Los Angeles)
California State U. (Sacramento)
California State U. (San Bernardino)
California, U. of (Irvine)
Castleton (VT)
Central Missouri
Chadron State (NE)
Chaminade (HI)
Columbia (MO)
Dayton, U. of (OH)
Delaware, U. of
Dillard (LA)
East Tennessee
Eastern Kentucky
Eastern Washington
Edinboro (PA)
Elmira (NY)
Fairmont State (WV)
Florida Atlantic
Florida Gulf Coast U.
Florida International
Florida Southern
Florida State
Gannon (PA)
George Washington (DC)
Georgia State
Grambling (LA)
Grand Valley (MI)
Great Falls, U. of (MT)
Guilford (NC)
Hamline (MN)
■ Hampden-Sydney (VA)
Hannibal-La Grange (MO)
Hardin-Simmons (TX)

* Husson (ME)
Illinois (Chicago)
Indiana
Indiana State
Iona (NY)
Jacksonville State (AL)
John Jay (CUNY) (NY)
Juniata (PA)
Kentucky Wesleyan
Kutztown (PA)
Lindenwood (MO)
Long Island U. (C.W. Post)(NY)
Longwood (VA)
Loras (IA)
Louisiana-Monroe
Louisville (KY)
Lycoming (PA)
Madonna (MI)
Mansfield (PA)
Marist (NY)
Marshall (WV)
Maryland
Massachusetts State College
   (Westfield)
Massachusetts, U. of (Lowell)
Mercy (NY)
Mercyhurst (PA)
Michigan State
Minnesota State U. (Mankato)
Minnesota State U. (Moorhead)
Missouri, U. of (St. Louis)
Mitchell (CT)
Mount Mercy (IA)
Nebraska, U. of (Omaha)
New Haven (CT)
New Mexico State
North Carolina (Charlotte)
North Carolina (Wilmington)
North Carolina Wesleyan
North Florida
North Michigan
Northeastern (MA)

* *Criminal Justice / Psychology*
   - Double Major (5-Year)

Military Leadership and
   National Security Studies

■ *Men Only*
▲ *Women Only*

CRIMINAL JUSTICE continues next page

CRIMINAL JUSTICE, continued

Northeastern State (OK)
Norwich (VT)
Ohio Northern
Old Dominion (VA)
Pittsburgh (Bradford)
Portland, U. of (OR)
Potsdam (SUNY) (NY)
Quinnipiac (CT)
Radford (VA)
Regis (CO)
Richard Stockton (NJ)
Richmond (VA)
Roanoke (VA)
Roger Williams (RI)
Rowan (NJ)
Sacred Heart (CT)
Saginaw Valley (MI)
St. Ambrose (IA)
St. Anselm (NH)
St. Cloud (MN)
St. Edward's (TX)
St. Francis (NY)
St. John's (NY)
St. Leo (FL)
Salem State (MA)
Salve Regina-The Newport College (RI)
Sam Houston State (TX)

San Diego State (CA)
San Jose State (CA)
Seton Hall (NJ)
Simpson (IA)
South Dakota, U. of
South Florida
Southern Illinois U.
    (Carbondale)
Southern Oregon
Southwest Texas
Tarleton State (TX)
Texas (El Paso)
Texas (Tyler)
Toledo (OH)
Washburn (KS)
Weber State (UT)
Western Carolina (NC)
Western Connecticut
Western Illinois
West Virginia Wesleyan
Wilmington (OH)
Wisconsin (Milwaukee)
Wisconsin (Platteville)
Wisconsin (Whitewater)
York (PA)
Youngstown State (OH)

DESIGN/COMMERCIAL ART

Alfred (NY)
Art Center College of Design (CA)
Arts, U. of the (PA)
Brenau (GA)
Brigham Young (UT)
California College of Arts & Crafts
California Inst. of the Arts
California Poly (SLO)
California, U. of (Davis)
Carnegie Mellon (PA)
Carthage (WI)
Central Oklahoma
Champlain (VT)
Chowan (NC)
Cincinnati, U. of (OH)
Cleveland Institute of Art (OH)
Columbia (IL)
Columbus College of Art & Design (OH)
Cornish (WA)
Creighton (NE)
Drake (IA)
Dubuque (IA)
Edgewood (WI)
Endicott (MA)
Fashion Inst. of Tech. (NY)
Flagler (FL)
Florida A&M
Fort Hays (KS)
Grand Valley (MI)
Illinois, U. of
Iowa State
John Brown (AR)
Kansas City Art Institute (MO)
Kean (NJ)
Kendall Coll. of Art & Design (MI)

Kent State (OH)
Long Island U. (C.W. Post)(NY)
Lyndon State (VT)
Maryland Institute - College of Art
Maryland, U. of
Maryville (MO)
Massachusetts College of Art
Massachusetts, U. of (Dartmouth)
Memphis College of Art
Milliken (IL)
Montserrat (MA)
Moore (PA)
Moravian (PA)
Morningside (IA)
** New Jersey, College of
New York Inst.of Technology
North Carolina State
Ohio State
Otis College of Art and Design (CA)
Parsons School of Design (NY)
Pratt (NY)
Purchase (SUNY) (NY)
Rhode Island School of Design
Ringling (FL)
Rochester Inst. of Tech. (NY)
* Roger Williams (RI)
St. Mary's (MN)
San Jose State (CA)
Southern Illinois U.
Texas Christian
Visual Arts, School of (NY)
** Woodbury (CA)

* *Graphic Design Communications*
** *Especially Graphic Design*
# *Digital Media Arts*

EAST ASIAN STUDIES

Bates (ME)
Berea (KY)
Binghamton (SUNY) (NY)
▲ Bryn Mawr (PA)
Bucknell (PA)
California, U. of (Davis)
California, U. of (Los Angeles)
California, U. of (San Diego)
Chicago, U. of (IL)
Coe (IA)
Colgate (NY)
Colorado College
Columbia (NY)
Connecticut College
Cornell (NY)
Denison (OH)
Denver, U. of (CO)
DePauw (IN)
Furman (SC)
George Washington (DC)
Hamilton (NY)
Hamline (MN)
Harvard (MA)
Hawaii, U. of
Hofstra (NY)
Illinois, U. of
Indiana
John Carroll (OH)
Kansas, U. of
Lawrence (WI)
Lehigh (PA)
Lewis & Clark (OR)
Macalester (MN)

Manhattanville (NY)
Maryland, U. of
Middlebury (VT)
▲ Mount Holyoke (MA)
New York U.
North Carolina
North Central (IL)
Oberlin (OH)
Occidental (CA)
Ohio State
Oregon, U. of
Pennsylvania, U. of
Pomona (CA)
Princeton (NJ)
Puget Sound (WA)
Redlands (CA)
Reed (OR)
Rice (TX)
Rutgers (NJ)
Sarah Lawrence (NY)
Stanford (CA)
Ursinus (PA)
Utah, U. of
Vassar (NY)
Washington & Lee (VA)
Washington U. (MO)
Washington, U. of
▲ Wellesley (MA)
Wesleyan (CT)
Western Washington
Westmont (CA)
Wisconsin, U. of
Wittenberg (OH)

E-COMMERCE

Bellevue (NE)
California State U.
   (Monterey Bay)
Carnegie Mellon (PA)
Castleton State (VT)
Champlain (VT)
Christopher Newport (VA)
Clarkson (NY)
DePaul (IL)
Emory (GA)
Harrisburg U. (PA)
Jacksonville State (AL)

▲ Judson (AL)
Misericordia (PA)
New Jersey Inst. of Tech.
North Dakota State
Northwestern Oklahoma
Old Dominion (VA)
San Jose State (CA)
Scranton (PA)
Seattle U. (WA)
Southern Alabama
Thomas (ME)
Utah State

■ *Men Only*
▲ *Women Only*

ENTOMOLOGY

Auburn (AL)
California State U.
    (Stanislaus)
California, U. of (Davis)
California, U. of (Riverside)
Colorado State
Cornell (NY)
Delaware, U. of
Florida A & M
Florida, U. of
Georgia, U. of
Harvard (MA)
Hawaii, U. of
Idaho, U. of
Illinois, U. of
Iowa State

Kentucky, U. of
Maine, U. of
Michigan State
Nebraska, U. of
New Mexico State
North Carolina State
Ohio State
Oklahoma State
Oregon State
Purdue (IN)
Rutgers (NJ)
San Jose State (CA)
Texas A & M
Utah State
Washington State
Wisconsin, U. of

ENTREPRENEUR STUDIES

American (DC)
American International (MA)
Arizona, U. of
Babson (MA)
Baylor (TX)
Black Hills State U. (SD)
Bradley (IL)
Brown (RI)
Buena Vista (IA)
California State U.
    (San Bernardino)
California, U. of (Riverside)
Canisius (NY)
Case Western Reserve (OH)
Catawba (NC)
Central Connecticut
Chowan (NC)
Colorado State
Columbia College (SC)
Connecticut, U. of
Creighton (NE)
Dayton (OH)
Duquesne (PA)
Eastern Michigan
Fairleigh Dickinson (NJ)
Ferris State U. (MI)
Florida State
Gannon (PA)
Gonzaga (WA)
Hampton (VA)
Hartford, U. of (CT)
Hawaii Pacific
Hofstra (NY)
Houston Baptist (TX)
Houston, U. of (TX)
Illinois
Indiana
Juniata (PA)
Louisiana State U.
Lourdes (OH)
Loyola Marymount (CA)
Lyndon State (VT)

Lynn (FL)
Marquette (WI)
Maryland, U. of
Miami (FL)
Middle Tennessee
Millikin (IL)
Mississippi U. for Women
Montana State
Muhlenberg (PA)
New Mexico
Northeastern (MA)
North Carolina (Greensboro)
North Central (IL)
North Dakota
North Texas
Northwood (MI)
Ohio University
Oklahoma, U. of
Oregon, U. of
Oregon Inst. of Tech.
Palm Beach Atlantic (FL)
Pennsylvania, U. of
Plattsburgh (SUNY) (NY)
Quinnipiac (CT)
Reinhardt (GA)
Rensselaer (NY)
Rider (NJ)
St. Mary's (TX)
▲ Seton Hill (PA)
Syracuse (NY)
Virginia Commonwealth
Washington & Jefferson (PA)
Washington State
Waynesburg (PA)
Western Carolina (NC)
Wheeling Jesuit (WV)
Wichita State (KS)
Winthrop (SC)
Wyoming
Xavier (LA)
Xavier (OH)

■ *Men Only*
▲ *Women Only*

ENVIRONMENTAL STUDIES

Adelphi (NY)
Alaska Pacific
Albion (MI)
Alfred (NY)
Allegheny (PA)
Antioch (OH)
Atlantic, College of the (ME)
Bates (ME)
Berry (GA)
Bethel (KS)
Birmingham-Southern (AL)
Bowdoin (ME)
Brenau (GA)
Briar Cliff (IA)
Brockport (SUNY)(NY)
Brown (RI)
California State U. (Channel Islands)
California, U. of (Davis)
California, U. of (Merced)
California, U. of (Riverside)
California, U. of (Santa Barbara)
California, U. of (Santa Cruz)
Carleton (MN)
Carroll (WI)
Case Western Reserve
Centenary (LA)
Central (IA)
Chestnut Hill (PA)
Chicago, U. of (IL)
Claremont McKenna (CA)
Clark (MA)
Clarkson (NY)
Colby (ME)
Colgate (NY)
Colorado, U. of
Connecticut College
Connecticut, U. of
Dartmouth (NH)
Davis & Elkins (WV)
Delaware Valley (PA)
Denison (OH)
Denver, U. of (CO)
DePaul (IL)
\# Depauw (IN)
Dickinson (PA)
Doane (NE)
Dordt (IA)
Drake (IA)
Dubuque (IA)
Duke (NC)
Earlham (IN)

Eastern Connecticut
Eastern Kentucky
Eckerd (FL)
Elizabethtown (PA)
Endicott (MA)
Evergreen State (WA)
Florida Gulf Coast
Florida, U. of
Florida Institute of Tech.
Franklin & Marshall (PA)
George Fox (OR)
Georgetown College (KY)
Georgia
Gettysburg (PA)
Green Mountain (VT)
Harvard (MA)
Hawaii Pacific
Hiram (OH)
Idaho
Jacksonville (FL)
Johnson State (VT)
Juniata (PA)
Knox (IL)
Lake Forest (IL)
Lawrence (WI)
Lesley (MA)
Lewis & Clark (OR)
Linfield (OR)
Long Island U. (C.W. Post)(NY)
Loyola (IL)
Lynchburg (VA)
Lyndon (VT)
Macalester (MN)
Manchester (IN)
Marietta (OH)
Marist (NY)
Maritime College (SUNY)(NY)
Maryville (MO)
Miami, U. of (FL)
Michigan, U. of
Michigan State
Michigan Tech.
Middlebury (VT)
Minnesota, U. of
Monmouth (IL)
Montana State (Billings)
Montreat (NC)
Moravian (PA)

\# *Environmental Geoscience*
π *Environmental & Occupational Health*

■ *Men Only*
▲ *Women Only*

ENVIRONMENTAL STUDIES continues next page

ENVIRONMENTAL STUDIES, continued

Nebraska, U. of
Nevada, U. of (Reno)
New Hampshire, U. of
New Mexico Inst. of Min. & Tech.
π New Mexico State
North Carolina (Asheville)
North Carolina (Greensboro)
North Carolina (Wilmington)
Northland (WI)
* Northwestern (IA)
Oberlin (OH)
Ohio Wesleyan
Oneonta (SUNY) (NY)
Oregon Inst. of Tech.
Oregon State
Pacific U. (OR)
Pennsylvania State
Pennsylvania, U. of
Pittsburgh (Bradford)
Pittsburgh, U. of (PA)
Pitzer (CA)
Plattsburgh (SUNY)(NY)
Portland State (OR)
Prescott (AZ)
Purchase (SUNY) (NY)
Ramapo (NJ)
Randolph (VA)
Redlands (CA)
Rensselaer (NY)
Rhode Island, U. of
Richard Stockton (NJ)
Ripon (WI)
Rochester Inst. of Tech. (NY)
Rocky Mountain (MT)
Rutgers (NJ)
Sacred Heart (CT)
St. Anselm (NH)
St. John's (NY)

St. Lawrence (NY)
St. Michael's (VT)
St. Norbert (WI)
Salisbury (MD)
Santa Fe, College of (NM)
Sarah Lawrence (NY)
Shepherd (WV)
South, U. of the (TN)
South Florida
Southwestern (TX)
Stanford (CA)
Stockton State (NJ)
SUNY College of Env.
    Sci. & Forestry
Susquehanna (PA)
Tarleton State (TX)
Texas (El Paso)
Unity (ME)
Utah State
Valparaiso (IN)
Vermont, U. of
Virginia, U. of
Warren Wilson (NC)
Washington State
Washington, U. of
Wesleyan (CT)
Western Washington
West Virginia Wesleyan
Westfield State (MA)
Westminster (MO)
Whitman (WA)
Wilson (PA)
Wisconsin
Wisconsin (Green Bay)
Worcester Poly (MA)
Yale (CT)

* *Environmental Science*
π *Environmental and Occupational Health*

EQUESTRIAN STUDIES

Averett (VA)
Bethany (WV)
Centenary (NJ)
Colorado State
Delaware Valley (PA)
Findlay (OH)
Johnson & Wales (RI)
▲ Judson (AL)
Lake Erie (OH)
Louisville
North Dakota State

Otterbein (OH)
Puerto Rico, U. of (Rio Piedras)
Rocky Mountain (MT)
St. Andrews (NC)
Salem International (WV)
▲ Stephens (MO)
Truman State (MO)
Virginia Intermont
William Woods (MO)
Wilson (PA)

■ *Men Only*
▲ *Women Only*

Equine Business

EXERCISE SCIENCE/WELLNESS/MOVEMENT

Abilene Christian (TX)
Adelphi (NY)
Adrian (MI)
Alma (MI)
Austin (TX)
Ball State (IN)
* Belhaven (MS)
Bloomsburg (PA)
Bluffton (OH)
Boston U.
Bridgewater (VA)
Buena Vista (IA)
Cal Poly (SLO)
California State U. (Fresno)
California State U. (Fullerton)
California State U.
   (Long Beach)
California State U.
   (San Bernardino)
California State U.
   (San Marcos)
Carthage (WI)
Castleton (VT)
Central (IA)
Chapman (CA)
Colby-Sawyer (NH)
Colorado, U. of
Concordia (NE)
Connecticut, U. of
Cumberland (KY)
Dayton (OH)
DePauw (IN)
Drury (MO)
East Stroudsburg (PA)
Eastern Nazarene (MA)
Evansville (IN)
Fitchburg (MA)
Florida Atlantic
Fort Lewis (CO)
Georgetown (KY)
George Washington (DC)
Gordon (MA)
Greensboro (NC)
Hendrix (AR)
High Point (NC)
Houston Baptist (TX)
Houston (TX)
Humboldt State (CA)
Idaho, U. of
Illinois, U. of (Chicago)
▲ Immaculata (PA)
Indiana Wesleyan
Ithaca (NY)
James Madison (VA)

Kennesaw State (GA)
Lipscomb (TN)
Linfield (OR)
Lynchburg (VA)
Lyndon State (VT)
Massachusetts, U. of
Massachusetts, U. of (Lowell)
▲ Meredith (NC)
Miami U. (OH)
Millersville (PA)
Mississippi U. for Women
Nevada, U. of (Las Vegas)
New Hampshire, U. of
New Jersey, College of
North Georgia
North Texas
Northeastern Illinois
Otterbein (OH)
Pacific U. (OR)
Pittsburgh, U. of (PA)
Puget Sound (WA)
Ripon (WI)
▲ St. Catherine (MN)
San Francisco State (CA)
Schreiner (TX)
Shaw (NC)
Slippery Rock (PA)
Southwestern (TX)
Southwest Texas State
Springfield (MA)
Stetson (FL)
Tampa, U. of (FL)
Tennessee, U. of
Texas A&M (Corpus Christi)
Texas A&M (Kingsville)
Toledo (OH)
Transylvania (KY)
Texas A&M (Commerce)
Texas (El Paso)
Texas Lutheran
Texas Women's
Utah
Westfield (MA)
Western State College of
   Colorado
Western Maryland
West Virginia U.
West Virginia Wesleyan
Whitworth (WA)
Willamette (OR)
Wisconsin (La Crosse)
Wyoming

■ *Men Only*
▲ *Women Only*

* *Exercise Science and*
Sports Medicine

FASHION DESIGN / MERCHANDISING

Akron, U. of (OH)
Albright (PA)
Auburn (AL)
Baylor (TX)
Bowling Green (OH)
Brenau (GA)
California College of
    Arts & Crafts
California State U. (Fresno)
California State U.
    (Sacramento)
Central Washington
Cincinnati (OH)
Colorado State
Columbus College of Art &
    Design (OH)
Delaware, U. of
Dominican (IL)
Drexel (PA)
Florida State
Framingham (MA)
Eastern Michigan
Hawaii, U. of
High Point (NC)
Illinois, U. of
Indiana (PA)
Iowa State
Kansas State

Kent State (OH)
Kentucky, U. of
Lasell (MA)
Lynn (FL)
Marist (NY)
Marymount (VA)
▲ Meredith (NC)
Moore College of Art (PA)
Nebraska, U. of
New Hampshire College
North Carolina (Greensboro)
Oklahoma State
Oregon State
Otis (CA)
Parsons (NY)
Pratt (NY)
Rhode Island School of Design
Rhode Island, U. of
▲ Stephens (MO)
Tarleton State (TX)
Texas Christian
Virginia Commonwealth U.
Washington State
Western Michigan
Wisconsin, U. of
Wisconsin, U. of (Stout)
Woodbury (CA)

 # Especially Interior Design

■ *Men Only*
▲ *Women Only*

FORENSIC SCIENCES / TECHNOLOGY

▲ Bay Path (MA)
Bemidji State (MN)
Central Florida
▲ Cedar Crest (PA)
Chaminade (HI)
Colorado (Colorado Springs)
Defiance (OH)
DeSales (PA)
Duquesne (PA)
Eastern Kentucky
Eastern Washington
Edinboro (PA)
Florida Gulf Coast U.
Great Falls, U. of (MT)
* Guilford (NC)
+ Gwynedd-Mercy (PA)
Hamline (MN)
Harrisburg U. (PA)
John Jay (CUNY)(NY)
Kansas State
Keystone (PA)

King (TN)
Long Island U. (C.W. Post)(NY)
Loyola (IL)
Marygrove (MI)
Mercyhurst (PA)
Miami, U. of (FL)
Mississippi, U. of
New Haven, U. of (CT)
**New Jersey, College of
North Dakota, U. of
Ohio U.
Pace (NY)
St. Francis (PA)
St. Scholastica (MN)
San Jose State (CA)
Seattle U. (WA)
**Towson (MD)
Virginia Commonwealth U.
Waynesburg (PA)
West Virginia U.
**Western New England (MA)

* Forensic Biology
* * Forensic Chemistry
+ Forensic Psychology
 # Forensic Biotechnology

GENETICS

Ball State (IN)
California, U. of (Berkeley)
California, U. of (Davis)
California, U. of (Irvine)
California, U. of (Los Angeles)
Carnegie Mellon (PA)
▲ Cedar Crest (PA)
Chicago, U. of (IL)
Connecticut, U. of
Cornell (NY)
Florida State
Fredonia (SUNY)(NY)
Georgia, U. of
Harvard (MA)
Illinois, U. of
Illinois, U. of (Chicago)

Iowa State
Kansas
Maryland, U. of
Minnesota
Ohio State
Ohio Wesleyan
Otterbein (OH)
Purdue (IN)
Rochester, U. of (NY)
Rutgers (NJ)
Texas A & M
Vermont, U. of
Washington State
Western Kentucky
Wisconsin, U. of

■ *Men Only*
▲ *Women Only*

GERONTOLOGY/GERIATRIC SERVICES

Alfred (NY)
Arkansas, U. of (Pine Bluff)
Bethune-Cookman (FL)
California (PA)
California State U. (Sacramento)
Case Western (OH)
Central Washington
East Stroudsburg (PA)
Florida Gulf Coast U.
Fort Hays (KS)
Gwynedd-Mercy (PA)
Ithaca (NY)
Kent State (OH)
King's (PA)
Langston (OK)
Lindenwood (VA)
Lourdes (OH)
Madonna (MI)
Massachusetts (Boston)
Miami U. (OH)
Minnesota State U. (Moorhead)

Mount St. Mary's (CA)
Mount St. Joseph (OH)
North Carolina (Greensboro)
North Colorado
North Texas
Oneonta (SUNY)(NY)
Quinnipiac (CT)
Roosevelt (IL)
Richard Stockton (NJ)
St. Mary's (CA)
San Diego State (CA)
Scranton (PA)
Shaw (NC)
South Florida
Southern California
Southwest Missouri
Springfield (MA)
Stephen F. Austin (TX)
Wagner (NY)
Washburn (KS)
Weber State (UT)

Also, Aging Services Administration
/ Social Work

HEALTH SERVICES ADMINISTRATION

Alfred (NY)
Appalachian State (NC)
Arcadia (PA)
Arizona
Creighton (NE)
Detroit Mercy (MI)
Eastern Michigan
Eastern Washington
Florida Atlantic
* Georgetown (DC)
Herbert Lehman (CUNY)(NY)
James Madison (VA)
Kentucky
Madonna (MI)
▲ Mary Baldwin (VA)
Michigan (Dearborn)
Missouri, U. of
Mount Mercy (IA)
North Carolina (Chapel Hill)

Northeastern (MA)
Ohio U.
Oregon State
Pennsylvania State
Providence College (RI)
Quinnipiac (CT)
Regis (CO)
Robert Morris (PA)
Saint Scholastica (MN)
Scranton (PA)
South Dakota, U. of
Springfield (MA)
Stonehill (MA)
Utah, U. of
Washburn (KS)
Washington, U. of
William Paterson (NJ)
Wisconsin (Eau Claire)

* Health Systems Administration
# Community Health

■ *Men Only*
▲ *Women Only*

HISPANIC STUDIES/LATIN AMERICAN STUDIES

Adelphi (NY)
Albany (SUNY) (NY)
American (DC)
Arizona, U. of
Assumption (MA)
Austin (TX)
Binghamton (SUNY) (NY)
California, U. of (Berkeley)
California, U. of
    (Santa Barbara)
California, U. of
    (Santa Cruz)
California State
    (Long Beach)
Chicago, U. of (IL)
City (CUNY) (NY)
Colby (ME)
Connecticut College
Connecticut, U. of
DePaul (IL)
Flagler (FL)
Gettysburg (PA)
George Fox (OR)
George Washington (DC)
Hobart & William Smith (NY)
Hunter (CUNY)(NY)
Johns Hopkins (MD)
Kansas, U. of
Loyola Marymount (CA)
Macalester (MN)
Michigan, U. of

Minnesota (Morris)
▲Mount Holyoke (MA)
Nebraska, U. of (Omaha)
New Mexico, U. of
North Carolina
Northern Colorado
Northridge State (CA)
Northwestern (IL)
Oberlin (OH)
Pennsylvania, U. of
Pomona (CA)
Rhodes (TN)
Rice (TX)
Rollins (FL)
Rutgers (NJ)
San Diego State (CA)
San Francisco State (CA)
▲Scripps (CA)
▲Smith (MA)
Sonoma State (CA)
Stetson (FL)
Texas, U. of
Texas, U. of (El Paso)
Tulane (LA)
Virginia, U. of
Washington, U. of
Wheaton (MA)
Whittier (CA)
Willamette (OR)
Wisconsin, U. of
Wisconsin (Eau Claire)

HORTICULTURE

Auburn (AL)
Arkansas, U. of
Berry (GA)
Brigham Young (UT)
Cal Poly (Pomona)
Cal Poly (San Luis Obispo)
California, U. of (Davis)
* California, U. of (Riverside)
Christopher Newport
Clemson (SC)
Colorado State
Connecticut, U. of
Cornell (NY)
Delaware Valley (PA)
Delaware, U. of
* Dordt (IA)
Florida, U. of
● Florida Southern
Georgia, U. of
Hawaii, U. of
Idaho, U. of
Illinois, U. of
Iowa State
Kansas State
Louisiana State
Maine, U. of
Maryland, U. of
Michigan State
Minnesota, U. of
Mississippi State

Missouri, U. of
Montana State (Bozeman)
Nebraska, U. of
New Hampshire, U. of
North Carolina State
North Dakota State
Northwest Missouri
Ohio State
Oklahoma State
Oregon State
Pennsylvania State
Purdue (IN)
Rhode Island, U. of
Rutgers (NJ)
South Dakota State
Southwest Missouri
Tarleton (TX)
Temple (PA)
Tennessee Tech
Tennessee, U. of
Texas A & M
Texas Tech
Utah State
Vermont, U. of
Virginia Poly
Washington State
Washington, U. of
Wisconsin, U. of
Wisconsin, U. of (River Falls)

* *Plant Science*
● *And Citrus*

HOTEL AND RESTAURANT MANAGEMENT

Ashland (OH)
Auburn (AL)
Berea (KY)
Bowling Green (OH)
Cal Poly (Pomona)
Central Florida
Champlain (VT)
Colorado State
Cornell (NY)
Delaware
Denver, U. of (CO)
East Stroudsburg (PA)
Endicott (MA)
Fairleigh Dickinson (NJ)
Findlay (OH)
Florida International U.
Florida State
Georgia Southern
* Green Mountain (VT)
Georgia State
Houston, U. of (TX)
Illinois, U. of
Indiana (PA)
Iowa State
π Johnson & Wales (RI)
Johnson State (VT)
Kansas State
Lasell (MA)
● Lyndon State (VT)
Massachusetts, U. of
Mercyhurst (PA)
Michigan State
Missouri, U. of
Nebraska
Nevada (Las Vegas)

New Hampshire College
New Hampshire, U. of
New Haven (CT)
New Mexico State
New Orleans, U. of (LA)
New York University
Niagara (NY)
North Dakota State
Northern Arizona
Northern Michigan
North Texas
Oklahoma State
Ozarks (MO)
π Paul Smith's (NY)
Penn State
Plattsburgh (SUNY)(NY)
Purdue (IN)
Robert Morris (PA)
Rochester Inst. of Tech. (NY)
Roosevelt (IL)
Siena Heights (MI)
South Carolina, U. of
South Dakota State U.
Southern Illinois
    (Carbondale)
Southern New Hampshire, U. of
Texas A&M (Kingsville)
Texas Tech.
Virginia Poly. Inst.
Washington State
Western Illinois
Western Kentucky
Widener (PA)
Wisconsin (Stout)

* *Resort Management*

● *Ski Resort Management*

Restaurant and Food Management

π *Also, Culinary Arts*

■ *Men Only*
▲ *Women Only*

HUMAN RESOURCES MANAGEMENT

American (DC)
Baylor (TX)
Birmingham-Southern (AL)
Boston College (MA)
Bowling Green (OH)
Briar Cliff (IA)
Cabrini (PA)
Cal. Poly. State U.
    (Pomona)
Cal. State (Los Angeles)
DeSales (PA)
Duquesne (PA)
Evansville (IN)
Findlay (OH)
Florida State
George Washington (DC)
Hastings (NE)
Hawaii Pacific
Holy Names (CA)
Houston (TX)
Indiana (PA)
Loras (IA)
LeMoyne (NY)
Lesley (MA)
Lindenwood (MO)
Lipscomb (TN)
Marietta (OH)
Marquette (WI)

Michigan State
Muhlenberg (PA)
Nevada, U. of (Las Vegas)
New Mexico, U. of
North Dakota State
Northeastern (MA)
Oakland (MI)
Oakland City (IN)
Ohio State
Ohio University
Oklahoma, U. of
Oswego (SUNY) (NY)
Point Park (PA)
Puerto Rico, U. of (Rio Piedras)
Rider (NJ)
Rockhurst (MO)
Roosevelt (IL)
Rowan (NJ)
St. Leo (FL)
St. Mary's (TX)
Southwestern (KS)
Tarleton State (TX)
Utah State
Washington U. (MO)
Western Illinois
Wichita State (KS)
Widener (PA)
Wisconsin (Oshkosh)

INDUSTRIAL ARTS

Auburn (AL)
Berea (KY)
California (PA)
π California State U. (Fresno)
Cal. Poly. (Pomona)
Central Michigan
Cincinnati, U. of (OH)
Clemson (SC)
Colorado State
Ferris State (MI)
Fitchburg (MA)
Florida A & M
Idaho
Indiana State
Iowa State
Louisiana State U.
Millersville (PA)

Montclair (NJ)
Nebraska, U. of
New Mexico, U. of
North Carolina State
Northern Colorado
Northern Illinois
Oklahoma State
Oswego (SUNY) (NY)
Pittsburgh, U. of (PA)
Purdue (IN)
Southern Illinois
Texas A&M
Western Michigan
Wisconsin, U. of (Stout)
Wyoming

■ *Men Only*
▲ *Women Only*

π *Also Construction Management*

INDUSTRIAL DESIGN

Alfred (NY)
Appalachian State (NC)
Arizona State
Arts, U. of the (PA)
Auburn (AL)
Brigham Young (UT)
California College of
    Arts & Crafts
California State U.
    (Long Beach)
Carnegie-Mellon (PA)
Cincinnati, U of (OH)
Georgia Inst. of Tech.
Illinois, U. of (Chicago)
Illinois, U. of
Kansas, U. of
Kent State (OH)
Metropolitan State (CO)

Michigan, U. of
North Carolina State
Pratt (NY)
Pittsburgh, U. of (PA)
Purdue (IN)
Rhode Island School
    of Design
Rochester Inst. of Tech. (NY)
San Houston State (TX)
San Jose State (CA)
Syracuse (NY)
Tufts (MA)
Virginia Poly
Washington U. (MO)
Western Michigan
Western Washington
Washington, U. of

INTERIOR DESIGN

Adrian (MI)
Akron, U. of (OH)
Alabama, U. of
Arcadia (PA)
Arizona State
Arkansas, U. of
Auburn (AL)
Bayor (TX)
Boston Architectural Center (MA)
Bowling Green (OH)
Bridgeport, U. of (CT)
California State U. (Fresno)
California State U.
    (Sacramento)
Centenary (NJ)
Central Michigan
Central Washington
Chaminade (HI)
Cincinnati, U. of (OH)
Cleveland Inst. of Art (OH)
Colorado State U.
Columbia College (IL)
Columbus College of Art &
    Design (OH)
Cornell (NY)
Drexel (PA)

Eastern Kentucky
Eastern Michigan
Fairmont (WV)
Fashion Inst. of Tech. (NY)
Ferris State (MI)
Florida, U. of
Florida International
Florida State
George Washington (DC)
Georgia, U. of
Georgia Southern
High Point (NC)
Houston, U. of (TX)
Howard (DC)
Idaho, U. of
Indiana U.
Iowa State
Kansas State
Kansas, U. of
Kean (NJ)
Kent State (OH)
Kentucky, U. of
Louisiana State
Louisiana, U. of (Lafayette)
Louisville, U. of (KY)

■ *Men Only*
▲ *Women Only*

INTERIOR DESIGN continues next page

INTERIOR DESIGN, continued

Maryland Inst. of Art
▲ Meredith (NC)
Miami (OH)
Michigan State
Michigan, U. of
Minnesota, U. of
Mississippi, U. of
Moore (PA)
Mt. Ida (MA)
Mt. St. Joseph (OH)
Murray State (KY)
Nevada, U. of (Las Vegas)
Nevada, U. of (Reno)
New Haven, U. of (CT)
NY Sch. of Interior Design
North Carolina (Greensboro)
North Dakota State U.
Northern Iowa
Ohio State
Ohio U.
Oklahoma, U. of
Oregon State
Parsons (NY)
Pratt Institute (NY)
Rhode Island School of
    Design

Ringling Sch. of Art &
    Design (FL)
Rochester Inst. of Tech. (NY)
▲ Salem (NC)
San Diego State (CA)
San Jose State
Seattle Pacific (WA)
South Dakota State U.
Southern Illinois (Carbondale)
Suffolk (MA)
Syracuse (NY)
Tennessee Tech. U
Tennessee, U. of
Texas A&M (Kingsville)
Texas Christian
Texas, U. of
Ursuline (OH)
Utah State
Virginia Commonwealth
Visual Arts, Sch. of (NY)
West Virginia, U. of
Western Carolina
Western Kentucky
Western Michigan
William Woods (MO)
Wisconsin, U. of

INTERNATIONAL RELATIONS/STUDIES

Adelphi (NY)
▲ Agnes Scott (GA)
American U. (DC)
+ Arcadia (PA)
☎ Arizona State
Austin (TX)
☎ Babson (MA)
π Belmont Abbey (NC)
Beloit (WI)
● Bentley (MA)
Bethany (WV)
Bethel (IN)
☎ Bethune-Cookman (FL)
Boise State (ID)
Boston U. (MA)
Bradley (IL)
Brown (RI)
☎ Bryant (RI)
▲ Bryn Mawr (PA)
Bucknell (PA)
☎ Butler (IN)
☎ Caldwell (NJ)
California State U. (Chico)
California State U.
　 (Long Beach)
California, U. of (Davis)
++ Carthage (WI)
π Central (IA)
▲ Chatham (PA)
City (CUNY) (NY)
+ Claremont McKenna (CA)
●● Clark (MA)
Colby (ME)
Colgate (NY)
Colorado
Connecticut College
☎ Cornell (IA)
Davidson (NC)
Dayton (OH)
Denison (OH)
☎ Denver, U. of (CO)
DePaul (IL)
☎ Dickinson (PA)
Dominican (CA)
☎ Drake (IA)
π D'Youville (NY)
✪ Earlham (IN)
Eckerd (FL)

☎ Elizabethtown (PA)
☎ Elmira (NY)
Emory (GA)
Evansville (IN)
Fairleigh Dickinson (NJ)
☎ Florida International
Franklin & Marshall (PA)
George Mason (VA)
+ George Washington (DC)
+ Georgetown (DC)
π Georgia
Georgia Tech.
Goucher (MD)
Grand Valley (MI)
Hamline (MN)
☎ Hawaii
+ Hawaii Pacific
☎ Hiram (OH)
☎ Hofstra (NY)
☎ Husson (ME)
Johns Hopkins (MD)
Juniata (PA)
☎ Illinois
Illinois State
Illinois Wesleyan
Indiana
Iowa, U. of
Kalamazoo (MI)
★ Kansas State
Kenyon (OH)
Knox (IL)
Lafayette (PA)
Lehigh (PA)
☎ Lenoir-Rhyne (NC)
Lewis & Clark (OR)
Linfield (OR)
Loras (IA)
Macalester (MN)
Maine (Farmington)
Manhattanville (NY)
▲ Mary Baldwin (VA)
☎ Marygrove (MI)
Massachusetts, U. of
▲ Meredith (NC)
**Miami, U. of (FL)

■ *Men Only*
▲ *Women Only*

INTERNATIONAL RELATIONS
continues next page

INTERNATIONAL RELATIONS/STUDIES, continued

☎ Michigan, U. of
Middlebury (VT)
++ Minnesota, U. of
☎ Minnesota State U. (Mankato)
**Mississippi, U. of
Missouri Southern
☎ Moravian (PA)
Mt. Holyoke (MA)
Mt. Mercy (IA)
Mt. St. Mary's (MD)
Muhlenberg (PA)
Nebraska
Nebraska (Omaha)
**New Jersey, College of
North Carolina (Chapel Hill)
North Central (IL)
π Northeastern (MA)
Occidental (CA)
Oglethorpe (GA)
Ohio U.
Ohio Wesleyan
π Oklahoma City U.
Pacific, U. of the (CA)
Pennsylvania, U. of
Pepperdine (CA)
Pittsburgh, U. of
Pitzer (CA)
Pomona (CA)
Princeton (NJ)
Providence (RI)
++ Puget Sound (WA)
Randolph College (VA)
Redlands (CA)
Reed (OR)
Richmond (VA)
Rhodes (TN)
☎ Rochester Inst. of Tech. (NY)
San Diego, U. of (CA)
++ San Diego State (CA)
Scranton, U. of (PA)
▲ Scripps (CA)
☎ South Carolina, U. of
+ Southern California, U. of
Southwestern (TX)

Spring Hill (AL)
☎ St. Andrews (NC)
▲ St. Catherine (MN)
☎ St. Louis U. (MO)
☎ St. Mary's (MN)
St. Mary's (TX)
St. Michael's (VT)
☎ St. Norbert (WI)
St. Olaf (MN)
☎ St. Peter's (NJ)
Stanford (CA)
▲ Stephens (MO)
☎ Stetson (FL)
▲ Sweet Briar (VA)
☎ Texas A&M (Kingsville)
▲ Trinity (DC)
Tufts (MA)
Tulane (LA)
U. S. Military Academy (NY)
Vassar (NY)
Virginia Poly. Institute
Virginia Wesleyan
Washington College (MD)
Washington, U. of
☎▲ Wesleyan (GA)
Westminster (MO)
π Westmont (CA)
☎ Westminster (UT)
Wheaton (MA)
Wheeling Jesuit (WV)
Whittier (CA)
William & Mary (VA)
William Jewell (MO)
Wilson (PA)
Wisconsin, U. of
Wisconsin (Oshkosh)
Wyoming, U. of

Global Studies
* *International Economics*
☎ *International Business*
★ *International Marketing*
✪ *Peace & Global Studies*
** *Also, International Business*
● *International Culture and Economy*
●● *Also, Global Environmental Studies*
π *International Business and Global Affairs*
+ *International Relations, also International Business*
++ *International Business, also International Political Economy*

■ *Men Only*
▲ *Women Only*

JAPANESE STUDIES

Boston U. (MA)	Linfield (OR)
Bucknell (PA)	Macalester (MN)
California, U. of (Berkeley)	Michigan, U. of
California, U. of (Irvine)	Middlebury (VT)
California, U. of (Los Angeles)	Minnesota, U. of
California, U. of (Santa Barbara)	North Central (IL)
Carnegie-Mellon (PA)	Oberlin (OH)
Case Western Reserve (OH)	Oregon, U. of
Colorado, U. of	Pacific, U. of the (CA)
Colorado State	San Diego State (CA)
Connecticut College	San Francisco State (CA)
DePaul (IL)	Sarah Lawrence (NY)
Dillard (LA)	Stanford (CA)
Earlham (IN)	Swarthmore (PA)
George Washington (DC)	Washington, U. of
Georgetown (DC)	Washington U. (MO)
Gettysburg (PA)	Willamette (OR)
Harvard (MA)	Wisconsin, U. of
Hawaii, U. of	Yale (CT)
Lawrence (WI)	

JAZZ

Alabama
Arizona State
Arizona, U. of
Auburn (AL)
Augustana (IL)
Bennington College (VT)
Berklee College of Music (MA)
Bowling Green (OH)
California Institute of the Arts
California State U. (Fullerton)
California State U. (Los Angeles)
California State U. (Northridge)
Cincinnati
Delaware
Denver, U. of
DePaul U. (IL)
Duquesne U. (PA)
Elmhurst (IL)
Five Towns College (NY)
Florida Atlantic
Georgia State
Hampshire College (MA)
Hartford (CT)
Idaho
Iowa
Indiana U.
Indiana U. (PA)
Jacksonville State (AL)
* Johns Hopkins (MD)
Julliard (NY)
Knox (IL)
Long Island U. (Brooklyn)(NY)
Louisville (KY)
Loyola U. (New Orleans) (LA)
Manhattan School of
    Music (NY)
Mannes College of Music (NY)
Marlboro College (VT)
Miami (FL)
Michigan, U. of

Michigan State
Middle Tennessee
Minnesota (Duluth)
Minnesota
Nevada, U. of (Reno)
New England Conservatory
    of Music (MA)
New Orleans, U. of (LA)
New York U. (NY)
North Carolina (Asheville)
North Carolina (Greensboro)
North Carolina (Wilmington)
North Central (IL)
North Florida
North Texas
Northeastern State (OK)
Oberlin College (OH)
Ohio State U. (OH)
Oneonta (SUNY) (NY)
Purchase (SUNY) (NY)
Rochester (NY)
Rowan (NJ)
Rutgers (NJ)
San Diego State (CA)
Shenandoah U. (VA)
South Florida
Southern California
Southwest Texas State
Temple U. (PA)
Tennessee
Texas (Arlington)
Virginia Commonwealth
Washington, U. of
Webster U. (MO)
Western Maryland
Western Michigan U.
Western Washington
Westfield State (MA)
William Paterson (NJ)

Jazz Performance

■ *Men Only*
▲ *Women Only*

LINGUISTICS

Alaska, U. of (Fairbanks)
Arizona, U. of
Beloit (WI)
Boston U. (MA)
Brown (RI)
Buffalo (SUNY) (NY)
California State U. (Fresno)
California, U. of (Berkeley)
California, U. of (Los Angeles)
California, U. of (San Diego)
California, U. of
    (Santa Barbara)
California, U. of (Santa Cruz)
Chicago, U. of (IL)
Clemson (SC)
Colorado, U. of
Connecticut, U. of
Cornell (NY)
Florida State
Florida, U. of
Georgetown (DC)
Georgia, U. of
Harvard (MA)
Hawaii, U. of
Illinois, U. of
Indiana U.
Iowa, U. of
Iowa State
Kansas, U. of
Kentucky, U. of
Lawrence (WI)
Macalester (MN)
Mary Washington (VA)
Maryland, U. of
Massachusetts, U. of
MIT (MA)
Michigan, U. of
Minnesota, U. of

Mississippi, U. of
Missouri, U. of
New Hampshire, U. of
New Mexico, U. of
New York U.
North Carolina, U. of
Northeastern (MA)
Northwestern (IL)
Oakland (MI)
Ohio State U.
Ohio U.
Oklahoma, U. of
Oregon, U. of
Pennsylvania, U. of
Pittsburgh, U. of (PA)
Pitzer (CA)
Pomona (CA)
Portland State (OR)
Queens (CUNY) (NY)
Rice (TX)
Rochester, U. of
Rutgers (NJ)
San Jose State (CA)
▲ Scripps (CA)
Southern California, U. of
Southern Maine, U. of
Stanford (CA)
Stony Brook (SUNY) (NY)
Tennessee, U. of
Texas, U. of
Tulane (LA)
Virginia, U. of
Washington, U. of
Wayne State (MI)
▲ Wellesley (MA)
Wisconsin, U. of
Yale (CT)

■ *Men Only*
▲ *Women Only*

MARINE SCIENCE

Alaska Pacific
American (DC)
Atlantic, College of the (ME)
Barry (FL)
Brown (RI)
California State U.
    (Long Beach)
California State U. (Stanislaus)
California, U. of (San Diego)
California, U. of
    (Santa Barbara)
California, U. of (Santa Cruz)
Coastal Carolina (SC)
College of Charleston (SC)
Eckerd (FL)
Fairleigh Dickinson (NJ)
Florida Inst. of Technology
Hawaii Pacific
Hawaii, U. of
Hawaii, U. of (Hilo)
Idaho, U. of
Jacksonville U. (FL)
▲ Judson (AL)
Juniata (PA)
Kutztown (PA)
Long Island U.
    (Southampton)(NY)
Maine, U. of
Maine, U. of (Machias)

Maine Maritime
★ Maritime College (SUNY)(NY)
Miami, U. of (FL)
North Carolina, U. of
    (Wilmington)
North Carolina State
Northern Michigan
∗∗ Northwest Missouri
Occidental (CA)
Rhode Island, U. of
Richard Stockton (NJ)
Roger Williams (RI)
Rollins (FL)
Samford (AL)
South Alabama
π South Carolina
South Florida
Southwest Texas State
Spring Hill (AL)
Stony Brook (NY)
Tampa, U. of (FL)
Texas A&M
Texas A&M (Galveston)
U.S. Coast Guard Academy (CT)
Unity (ME)
Washington, U. of
West Florida
∗∗ Wisconsin, U. of (Whitewater)

∗∗ *Marine Biology*

π *Also, Oceanography*

★ *and Marine Environmental Science*

■ *Men Only*
▲ *Women Only*

MEDICAL TECHNOLOGY

Alabama, U. of (Birmingham)
Alaska, U. of (Anchorage)
American International (MA)
Avila (MO)
Barry (FL)
Bowling Green (OH)
Bradley (IL)
Briar Cliff (IA)
Buffalo (SUNY) (NY)
Carroll (WI)
Cincinnati (OH)
Connecticut
East Tennessee
Edgewood (WI)
Elon (NC)
Fairmont (WV)
Florida Atlantic
Florida International
Fredonia (SUNY) (NY)
Gwynedd-Mercy (PA)
Hartwick (NY)
▲ Hood (MD)
Houston (TX)
Humboldt (CA)
Indiana Wesleyan
Kansas, U. of
King (TN)
Loma Linda (CA)
Marist (NY)
▲ Mary Baldwin (VA)

Massachusetts, U. of (Boston)
Mercy (NY)
Miami U. (OH)
Michigan
Michigan State
Midwestern State (TX)
Minnesota, U. of
Minnesota State U. (Mankato)
North Carolina (Greensboro)
Pacific U. (OR)
Pittsburgh (PA)
Plattsburgh (SUNY) (NY)
St. Leo (FL)
St. Mary's (NE)
▲ St. Mary's (IN)
Salisbury (MD)
Sciences, U. of the (PA)
Scranton (PA)
Springfield (MA)
Stetson (FL)
Suffolk (MA)
Texas
Texas A&M (Corpus Christi)
Thomas More (KY)
Tuskegee (AL)
Virginia Commonwealth
Washington, U. of
Western Connecticut
West Virginia U.
Wisconsin, U. of

MIDDLE EASTERN STUDIES

Arizona, U. of
Arkansas, U. of
Barnard (NY)
Binghamton (SUNY) (NY)
Brandeis (MA)
Brigham Young (UT)
Brown (RI)
California, U. of (Berkeley)
California, U. of (Los Angeles)
California, U. of (Santa Barbara)
Chicago, U. of
Columbia (NY)
Connecticut, U. of
Cornell (NY)
Emory (GA)
Florida State
Fordham (NY)
George Washington (DC)
Hampshire (MA)

Harvard (MA)
Indiana, U. of
Johns Hopkins (MD)
Lycoming (PA)
Massachusetts, U. of
Michigan, U. of
Minnesota, U. of
New York U.
Princeton (NJ)
Rutgers (NJ)
Southwest Texas State
Texas, U. of
Toledo, U. of (OH)
U.S. Military Academy (NY)
Utah, U. of
Washington, U. of
Washington U (MO)
Wooster (OH)
Yale (CT)

■ *Men Only*
▲ *Women Only*

MORTUARY SCIENCE/FUNERAL SERVICES

Central Oklahoma
Cincinnati Coll. of Mort. Sci.
π District of Columbia, U. of the
π Ferris State (MI)
Gannon (PA)
π Lynn (FL)

Minnesota, U. of
Mount Ida (MA)
Point Park (PA)
Southern Illinois
St. John's (NY)
Wayne State (MI)

π *Two Year Only*

MUSIC THERAPY

Alabama, U. of
Alverno (WI)
Anna Maria (MA)
Arizona State
Augsburg (MN)
Baldwin-Wallace (OH)
Berklee Coll. of Music (MA)
Charleston Southern (SC)
Colorado State
Dayton (OH)
Drury (MO)
Duquesne (PA)
East Carolina (NC)
Eastern Michigan (MI)
Elizabethtown (PA)
Evansville (IN)
Florida State
Fredonia (SUNY)(NY)
Georgia
Howard (DC)
Immaculata (PA)
Incarnate Word (TX)
Iowa
Kansas
Louisville (KY)
Loyola (LA)
Mansfield (PA)
Maryville, U. of

(St. Louis)(MO)
Miami, U. of (FL)
Michigan State
Minnesota
Mississippi U. for Women
Missouri, U. of (Kansas City)
Molloy (NY)
Montclair (NJ)
Nazareth (NY)
New Paltz (SUNY)(NY)
North Dakota, U. of
Ohio U.
Pacific, U. of the (CA)
Queens (NC)
Shenandoah (VA)
Slippery Rock (PA)
Southern Methodist (TX)
Southwestern Oklahoma
Temple (PA)
Texas Women's
Utah State
Wartburg (IA)
Western Illinois
Western Michigan
Wisconsin, U. of (Eau Claire)
Wisconsin, U. of (Oshkosh)
Wooster (OH)

■ *Men Only*
▲ *Women Only*

MUSICAL THEATER

Adrian (MI)
American Academy of
    Dramatic Arts (NY)
Arizona, U. of
Baldwin-Wallace (OH)
Boston Conservatory (MA)
California State (Fullerton)
Carnegie Mellon (PA)
Catholic U. (DC)
Central Florida
Central Michigan
Central Oklahoma
Cincinnati, U. of (OH)
Coastal Carolina (SC)
Elmhurst (IL)
Elon (NC)
Emerson (MA)
Florida
Florida State
Fredonia (SUNY)(NY)
Illinois State
Illinois Wesleyan
Ithaca (NY)
Jacksonville (FL)
James Madison (VA)
▲ Meredith (NC)
Miami, U. of (FL)
Michigan, U. of
Missouri State
Mobile, U. of (AL)
Montclair (NJ)

Muhlenberg (PA)
Nazareth (NY)
North Colorado
Northwestern (IL)
Nebraska, U. of (Kearney)
New York U.
Oklahoma, U. of
Oklahoma City U.
Otterbein (OH)
Ouachita (AR)
Point Park (PA)
Rochester, U. of (NY)
Roosevelt (IL)
Russell Sage (NY)
Santa Clara (CA)
Sarah Lawrence (NY)
Shenandoah (VA)
Southern Illinois U.
    (Carbondale)
Southwest Missouri State
Syracuse (NY)
Texas Christian
Texas, U. of (El Paso)
Trinity (CT)
West Virginia Wesleyan
Weber State (UT)
Western Illinois
Western Michigan
Wilkes (PA)
Wisconsin (Stevens Point)

NAVAL ARCHITECTURE

California Maritime
    Academy
Michigan, U. of
New Orleans, U. of (LA)
SUNY Maritime College (NY)
Texas A&M (Galveston)

U.S. Coast Guard Academy (CT)
U.S. Merchant Marine
    Academy (NY)
U.S. Naval Academy (MD)
Webb Institute (NY)

■ *Men Only*
▲ *Women Only*

NEUROSCIENCE

Allegheny (PA)
Amherst (MA)
Baldwin-Wallace (OH)
Bowling Green (OH)
Bowdoin (ME)
Brown (RI)
California, U. of
    (Los Angeles)
Carthage (WI)
Central Michigan
Claremont McKenna (CA)
Colby (ME)
Colgate (NY)
Colorado College
Connecticut, U. of
Dickinson (PA)
Drake (IA)
Drew (NJ)
Emory (GA)
Florida State
Harvey Mudd (CA)
Kenyon (OH)
King (TN)

Lafayette (PA)
Macalester (MN)
Michigan
Middlebury (VT)
MIT (MA)
Minnesota, U. of
Montana State
Muskingum (OH)
New College (FL)
Northeastern (MA)
Northwestern (IL)
Oberlin (OH)
Pittsburgh (PA)
Pitzer (CA)
Pomona (CA)
Queens (CUNY) (NY)
Regis (CO)
Rochester, U. of (NY)
▲Scripps (CA)
Texas, U. of (Dallas)
Union (NY)
Ursinus (PA)
Wesleyan (CT)

■ *Men Only*
▲ *Women Only*

NUTRITIONAL SCIENCE

Alabama, U. of
Andrews (MI)
Arizona, U. of
Auburn (AL)
Ball State (IN)
Boston U. (MA)
Bridgewater (VA)
Cal Poly (SLO)
California, U. of (Berkeley)
California, U. of (Davis)
Case Western Reserve (OH)
Chapman (CA)
Clemson (SC)
Colorado State
Connecticut, U. of
Cornell (NY)
Delaware
Dominican (IL)
Florida, U. of
Framingham State (MA)
Georgia, U. of
Hawaii, U. of
Illinois
Iowa State
Kansas State
Long Island U.
   (C.W. Post)(NY)
Maine, U. of
Marygrove (MI)
Maryland, U. of
Marywood (PA)
Massachusetts, U. of (Lowell)
Minnesota, U. of
Mississippi State

Missouri, U. of
Montclair (NJ)
Nebraska, U. of
New Hampshire, U. of
New York Inst. of Tech.
New York U.
North Carolina, U. of
North Carolina, U. of
   (Greensboro)
Ohio State
Oklahoma State
Oneonta (SUNY) (NY)
Oregon State
Pittsburgh, U. of (PA)
Purdue (IN)
Rhode Island, U. of
Rutgers (NJ)
▲ Sage Colleges
   (Russell Sage)(NY)
St. John's/St. Benedict (MN)
St. Louis U. (MO)
San Jose State
Seattle Pacific (WA)
▲ Simmons (MA)
Tennessee Tech
Tennessee, U. of
Texas A&M
Texas A&M (Kingsville)
Texas Tech
Virginia Poly
Viterbo (WI)
Winthrop (SC)
Wisconsin, U. of
Wisconsin, U. of (Stout)

■ *Men Only*
▲ *Women Only*

OCCUPATIONAL THERAPY

American International (MA)
▲ Bay Path (MA)
Boston U. (MA)
Brenau (GA)
Buffalo (SUNY) (NY)
Cleveland State (OH)
Colorado State
Dominican (CA)
Eastern Carolina
Eastern Kentucky
Elizabethtown (PA)
Findlay (OH)
Florida Gulf Coast
Florida, U. of
Gannon (PA)
Illinois (Chicago)
I.U.- P.U.- Indianapolis (IN)
Ithaca (NY)
Kansas, U. of
Lenoir-Rhyne (NC)
Long Island U. (Brooklyn)(NY)
Louisiana-Monroe
Maryville (St. Louis)(MO)
McKendree (IL)
Minnesota, U. of
Missouri
New England, U. of (ME)
New Hampshire, U. of
New Mexico, U. of
Newman (KS)
New York Inst. of Tech.
North Carolina, U. of
North Dakota, U. of
Ohio State
Penn State

Pittsburgh, U. of (PA)
Puget Sound (WA)
St. Ambrose (IA)
▲ St. Catherine (MN)
St. Francis (PA)
St. Louis U. (MO)
▲ St. Mary (NE)
St. Scholastica (MN)
Salem State (MA)
San Jose State (CA)
Sciences, U. of the (PA)
Scranton (PA)
South Dakota
Southern California
Stony Brook (SUNY)(NY)
Temple (PA)
Texas A&M (Corpus Christi)
Texas, U. of (El Paso)
▲ Texas Woman's
Texas U. of (Health Sci.Ctr.-
San Antonio)
Towson (MD)
Tuskegee (AL)
Utica College (NY)
Washington U. (MO)
Washington, U. of
Wayne State (MI)
Western Michigan
Wisconsin, U. of
Wisconsin, U. of
(La Crosse)
Wisconsin, U. of
(Milwaukee)
Worcester State (MA)
Xavier (OH)

ORTHOTICS / PROSTHETICS

California State
(Dominguez Hills)
Florida International

Texas, U. of, S.W. Med Ctr.
(Dallas)
Washington, U. of

■ *Men Only*
▲ *Women Only*

PARKS AND RECREATION SERVICES

π Alaska Pacific
Alderson-Broaddus (WV)
Arizona State
Aurora (IL)
Bowling Green (OH)
Cal. Poly. State U. (Pomona)
Cal. Poly. State U. (SLO)
California State U.
    (Dominguez Hills)
California State U. (Fresno)
California State U.
    (Los Angeles)
California State U.
    (Northridge)
California State U.
    (Sacramento)
Catawba (NC)
Central Michigan
Clemson (SC)
Colorado State
Connecticut
East Stroudsburg (PA)
Florida International
Florida State
Franklin (IN)
Georgia State
Georgia, U. of
Gordon (MA)
Green Mountain (VT)
* Houghton (NY)
Idaho
Illinois State
Illinois, U. of
Indiana U.
Indiana Wesleyan
Kansas State
Kean (NJ)
Lock Haven (PA)
• Lyndon (VT)
Maine, U. of
Mankato State (MN)

Maryland, U. of
Mesa State (CO)
Michigan State
Minnesota
** Minnesota (Duluth)
Minnesota State U. (Mankato)
Missouri
Montana
Montreat (NC)
Nevada (Reno)
New Hampshire, U. of
New York U.
North Carolina (Greensboro)
North Carolina (Wilmington)
North Carolina State
Northern Arizona
Northern Iowa
π Northland (WI)
Ohio U.
Pfeiffer (NC)
Pittsburgh (Bradford)
Purdue (IN)
San Diego State (CA)
San Jose State (CA)
Science & Arts of Oklahoma
Shepherd (WV)
Slippery Rock (PA)
Southern Conneccticut
Southwest Missouri
Springfield College (MA)
Taylor (IN)
Texas A&M
Virginia Wesleyan
West Virginia U.
Western Carolina (NC)
Western State College of
    Colorado
Western Washington
Wingate (NC)
Winona State (MN)
Wisconsin (LaCrosse)

π *Outdoor Studies*
** *Outdoor Education*
# *Resort Management*
• *Also Ski Resort Management*
* *Also Equestrian Studies Option*

■ *Men Only*
▲ *Women Only*

PEACE AND CONFLICT STUDIES

American (DC)
Bethel (KS)
Bluffton (OH)
California, U. of (Berkeley)
Chapman (CA)
π Clark (MA)
Colgate (NY)
DePauw (IN)
Earlham (IN)
Eastern Mennonite (PA)
Goshen (IN)
Goucher (MD)
Guilford (NC)
Hamline (MN)
Hampshire (MA)
Juniata (PA)
Kent State (OH)
LeMoyne (NY)

Maine, U. of
Manchester (IN)
Manhattan (NY)
Missouri, U. of
Molloy (NY)
Mount St. Clair (IA)
North Carolina, U. of
Northland (WI)
North Texas
Norwich (VT)
Quincy (IL)
St. Benedict/St. John's (MN)
St. Thomas (MN)
Washington, U. of
▲ Wellesley (MA)
Whitworth (WA)
Youngstown State (OH)

π *Also Global Environmental Studies*

PHOTOJOURNALISM

Boston U. (MA)
Indiana U.
Missouri, U. of
Montana, U. of
Northern Illinois U.
Ohio U.

Rochester Inst. of Tech. (NY)
\# St. Edward's (TX)
San Jose State (CA)
Southern Illinois
Texas
Western Kentucky

\# *Photocommunications*

■ *Men Only*
▲ *Women Only*

PHYSICAL EDUCATION

Adelphi (NY)	Kutztown (PA)
Alderson-Broaddus (WV)	Lebanon Valley (PA)
Asbury (KY)	LeTourneau (TX)
Augsburg (MN)	Linfield (OR)
Baker (KS)	Lock Haven (PA)
Bemidji State (MN)	Longwood (VA)
Berea (KY)	Louisiana College
Berry (GA)	Luther (IA)
Bethany (WV)	Maine, U. of
Blackburn (IL)	McPherson (KS)
Bridgewater (MA)	Michigan State
Brockport (SUNY) (NY)	Monmouth (IL)
Castleton (VT)	Muskingum (OH)
Chowan (NC)	Nebraska, U. of
Coe (IA)	Nevada (Reno)
Colorado, U. of	North Carolina, U. of
Colorado State	North Central (IL)
Cornell (IA)	North Georgia
Cortland State (NY)	Norwich (VT)
Dana (NE)	Occidental (CA)
Davis & Elkins (WV)	Ohio U.
Denison (OH)	Oregon State
Doane (NE)	Otterbein (OH)
East Stroudsburg (PA)	Ozarks (MO)
Elon (NC)	Pacific U. (OR)
Eureka (IL)	Pennsylvania State
Faulkner (AL)	Peru State (NE)
Findlay (OH)	Plymouth State (NH)
Florida Southern	Puerto Rico, U. of
Florida State	(Mayaguez)
Florida, U. of	Purdue (IN)
Franklin (IN)	Randolph College (VA)
Georgia, U. of	Rockford (IL)
Goshen (IN)	St. Leo (FL)
Graceland (IA)	Skidmore (NY)
Grambling (LA)	Slippery Rock (PA)
Hamline (MN)	South Florida, U. of
Hanover (IN)	Springfield (MA)
Hardin-Simmons (TX)	Sterling (KS)
Illinois College	Texas, U. of
Illinois, U. of (Chicago)	Union (TN)
Indiana (PA)	Ursinus (PA)
Iowa, U. of	Walsh (OH)
Ithaca (NY)	Washington State
Jacksonville (FL)	Western Illinois
Jamestown (ND)	Western Washington
Johnson C. Smith (NC)	Westmont (CA)
Kansas State	West Virginia U.
Kansas, U. of	West Virginia Wesleyan
Kean (NJ)	William & Mary (VA)
Kennesaw State (GA)	Wisconsin (LaCrosse)
Kentucky Wesleyan	Wisconsin, U. of
King (TN)	

■ *Men Only*
▲ *Women Only*

PHYSICAL THERAPY

American International (MA)
Azusa Pacific (CA)
Barry (FL)
Boston University (MA)
Bowling Green (OH)
Bradley (IL)
Buffalo (SUNY) (NY)
California State U. (Fresno)
California State U.
   (Sacramento)
Carroll (MT)
Clarke (IA)
Clarkson (NY)
Connecticut, U. of
Dayton (OH)
D'Youville (NY)
Daemen (NY)
Duquesne (PA)
Evansville (IN)
Fairmont State (WV)
Florida Gulf Coast U.
Florida International
Florida, U. of
Grambling (LA)
Grand Valley (MI)
Hartford (CT)
Houston, U. of (TX)
Hunter (CUNY) (NY)
Huntington (AL)
Husson (ME)
Illinois (Chicago)
Indiana State
I.U.-P.U.- Indianapolis (IN)
Ithaca (NY)
Kentucky, U. of
Lebanon Valley (PA)
Louisiana-Lafayette
Louisville, U. of (KY)
Manhattan (NY)
Marquette (WI)

Maryville (St. Louis) (MO)
Miami, U. of (FL)
Midwestern State (TX)
Minnesota, U. of
Missouri, U. of
Mount St. Joseph (OH)
Mt. St. Mary's (CA)
Nazareth (NY)
Nebraska, U. of
New England, U. of (ME)
New Mexico, U. of
North Dakota, U. of
Northeastern (MA)
Northern Illinois
Ohio State U.
Ohio University
Pacific (OR)
Pittsburgh, U. of (PA)
Regis (CO)
Russell Sage (NY)
St. Francis (PA)
St. Louis U. (MO)
Saint Scholastica (MN)
San Diego State (CA)
San Francisco State (CA)
Sciences, U. of the (PA)
Scranton, U. of (PA)
Slippery Rock (PA)
Springfield College (MA)
Texas Southern
Texas U. of (Health Sci.Ctr.-
   San Antonio)
Toledo (OH)
Utah
Washington U. (MO)
Waynesburg (PA)
Wayne State (MI)
West Virginia U.
Western Carolina (NC)
Wisconsin, U. of

■ *Men Only*
▲ *Women Only*

PHYSICIAN ASSISTANT

Alderson-Broaddus (WV)
Augsburg (MN)
Butler (IN)
Daeman (NY)
DeSales (PA)
D'Youville (NY)
East Carolina
Findlay (OH)
Gannon (PA)
George Washington (DC)
High Point (NC)
Hofstra (NY)
Howard (DC)
Idaho State
Kentucky
King's (PA)
LeMoyne (NY)
Long Island U. (Brooklyn)(NY)
Miami, U. of (FL)

New York Inst. of Tech.
Nova Southeastern (FL)
Pace (NY)
Pacific (OR)
Rochester Inst. of Tech. (NY)
Rocky Mountain (MT)
St. Francis (NY)
St. Francis (PA)
St. Louis (MO)
Sciences, U. of the (PA)
▲ Seton Hill (PA)
South Dakota
Southern California
Springfield (MA)
Stony Brook (SUNY)(NY)
Union (NE)
Wichita State (KS)
Wisconsin

PRE-VETERINARY

Arkansas, U. of
Auburn (AL)
California, U. of (Davis)
Cal. Poly. State U.
    (San Luis Obispo)
Clemson (SC)
Colorado State
Delaware Valley (PA)
Elmhurst (IL)
Evansville, U. of (IN)
Findlay (OH)
Fort Lewis (CO)
Georgia, U. of
Goucher (MD)
▲ Hollins (VA)
Humboldt State (CA)
Idaho, U. of
Illinois, U. of
Iowa State
Juniata (PA)
Kansas State
Lawrence (WI)
Louisiana-Lafayette
Loyola (CA)
MacMurray (IL)
Maryland, U. of
Massachusetts, U. of
Mercy (NY)
Michigan State
Minnesota, U. of
Montana, U. of
Moravian (PA)
π Mount Ida (MA)
Murray State (KY)

Muskingum (OH)
Nebraska, U. of
Nebraska, U. of (Kearney)
Nevada, U. of (Reno)
New Hampshire, U. of
New Mexico State
Northland (WI)
North Dakota State
Oklahoma State
Oregon, U. of
Purdue (IN)
Rhode Island, U. of
▲ Russell Sage
    (The Sage Colleges)(NY)
St. Francis (PA)
▲ Salem (NC)
South Dakota State U.
Southern Mississippi, U. of
Susquehanna (PA)
Tennessee, U. of
Texas A & M
Tuskegee (AL)
Utah State
Vermont, U. of
Virginia Wesleyan
Warren Wilson (NC)
Washington & Jefferson (PA)
Washington State
West Virginia Wesleyan
Wilmington (OH)
Wingate (NC)
Winona State (MN)
Wyoming, U. of

■ *Men Only*
▲ *Women Only*

π *Veterinary Technician*

PUBLIC HEALTH

American (DC)
Baylor (TX)
Bethel (MN)
Brown (RI)
Central Oklahoma
Central State (OH)
Central Washington
Delaware State
Dillard (LA)
Florida State
Hofstra (NY)
Holy Family (PA)
* Hunter (CUNY) (NY)
Idaho, U. of
Indiana U.
Ind. U.-Pur U.-Ind U. (IN)
Johns Hopkins(MD)
Kansas, U. of
Kent State (OH)
Moorhead State (MN)
Nevada, U. of (Reno)
New Mexico State
New Orleans, U. of (LA)
North Carolina (Greensboro)

Northern Illinois
Ohio U.
Potsdam (SUNY) (NY)
Purdue (IN)
Richard Stockton (NJ)
Rutgers (NJ)
St. Cloud (MN)
St. Joseph's (NY)
Salem-Teikyo (WV)
San Francisco State (CA)
San Jose State (CA)
▲ Simmons (MA)
Southern Connecticut State
Texas Women's
Utah State
Virginia Commonwealth
West Chester (PA)
Western Illinois
Western Kentucky
Western Michigan
Western Washington
Wisconsin (Eau Claire)
Worcester State (MA)

* *Urban Public Health*
# *Health Ecology*

PUBLIC RELATIONS

Alabama, U. of
American (DC)
Auburn (AL)
Boston U. (MA)
Champlain (VT)
Coe (IA)
Dayton (OH)
Drake (IA)
Duquesne (PA)
Florida, U. of
Florida State
Georgia, U. of
Hawaii Pacific
Illinois, U. of
Louisiana-Lafayette
Marietta (OH)
Marquette (WI)
Miami, U. of (FL)
Michigan State

Monmouth (IL)
Northern Arizona
Oklahoma, U. of
Oregon, U. of
Pennsylvania State
Quinnipiac (CT)
Rhode Island, U. of
St. Scholastica (MN)
San Diego State (CA)
San Jose State (CA)
Southern California, U. of
Syracuse (NY)
Tennessee, U. of
Texas Tech.
Texas, U. of
Valparaiso (IN)
Vermont, U. of
West Virginia

■ *Men Only*
▲ *Women Only*

RANGE MANAGEMENT

Brigham Young (UT)
California, U. of
   (Berkeley)
California, U. of (Davis)
Colorado State
Eastern Oregon
Humboldt State (CA)
Idaho, U. of
Montana State (Bozeman)
Nebraska, U. of
New Mexico State U.
North Dakota State U.

Oregon State U.
South Dakota State U.
Stephen F. Austin State U. (TX)
Tarleton State (TX)
Texas A&M
Texas A&M (Kingsville)
Texas Christian
Texas Tech.
Utah State
Washington State
Wyoming, U. of

SOCIAL AND REHABILITATION SERVICES

Arizona, U. of
Assumption (MA)
Boston U. (MA)
California State U.
   (Los Angeles)
Gustavus Adolphus (MN)
Iowa, U. of
Louisiana State
Maine (Farmington)
Marshall (WV)
\# Marysville U.-St. Louis (MO)
Montana, U. of
Northern Colorado
North Texas

Ohio State
Pittsburgh, U. of (PA)
Seattle (WA)
South Florida, U. of
Southern Mississippi
Springfield College (MA)
Texas, U. of (Austin)
Virginia Commonwealth
Wartburg (IA)
West Virginia Wesleyan
Wilberforce (OH)
Wisconsin
Wright State (OH)

\# *Business and Rehabilitation Services*

SOCIAL WORK

Adelphi (NY)
Alabama, U. of
Alaska, U. of (Anchorage)
Alaska, U. of (Fairbanks)
Albany (SUNY) (NY)
Andrews (MI)
Arizona State
Arkansas, U. of
Ashland (OH)
Augsburg (MN)
Azusa Pacific (CA)
Ball State (IN)
Barry (FL)
Baylor (TX)
Belmont (TN)
Bemidji State (MN)
▲ Bennett (NC)
Bethany (KS)
Bethany (WV)
Bethel (KS)
Boise State (ID)
Brescia (KY)
Brigham Young (UT)
Brockport (SUNY) (NY)
Buena Vista (IA)
California (PA)
California (Berkeley)
California State U. (Chico)
California State U. (Fresno)
California State U. (Fullerton)
California State U.
    (Los Angeles)
California State U.
    (Sacramento)
California State U.
    (San Bernardino)
Carroll (WI)
Castleton (VT)
Catholic (DC)
Clarke (IA)
Colorado State
Connecticut, U. of
Creighton (NE)
Cumberland (KY)
Dana (NE)
David Lipscomb (TN)
Dillard (LA)
Eastern Michigan
Eastern Nazarene (MA)

Eastern Washington
Elizabethtown (PA)
Elmira (NY)
Elms (MA)
Ferris State (MI)
Findlay (OH)
Florida Atlantic
Florida International
Florida State
Fordham (NY)
Fort Hays (KS)
Franciscan U. of Steubenville (OH)
Fredonia (SUNY) (NY)
Georgia State
Georgia U. of
Gordon (MA)
Grand Valley (MI)
Hawaii, U. of
Hawaii Pacific
Hood (MD)
Hope (MI)
Humboldt State (CA)
Illinois, U. of
Illinois, U. of (Chicago)
Illinois, U. of (Springfield)
Indiana
Indiana U.-Purdue U.-
    Indianapolis (IN)
Indiana Wesleyan
Iowa, U. of
Jacksonville State (AL)
Johnson C. Smith (NC)
Juniata (PA)
Kansas State
Kansas, U. of
Kean (NJ)
Kentucky
Lewis-Clark (ID)
Lindenwood (MO)
Lipscomb (TN)
Lock Haven (PA)
Longwood (VA)
Loras (IA)
Louisiana-Monroe
Lourdes (OH)
Loyola (IL)
MacMurray (IL)

■ *Men Only*
▲ *Women Only*

SOCIAL WORK continues next page

SOCIAL WORK, continued

Madonna (MI)
Maine, U. of
Manchester (IN)
Mansfield (PA)
Marquette (WI)
Marshall (WV)
▲ Mary Baldwin (VA)
Marygrove (MI)
Maryland (Baltimore Co.)
Marywood (PA)
McDaniel (MD)
Mercyhurst (PA)
▲ Meredith (NC)
Michigan State
Michigan, U. of
Middle Tennessee
Millersville (PA)
Minnesota (Duluth)
Minnesota State U.
    (Moorhead)
Misericordia (PA)
Missouri, U. of
Montana, U. of
Mount St. Joseph (OH)
Nazareth (NY)
Nevada, U. of (Las Vegas)
Nevada, U. of (Reno)
New Mexico State
New York University
Niagara (NY)
North Carolina (Greensboro)
North Carolina (Pembroke)
North Carolina State
Northern Iowa
Northwestern State (LA)
Ohio U.
Oklahoma, U. of
Oral Roberts (OK)
Pittsburgh, U. of (PA)
Portland, U. of (OR)
Presentation (SD)
Providence (RI)
Radford (VA)
Ramapo (NJ)
Rhode Island College
Richard Stockton (NJ)
Rochester Inst. of Tech. (NY)
Rockford (IL)
Sacred Heart (CT)

Saginaw Valley (MI)
▲ St. Catherine (MN)
St. Edward's (TX)
St. Francis (IN)
St. Francis (PA)
St. Leo (FL)
St. Louis (MO)
St. Olaf (MN)
St. Scholastica (MN)
St. Thomas (MN)
Salem State (MA)
Salisbury (MD)
San Francisco State (CA)
Shepherd (WV)
Shippensburg U. of (PA)
South Florida, U. of
Southern Connecticut
Southwestern Oklahoma State U.
Stony Brook (SUNY) (NY)
Tarleton State (TX)
Tennessee, U. of
Texas A&M (Kingsville)
Texas, U. of (Arlington)
Texas, U. of (Austin)
Texas Women's
Utah State
Valparaiso (IN)
Vermont, U. of
Walla Walla (WA)
Warren Wilson (NC)
Wartburg (IA)
Washburn (KS)
Washington U. (MO)
Washington, U. of
Wayne State (MI)
West Florida
Western Carolina (NC)
Western Maryland
Western Michigan
Western New England (MA)
William Woods (MO)
Winona State (MN)
Winthrop (SC)
Wisconsin, U. of
Wisconsin, U. of (Milwaukee)
Wisconsin, U. of (Superior)
Wisconsin, U. of (Whitewater)
Wyoming, U. of

■ *Men Only*
▲ *Women Only*

SPECIAL EDUCATION

Alabama, U. of
Alderson-Broaddus (WV)
American International (MA)
Arizona State
Arizona, U. of
Arkansas
Auburn (AL)
Augustana (SD)
Bemidji State (MN)
π Bethel (IN)
Boston U. (MA)
Brenau (GA)
Bridgewater State (MA)
California State (Fresno)
π California State
   (Northridge)
Central (CT)
Clarke (IA)
Clarion (PA)
Columbia (SC)
Connecticut, U. of
▲ Converse (SC)
Culver-Stockton (MO)
Curry (MA)
Dana (NE)
Delaware State
Doane (NE)
Eastern Kentucky
Eastern Illinois
Eastern Michigan
Edinboro (PA)
Emporia State (KS)
Fitchburg (MA)
π Flagler (FL)
Florida Atlantic
Florida Gulf Coast
Florida, U. of
Fontbonne (MO)
Fort Hays (KS)
Geneseo (SUNY) (NY)
Georgia Southwestern
Georgia, U. of
Gonzaga (WA)
Grand Valley (MI)
Hartford (CT)
Hofstra (NY)
Holy Names (CA)

Hood (MD)
Idaho, U. of
Illinois State
Indiana U.
James Madison (VA)
Juniata (PA)
Kansas State
Kansas Wesleyan
Kean (NJ)
Keene (NH)
Kentucky, U. of
Kutztown (PA)
Landmark College (VT)
Lasell (MA)
Lesley (MA)
Lindenwood (MO)
Lock Haven (PA)
Longwood (VA)
Loras (IA)
Louisiana State U.
Lyndon State (VT)
MacMurray (IL)
Maine, U. of (Farmington)
Malone (OH)
Mansfield (PA)
Marygrove (MI)
Maryland, U. of
Mercyhurst (PA)
Miami, U. of (FL)
Michigan State
Michigan, U. of
Millersville (PA)
Montana State (Billings)
Muskingum (OH)
Nebraska, U. of
Nebraska, U. of (Omaha)
New Mexico State
Nevada, U. of (Las Vegas)
Nevada, U. of (Reno)
North Florida
North Georgia
North Texas
Northern Colorado, U. of
Northern Illinois

π *Also Deaf Studies*

■ *Men Only*
▲ *Women Only*

SPECIAL ED. continues next page

SPECIAL EDUCATION, continued

Northern Iowa
Nyack (NY)
Oklahoma, U. of
Old Dominion (VA)
Pennsylvania State
Peru State (NE)
Presbyterian (SC)
Providence (RI)
Quincy (IL)
Rhode Island College
Rockford (IL)
Rowan (NJ)
St. Cloud (MN)
St. Elizabeth (NJ)
St. Francis (IN)
▲ St. Joseph (CT)
St. Louis U. (MO)
St. Martin's (WA)
Silver Lake (WI)
▲ Simmons (MA)
Southern Connecticut
South Florida
Southern Illinois U.
    (Carbondale)

Southern Utah
Tennessee, U. of
Texas, U. of
▲ Trinity (DC)
Utah State
Utah, U. of
Vanderbilt (TN)
Walsh (OH)
West Chester (PA)
West Florida
Western Carolina
Western Washington
Westfield (MA)
Wisconsin, U. of
Wisconsin, U. of (Eau Claire)
Wisconsin, U. of (Milwaukee)
Wisconsin, U. of (Oshkosh)
Wisconsin, U. of (Whitewater)
Winona (MN)
Wittenberg (OH)
Wyoming, U. of
Xavier (LA)

■ *Men Only*
▲ *Women Only*

SPORTS MEDICINE/ATHLETIC TRAINING

Alderson-Broaddus (WV)
Alfred (NY)
Baldwin Wallace (OH)
Ball State (IN)
Belmont Abbey (NC)
Boise State (ID)
Bryan (TN)
California (PA)
California Lutheran
Canisius (NY)
Carthage (WI)
Castleton (VT)
Catawba (NC)
Charleston, College of (SC)
Charleston, U. of (WV)
Chowan (NC)
Clarke (IA)
Coe (IA)
Colby-Sawyer (NH)
Colorado State
Connecticut, U. of
East Stroudsburg (PA)
Eastern Nazarene (MA)
Elon (NC)
Endicott (MA)
Eureka (IL)
Evansville (IN)
Findlay (OH)
Florida Southern
Florida State
Gardner-Webb (NC)
George Fox (OR)
Gustavus Adolphus (MN)
Heidelberg (OH)
High Point (NC)
Hope (MI)
Houston Baptist (TX)
Illinois (Chicago)
Indiana U.
Indiana Wesleyan
James Madison (VA)
Kansas Wesleyan
King's (PA)
LaSell (MA)
Laverne (CA)
Lees-McCrae (NC)
Lindenwood (MO)
Linfield (OR)
Lipscomb (TN)
Long Island U. (Brooklyn)(NY)
Louisiana College

Lynchburg (VA)
Manchester (IN)
Manhattan (NY)
Marietta (OH)
McKendree (IL)
Merrimack (MA)
Mercyhurst (PA)
Minnesota State U. (Mankato)
Missouri Baptist
Mobile, U. of (AL)
Mount Union (OH)
Neumann (PA)
Nevada, U. of (Las Vegas)
New Mexico State
North Dakota
North Georgia
Northeastern (MA)
Northwestern (IA)
Norwich (VT)
Ohio Northern
Ohio State
Otterbein (OH)
Palm Beach Atlantic (FL)
Pepperdine (CA)
Quincy (IL)
Quinnipiac (CT)
Roanoke (VA)
St. Andrews (NC)
Samford (AL)
Slippery Rock (PA)
Southern Maine
Southwest Missouri
Southwest Texas State
Springfield (MA)
Sterling (KS)
Stony Brook (SUNY) (NY)
Taylor (IN)
Texas (Arlington)
Towson (MD)
Tusculum (TN)
Tulsa (OK)
Union (TN)
Waynesburg (PA)
West Virginia Wesleyan
West Chester (PA)
Whitworth (WA)
William Woods (MO)
Wilmington (OH)
Wingate (NC)
Wisconsin (La Crosse)
Xavier (OH)

■ *Men Only*
▲ *Women Only*

SPORTS SCIENCES / MANAGEMENT

Alabama, U. of
Alderson-Broaddus (WV)
Aquinas (MI)
Arizona State
Averett (VA)
Belmont Abbey (NC)
Bemidji (MN)
Berry (GA)
Bowling Green (OH)
Briar Cliff (IA)
Buena Vista (IA)
Cabrini (PA)
Carthage (WI)
Castleton (VT)
Central Washington
Chowan (NC)
✳ Coastal Carolina (SC)
Colby-Sawyer (NH)
Concordia (CA)
Connecticut, U. of
Dallas, U. of (TX)
Eastern Connecticut
Elon (NC)
Endicott (MA)
Faulkner (AL)
Flagler (FL)
Florida Southern
Florida, U. of
Guilford (NC)
High Point (NC)
Husson (ME)
Idaho, U. of
Incarnate Word (TX)
Indiana U.
Ithaca (NY)
Kansas, U. of
Kentucky Wesleyan
Knox (IL)
Liberty (VA)
Lock Haven (PA)
Louisville (KY)
Lynchburg (VA)
Lynn (FL)
MacMurray (IL)
Malone (OH)
Marian (WI)
Massachusetts, U. of
Michigan, U. of
Millersville (PA)

Misericordia (PA)
Mississippi U. for Women
Missouri Baptist
Mount Union (OH)
\# Nebraska, U. of
Neumann (PA)
✳✳ North Carolina State
North Michigan
Ohio Northern
Ohio State
Ohio U.
Oklahoma
Oregon, U. of
Pfeiffer (NC)
Principia (IL)
Richmond (VA)
Robert Morris (PA)
Rutgers (NJ)
Seton Hall (NJ)
Shepherd (WV)
Simpson (IA)
South Carolina, U. of
Southern New Hampshire, U. of
Southwest Baptist (MO)
Springfield (MA)
St. Ambrose (IA)
St. John's (NY)
St. Leo (FL)
St. Olaf (MN)
St. Thomas U. (FL)
Stetson (FL)
Tampa, U. of (FL)
Tarleton State (TX)
Taylor (IN)
Temple (PA)
Tennessee
Texas Christian
Towson (MD)
Tulsa (OK)
Union (TN)
West Virginia U.
Western Carolina
Western New England (MA)
Wingate (NC)
Wisconsin (La Crosse)
Xavier (OH)

■ *Men Only*
▲ *Women Only*

\# *PGA Golf Management*
✳ *Professional Golf Management*
✳✳ *Also, Professional Golf Management*

URBAN STUDIES

Akron, U. of (OH)
Albany (SUNY)(NY)
Aquinas (MI)
Augsburg (MN)
▲ Barnard (NY)
Boston U. (MA)
Brown (RI)
▲✪ Bryn Mawr (PA)
California State U. (Northridge)
California, U. of (San Diego)
★ Cal Poly State U. (SLO)
Canisius (NY)
Cincinnati, U. of (OH)
Cleveland State (OH)
College of Charleston (SC)
Columbia (NY)
Connecticut College
Connecticut, U. of
Cornell (NY)
David Lipscomb (TN)
DePaul (IL)
Eastern Washington
Elmhurst (IL)
Florida International
Florida, U. of
Furman (SC)
Georgia State
Grambling (LA)
Hamline (MN)
Hampshire (MA)
Harvard (MA)
Hunter (CUNY)(NY)
Illinois (Chicago)
Indiana State
Lehigh (PA)
Lipscomb (TN)
Loyola Marymount (CA)
Macalester (MN)
Malone (OH)
Manhattan (NY)

Maryland, U. of
Michigan State
Minnesota, U. of
π Minnesota State U. (Mankato)
■ Morehouse (GA)
Mount Mercy (IA)
Nebraska, U. of
New School U. (NY)
New York U.
Northwestern (IL)
Ohio State
Pennsylvania, U. of
Pittsburgh, U. of (PA)
✶✶ Portland State (OR)
Queens (CUNY) (NY)
Rockford (IL)
Rutgers (NJ)
Rutgers (Camden) (NJ)
St. Louis (MO)
St. Peter's (NJ)
San Francisco State U. (CA)
Shippensburg (PA)
Stanford (CA)
Tampa, U. of (FL)
Towson State (MD)
Trinity (TX)
Vanderbilt (TN)
Vassar (NY)
Virginia Commonwealth
Virginia Poly
Washington U. (MO)
Wayne State (MI)
Western Washington
π Westfield State (MA)
Wisconsin, U. of
   (Green Bay)
Wittenberg (OH)
Wooster (OH)
Worcester State (MA)
Wright State (OH)

π *Regional Planning*
And Regional Planning
★ *City & Regional Planning*
✶✶ *Community Development*
✪ *Growth and Structure of Cities*

■ *Men Only*
▲ *Women Only*

VOICE

Ball State (IN)	New England Conservatory (MA)
Bucknell (PA)	New Hampshire, U. of
Catholic (DC)	New York U.
Chapman (CA)	North Carolina (Greensboro)
Cincinnati, U. of (OH)	North Carolina School of the Arts
Cleveland Inst. of Music (OH)	North Texas
Connecticut College	Northwestern (IL)
Florida Southern	Nyack (NY)
Florida State	Oberlin (OH)
Fredonia (SUNY)(NY)	Ohio U.
Furman (SC)	Oklahoma City U.
Illinois, U. of	Ouachita (AR)
Illinois Wesleyan	Pacific Lutheran (WA)
Ithaca (NY)	Palm Beach Atlantic (FL)
Indiana U.	Purchase (SUNY) (NY)
Julliard (NY)	Rice (TX)
Kansas, U. of	Rider (Westminster) (NJ)
Manhattan Sch. of Music (NY)	Roosevelt (IL)
Mannes (NY)	Samford (AL)
Mercer (GA)	San Francisco Conserv. of
▲ Meredith (NC)	Music (CA)
Miami, U. of (FL)	Southern California
Michigan, U. of	Syracuse (NY)
Middle Tennessee	Temple (PA)
Millersville (PA)	Tulsa, U. of (OK)
Missouri, U. of (Kansas City)	Weber State (UT)
Missouri State	Wheaton (IL)
Nebraska Wesleyan	

■ *Men Only*
▲ *Women Only*

WILDLIFE/WILDLANDS MANAGEMENT

Alaska (Fairbanks)
Arizona, U. of
Auburn (AL)
Ball State (IN)
Brevard (NC)
California, U. of (Davis)
Clemson (SC)
Colorado State
Connecticut, U. of
Cornell (NY)
Eastern Kentucky
Eastern New Mexico
Florida, U. of
Frostburg State (MD)
Georgia, U. of
π Grand Valley (MI)
Humboldt State (CA)
Idaho, U. of
Kansas State
Louisiana State
Maine, U. of
Massachusetts, U. of
Michigan State
Michigan Tech
Michigan, U. of
Minnesota, U. of
Mississippi State
Missouri, U. of
Montana, U. of

Montana State
Nebraska, U. of
New Hampshire, U. of
New Mexico State
North Carolina State
Ohio State
Oklahoma State
Oregon State
Penn State
Purdue (IN)
Rhode Island, U. of
Rutgers (NJ)
South Dakota State
Tarleton State (TX)
Tennessee Tech
Tennessee, U. of
Texas A&M
Texas Tech.
Unity (ME)
Utah State
Vermont, U. of
Virginia Poly Tech
Washington State
Washington, U. of
West Virginia U.
Wisconsin, U. of
Wisconsin, U. of
    (Stevens Point)
Wyoming, U. of

π *Natural Resources Management*

■ *Men Only*
▲ *Women Only*

WOMEN'S STUDIES

▲Agnes Scott (GA)
Antioch (OH)
Arizona State
Arizona, U. of
▲Barnard (NY)
Bates (ME)
Beloit (WI)
Berea (WV)
Bowling Green (OH)
Brandeis (MA)
Brown (RI)
Cal Poly State U. (Pomona)
California State U. (Fresno)
California State U.
   (Long Beach)
California, U. of (Berkeley)
California, U. of (Davis)
California, U. of (Riverside)
California, U. of
   (Santa Barbara)
California, U. of (Santa Cruz)
Carleton (MN)
Colby (ME)
Colorado College
Colorado, U. of
Connecticut College
Connectut, U. of
Dartmouth (NH)
Delaware, U. of
Denver, U. of (CO)
DePauw (IN)
Drew (NJ)
Duke (NC)
Emory (GA)
Florida, U. of
Florida International
Florida State
Franklin & Marshall (PA)
Fredonia (SUNY) (NY)
Georgetown (DC)
Goucher (MD)
Harvard (MA)
Hawaii, U. of
Hobart & William Smith (NY)
▲Hollins (VA)

Hope (MI)
Iowa, U. of
Iowa State
Kansas, U. of
Kansas State
Kalamazoo (MI)
Kenyon (OH)
Lawrence (WI)
Louisiana State
Louisville (KY)
π Loyola (IL)
Loyola Marymount (CA)
Macalester (MN)
Maine, U. of
Maine, U. of (Farmington)
Maryland, U. of
Massachusetts, U. of
Mercer (GA)
▲Meredith (NC)
Michigan, U. of
Middlebury (VT)
▲Mills (CA)
Minnesota (Duluth)
Minnesota (Morris)
Missouri, U. of
▲Mt. Holyoke (MA)
Nebraska, U. of
Nebraska Wesleyan
Nevada, U. of (Las Vegas)
Nevada, U. of (Reno)
New College (FL)
New Hampshire, U. of
New Jersey, College of
New Mexico, U. of
Northwestern (IL)
Oakland (MI)
Oberlin (OH)
Ohio State
Ohio Wesleyan
Oklahoma, U. of
Old Dominion (VA)

Gender Studies
π *Must be a Second Major*

■ *Men Only*
▲ *Women Only*

WOMEN'S STUDIES continues next page

WOMEN'S STUDIES

Oregon, U. of
Pennsylvania, U. of
Pittsburgh, U. of (PA)
Pitzer (CA)
Pomona (CA)
Portland State (OR)
Purchase (SUNY) (NY)
Randolph College (VA)
Regis (CO)
Rhode Island, U. of
Rhode Island College
Rice (TX)
Rochester, U. of (NY)
▲Rosemont (PA)
Rutgers (NJ)
San Francisco State (CA)
Sarah Lawrence (NY)
▲Scripps (CA)
▲Simmons (MA)
Skidmore (NY)
▲Smith (MA)
Southern California
Southern Maine

Southwestern (TX)
▲Spelman (GA)
Stanford (CA)
Stony Brook (SUNY) (NY)
Syracuse (NY)
Towson (MD)
Vassar (NY)
Washington State
Washington U. (MO)
Washington, U. of
▲Wellesley (MA)
Wells (NY)
Wesleyan (CT)
West Chester (PA)
Wheaton (MA)
Wisconsin, U. of
Wisconsin, U. of
  (Milwaukee)
Wisconsin, U. of
  (Whitewater)
Wooster (OH)
Wyoming, U. of
Yale (CT)

SECTION THREE

AVERAGE SAT-1/
EXPECTED AVERAGE NEW SAT-1/
ACT TOTALS
RECOMMENDED MAJORS

ABILENE CHRISTIAN UNIVERSITY (TX) .... acu.edu **1110/1665/24**
Art, Bus Admin, Chem, Nurs, Reli Stu

ADELPHI COLLEGE (NY) .... adelphi.edu **1120/1680/24**
Chem, Communic, Comp Sci, Drama, Ed, Nurs, Physics, Psych

ADRIAN COLLEGE (MI) .... adrian.edu **1040/1560/22**
Art, Bus Admin, Comp Sci, Ed, English, Math, Poli Sci, Pre-Law, Soc

AGNES SCOTT COLLEGE (GA) .... agnesscott.edu **1220/1830/27**
*Art, Bio, Bus Admin, Classics, Econ, English, For Lang, Hist, Math, Physics,
Poli Sci, Pre-Law, Pre-Med/Pre-Dental, Psych*

AKRON, UNIVERSITY OF (OH) .... uakron.edu **1000/1500/21**
Bus Admin, Chem, Drama, Ed, Engine, Hist, Home Ec, Nurs, Soc

ALABAMA, UNIVERSITY OF (AL) .... ua.edu **1105/1660/24**
*Amer St, Anthro, Art, Bot, Bus Admin, Communic, Drama, Engine, English,
For Lang, Geol, Hist, Music, Philo, Pre-Law, Pre-Med/Pre-Dental, Psych*

ALABAMA, UNIVERSITY OF (BIRMINGHAM) .... uab.edu **1060/1600/23**
Bus Admin, Chem, Comp Sci, Drama, Engine, English, Nurs, Philo, Psych

ALABAMA, UNIVERSITY OF (HUNTSVILLE) .... uah.edu **1150/1725/25**
Bus Admin, Chem, Communic, Comp Sci, Engine, English, Math, Nurs, Philo, Physics, Psych

ALASKA PACIFIC UNIVERSITY (AK) .... alaskapacific.edu **1040/1560/22**
Bus Admin, Ed, Music, Psych, Reli Stu

ALASKA, UNIVERSITY OF (ANCHORAGE) (AK) .. uaa.alaska.edu **1000/1545/21**
Art, Bus Admin, Econ, Ed

ALASKA, UNIVERSITY OF (FAIRBANKS) (AK) .... uaf.edu **1030/1545/22**
Anthro, Bio, Bus Admin, Drama, Engine, Geol, Nurs

ALBANY COLLEGE OF PHARMACY (NY) .... acp.edu **1140/1715/25**
Pharm

ALBERTSON COLLEGE OF IDAHO (ID) .... albertson.edu **1170/1750/26**
*Bio, Bus Admin, Chem, Ed, English, Hist, Math, Music, Poli Sci, Pre-Law,
Pre-Med/Pre-Dental, Zoo*

ALBION COLLEGE (MI) .... albion.edu **1150/1725/25**
Econ, English, Hist, Math, Philo, Poli Sci, Pre-Law, Pre-Med/Pre-Dental,

ALBRIGHT COLLEGE (PA) .... albright.edu **1030/1550/22**
*Art, Biochem, Bio, Bus Admin, Poli Sci, Pre-Law, Pre-Med/Pre-Dental,
Psych, Soc*

ALDERSON-BROADDUS COLLEGE (WV) .... ab.edu **1030/1545/22**
Bus Admin, Ed, Music, Nurs

ALFRED UNIVERSITY (NY) .... alfred.edu **1140/1715/25**
*Art, Bio, Bus Admin, Chem, Communic, Ed, Engine, English, Hist, Pre-Law,
Pre-Med/Pre-Dental, Psych*

ALLEGHENY COLLEGE (PA) .... alleg.edu **1210/1815/26**
Bio, Chem, Comp Sci, Drama, Econ, English, For Lang, Geol, Hist, Philo,
Physics, Pre-Law, Pre-Med/Pre-Dental, Psych

ALMA COLLEGE (MI) .... alma.edu **1140/1710/25**
Art, Bio, Bus Admin, Chem, Communic, Comp Sci, Ed, English, Hist,
Poli Sci, Pre-Law, Pre-Med/Pre-Dental, Psych

ALVERNO COLLEGE (WI) .... alverno.edu **1000/1500/21**
Bio, Communic, Bus Admin, Ed, English, Nurs, Psych

AMERICAN ACADEMY OF DRAMATIC ARTS (NY) ..... aada.org **1205/1810/27**
Drama

AMERICAN INTERNATIONAL COLLEGE (MA) .... aic.edu **1000/1500/21**
Bus Admin, Pre-Med/Pre-Dental, Psych

AMERICAN UNIVERSITY (DC) .... american.edu **1260/1890/27**
Amer St, Anthro, Art, Bus Admin, Drama, Econ, Communic, Hist, Math,
Poli Sci, Pre-Law, Pre-Med/Pre-Dental

AMHERST COLLEGE (MA) .... amherst.edu **1440/2160/32**
Amer St, Astro, Bio, Chem, Classics, Drama, Econ, English, Geol, Hist,
Philo, Physics, Poli Sci, Pre-Law, Pre-Med/Pre-Dental, Psych, Soc

ANDERSON UNIVERSITY (IN) .... anderson.edu **1062/1593/23**
Ed, Music

ANDREWS UNIVERSITY (MI) .... andrews.edu **1080/1620/23**
Arch, Chem, Music, Nurs, Reli Stu

ANNA MARIA COLLEGE (MA) .... annamaria.edu **1000/1500/21**
Art, Bus Admin, Music

APPALACHIAN STATE UNIVERSITY (NC) .... appstate.edu **1100/1650/24**
Bus Admin, Communic, Ed, English, Hist, Poli Sci

AQUINAS COLLEGE (MI) .... aquinas.edu **1060/1590/23**
Art, Bio, Bus Admin, Chem, Drama, English, Geog, Music, Psych, Reli Stu

ARCADIA UNIVERSITY (PA) .... arcadia.edu **1048/1572/22**
Art, Bio, Chem, Comp Sci, Ed, English, Math, Poli Sci, Pre-Law, Psych

ARIZONA, UNIVERSITY OF (AZ) .... arizona.edu **1100/1650/24**
Ag, Amer St, Anthro, Arch, Art, Astro, Bio, Bus Admin, Chem, Communic, Drama,
Ed, Engine, English, Forest, For Lang, Geol, Hist, Nurs, Pharm, Philo, Pre-Law,
Pre-Med/Pre-Dental, Psych, Soc

ARIZONA STATE UNIVERSITY (AZ) .... asu.edu **1105/1655/24**
Anthro, Arch, Art, Biochem, Bio, Bus Admin, Communic, Comp Sci,
Drama, Ed, Engine, English, For Lang, Geog, Geol, Hist, Math, Music,
Nurs, Physics, Poli Sci, Pre-Med/Pre-Dental, Psych, Reli Stu, Zoo

ARKANSAS, UNIVERSITY OF (AR) .... uark.edu **1163/1750/25**
Ag, Anthro, Arch, Bus Admin, Communic, Comp Sci, Econ, Ed, Engine,
English, Hist, Music, Physics, Pre-Law, Psych

ART CENTER COLLEGE OF DESIGN (CA) .... artcenter.edu **1110/1660/24**
Art

ART INSTITUTE OF CHICAGO (IL) .... artic.edu/saic **1100/1650/24**
Art

ARTS, UNIVERSITY OF THE (PA) .... uarts.edu **1060/1590/23**
Art, Drama, Music

ASBURY COLLEGE (KY) .... asbury.edu **1150/1725/25**
Art, Bus Admin, Communic, Ed, Music, Philo, Reli Stu, Soc

ASHLAND UNIVERSITY (OH) .... ashland.edu **1060/1600/23**
Bus Admin, Chem, Ed

ASSUMPTION COLLEGE (MA) .... assumption.edu **1090/1635/23**
Bus Admin, Econ, Ed, English, Hist, Philo

AUBURN UNIVERSITY (AL) ....auburn.edu **1120/1680/24**
Ag, Arch, Art, Bus Admin, Communic, Comp Sci, Econ, Ed, Engine,
English, Forest, Hist, Math, Pharm, Physics, Poli Sci

AUGSBURG COLLEGE (MN) .... augsburg.edu **1080/1620/23**
Bus Admin, Communic, Comp Sci, Ed, English, Physics, Pre-Law, Soc

AUGUSTA STATE UNIVERSITY (GA) .... aug.edu **1000/1500/21**
English, Soc

AUGUSTANA COLLEGE (IL) .... augustana.edu **1180/1770/26**
Art, Bio, Bus Admin, Ed, English, Music, Pre-Law

AUGUSTANA COLLEGE (SD) .... augie.edu **1120/1680/24**
Bio, Chem, Ed, English, Music, Pre-Med/Pre-Dental, Reli Stu

AUSTIN COLLEGE (TX) .... austincollege.edu **1240/1860/28**
Biochem, Bio, Bus Admin, Chem, Ed, Hist, Philo, Poli Sci, Pre-Med/Pre-Dental, Reli Stu

AVERETT UNIVERSITY (VA) .... averett.edu **1000/1500/21**
Bus Admin, Ed, Math, Psych

AVILA UNIVERSITY (MO) ....avila.edu **1000/1500/21**
Bus Admin, Ed, Nurs

AZUSA PACIFIC (CA) .... apu.edu **1100/1650/24**
Bio, Bus Admin, English, Music, Nurs, Poli Sci

BABSON COLLEGE (MA) .... babson.edu **1260/1890/29**
Bus Admin, Econ

BAKER UNIVERSITY (KS) .... bakeru.edu **1080/1620/23**
Bio, Bus Admin, Comp Sci, Ed, Music, Nurs, Poli Sci, Psych

BALDWIN-WALLACE COLLEGE (OH) .... bw.edu **1100/1650/24**
Bus Admin, Chem, Comp Sci, Econ, Ed, English, Hist, Math, Music, Poli Sci, Pre-Law, Psych

BALL STATE UNIVERSITY (IN) .... bsu.edu **1030/1550/22**
Anthro, Art, Bio, Botany, Communic, Comp Sci, Ed, Geog, Math, Nurs, Physics, Poli Sci, Psych

BARD COLLEGE (NY) .... bard.edu **1340/2010/30**
Art, Drama, English, For Lang, Hist, Music, Pre-Law, Psych, Soc

BARNARD COLLEGE (NY) .... barnard.edu **1360/2040/31**
*Anthro, Arch, Art Hist, Biochem, Bio, Chem, Classics, Drama, Econ, Engine, English,
For Lang, Hist, Math, Music, Philo, Physics, Poli Sci, Pre-Law, Psych, Reli Stu, Soc*

BARRY UNIVERSITY (FL) .... barry.edu **1000/1500/21**
Bio, Bus Admin, Drama, Ed, Nurs

BATES COLLEGE (ME) .... bates.edu **1350/2020/30**
*Art, Bio, Chem, Econ, English, For Lang, Geol, Hist, Math, Philo, Physics, Poli Sci, Pre-Law,
Pre-Med/Pre-Dental, Psych, Rel Stu*

BAYLOR UNIVERSITY (TX) .... baylor.edu **1195/1790/26**
*Bus Admin, Chem, Classics, Drama, Ed, Engine, English, Hist, Math,
Music, Nurs, Pre-Law, Pre-Med/Pre-Dental, Reli Stu*

BAY PATH COLLEGE (MA) .... baypath.edu **1010/1515/21**
Bus Admin, Psych

BELHAVEN COLLEGE (MS) .... belhaven.edu **1080/1620/23**
Art, Bus Admin, Comp Sci, Drama, Ed, Music

BELLARMINE UNIVERSITY (KY) .... bellarmine.edu **1100/1650/24**
Bus Admin, Econ, Ed, English, Hist, Math, Nurs, Philo

BELMONT ABBEY COLLEGE (NC) .... belmontabbeycollege.edu **1020/1565/22**
Bus Admin, Poli Sci, Pre-Law, Soc

BELMONT UNIVERSITY (TN) .... belmont.edu **1130/1700/25**
*Art, Bio, Bus Admin, Ed, English, Math, Music, Nurs, Philo, Poli Sci,
Pre-Law, Psych, Reli Stu, Soc*

BELOIT COLLEGE (WI) .... beloit.edu **1250/1875/28**
Anthro, Biochem, Bio, Classics, Drama, Econ, English, For Lang, Hist, Geol, Music, Physics, Psych, Soc

BEMIDJI STATE UNIVERSITY (MN) .... bemidji.msus.edu **1040/1555/22**
Chem, Communic, Comp Sci, Ed, English, Geog, Music

BENEDICTINE COLLEGE (KS) .... benedictine.edu **1030/1545/22**
Astro, Bus Admin, Chem, Comp Sci, Drama, Ed, Music, Philo, Reli Stu, Soc

BENEDICTINE UNIVERSITY (IL) .... ben.edu **1075/1615/23**
Bio, Bus Admin, Comp Sci, Ed, Math, Pre-Med/Pre-Dental

BENNETT COLLEGE (NC) .... bennett.edu **1000/1500/21**
Bus Admin, Comp Sci, Ed, Math, Poli Sci, Pre-Law, Pre-Med/Pre-Dental

BENNINGTON COLLEGE (VT) .... bennington.edu **1200/1800/26**
Drama, English, Music, Pre-Law

BENTLEY COLLEGE (MA) .... bentley.edu **1170/1755/26**
Bus Admin, Econ, English, Math

BEREA COLLEGE (KY) .... berea.edu **1095/1645/24**
Ag, Bio, Bus Admin, Chem, Econ, Ed, English, Home Ec, Music, Nurs, Reli Stu

BERKLEE COLLEGE OF MUSIC (MA) .... berklee.edu **1100/1650/24**
Music

BERRY COLLEGE (GA) .... berry.edu **1150/1725/25**
Bio, Bus Admin, Chem, Ed, English, Forest, Pre-Med/Pre-Dental, Psych

BETHANY COLLEGE (KS) bethany2b.edu **1080/1620/23**
Chem, Ed, Music

BETHANY COLLEGE (WV) .... bethanycollege.edu **1040/1560/22**
Bio, Chem, Communic, Drama, Econ, Ed, English, For Lang, Music,
Physics, Poli Sci, Pre-Law, Pre-Med/Pre-Dental, Psych, Reli Stu

BETHEL COLLEGE (IN) .... bethelcollege.edu **1060/1590/23**
Bio, Drama, Ed, English, Music, Nurs, Philo, Reli Stu

BETHEL COLLEGE (KS) .... bethelks.edu **1100/1650/24**
Ed, Music, Nurs

BETHEL COLLEGE (MN) .... bethel.edu **1160/1740/25**
Biochem, Bio, Bus Admin, Ed, Nurs, Philo, Psych, Reli Stu

BIOLA UNIVERSITY (CA) .... biola.edu **1120/1680/24**
Ed, Philo, Psych, Soc

BIRMINGHAM-SOUTHERN COLLEGE (AL) .... bsc.edu **1185/1775/26**
Art, Bio, Bus Admin, Chem, Drama, Ed, English, Hist, Math, Music, Pre-Law,
Pre-Med/Pre-Dental, Psych, Reli Stu

BLACKBURN COLLEGE (IL) .... blackburn.edu **1040/1560/22**
Bio, Bus Admin, Ed, Pre-Med/Pre-Dental, Psych

BLOOMSBURG UNIVERSITY (PA) .... bloomu.edu **1040/1560/22**
Art, Bus Admin, Chem, Comp Sci, Ed, Geog, Geol, Nurs

BLUFFTON COLLEGE (OH) .... bluffton.edu **1050/1575/22**
Bus Admin, Chem, Ed, Math, Music

BOISE STATE UNIVERSITY (ID) .... boisestate.edu **1060/1600/22**
Art, Bus Admin, Drama, Ed, Engine, Geol, Hist, Math, Nurs

BOSTON ARCHITECTURAL CENTER (MA) .... the-bac.edu **1100/1650/24**
Arch

BOSTON COLLEGE (MA) .... bc.edu **1340/2010/30**
Art, Bio, Bus Admin, Chem, Communic, Comp Sci, Drama, Econ, Ed, English, For Lang,
Hist, Music, Nurs, Philo, Poli Sci, Pre-Law, Pre-Med/Pre-Dental, Reli Stu, Soc

BOSTON CONSERVATORY OF MUSIC (MA) .. bostonconservatory.edu **1050/1575/22**
Music

BOSTON UNIVERSITY (MA) .... bu.edu **1270/1905/28**
Anthro, Art, Art Hist, Astro, Bio, Bus Admin, Chem, Communic, Drama, Econ, Ed, Engine, For
Lang, Geog, Hist, Math, Music, Philo, Physics, Poli Sci, Pre-Law, Pre-Med/Pre-Dental, Psych

BOWDOIN COLLEGE (ME) .... bowdoin.edu **1370/2055/31**
Anthro, Art Hist, Biochem, Bio, Chem, Classics, Econ, English, For Lang, Geol,
Hist, Math, Music, Philo, Poli Sci, Pre-Law, Pre-Med/Pre-Dental, Reli Stu, Soc

BOWLING GREEN STATE UNIVERSITY (OH) .... bgsu.edu **1030/1550/22**
Amer St, Art, Bus Admin, Ed, Geol, Math, Music, Philo, Psych

BRADLEY UNIVERSITY (IL) .... bradley.edu **1175/1660/26**
Art, Bus Admin, Chem, Comp Sci, Econ, Ed, Engine, English, Nurs,
Physics, Poli Sci, Pre-Law

BRANDEIS UNIVERSITY (MA) .... brandeis.edu **1370/2010/30**
Amer St, Anthro, Biochem, Bio, Chem, Comp Sci, Drama, Econ, English, Hist, Math,
Music, Physics, Poli Sci, Pre-Law, Pre-Med/Pre-Dental, Psych

BRENAU UNIVERSITY (GA) .... brenau.edu **1020/1580/22**
Drama, Music

BRESCIA UNIVERSITY (KY) .... brescia.edu **1020/1580/22**
Art, Bus Admin, Ed, English, Reli Stu

BRIAR CLIFF UNIVERSITY (IA) .... briarcliff.edu **1040/1550/22**
Art, Bio, Bus Admin, English, Hist, Math, Music, Nurs

BRIDGEWATER COLLEGE (VA) .... bridgewater.edu **1010/1510/22**
Bus Admin, Hist, Music, Psych, Soc

BRIDGEWATER STATE COLLEGE (MA) .... bridgew.edu **1030/1550/22**
Communic, Ed, Geog, Hist, Poli Sci, Psych, Soc

BRIGHAM YOUNG UNIVERSITY (UT) .... byu.edu **1240/1860/28**
Art, Astro, Bus Admin, Chem, Econ, Ed, Engine, English, For Lang, Geol,
Home Ec, Music, Pre-Law, Pre-Med, Reli Stu, Psych, Zoo

BROWN UNIVERSITY (RI) .... brown.edu **1420/2130/32**
Amer St, Anthro, Art, Art Hist, Bio, Biochem, Chem, Classics, Comp Sci, Econ, Engine, English,
For Lang, Geol, Hist, Philo, Poli Sci, Physics, Pre-Law, Pre-Med/Pre-Dental, Reli Stu, Soc

BRYAN COLLEGE (TN) .... bryan.edu **1100/1650/24**
Communic, Ed, Hist, Music, Reli Stu

BRYANT UNIVERSITY (RI) .... bryant.edu **1120/1680/24**
Bus Admin, Comp Sci, Math

BRYN ATHYN COLL. OF THE NEW CHURCH (PA) newchurch.edu/college **1150/1725/25**
English, Hist, Reli Stu

BRYN MAWR COLLEGE (PA) ....brynmawr.edu **1310/1970/29**
Art, Art Hist, Astro, Bio, Chem, Classics, Econ, English, For Lang,
Geol, Hist, Math, Physics, Pre-Law, Pre-Med/Pre-Dental, Psych, Soc

BUCKNELL UNIVERSITY (PA) .... bucknell.edu **1310/1970/29**
Bio, Bus Admin, Chem, Comp Sci, Drama, Econ, Ed, Engine, English, Hist, Math, Music,
Philo, Pre-Law, Pre-Med/Pre-Dental, Psych, Soc

BUENA VISTA UNIVERSITY (IA)................................... bvu.edu **1050/1590/23**
Bus Admin, Communic, Comp Sci, Ed

BUTLER UNIVERSITY (IN) .... butler.edu **1190/1785/26**
Art, Bus Admin, Chem, Communic, Comp Sci, Drama, Ed, Engine, Music, Pharm,
Pre-Law, Pre-Med/Pre-Dental

CALDWELL COLLEGE (NJ) .... caldwell.edu **1000/1500/21**
Bus Admin, Ed, Psych

CALIFORNIA COLLEGE OF THE ARTS (CA) .... cca.edu **1070/1610/23**
Arch, Art

CALIFORNIA INSTITUTE OF TECHNOLOGY (CA) . caltech.edu **1520/2220/34**
Astro, Bio, Chem, Engine, Geol, Math, Physics, Pre-Med/Pre-Dental

CALIFORNIA INSTITUTE OF THE ARTS (CA) .... calarts.edu **1100/1650/24**
Art, Drama, Music

CALIFORNIA, UNIVERSITY OF, AT
    BERKELEY .... berkeley.edu **1320/1980/29**
    Anthro, Arch, Biochem, Bio, Bot, Bus Admin, Chem, Comp Sci, Engine,
    English, For Lang, Geog, Geol, Hist, Math, Music, Philo, Poli Sci, Physics,
    Pre-Law, Pre-Med/Pre-Dental, Psych, Reli Stu, Soc, Zoo
    DAVIS .... ucdavis.edu **1180/1770/25**
    Ag, Anthro, Art, Bio, Biochem, Bot, Chem, Econ, Engine, English, Geol,
    Hist, Math, Physics, Poli Sci, Pre-Law, Pre-Med/Pre-Dental, Zoo
    IRVINE .... uci.edu **1220/1830/27**
    Anthro, Art, Bio, Chem, Comp Sci, Drama, Engine, English, Math, Physics, Pre-Law,
    Pre-Med/Pre-Dental, Psych
    LOS ANGELES .... ucla.edu **1300/1950/29**
    Anthro, Art Hist, Bio, Biochem, Bus Admin, Chem, Communic, Comp Sci, Drama,
    Econ, Engine, English, For Lang, Hist, Math, Music, Philo, Poli Sci, Pre-Law,
    Pre-Med/Pre-Dental, Psych, Soc
    MERCED .... ucmerced.edu **1150/1725/25**
    Bio, Comp Sci, Econ, Engine, Hist, Psych
    RIVERSIDE .... ucr.edu **1115/1680/24**
    Ag, Art Hist, Biochem, Bio, Bot, Bus Admin, Drama, Ed, Engine, Hist,
    Math, Music, Poli Sci, Pre-Law, Pre-Med/Pre-Dental, Psych
    SAN DIEGO .... ucsd.eu **1270/1910/28**
    Amer St, Biochem, Bio, Chem, Communic, Comp Sci, Drama, Econ, Engine,
    Math, Music, Physics, Poli Sci, Pre-Law, Pre-Med/Pre-Dental, Psych
    SANTA BARBARA...ucsb.edu **1230/1840/27**
    Art, Art Hist, Bio, Bus Admin, Chem, Classics, Comp Sci, Ed, Econ, Engine,
    For Lang, Geog, Geol, Music, Philo, Physics, Poli Sci, Pre-Law,
    Pre-Med/Pre-Dental, Psych, Reli Stu, Soc, Zoo
    SANTA CRUZ ....ucsc.edu **1175/1765/26**
    Amer St, Anthro, Art Hist, Bio, Chem, Comp Sci, Econ, English, Hist,
    Math, Music, Philo, Physics, Pre-Med/Pre-Dental, Psych

CALIFORNIA LUTHERAN UNIVERSITY (CA) .... clunet.edu **1070/1605/23**
Bus Admin, Communic, Ed, Psych

CALIFORNIA MARITIME ACADEMY (CA) .... csum.edu **1030/1540/22**
Bus Admin, Engine

CALIFORNIA POLYTECHNIC U. AT POMONA (CA) csupomona.edu **1020/1530/22**
Ag, Arch, Bio, Bus Admin, Comp Sci, Engine, Physics, Zoo

CALIFORNIA POLYTECHNIC U. AT SAN LUIS OBISPO (CA) calpoly.edu **1230/1850/27**
Ag, Arch, Biochem, Bio, Bus Admin, Comp Sci, Communic, Drama, Engine,
English, Hist, Math, Music, Physics, Psych

CALIFORNIA STATE UNIVERSITY, AT:

BAKERSFIELD .... csubak.edu **1000/1500/21**
Bus Admin, Econ, Ed, English, Geol, Nurs, Psych

CHANNEL ISLANDS (CAMARILLO)(CA) .... csuci.edu **1000/1500/21**
Art, Bio, Bus Admin, Econ, Ed, English, Hist, Math, Pre-Law,
Pre-Med/Pre-Dental, Psych

CHICO .... csuchico.edu **1020/1530/22**
Ag, Anthro, Bio, Chem, Comp Sci, Econ, Geog, Geol, Nurs, Poli Sci, Psych, Reli Stu

DOMINGUEZ HILLS .... csudh.edu **1000/1500/21**
Bus Admin, Chem, Math, Nurs, Philo, Physics, Psych

EAST BAY .... csueb.edu **1000/1500/21**
Art, Bus Admin, Comp Sci, Econ, English, Geol, Hist, Music, Soc

FRESNO .... csufresno.edu **1000/1500/21**
Ag, Amer St, Art, Bus Admin, Chem, Ed, Engine, English, Home Ec,
Music, Nurs, Philo, Soc

FULLERTON .... fullerton.edu **1000/1500/21**
Amer St, Anthro, Bus Admin, Chem, Communic, Engine, English, Hist,
Music, Nurs, Poli Sci, Pre-Med/Pre-Dental, Soc

LONG BEACH .... csulb.edu **1000/1500/21**
Anthro, Art, Art Hist, Chem, Classics, Communic, Drama, Econ, Hist, Music,
Poli Sci, Pre-Law, Psych

LOS ANGELES .... calstatela.edu **1000/1500/21**
Art, Bus Admin, Ed, Engine, Nurs, Psych, Soc

MONTEREY BAY .... scumb.edu **1000/1500/21**
Art, Bio, Comp Sci, Ed, English, Math, Pre-Law, Pre-Med/Pre-Dental

NORTHRIDGE .... csun.edu **1000/1500/21**
Art, Art Hist, Bus Admin, Comp Sci, Communic, Drama, Econ, Engine,
English, Geog, Music, Philo, Physics, Poli Sci, Pre-Law, Psych, Soc

SACRAMENTO .... csus.edu **1000/1500/21**
Anthro, Bus Admin, Communic, Comp Sci, Drama, Ed, Engine, English,
For Lang, Geol, Home Ec, Music, Poli Sci, Psych, Soc

SAN BERNARDINO .... csusb.edu **1000/1500/21**
Art, Bus Admin, Communic, Comp Sci, Ed, Psych, Soc

SAN JOSE .... sjsu.edu **1000/1500/21**
Art, Bus Admin, Chem, Communic, Comp Sci, Math, Music, Nurs,
Physics, Pre-Med/Pre-Dental, Zoo

SAN MARCOS .... csusm.edu **1000/1500/21**
Bus Admin, Chem, Comp Sci, Ed, Hist, Poli Sci, Psych, Soc

STANISLAUS .... csustan.edu **1000/1500/21**
Bus Admin, Comp Sci, Ed, Poli Sci, Psych

CALIFORNIA UNIVERSITY OF PENNSYLVANIA (PA) . cup.edu **1000/1500/21**
Chem, Ed, English, Nurs, Psych

CALVIN COLLEGE (MI) .... calvin.edu **1190/1770/26**
Ed, Engine, English, For Lang, Hist, Nurs, Philo, Physics, Pre-Law

CAMPBELL UNIVERSITY (NC) .... campbell.edu **1040/1550/22**
Bus Admin, English, Hist, Pharm, Poli Sci, Pre-Law

CANISIUS COLLEGE (NY) .... canisius.edu **1140/1710/25**
Bio, Bus Admin, Communic, Comp Sci, Ed, English, Hist, Pre-Med/Pre-Dental, Psych

CAPITAL UNIVERSITY (OH) .... capital.edu **1080/1620/23**
Bus Admin, Chem, Communic, Comp Sci, Ed, Hist, Music, Nurs, Reli Stu

CARLETON COLLEGE (MN) .... carleton.edu **1400/2100/31**
Amer St, Bio, Chem, Classics, Comp Sci, Drama, Econ, English, For Lang, Geol, Hist, Math, Music, Philo, Physics, Poli Sci, Pre-Law, Pre-Med/Pre-Dental, Psych, Reli Stu

CARNEGIE MELLON UNIVERSITY (PA) .... cmu.edu **1360/2040/30**
Arch, Art, Bus Admin, Chem, Comp Sci, Drama, Econ, Engine, English, Hist, Math, Music, Philo, Physics, Pre-Law, Pre-Med/Pre-Dental, Psych

CARROLL COLLEGE (MT) .... carroll.edu **1090/1630/24**
Bio, Chem, Comp Sci, Engine, Hist, Math, Nurs, Philo, Pre-Med/Pre-Dental

CARROLL COLLEGE (WI) .... cc.edu **1070/1605/23**
Art, Chem, Comp Sci, Ed, Nurs, Pre-Med/Pre-Dental, Psych

CARSON-NEWMAN COLLEGE (TN) .... cn.edu **1075/1605/23**
Chem, Ed, English, Hist, Music, Nurs, Pre-Med/Pre-Dental, Psych

CARTHAGE COLLEGE (WI) .... carthage.edu **1090/1630/24**
Bus Admin, For Lang, Geog, Music, Physics, Poli Sci, Psych, Reli Stu

CASE WESTERN RESERVE UNIVERSITY (OH) .... cwru.edu **1330/2000/30**
Amer St, Anthro, Art, Art Hist, Astro, Biochem, Bio, Bus Admin, Chem, Classics, Comp Sci, Drama, Econ, Engine, Hist, Math, Music, Nurs, Physics, Pre-Law, Pre-Med/Pre-Dental, Psych, Reli Stu

CASTLETON STATE COLLEGE (VT) .... castleton.edu **1000/1500/21**
Art, Bus Admin, Communic, Ed, Psych, Soc

CATAWBA COLLEGE (NC) .... catawba.edu **1000/1500/21**
Bus Admin, Comp Sci, Drama, Ed

CATHOLIC UNIVERSITY OF AMERICA (DC) .... cua.edu **1165/1755/26**
Arch, Classics, Drama, Engine, English, For Lang, Music, Nurs, Philo, Physics, Poli Sci, Pre-Law, Psych, Reli Stu, Soc

CEDAR CREST COLLEGE (PA) .... cedarcrest.edu **1080/1620/23**
At, Bio, Nurs, Psych

CEDARVILLE UNIVERSITY (OH) .... cedarville.edu **1160/1730/25**
Bus Admin, Ed, Music, Nurs

CENTENARY COLLEGE OF LOUISIANA (LA) ...... centenary.edu **1160/1740/25**
Art, Bio, Bus Admin, Chem, Ed, English, Geol, Music

CENTRAL ARKANSAS, UNIVERSITY OF (AR) .... uca.edu **1070/1600/23**
Bus Admin, Nurs

CENTRAL COLLEGE (IA) .... central.edu **1108/1660/24**
Bio, Chem, Comp Sci, Ed, English, For Lang, Music, Philo, Reli Stu

CENTRAL CONNECTICUT STATE UNIVERSITY (CT) ccsu.edu **1000/1500/21**
Bus Admin, Ed, Engine, Geog, Hist, Music, Psych, Soc

CENTRAL FLORIDA, UNIVERSITY OF (FL) .... ucf.edu **1190/1780/26**
Bus Admin, Comp Sci, Communic, Drama, Ed, Engine, English, Music, Philo, Physics, Psych

CENTRAL MICHIGAN UNIVERSITY (MI) .... cmich.edu **1050/1570/22**
Bio, Communic, Drama, Ed, English, Home Ec, Geog, Music, Psych

CENTRAL MISSOURI STATE UNIVERSITY (MO) ...... cmsu.edu　**1020/1530/22**
Communic, Econ, Nurs

CENTRAL OKLAHOMA, UNIVERSITY OF (OK).......... ucok.edu　**1000/1500/21**
Bus Admin, Econ, Ed, Music

CENTRAL WASHINGTON UNIVERSITY .... cwu.edu　**1030/1545/22**
Anthro, Bus Admin, Chem, English, Geog, Music, Psych

CENTRE COLLEGE (KY) .... centre.edu　**1240/1860/27**
Art, Biochem, Bio, Chem, Classics, Econ, Ed, English, For Lang, Hist, Philo, Physics, Poli Sci, Pre-Law, Pre-Med/Pre-Dental, Psych, Reli Stu

CHAMINADE UNIVERSITY OF HONOLULU (HI) . chaminade.edu　**1000/1500/21**
Bus Admin, Ed

CHAMPLAIN COLLEGE (VT) .... champlain.edu　**1060/1590/23**
Bus Admin, Comp Sci

CHAPMAN UNIVERSITY (CA) .... chapman.edu　**1210/1820/26**
Art Hist, Bus Admin, Communic, Econ, Music, Pre-Law, Pre-Med/Pre-Dental, Psych

CHARLESTON, COLLEGE OF (SC) .... cofc.edu　**1180/1770/26**
Bio, Bus Admin, Chem, Communic, Drama, Ed, For Lang, Geol, Math, Poli Sci, Pre-Med/Pre-Dental, Psych, Soc

CHARLESTON SOUTHERN UNIVERSITY (SC)....... csuniv.edu　**1060/1590/23**
Comp Sci, Ed, English, Music

CHARLESTON, UNIVERSITY OF (WV) .... uchaswv.edu　**1030/1545/22**
Hist, Nurs

CHATHAM COLLEGE (PA) .... chatham.edu　**1070/1600/23**
Art, Bio, Bus Admin, Communic, English, Hist, Poli Sci, Pre-Law

CHESTNUT HILL COLLEGE (PA) .... chc.edu　**1000/1500/21**
Ed, English, Pre-Law

CHEYNEY UNIVERSITY OF PENNSYLVANIA (PA) .. cheney.edu　**1000/1500/21**
Ed

CHICAGO, UNIVERSITY OF (IL) .... uchicago.edu　**1450/2175/33**
Amer St, Anthro, Art, Art Hist, Biochem, Bio, Chem, Classics, Comp Sci, Econ, English, For Lang, Geog, Geol, Hist, Math, Music, Philo, Physics, Poli Sci, Pre-Law, Pre-Med/Pre-Dental, Psych, Reli Stu, Soc

CHOWAN COLLEGE (NC) .... chowan.edu　**900/1350/20**
Art, Bus Admin, Comp Sci, English

CHRISTIAN BROTHERS UNIVERSITY (TN) .... cbu.edu　**1100/1650/24**
Bus Admin, Ed, Engine, Reli Stu

CHRISTENDOM COLLEGE (VA)....................... christendom.edu　**1220/1830/27**
Hist, Philo, Reli Stu

CHRISTOPHER NEWPORT UNIVERSITY (VA) ....cnu.edu　**1150/1725/25**
Bus Admin, Comp Sci, English, Math, Music, Philo, Physics, Poli Sci

CINCINNATI, UNIVERSITY OF (OH) .... uc.edu **1100/1650/24**
Arch, Art, Bus Admin, Classics, Ed, Engine, English, Hist, Math, Music, Nurs, Pharm, Psych, Soc

CITADEL, THE (SC) .... citadel.edu **1090/1635/24**
Bus Admin, Chem, Ed, Engine, English, Pre-Law

CLAFLIN UNIVERSITY (SC) .... claflin.edu **1000/1500/21**
Ed

CLAREMONT MCKENNA COLLEGE (CA) .... mckenna.edu **1400//2100/31**
Bio, Bus Admin, Chem, Econ, English, Hist, Philo, Poli Sci, Pre-Law,
Pre-Med/Pre-Dental, Psych, Reli Stu

CLARK ATLANTA UNIVERSITY (GA) .... cau.edu **1000/1500/21**
Bus Admin, Comp Sci, Ed, Math, Physics

CLARK UNIVERSITY (MA) .... clarku.edu **1240/1860/28**
Bio, Biochem, Bus Admin, Chem, Communic, Econ, English, For Lang,
Geog, Music, Physics, Poli Sci, Pre-Law, Pre-Med/Pre-Dental, Psych

CLARKE COLLEGE (IA) .... clarke.edu **1100/1650/24**
Art, Art Hist, Bio, Chem, Communic, Comp Sci, Drama, Ed, Music, Nurs, Philo

CLARKSON UNIVERSITY (NY) .... clarkson.edu **1190/1790/26**
Bio, Biochem, Bus Admin, Chem, Comp Sci, Engine, Math, Physics, Pre-Law, Psych, Soc

CLEMSON UNIVERSITY (SC) .... clemson.edu **1195/1785/26**
Ag, Arch, Bio, Bus Admin, Chem, Comp Sci, Econ, Ed, Engine, English,
Forest, For Lang, Physics, Poli Sci, Soc, Zoo

CLEVELAND INSTITUTE OF ART (OH) .... cia.edu **1040/1560/22**
Art

CLEVELAND INSTITUTE OF MUSIC (OH) .... cim.edu **1220/1840/27**
Music

COASTAL CAROLINA UNIVERSITY (SC) .... coastal.edu **1050/1575/22**
Art, Bus Admin, Comp Sci, Ed, Philo

COE COLLEGE (IA) .... coe.edu **1170/1755/26**
Art, Bio, Bus Admin, Chem, Drama, Ed, English, Hist, Music, Nurs, Physics, Psych

COGSWELL POLYTECHNIC COLLEGE (CA) .... cogswell.edu **1000/1500/21**
Comp Sci, Engine

COKER COLLEGE (SC) .... coker.edu **1000/1500/21**
Art, Bus Admin, Drama, Ed, Music, Psych, Soc

COLBY COLLEGE (ME) .... colby.edu **1360/2040/30**
Art, Bio, Chem, Econ, English, For Lang, Math, Music, Philo,
Physics, Poli Sci, Pre-Law, Pre-Med/Pre-Dental, Psych, Soc, Reli Stu

COLBY-SAWYER COLLEGE (NH) .... colby-sawyer.edu **1010/1510/21**
Bio, Ed, English, Nurs, Psych

COLGATE UNIVERSITY (NY) .... colgate.edu **1380/2080/31**
Art, Art Hist, Bio, Chem, Classics, Comp Sci, Drama, Econ, English,
For Lang, Geog, Geol, Hist, Math, Philo, Poli Sci, Pre-Law,
Pre-Med/Pre-Dental, Psych, Reli Stu

COLORADO COLLEGE (CO) ....coloradocollege.edu **1300/1950/29**
Anthro, Art, Art Hist, Bio, Chem, Drama, Econ, English, Geol, Hist,
Math, Philo, Poli Sci, Pre-Law, Pre-Med/Pre-Dental, Psych, Soc

COLORADO, UNIVERSITY OF (CO) .... colorado.edu **1170/1755/25**
Anthro, Astro, Bio, Biochem, Bus Admin, Chem, Communic, Econ, Engine, English,
Hist, Geog, Geol, Math, Music, Nurs, Physics, Pre-Med/Pre-Dental, Psych, Soc

COLORADO, UNIVERSITY OF (COLORADO SPRINGS) . uccs.edu **1060/1590/23**
Anthro, Bus Admin, Chem, Communic, Comp Sci, Ed, Engine, Geog, Nurs, Physics, Psych, Soc

COLORADO, UNIVERSITY OF (DENVER) .... cudenver.edu **1060/1590/23**
Art, Bio, Bus Admin, Comp Sci, Math, Psych

COLORADO SCHOOL OF MINES (CO) .... mines.edu **1240/1860/28**
Comp Sci, Econ, Engine, Geol, Math, Physics, Pre-Med/Pre-Dental

COLORADO STATE UNIVERSITY (CO) .... colostate.edu **1110/1660/24**
Ag, Anthro, Art, Art Hist, Bot, Bus Admin, Comp Sci, Engine, Forest, Geol, Poli Sci, Psych, Zoo

COLUMBIA COLLEGE (IL) .... colum.edu **1000/1500/21**
Art Hist, Communic, Drama

COLUMBIA COLLEGE (MO) ....ccis.edu **1000/1500/21**
Art, Bus Admin

COLUMBIA COLLEGE (SC) .... columbiacollegesc.edu **1020/1530/22**
Bio, Bus Admin, Drama, Ed, Music, Pre-Law, Pre-Med/Pre-Dental, Psych, Reli Stu

COLUMBIA UNIVERSITY (NY) .... columbia.edu **1430/2150/32**
Anthro, Arch, Art Hist, Biochem, Bio, Chem, Classics, Drama, Econ, Engine,
English, For Lang, Geol, Hist, Math, Music, Philo, Physics, Poli Sci, Pre-Law,
Pre-Med/Pre-Dental, Psych, Reli Stu, Soc

CONCORDIA COLLEGE-MOORHEAD (MN) .... cord.edu **1120/1680/24**
Bio, Bus Admin, Chem, Ed, English, For Lang, Math, Music,
Pre-Med/Pre-Dental, Psych, Reli Stu, Soc

CONCORDIA UNIVERSITY (NE)................................... cune.edu **1070/1600/23**
Bus Admin, Ed, Reli Stu

CONCORDIA UNIVERSITY (CA) .... cui.edu **1020/1530/22**
Bus Admin, Music, Reli Stu

CONNECTICUT, UNIVERSITY OF (CT) .... uconn.edu **1185/1775/26**
Ag, Art, Biochem, Bio, Bot, Bus Admin, Communic, Econ, Ed, Engine, Forest, Hist,
Home Ec, Nurs, Poli Sci, Pharm, Pre-Law, Pre-Med/Pre-Dental, Psych, Soc, Zoo

CONNECTICUT COLLEGE (CT) .... conncoll.edu **1300/1900/28**
Anthro, Art, Art Hist, Biochem, Bio, Bot, Chem, Classics, Drama,
Econ, Ed, English, For Lang, Hist, Math, Music, Philo, Physics,
Poli Sci, Pre-Law, Pre-Med/Pre-Dental, Psych, Soc

CONVERSE COLLEGE (SC) .... converse.edu **1090/1635/24**
Art, Chem, Drama, Ed, Music, Poli Sci

THE COOPER UNION (NY) .... cooper.edu **1420/2130/32**
Arch, Art, Engine

CORNELL COLLEGE (IA) .... cornell-iowa.edu **1210/1815/26**
Art, Bio, Econ, Ed, English, Geol, Hist, Philo, Poli Sci, Pre-Law, Pre-Med/Pre-Dental, Psych, Soc

CORNELL UNIVERSITY (NY) .... cornell.edu **1380/2070/31**
Ag, Arch, Art, Astro, Biochem, Bio, Bot, Bus Admin, Chem, Comp Sci, Drama, Econ, Engine, English, Hist, Philo, Physics, Pre-Law, Pre-Med/Pre-Dental, Zoo

CORNISH COLLEGE OF THE ARTS (WA) .... cornish.edu **1100/1650/24**
Art, Drama, Music

COVENANT COLLEGE (GA) .... covenant.edu **1150/1725/25**
Hist, Music, Soc

CREIGHTON UNIVERSITY (NE) .... creighton.edu **1195/1795/26**
Art, Bio, Bus Admin, Chem, Classics, Communic, Drama, Ed, English, Music, Nurs, Pharm, Philo, Physics, Poli Sci, Pre-Law, Pre-Med/Pre-Dental, Psych, Reli Stu

CULVER-STOCKTON COLLEGE (MO) .... culver.edu **1000/1500/21**
Art, Bus Admin

CUMBERLAND COLLEGE (KY) .... cumber.edu **1050/1575/22**
Chem, Ed, Hist, Music, Reli Stu

CURTIS INSTITUTE OF MUSIC (PA) .... curtis.edu **1100/1650/24**
Music

DAEMEN COLLEGE (NY) .... daemen.edu **1000/1500/21**
Bio, Bus Admin, Ed, English, Nurs

DALLAS, UNIVERSITY OF (TX) .... udallas.edu **1210/1815/27**
Art, Bio, Biochem, Classics, Comp Sci, Drama, Econ, Ed, English, For Lang, Hist, Philo, Poli Sci, Pre-Law, Pre-Med/Pre-Dental, Psych

DANA COLLEGE (NE) .... dana.edu **1020/1530/22**
Art, Communic, Drama, Ed, English, Music, Reli Stu

DARTMOUTH COLLEGE (NH) .... dartmouth.edu **1435/2150/32**
Anthro, Art, Bio, Chem, Classics, Comp Sci, Drama, Econ, Engine, English, For Lang, Geog, Geol, Hist, Math, Physics, Poli Sci, Pre-Law, Pre-Med/Pre-Dental, Psych, Reli Stu, Soc

DAVIDSON COLLEGE (NC) .... davidson.edu **1360/2040/31**
Bio, Chem, Drama, Econ, English, Hist, Math, Philo, Poli Sci, Pre-Law, Pre-Med/Pre-Dental, Psych, Reli Stu

DAYTON, UNIVERSITY OF (OH) .... udayton.edu **1170/1755/26**
Bus Admin, Communic, Ed, Engine, Geol, Music, Philo, Poli Sci, Pre-Law, Pre-Med/Pre-Dental, Reli Stu, Soc

DELAWARE STATE UNIVERSITY .... dsc.edu **1000/1500/21**
Hist, Psych

DELAWARE, UNIVERSITY OF (DE) .... udel.edu   **1195/1790/26**
Art, Art Hist, Bio, Bot, Bus Admin, Chem, Communic, Econ, Ed, Engine, English, Hist, Nurs, Poli Sci, Pre-Law, Pre-Med/Pre-Dental, Psych

DELAWARE VALLEY COLLEGE (PA) .... devalcol.edu   **1000/1500/21**
Ag, Bio, Bus Admin, Chem, English, Pre-Med/Pre-Dental

DENISON UNIVERSITY (OH) .... denison.edu   **1210/1810/27**
Art, Art Hist, Bio, Biochem, Comp Sci, Drama, Econ, English, Geol, Hist, Music, Philo, Physics, Poli Sci, Pre-Law, Pre-Med/Pre-Dental, Psych, Soc

DENVER, UNIVERSITY OF (CO) .... du.edu   **1210/1815/27**
Art, Art Hist, Bio, Bus Admin, Chem, Communic, Comp Sci, Engine, English, Geog, Hist, Music, Physics, Pre-Law, Pre-Med/Pre-Dental, Psych, Reli Stu, Soc

DePAUL UNIVERSITY (IL) .... depaul.edu   **1140/1710/25**
Amer St, Bus Admin, Chem, Communic, Comp Sci, Drama, Ed, English, Geog, Hist, Math, Music, Philo, Poli Sci, Pre-Law, Pre-Med/Pre-Dental, Psych, Reli Stu

DePAUW UNIVERSITY (IN) .... depauw.edu   **1235/1855/28**
Art, Biochem, Bio, Chem, Communic, Comp Sci, Econ, English, For Lang, Hist, Music, Philo, Physics, Poli Sci, Pre-Law, Pre-Med/Pre-Dental, Psych, Reli Stu, Soc

DeSALES UNIVERSITY (PA) .... desales.edu   **1095/1640/24**
Bio, Chem, Drama, English, Nurs, Philo, Pre-Med/Pre-Dental, Reli Stu

DETROIT MERCY, UNIVERSITY OF (MI) .... udmercy.edu   **1090/1640/24**
Arch, Engine, Nurs, Philo, Reli Stu

DICKINSON COLLEGE (PA) .... dickinson.edu   **1275/1958/29**
Bio, Comp Sci, Ed, English, For Lang, Hist, Math, Physics, Poli Sci, Pre-Law, Pre-Med/Pre-Dental, Psych, Reli Stu

DILLARD UNIVERSITY (LA) .... dillard.edu   **1030/1540/22**
Bio, Bus Admin, Ed, Nurs, Pre-Med/Pre-Dental

DIXIE STATE COLLEGE (UT) .... dixie.edu   **1000/1500/21**
Nurs

DOANE COLLEGE (NE) .... doane.edu   **1075/1610/23**
Bio, Bus Admin, Ed, English, Music, Philo, Physics, Reli Stu, Soc

DOMINICAN UNIVERSITY OF CALIFORNIA (CA) ... dominican.edu   **1030/1550/22**
Ed, Nurs, Psych

DOMINICAN UNIVERSITY (IL) .... dom.edu   **1070/1600/23**
Bus Admin, Psych

DORDT COLLEGE (IA) .... dordt.edu   **1130/1690/25**
Ag, Art, Ed, Engine, English, Reli Stu

DRAKE UNIVERSITY (IA) .... drake.edu   **1190/1780/26**
Art, Astro, Bio, Bus Admin, Chem, Communic, Drama, Econ, Ed, English, For Lang, Hist, Music, Pharm, Poli Sci, Pre-Law, Soc

DREW UNIVERSITY (NJ) .... drew.edu   **1210/1805/27**
Art, Chem, Classics, Drama, Econ, English, For Lang, Hist, Poli Sci, Pre-Law, Pre-Med/Pre-Dental, Psych, Reli Stu

DREXEL UNIVERSITY (PA) .... drexel.edu **1200/1800/26**
Arch, Comp Sci, Engine

DRURY UNIVERSITY (MO) .... drury.edu **1130/1690/25**
Arch, Bio, Ed, English, Music, Pre-Law, Reli Stu

DUBUQUE, UNIVERSITY OF (IA) .... dbq.edu **1020/1530/22**
Bus Admin, Communic, English, Ed, Psych

DUKE UNIVERSITY (NC) .... duke.edu **1430/2145/32**
*Anthro, Bio, Bot, Chem, Classics, Econ, Engine, English, Hist, Math, Nurs, Philo, Poli Sci,
Pre-Law, Pre-Med/Pre-Dental, Psych, Reli Stu, Soc*

DUQUESNE UNIVERSITY (PA) .... duq.edu **1100/1650/24**
Bio, Bus Admin, Chem, Classics, Communic, Ed, Music, Nurs, Pharm, Pre-Med/Pre-Dental, Reli Stu

D'YOUVILLE COLLEGE (NY) .... dyc.edu **1000/1500/21**
Bio, Ed, English, Nurs, Psych, Soc

EARLHAM COLLEGE (IN) .... earlham.edu **1240/1860/28**
*Anthro, Astro, Bio, Chem, Ed, English, For Lang, Geol, Math, Philo, Pre-Med/Pre-Dental,
Psych, Reli Stu, Soc*

EAST CAROLINA UNIVERSITY (NC) .... ecu.edu **1080/1620/23**
Art, Art Hist, Econ, Ed, Engine, Hist, Math, Music, Nurs, Pre-Med/Pre-Dental, Psych

EAST CENTRAL UNIVERSITY (OK) .... ecok.edu **1000/1500/21**
Ed, English

EAST STROUDSBURG UNIVERSITY (PA) .... esu.edu **1000/1500/21**
Bio, Chem, Comp Sci, Ed, Nurs, Physics

EAST TENNESSEE STATE UNIVERSITY (TN) .... etsu.edu **1030/1540/22**
Art, Bio, Bus Admin, Communic, Econ, English, Hist, Math, Nurs, Philo

EASTERN UNIVERSITY (PA) .... eastern.edu **1090/1630/24**
Bus Admin, Nurs, Soc

EASTERN CONNECTICUT STATE UNIVERSITY (CT) easternct.edu **1040/1560/22**
*Amer St, Art Hist, Bio, Bot, Bus Admin, Communic, Comp Sci, Econ, Ed, Hist, Math,
Poli Sci, Psych, Soc*

EASTERN ILLINOIS UNIVERSITY (IL) .... eiu.edu **1030/1540/22**
Art, Bot, Bus Admin, Chem, Communic, Ed, English, Home Ec, Math, Poli Sci, Psych, Zoo

EASTERN KENTUCKY UNIVERSITY (KY) .... eku.edu **1000/1500/21**
Communic, Ed, Nurs, Poli Sci

EASTERN MENNONITE UNIVERSITY (VA) .... emu.edu **1070/1600/23**
Ed, Nurs, Reli Stu

EASTERN MICHIGAN UNIVERSITY (MI) .... emich.edu **1010/1510/21**
Bus Admin, Chem, Comp Sci, Ed, English, Hist, Music, Nurs, Physics, Poli Sci, Psych

EASTERN NAZARENE COLLEGE (MA) .... enc.edu **1040/1560/22**
Bus Admin, English

EASTERN OREGON UNIVERSITY (OR) .... eou.edu **1000/1500/21**
Bio, Bus Admin, Ed, English, Nurs

EASTERN WASHINGTON UNIVERSITY (WA) .... ewu.edu **1000/1500/21**
Chem, Econ, English, For Lang, Geol, Math, Nurs

ECKERD COLLEGE (FL) .... eckerd.edu **1140/1715/25**
Bio, Bus Admin, Comp Sci, English, For Lang, Pre-Med/Pre-Dental, Reli Stu

EDGEWOOD COLLEGE (WI) .... edgewood.edu **1040/1560/22**
Art, Ed, Music, Nurs

EDINBORO UNIVERSITY OF PENNSYLVANIA (PA) .... edinboro.edu **1000/1500/21**
Art, Art Hist, Ed, English, Geog, Geol, Philo, Physics

ELIZABETHTOWN COLLEGE (PA) .... etown.edu **1140/1710/25**
Bio, Bus Admin, Chem, Ed, English, Music, Pre-Law, Reli Stu

ELMHURST COLLEGE (IL) .... elmhurst.edu **1060/1590/23**
Bio, Chem, Ed, Geog, Music, Nurs, Physics, Pre-Med/Pre-Dental, Psych

ELMIRA COLLEGE (NY) .... elmira.edu **1130/1700/25**
Art, Bus Admin, Ed, Hist, Nurs, Psych

ELMS COLLEGE (MA) .... elms.edu **1000/1500/21**
Ed, Nurs

ELON UNIVERSITY (NC) .... elon.edu **1200/1800/26**
Bio, Bus Admin, Communic, Drama, Ed, Philo, Poli Sci, Psych

EMBRY-RIDDLE AERONAUTICAL UNIVERSITY (FL) emu.edu **1110/1660/24**
Comp Sci, Engine

EMERSON COLLEGE (MA) .... emerson.edu **1220/1830/27**
Communic, Drama, English, Poli Sci, Pre-Law

EMMANUEL COLLEGE (MA) .... emmanuel/edu **1040/1560/22**
Art, Bio

EMORY & HENRY COLLEGE (VA) .... ehc.edu **1020/1530/22**
Bus Admin, For Lang

EMORY UNIVERSITY (GA) .... emory.edu **1370/2055/31**
*Amer St, Anthro, Art Hist, Bio, Bus Admin, Chem, Classics, Econ, English, For Lang,
Hist, Nurs, Poli Sci, Pre-Law, Pre-Med/Pre-Dental, Psych, Reli Stu, Soc*

EMPORIA STATE UNIVERSITY (KS) .... emporia.edu **1040/1560/22**
Art, Chem, Ed, Geol, Nurs

ENDICOTT COLLEGE (MA) .... endicott.edu **1050/1575/22**
Art, Bus Admin, Communic

ERSKINE COLLEGE (SC) .... erskine.edu **1100/1650/24**
Bio, Bus Admin, Ed, Hist, Pre-Med/Pre-Dental

EUREKA COLLEGE (IL) .... eureka.edu **1050/1575/22**
Bus Admin, Comp Sci, Ed, English

EVANSVILLE, UNIVERSITY OF (IN) .... evansville.edu   **1130/1695/25**
Bio, Bus Admin, Chem, Comp Sci, Drama, Ed, English, Math, Music, Nurs, Physics, Pre-Med/Pre-Dental

FAIRFIELD UNIVERSITY (CT) .... fairfield.edu   **1190/1780/26**
Bio, Bus Admin, Communic, Math, Nurs, Physics, Pre-Med/Pre-Dental, Psych

FAIRLEIGH DICKINSON (NJ) .... fdu.edu   **1030/1545/22**
Art, Bus Admin, English, Poli Sci, Pre-Law

FAIRMONT STATE COLLEGE (WV) .... fscwv.edu   **1000/1500/21**
Bus Admin, Ed, Hist, Nurs, Psych

FAULKNER UNIVERSITY (AL) .... faulkner.edu   **1000/1500/21**
Bus Admin

FERRIS STATE UNIVERSITY (MI) .... ferris.edu   **1010/1515/21**
Bus Admin, Comp Sci, Nurs, Pharm

FINDLAY, UNIVERSITY OF (OH) .... findlay.edu   **1070/1600/23**
Bio, Bus Admin, Ed, Math, Pre-Med/Pre-Dental, Psych

FISK UNIVERSITY (TN) .... fisk.edu   **1010/1510/21**
Bus Admin, Math, Physics, Pre-Law, Soc

FITCHBURG STATE COLLEGE (MA) .... fsc.edu   **1020/1530/22**
Bio, Communic, Comp Sci, Ed, Hist, Math, Nurs, Psych

FIVE TOWNS COLLEGE (NY) .... ftc.edu   **1000/1500/21**
Music

FLAGLER COLLEGE (FL) .... flagler.edu   **1100/1650/24**
Bus Admin, Communic, Ed, English, Pre-Law, Psych

FLORIDA, UNIVERSITY OF (FL) .... ufl.edu   **1300/1950/29**
Ag, Anthro, Arch, Art, Astro, Bot, Bus Admin, Classics, Communic, Drama, Engine, English, Forest, For Lang, Geol, Hist, Math, Music, Nurs, Pharm, Philo, Physics, Poli, Sci, Pre-Law, Pre-Med/Pre-Dental, Soc, Zoo

FLORIDA A&M (FL) .... famu/edu   **1000/1500/21**
Arch, Bus Admin, Communic, Ed, Engine, English, Pharm, Physics, Pre-Law, Pre-Med/Pre-Dental

FLORIDA ATLANTIC UNIVERSITY (FL) .... fau.edu   **1050/1575/22**
Bus Admin, Comp Sci, Econ, Ed, Engine, Hist, Math, Nurs, Psych

FLORIDA GULF COAST UNIVERSITY (FL) .... fgcu.edu   **1040/1560/22**
Bus Admin, Comp Sci, Ed, English, Nurs

FLORIDA INSTITUTE OF TECHNOLOGY (FL) .... fit.edu   **1150/1725/25**
Astro, Bio, Biochem, Bus Admin, Chem, Communic, Comp Sci, Engine, Physics, Psych

FLORIDA INTERNATIONAL UNIVERSITY (FL) .... fiu.edu   **1160/1740/25**
Arch, Art, Bio, Bus Admin, Ed, Engine, Geog, Nurs, Poli Sci, Psych, Soc

FLORIDA SOUTHERN COLLEGE (FL) .... flsouthern.edu   **1050/1575/22**
Bio, Chem, Communic, Drama, Ed, Music, Pre-Med/Pre-Dental

FLORIDA STATE UNIVERSITY (FL) .... fsu.edu **1195/1790/26**
Amer St, Art, Art Hist, Bus Admin, Chem, Classics, Comp Sci, Drama, Econ, Ed, English, Hist, Home Ec, Music, Philo, Physics, Pre-Med/Pre-Dental, Psych, Reli Stu

FONTBONNE UNIVERSITY (MO) .... fontbonne.edu **1050/1575/22**
Art, Bus Admin, Communic, Drama, Ed, Math

FORDHAM UNIVERSITY (NY) .... fordham.edu **1200/1800/26**
Bus Admin, Classics, Communic, Drama, English, Philo, Pre-Law, Pre-Med/Pre-Dental, Reli Stu

FORT HAYS STATE UNIVERSITY (KS) .... fhsu.edu **1050/1575/22**
Art, Ed, English, Music, Nurs, Philo, Soc

FORT LEWIS COLLEGE (CO) .... fortlewis.edu **1000/1500/21**
Anthro, Art, Bio, English, Geol, Physics, Pre-Law, Reli Stu

FRAMINGHAM STATE COLLEGE (MA) .... framingham.edu **1060/1590/23**
Bio, Biochem, Bus Admin, Chem, Econ, Ed, Psych

FRANCISCAN UNIVERSITY OF STEUBENVILLE (OH) franuniv.edu **1150/1725/25**
English, Nurs, Philo, Psych, Reli Stu

FRANKLIN COLLEGE (IN) .... franklincollege.edu **1030/1550/22**
Communic, Drama, Ed, Pre-Med

FRANKLIN & MARSHALL COLLEGE (PA) .... fandm.edu **1270/1910/28**
Amer Stu, Astro, Bio, Bus Admin, Chem, Classics, Econ, English, For Lang, Geol, Physics, Poli Sci, Pre-Law, Pre-Med/Pre-Dental, Psych, Soc

FREED-HARDEMAN UNIVERSITY (TN) .... fhu.edu **1080/1620/23**
Bus Admin, Ed, Pre-Med/Pre-Dental, Reli Stu

FRIENDS UNIVERSITY (KS) .... friends.edu **1050/1575/22**
Ed, English, Music

FROSTBURG STATE UNIVERSITY (MD) .... frostburg.edu **1015/1520/21**
Art, Bus Admin, Comp Sci, Ed, Geog, Philo

FURMAN UNIVERSITY (SC) .... furman.edu **1280/1920/29**
Art, Bio, Bus Admin, Chem, Comp Sci, Econ, Geol, Hist, Music, Physics, Poli Sci, Pre-Law, Pre-Med/Pre-Dental, Psych, Reli Stu

GANNON UNIVERSITY (PA) .... gannon.edu **1060/1640/23**
Bio, Bus Admin, Chem, Comp Sci, Ed, Engine, Nurs, Pre-Med/Pre-Dental, Reli Stu

GARDNER-WEBB UNIVERSITY (NC) .... gardner-webb.edu **1040/1560/23**
Bus Admin, Comp Sci, Poli Sci, Pre-Med/Pre-Dental, Soc

GENEVA COLLEGE (PA) .... geneva.edu **1100/1650/24**
Chem, Communic, Ed, Engine, Reli Stu

GEORGETOWN COLLEGE (KY) .... georgetowncollege.edu **1080/1620/23**
Bio, Bus Admin, Chem, Communic, Ed, English, Hist, Pre-Law, Soc

GEORGETOWN UNIVERSITY (DC) .... georgetown.edu **1380/2070/31**
Amer St, Anthro, Art Hist, Biochem, Bio, Bus Admin, Chem, Classics, Econ, English, For Lang, Hist, Nurs, Philo, Physics, Poli Sci, Pre-Law, Pre-Med/Pre-Dental, Psych, Reli Stu, Soc

GEORGE FOX UNIVERSITY (OR) .... georgefox.edu   **1120/1680/24**
Art, Bio, Bus Admin, Ed, Psych, Reli Stu, Soc

GEORGE MASON UNIVERSITY (VA) .... gmu.edu   **1140/1710/25**
*Amer St, Anthro, Art Hist, Bus Admin, Communic, Comp Sci, Drama,
Econ, English, Math, Nurs, Philo, Physics, Poli Sci, Psych, Pre-Law*

GEORGE WASHINGTON UNIVERSITY (DC) .... gwu.edu   **1260/1890/28**
*Amer St, Anthro, Art Hist, Bus Admin, Chem, Comp Sci, Drama, Econ, Engine,
Geog, Hist, Philo, Poli Sci, Pre-Law, Psych, Soc*

GEORGIA, UNIVERSITY OF (GA) .... uga.edu   **1195/1780/26**
*Ag, Art Hist, Astro, Bio, Biochem, Chem, Classics, Communic, Drama, Econ, Ed,
English, For Lang, Forest, Geog, Hist, Home Ec, Music, Pharm, Philo, Poli Sci, Pre-Law,
Pre-Med/Pre-Dental, Psych, Zoo*

GEORGIA INSTITUTE OF TECHNOLOGY (GA) ....gatech.edu   **1330/1990/30**
Arch, Bus Admin, Chem, Comp Sci, Econ, Engine, Hist, Math, Physics, Psych

GEORGIA SOUTHERN UNIVERSITY (GA) .... gasou.edu   **1030/1550/22**
Art, Bus Admin, Ed, Hist, Home Ec, Nurs

GEORGIA SOUTHWESTERN STATE UNIVERSITY (GA) ... gsw.edu   **1000/1500/21**
Ed, English, Nurs

GEORGIA STATE UNIVERSITY (GA) .... gsu.edu   **1060/1590/23**
*Astro, Bio, Bus Admin, Chem, Communic, Comp Sci, Econ, Ed, Math, Music,
Nurs, Philo, Physics, Psych, Soc*

GETTYSBURG COLLEGE (PA) .... gettysburg.edu   **1260/1890/28**
*Bio, Bus Admin, Communic, Drama, Econ, English, Hist, Philo, Physics,
Poli Sci, Pre-Law, Pre-Med/Pre-Dental, Psych, Soc*

GONZAGA UNIVERSITY (WA) .... gonzaga.edu   **1195/1795/26**
*Bio, Bus Admin, Chem, Communic, Ed, Engine, English, Hist, Philo, Poli Sci, Pre-Law,
Pre-Med/Pre-Dental, Reli Stu*

GORDON COLLEGE (MA) .... gordon.edu   **1199/1800/26**
Art, Bio, Ed, English, Music, Philo, Reli Stu, Soc

GOSHEN COLLEGE (IN) .... goshen.edu   **1140/1710/25**
English, Music, Nurs, Physics

GOUCHER COLLEGE (MD) .... goucher.edu   **1170/1755/26**
*Art, Bus Admin, Chem, Comp Sci, Drama, Ed, English, Hist, Poli Sci,
Pre-Law, Pre-Med/Pre-Dental*

GRACELAND UNIVERSITY (IA) .... graceland.edu   **1001/1500/21**
Bus Admin, Ed, Hist, Nurs

GRAMBLING STATE UNIVERSITY (LA) .... gram.edu   **1000/1500/21**
Bus Admin, Ed, Nurs, Poli Sci, Soc

GREAT FALLS, UNIVERSITY OF (MT) .... ugf.edu   **1000/1500/21**
Comp Sci, Ed

GRAND VALLEY STATE UNIVERSITY (MI) .... gvsu.edu **1120/1680/24**
Anthro, Art, Bio, Drama, Ed, Engine, English, For Lang, Math, Pre-Law, Psych

GREEN MOUNTAIN COLLEGE (VT) .... greenmtn.edu **1020/1530/22**
Bus Admin

GREENSBORO COLLEGE (NC) .... gborocollege.edu **1000/1500/21**
Art, Drama, Ed, Reli Stu

GRINNELL COLLEGE (IA) .... grinnell.edu **1340/2010/30**
Anthro, Bio, Chem, Classics, Comp Sci, Econ, English, For Lang, Hist, Math,
Physics, Poli Sci, Pre-Law, Pre-Med/Pre-Dental, Psych, Reli Stu, Soc

GROVE CITY COLLEGE (PA) .... gcc.edu **1270/1900/28**
Bio, Bus Admin, Econ, Ed, Engine, English, Poli Sci

GUILFORD COLLEGE (NC) .... guilford.edu **1130/1700/25**
Art, Bio, Bus Admin, Econ, Ed, English, Geol, Hist, Physics, Poli Sci,
Pre-Law, Pre-Med/Pre-Dental, Psych, Reli Stu

GUSTAVUS ADOLPHUS COLLEGE (MN) .... gustavus.edu **1200/1800/26**
Bio, Bus Admin, Chem, Classics, Ed, English, For Lang, Geol, Hist, Music, Nurs, Physics, Psych, Reli Stu

GWYNEDD-MERCY COLLEGE (PA) .... gmc.edu **1000/1500/21**
Bio, Communic, English, Nurs, Pre-Law

HAMILTON COLLEGE (NY) .... hamilton.edu **1350/2025/30**
Bio, Chem, Comp Sci, Drama, Econ, English, Geol, Hist, Philo, Physics,
Poli Sci, Pre-Law, Pre-Med/Pre-Dental, Reli Stu

HAMLINE UNIVERSITY (MN) .... hamline.edu **1120/1680/24**
Anthro, Art, Bio, Chem, Ed, English, Hist, Physics, Philo, Pre-Law,
Pre-Med/Pre-Dental, Psych, Reli Stu, Soc

HAMPDEN-SYDNEY COLLEGE (VA) .... hsc.edu **1120/1680/24**
Bio, Chem, Classics, Econ, English, Hist, Poli Sci, Pre-Law, Pre-Med/Pre-Dental, Reli Stu

HAMPTON UNIVERSITY (VA) .... hamptonu.edu **1040/1560/22**
Bio, Bus Admin, Chem, Communic, English, Psych, Pre-Law

HANNIBAL-LA GRANGE COLLEGE (MO) .... hlg.edu **1000/1500/21**
Ed, Music

HANOVER COLLEGE (IN) .... hanover.edu **1190/1785/26**
Bus Admin, Classics, Communic, Drama, Econ, Ed, English, Hist, Philo,
Physics, Psych, Soc, Reli Stu

HARDIN-SIMMONS UNIVERSITY (TX) .... hsutx.edu **1020/1530/22**
Bio, Communic, Econ, Ed, Music, Nurs, Reli Stu

HARDING UNIVERSITY (AR) .... harding.edu **1120/1680/24**
Bus Admin, Ed, Music, Nurs, Reli Stu

HARRISBURG UNIVERSITY (PA) .... harrisburg.edu **1100/1650/24**
Bio, Chem, Comp Sci, Geog, Pre-Med/Pre-Dental

HARTFORD, UNIVERSITY OF (CT) .... hartford.edu   **1060/1600/23**
Bus Admin, Communic, Drama, Ed, Engine, Music, Soc

HARTWICK COLLEGE (NY) .... hartwick.edu   **1130/1700/25**
Bus Admin, Drama, Geol, Music, Nurs, Poli Sci, Pre-Law, Soc

HARVARD UNIVERSITY (MA) .... harvard.edu   **1485/2230/33**
*Amer St, Anthro, Art, Art Hist, Astro, Biochem, Bio, Chem, Classics, Comp Sci, Econ,
English, For Lang, Geol, Hist, Math, Music, Philo, Physics, Poli Sci, Pre-Law,
Pre-Med/Pre-Dental, Psych, Soc*

HARVEY MUDD COLLEGE (CA) .... hmc.edu   **1470/2200/33**
Bio, Chem, Comp Sci, Engine, Math, Physics, Pre-Med/Pre-Dental

HASTINGS COLLEGE (NE) .... hastings.edu   **1090/1635/24**
Art, Bus Admin, Communic, Ed, Hist, Music, Physics, Reli Stu

HAVERFORD COLLEGE (PA) .... haverford.edu   **1380/2080/31**
*Art, Astro, Bio, Chem, Classics, Econ, English, For Lang, Hist, Math, Philo,
Physics, Poli Sci, Pre-Law, Pre-Med/Pre-Dental, Psych, Reli Stu*

HAWAII, UNIVERSITY OF (HILO) (HI) .... hilo.hawaii.edu   **1000/1500/21**
Pharm, Psych

HAWAII, UNIVERSITY OF (MANOA) (HI) .... uhm.hawaii.edu   **1100/1650/24**
*Ag, Amer St, Anthro, Art, Astro, Bot, Comp Sci, Drama, English, For Lang,
Hist, Poli Sci, Pre-Law, Soc, Zoo*

HAWAII PACIFIC UNIVERSITY (HI) .... hpu.edu   **1030/1550/22**
Bus Admin, Communic, Comp Sci, Econ, English, Nurs, Pre-Med/Pre-Dental

HEIDELBERG COLLEGE (OH) .... heidelberg.edu   **1050/1575/22**
Bio, Bus Admin, Comp Sci, Econ, Ed, Hist, Music, Poli Sci, Pre-Law, Pre-Med/Pre-Dental

HENDERSON STATE UNIVERSITY (AR) .... hsu.edu   **1030/1545/22**
Art, Bus Admin, Chem, Ed, Nurs

HENDRIX COLLEGE (AR) .... hendrix.edu   **1240/1860/28**
*Bio, Bus Admin, Chem, Comp Sci, Econ, English, Math, Physics, Poli Sci,
Pre-Law, Pre-Med/Pre-Dental, Psych, Reli Stu, Soc*

HIGH POINT UNIVERSITY (NC) .... highpoint.edu   **1030/1550/22**
Chem, Comp Sci, Ed, Math, Reli Stu

HILLSDALE COLLEGE (MI) .... hillsdale.edu   **1190/1790/26**
Amer St, Bio, Bus Admin, Econ, Ed, English, For Lang, Hist, Poli Sci

HIRAM COLLEGE (OH) .... hiram.edu   **1100/1650/24**
Bio, Chem, Comp Sci, Ed, English, Hist, Math, Music, Pre-Law, Pre-Med/Pre-Dental, Reli Stu

HOBART & WILLIAM SMITH COLLEGE (NY) .... hws.edu   **1180/1770/26**
*Amer Stu, Art, Bio, Chem, Econ, English, Hist, Philo, Poli Sci, Pre-Law,
Pre-Med/Pre-Dental, Psych, Soc*

HOFSTRA UNIVERSITY (NY) .... hofstra.edu   **1110/1660/24**
*Anthro, Art, Bus Admin, Communic, Comp Sci, Drama, Ed, English, Music,
Poli Sci, Pre-Law, Pre-Med/Pre-Dental, Psych, Soc*

HOLLINS UNIVERSITY (VA) .... hollins.edu **1140/1710/25**
Art, Art Hist, Chem, Classics, Drama, Econ, English, For Lang, Hist, Poli Sci,
Pre-Law, Pre-Med/Pre-Dental, Soc, Psych

HOLY CROSS, COLLEGE OF THE (MA) .... holycross.edu **1270/1905/28**
Bio, Chem, Classics, Econ, English, For Lang, Hist, Math, Philo, Physics,
Poli Sci, Pre-Law, Pre-Med/Pre-Dental, Psych, Reli Stu, Soc

HOLY NAMES UNIVERSITY (CA) .... hnu.edu **1000/1500/21**
Bio, Ed, Hist, Music, Nurs, Psych, Reli Stu

HOOD COLLEGE (MD) .... hood.edu **1130/1700/25**
Art, Bio, Bus Admin, Ed, English, Hist, Philo, Poli Sci, Pre-Law, Pre-Med/Pre-Dental, Psych

HOPE COLLEGE (MI) .... hope.edu **1190/1790/26**
Bio, Chem, Classics, Drama, English, For Lang, Geol, Music, Nurs,
Physics, Poli Sci, Pre-Law, Pre-Med/Pre-Dental, Psych, Reli Stu

HOUGHTON COLLEGE (NY) .... houghton.edu **1160/1740/25**
Art, Bio, Chem, Ed, English, Hist, Music, Pre-Med/Pre-Dental, Psych, Reli Stu

HOUSTON BAPTIST UNIVERSITY (TX) .... hbu.edu **1040/1560/23**
Bio, Chem, Music, Nurs, Pre-Med/Pre-Dental

HOUSTON, UNIVERSITY OF (TX) .... uh.edu **1060/1590/23**
Arch, Art, Bio, Bus Admin, Chem, Communic, Drama, Ed, Engine, English, Geol, Hist,
Music, Pharm, Physics, Pre-Med/Pre-Dental, Psych

HOWARD UNIVERSITY (DC) .... howard.edu **1060/1590/23**
Arch, Bus Admin, Chem, Classics, Communic, Engine, English, Nurs, Pharm,
Poli Sci, Pre-Law, Pre-Med/Pre-Dental, Soc, Zoo

HUMBOLDT STATE UNIVERSITY (CA) .... humboldt.edu **1060/1590/23**
Anthro, Art, Bio, Bot, Chem, Forest, Geog, Geol, Math, Physics, Zoo

HUNTINGDON COLLEGE (AL) .... huntingdon.edu **1100/1650/24**
Chem, Ed, Music, Pre-Med/Pre-Dental, Reli Stu

HUNTINGTON UNIVERSITY (IN) .... huntcol.edu **1070/1600/23**
Art, Ed, Music

HUSSON COLLEGE (ME) .... husson.edu **1000/1500/21**
Bus Admin, Comp Sci, Ed, Nurs

IDAHO, UNIVERSITY OF (ID) .... uidaho.edu **1100/1650/24**
Ag, Arch, Bus Admin, Communic, Comp Sci, Engine, Forest, Geol, Music, Physics

IDAHO STATE UNIVERSITY (ID) .... isu.edu **1000/1500/21**
Nurs, Pharm

ILLINOIS, UNIVERSITY OF, AT:
      URBANA-CHAMPAIGN .... uiuc.edu **1270/1900/28**
      Ag, Anthro, Arch, Astro, Bus Admin, Chem, Communic, Comp Sci, Drama,
      Ed, Engine,English, Forest, For Lang, Hist, Math, Music, Nurs, Pharm,
      Physics, Poli Sci, Pre-Law, Pre-Med/Pre-Dental, Psych, Soc

ILLINOIS, UNIVERSITY OF, AT: *(Continued)*
  CHICAGO .... uic.edu **1100/1650/24**
  Arch, Art, Art Hist, Bio, Bus Admin, Classics, Econ, Engine, English, For Lang, Hist,
  Math, Music, Nurs, Pharm, Philo, Poli Sci, Pre-law, Pre-Med/Pre-Dental, Psych
  SPRINGFIELD .... uis.edu **1160/1740/25**
  Bus Admin, Comp Sci

ILLINOIS COLLEGE (IL) .... ic.edu **1130/1695/25**
Bio, Bus Admin, Communic, Comp Sci, Econ, Ed, English, For Lang, Hist, Math,
Poli Sci, Pre-Law, Soc

ILLINOIS INSTITUTE OF TECHNOLOGY (IL) .... iit.edu **1240/1860/28**
Arch, Chem, Comp Sci, Engine, English, Math, Music, Physics, Soc

ILLINOIS STATE UNIVERSITY (IL) .... ilstu.edu **1080/1620/24**
Drama, Ed, Poli Sci, Pre-Law

ILLINOIS WESLEYAN UNIVERSITY (IL) .... iwu.edu **1270/1900/28**
Bio, Chem, Drama, Econ, English, Music, Nurs, Philo, Physics, Pre-Law,
Pre-Med/Pre-Dental, Psych

IMMACULATA UNIVERSITY (PA) .... immaculata.edu **1030/1550/22**
Bio, Bus Admin, Ed, Music, Nurs

INDIANA STATE UNIVERSITY (IN) .... indstate.edu **1000/1500/21**
Art, Bus Admin, Communic, Drama, Ed, Geog, Math, Music, Physics

INDIANA UNIVERSITY (IN) .... indiana.edu **1120/1680/24**
Bio, Bus Admin, Chem, Communic, Drama, Ed, For Lang, Geog, Geol, Hist, Music,
Nurs, Pre-Med/Pre-Dental, Psych, Soc, Zoo

INDIANA UNIVERSITY OF PENNSYLVANIA .... iup.edu **1150/1725/25**
Anthro, Art, Art Hist, Biochem, Bio, Bus Admin, Communic, Ed, Geog, Hist, Math,
Music, Nurs, Philo, Physics, Soc

INDIANA U./PURDUE U./INDIANAPOLIS (IN) .... iupui.edu **1000/1500/21**
Communic, Econ, Ed, Engine, English, Hist, Math, Nurs, Soc

INDIANA INSTITUTE OF TECHNOLOGY (IN) ... indianatech.edu **1100/1650/24**
Bus Admin, Comp Sci

INDIANA WESLEYAN UNIVERSITY (IN) .... indwes.edu **1060/1590/23**
Bus Admin, Pre-Med/Pre-Dental, Reli Stu

IONA COLLEGE (NY) .... iona.edu **1070/1605/23**
Bus Admin, Communic, Comp Sci, Ed, Poli Sci

IOWA, UNIVERSITY OF .... uiowa.edu **1160/1740/25**
Amer St, Anthro, Art, Astro, Biochem, Bus Admin, Chem, Communic,
Comp Sci, Drama, Ed, Engine, English, For Lang, Hist, Music, Nurs, Pharm,
Physics, Poli Sci, Pre-Law, Pre-Med/Pre-Dental, Psych, Reli Stu

IOWA STATE UNIVERSITY (IA) .... iastate.edu **1160/1740/25**
Ag, Arch, Art, Bio, Bus Admin, Chem, Comp Sci, Econ, Ed, Engine, English, Forest, Home Ec,
Music, Philo, Physics, Pre-Law, Pre-Med/Pre-Dental, Soc, Zoo

ITHACA COLLEGE (NY)... ithaca.edu **1183/1770/26**
Anthro, Biochem, Bio, Bus Admin, Chem, Communic, Drama, Music, Pre-Med/Pre-Dental

JACKSONVILLE STATE (AL)..jsu.edu **1000/1500/21**
Bio, Comp Sci, Ed, Music, Nurs

JACKSONVILLE UNIVERSITY (FL) .... ju.edu **1040/1560/22**
Art, Bio, Bus Admin, Communic, Comp Sci, Drama, Ed, Music, Nurs, Physics, Pre-Med/Pre-Dental

JAMES MADISON UNIVERSITY (VA).............................. jmu.edu **1170/1755/26**
Anthro, Art, Bus Admin, Communic, Comp Sci, Drama, Ed, For Lang, Hist, Math, Music, Poli Sci, Pre-law, Pre-Med/Pre-Dental, Psych, Soc

JAMESTOWN COLLEGE (ND)..................................... jc.edu **1050/1575/22**
Bus Admin, Comp Sci, Ed, English, Nurs

JOHN BROWN UNIVERSITY (AR) .... jbu.edu **1100/1650/24**
Music, Reli Stu

JOHN CARROLL UNIVERSITY (OH)................................jcu.edu **1120/1680/24**
Bus Admin, Chem, Communic, Econ, English, Hist, Math, Philo, Poli Sci, Psych, Reli Stu, Soc

JOHNS HOPKINS UNIVERSITY (MD) .... jhu.edu **1400/2100/31**
Amer St, Anthro, Art Hist, Bio, Chem, Classics, Comp Sci, Engine, Geog, Hist, Music, Nurs, Philo, Physics, Poli Sci, Pre-Law, Pre-Med/Pre-Dental, Psych, Soc

JOHNSON C. SMITH (NC) .... jcsu.edu **1000/1500/21**
Communic, Comp Sci, Psych, Soc

JOHNSON STATE COLLEGE (VT)............................ jsc.vsc.edu **1000/1500/21**
Art, Drama, Ed, English, Music

JUDSON COLLEGE (AL) .... judson.edu **1030/1540/22**
Art, Bus Admin, Communic, Ed, English, Music, Psych, Reli Stu

JUILLIARD SCHOOL(NY) ....juilliard.edu **1120/1680/24**
Drama, Music

JUNIATA COLLEGE (PA).. juniata.edu **1170/1755/26**
Art, Art Hist, Bio, Bus Admin, Chem, Communic, Comp Sci, Ed, English, Geol, Hist, Math, Pre-Law, Pre-Med/Pre-Dental

KALAMAZOO COLLEGE (MI) .... kzoo.edu **1300/1950/28**
Amer St, Anthro, Bio, Chem, Classics, Econ, English, For Lang, Hist, Music, Physics, Poli Sci, Pre-Law, Pre-Med/Pre-Dental, Psych, Soc

KANSAS CITY ART INSTITUTE (MO) .... kcai.edu **1080/1620/23**
Art

KANSAS, UNIVERSITY OF (KS)................................. ukans.edu **1100/1650/24**
Amer St, Anthro, Arch, Art, Art Hist, Astro, Bio, Bus Admin, Chem, Communic, Drama, Econ, Ed, Engine, For Lang, Geog, Hist, Music, Nurs, Pharm, Physics, Poli Sci, Pre-Med/Pre-Dental, Psych, Zoo

KANSAS STATE UNIVERSITY (KS) .... ksu.edu **1100/1650/24**
Ag, Anthro, Arch, Art, Bio, Biochem, Bus Admin, Communic, Comp Sci, Drama, Ed, Engine, English, For Lang, Geog, Hist, Home Ec, Math, Music, Philo, Physics, Pre-Law, Pre-Med/Pre-Dental, Psych, Soc

KANSAS WESLEYAN UNIVERSITY (KS) .... kwu.edu **1050/1575/22**
Bus Admin, Chem, Comp Sci, Ed, Nurs

KEAN UNIVERSITY (NJ) .... kean.edu **1010/1510/21**
Art, Ed, English, Nurs, Psych, Soc

KEENE STATE COLLEGE (NH) .... keene.edu **1000/1500/21**
Art, Communic, Drama, Ed, English, Geog, Music, Psych, Soc

KENNESAW STATE UNIVERSITY (GA) .... kennesaw.edu **1090/1635/24**
Bus Admin, Chem, Comp Sci, Ed, English, Hist, Math, Nurs, Poli Sci

KENT STATE UNIVERSITY (OH) .... kent.edu **1030/1545/22**
Arch, Art, Chem, Communic, Comp Sci, Ed, English, Music, Nurs, Philo, Physics, Poli Sci

KENTUCKY, UNIVERSITY OF (KY) .... uky.edu **1130/1700/25**
Ag, Arch, Bio, Bus Admin, Classics, Communic, Comp Sci, Ed, Engine, English, Forest, Hist, Music, Nurs, Pharm, Pre-Med/Pre-Dental, Psych, Zoo

KENTUCKY WESLEYAN COLLEGE (KY) .... kwc.edu **1030/1540/22**
Bio, Bus Admin, Chem, Communic, Ed, English, Hist, Music, Pre-Med/Pre-Dental, Psych, Reli Stu

KENYON COLLEGE (OH) .... kenyon.edu **1290/1935/29**
Anthro, Art, Biochem, Bio, Chem, Classics, Drama, Econ, English, Hist, Math, Music, Philo, Physics, Poli Sci, Pre-Law, Pre-Med/Pre-Dental, Psych, Reli Stu, Soc

KETTERING UNIVERSITY (MI) .... kettering.edu **1200/1800/26**
Engine, Physics

KING COLLEGE (TN) .... king.edu **1100/1650/24**
Chem, Ed, English, Nurs, Reli Stu

KING'S COLLEGE (PA) .... kings.edu **1040/1560/22**
Bio, Bus Admin, Chem, Ed, English

KNOX COLLEGE (IL) .... knox.edu **1250/1875/28**
Amer St, Anthro, Art, Bio, Biochem, Chem, Drama, Econ, English, Hist, Math, Music, Physics, Poli Sci, Pre-Law, Pre-Med/Pre-Dental, Soc

KUTZTOWN UNIVERSITY (PA) .... kutztown.edu **1000/1500/21**
Art, Ed, English, Hist, Music, Philo, Poli Sci, Psych

LAFAYETTE COLLEGE (PA) .... lafayette.edu **1300/1950/29**
Anthro, Art, Bio, Bus Admin, Chem, Comp Sci, Econ, Engine, English, Geol, Hist, Math, Poli Sci, Pre-Law, Pre-Med/Pre-Dental, Psych

LAKE FOREST COLLEGE (IL) .... lfc.edu **1200/1800/26**
Art, Art Hist, Bio, Chem, Econ, Ed, English, For Lang, Hist, Music, Philo, Poli Sci,Pre-Law, Pre-Med/Pre-Dental, Psych, Soc

LAMAR UNIVERSITY (TX) .... lamar.edu **1000/1500/21**
Chem, Comp Sci, Ed, Engine, Geol, Nurs, Soc

LAMBUTH UNIVERSITY (TN) .... lambuth.edu **1080/1620/23**
Art, Bio, Chem, Ed, Hist, Reli Stu

LA SALLE UNIVERSITY (PA) ....lasalle.edu **1100/1650/24**
Amer St, Bus Admin, Chem, Communic, Comp Sci, Ed, English, Math, Nurs,
Philo, Pre-Law, Psych, Reli Stu

LASELL COLLEGE (MA) .... lasell.edu **1000/1500/21**
Bus Admin, Ed

LA VERNE, UNIVERSITY OF (CA) .... ulv.edu **1010/1510/21**
Bus Admin, Comp Sci, Ed, Poli Sci, Pre-Law, Psych

LAWRENCE UNIVERSITY (WI) ....lawrence.edu **1300/1950/28**
Anthro, Art, Art Hist, Bio, Chem, Drama, Econ, English, For Lang, Hist, Music,
Philo, Physics, Pre-Law, Pre-Med/Pre-Dental, Reli Stu

LEBANON VALLEY COLLEGE OF PENNSYLVANIA (PA) . lvc.edu **1100/1650/24**
Amer St, Art, Art Hist, Bus Admin, Chem, Math, Music, Nurs, Pre-Law, Pre-Med/Pre-Dental,
Psych, Soc

LEHIGH UNIVERSITY (PA) .... lehigh.edu **1300/1950/29**
Amer St, Arch, Biochem, Bio, Bus Admin, Chem, Comp Sci, Econ, Engine,
English, Geol, Hist, Math, Physics, Poli Sci, Psych

LEMOYNE COLLEGE (NY) .... lemoyne.edu **1130/1695/25**
Bio, Bus Admin, Chem, Communic, Drama, Ed, English, Hist, Psych, Reli Stu

LENOIR-RHYNE COLLEGE (NC) .... lrc.edu **1020/1530/22**
Bus Admin, Comp Sci, Music, Nurs, Soc

LESLEY UNIVERSITY (MA) .... lesley.edu **1000/1500/21**
Art, Bus Admin, Comp Sci, Ed

LETOURNEAU COLLEGE (TX) .... letu.edu **1170/1755/26**
Bus Admin, Comp Sci, Ed, Engine

LEWIS & CLARK COLLEGE (OR) .... lclark.edu **1240/1860/28**
Bio, Biochem, Bus Admin, Chem, Communic, Drama, English, For Lang, Hist,
Music, Philo, Physics, Pre-Med/Pre-Dental, Soc

LEWIS-CLARK STATE COLLEGE (ID) .... lcsc.edu **1000/1500/21**
Art, Bio, Chem, Communic, Ed, English, Math, Nurs

LIBERTY UNIVERSITY (VA) .... liberty.edu **1030/1550/22**
Communic, Comp Sci, Ed, Hist, Nurs, Psych, Reli Stu

LINDENWOOD UNIVERSITY (MO) .... lindenwood.edu **1060/1600/23**
Art, Bus Admin, Communic, Drama, Ed, English, Psych

LINFIELD COLLEGE (OR) ....linfield.edu **1120/1680/24**
Bio, Bus Admin, Chem, Comp Sci, Econ, Ed, For Lang, Hist, Math, Music, Physics

LIPSCOMB UNIVERSITY (TN) .... lipscomb.edu **1120/1680/24**
Bio, Bus Admin, Chem, Ed, Engine, English, Nurs, Poli Sci, Pre-Med/Pre-Dental, Reli Stu

LOCK HAVEN UNIVERSITY (PA) .... lhup.edu **1015/1525/22**
Art, Bio, Chem, Ed, Hist, Music, Poli Sci, Psych

LONG ISLAND UNIVERSITY (BROOKLYN) (NY) .... liu.edu **1000/1500/21**
Chem, Comp Sci, Drama, Ed, English, Pharm, Nurs

LONG ISLAND UNIVERSITY (C.W.POST) (NY) .... liu.edu **1030/1550/22**
Art, Bio, Bus Admin, Chem, Comp Sci, Drama, Ed, English, Math, Music, Psych

LONGWOOD UNIVERSITY (VA) .... lwc.edu **1080/1620/23**
Art, Bus Admin, Drama, Ed, English, Music, Pre-Law, Psych, Soc

LORAS COLLEGE (IA) .... loras.edu **1050/1575/22**
Art, Bio, Bus Admin, Chem, Communic, Comp Sci, Econ, Ed, English, Hist, Philo, Physics,
Pre-Law, Psych, Reli Stu

LOUISIANA COLLEGE (LA) .... lacollege.edu **1050/1575/22**
Ed, English, Hist, Music, Nurs, Pre-Law, Pre-Med/Pre-Dental, Reli Stu

LOUISIANA-LAFAYETTE, UNIVERSITY OF (LA) . louisiana.edu **1080/1620/22**
Arch, Art, Bio, Bus Admin, Chem, Comp Sci, Econ, Ed, Engine, English, Geol,
Math, Music, Nurs, Physics, Pre-Med/Pre-Dental, Zoo

LOUISIANA-MONROE, UNIVERSITY OF (LA) .... ulm.edu **1000/1500/21**
Communic, Ed, Music, Pharm

LOUISIANA STATE UNIVERSITY (LA) .... lsu.edu **1150/1725/25**
Ag, Anthro, Arch, Art, Astro, Biochem, Bot, Chem, Communic, Comp Sci,
Econ, Engine, English, Geog, Geol, Hist, Math, Music, Philo, Physics, Poli Sci,
Pre-Law, Pre-Med/Pre-Dental, Psych, Reli Stu, Soc, Zoo

LOUISIANA TECH. UNIVERSITY (LA) .... latech.edu **1070/1605/23**
Bus Admin, Ed, Geog

LOUISVILLE, UNIVERSITY OF (KY) .... louisville.edu **1100/1650/24**
Art, Bus Admin, Chem, Engine, Music, Nurs, Poli Sci, Soc

LOYOLA COLLEGE (MD) .... loyola.edu **1210/1815/27**
Bio, Bus Admin, Chem, Classics, Communic, Comp Sci, Ed, Engine, For Lang,
Philo, Psych, Pre-Law, Pre-Med/Pre-Dental

LOYOLA MARYMOUNT UNIVERSITY (CA) .... lmu.edu **1150/1725/25**
Amer St, Art, Bus Admin, Classics, Communic, Econ, Engine, English, Hist, Math, Reli Stu, Soc

LOYOLA UNIVERSITY OF CHICAGO (IL) .... luc.edu **1140/1710/25**
Anthro, Art, Bio, Communic, Classics, Drama, Hist, Math, Music, Nurs, Philo,
Physics, Pre-Med/Pre-Dental, Psych, Reli Stu

LOYOLA UNIVERSITY OF NEW ORLEANS (LA) .... loyno.edu **1230/1840/27**
Art, Bio, Bus Admin, Chem, Comp Sci, Communic, Econ, English, Hist,
Music, Philo, Pre-Law, Pre-Med/Pre-Dental, Reli Stu

LUTHER COLLEGE (IA) .... luther.edu **1170/1750/26**
Anthro, Bio, Bus Admin, Drama, Ed, English, Hist, Math, Music, Nurs, Psych, Reli Stu

LYCOMING COLLEGE (PA) .... lycoming.edu **1100/1650/24**
Art, Astro, Bio, Chem, Drama, English, Philo, Pre-Med/Pre-Dental, Psych, Reli Stu

LYNCHBURG COLLEGE (VA) .... lynchburg.edu **1030/1545/22**
Bio, Communic, Comp Sci, Ed, English, Math, Music, Pre-Law, Pre-Med/Pre-Dental, Soc

LYNDON STATE COLLEGE (VT) .... lsc.vsc.edu **1000/1500/21**
Bio, Bus Admin, Communic, English, Psych

LYON COLLEGE (AR) .... lyon.edu **1170/1755/26**
Chem, Drama, Econ, Ed, English, For Lang, Math, Poli Sci, Psych

MACALESTER COLLEGE (MN) .... macalester.edu **1340/2000/30**
*Anthro, Art, Bio, Chem, Classics, Communic, Comp Sci, Drama, Econ, English, For Lang,
Geog, Hist, Math, Philo, Physics, Poli Sci, Pre-Law, Pre-Med/Pre-Dental, Psych, Reli Stu*

MacMURRAY COLLEGE (IL) .... mac.edu **1040/1560/22**
Ed, Nurs

MAINE, UNIVERSITY OF (ME) .... umaine.edu **1090/1630/24**
*Ag, Anthro, Biochem, Bot, Bus Admin, Chem, Communic, Comp Sci, Drama, Econ,
Ed, Engine, Forest, Music, Nurs, Philo, Physics, Psych*

MAINE, UNIVERSITY OF (FARMINGTON) (ME) . umf.maine.edu **1070/1605/23**
Bus Admin, Ed, English, Geog, Psych

MALONE COLLEGE (OH) .... malone.edu **1050/1575/22**
Bus Admin, Math, Music, Nurs

MANCHESTER COLLEGE (IN) .... manchester.edu **1050/1575/22**
Bus Admin, Ed, Hist, Poli Sci, Psych, Soc

MANHATTAN COLLEGE (NY) .... manhattan.edu **1100/1650/24**
Bus Admin, Chem, Comp Sci, Ed, Engine, Math, Poli Sci, Pre-Law, Pre-Med/Pre-Dental, Reli Stu

MANHATTAN SCHOOL OF MUSIC (NY) .... msmnyc.edu **1100/1650/24**
Music

MANHATTANVILLE COLLEGE (NY) .... manhattanville.edu **1070/1600/23**
*Amer St, Art, Art Hist, Bus Admin, Drama, Econ, Ed, English, Hist, Music,
Poli Sci, Psych, Reli Stu, Soc*

MANNES SCHOOL OF MUSIC (NEW SCHOOL U.) (NY) mannes.edu **1100/1650/24**
Music

MANSFIELD UNIVERSITY OF PENNSYLVANIA (PA) mnsfld.edu **1000/1500/21**
Chem, Communic, Ed, English, For Lang, Geog, Hist, Music, Philo, Physics

MARIETTA COLLEGE (OH) .... marietta.edu **1085/1625/23**
Art, Bus Admin, Chem, Communic, Ed, Engine, English, Physics, Pre-Law

MARIST COLLEGE (NY) .... marist.edu **1180/1770/26**
Bio, Bus Admin, Chem, Comp Sci, Communic, Math, Poli Sci, Psych

MARQUETTE UNIVERSITY (WI) .... marquette.edu **1180/1770/26**
*Bio, Bus Admin, Chem, Communic, Comp Sci, Ed, English, Engine, Hist,
Math, Nurs, Philo, Poli Sci, Pre-Law, Pre-Med/Pre-Dental, Psych, Reli Stu*

MARSHALL UNIVERSITY (WV) .... marshall.edu **1050/1575/22**
Bus Admin, Chem, Communic, Econ, Ed, Math, Nurs, Psych

MARY BALDWIN COLLEGE (VA) .... mbc.edu **1060/1590/23**
Art, Bus Admin, Chem, Communic, Drama, English, Hist, Physics, Poli Sci, Psych, Soc

MARYGROVE COLLEGE (MI) .... marygrove.edu **1000/1500/21**
Comp Sci, Ed, English

MARYLAND INSTITUTE-COLLEGE OF ART (MD) ...... mica.edu **1140/1710/25**
Art

MARYLAND, UNIVERSITY OF (MD) .... maryland.edu **1260/1890/27**
Ag, Amer St, Anthro, Arch, Astro, Bot, Bus Admin, Communic, Comp Sci, Econ, Ed, Engine, English, For Lang, Geog, Hist, Music, Pharm, Philo, Physics, Poli Sci, Pre-Law, Soc, Zoo

MARYLAND, UNIVERSITY OF (BALTIMORE COUNTY) (MD) umbc.edu **1230/1840/27**
Amer St, Art, Chem, Classics, Comp Sci, Drama, Econ, Ed, Hist, Math, Nurs, Physics, Poli Sci, Pre-Law

MARYMOUNT MANHATTAN COLLEGE (NY) .... mmm.edu **1060/1590/23**
Art, Communic, Drama, Psych

MARYMOUNT UNIVERSITY (VA) ....marymount.edu **1000/1500/21**
Nurs, Psych

MARYVILLE COLLEGE (TN) .... maryvillecollege.edu **1090/1635/24**
Bio, Chem, Hist, Music, Psych, Reli Stu

MARYVILLE UNIVERSITY-ST. LOUIS (MO) .... maryville.edu **1110/1650/24**
Art, Ed, Nurs

MARY WASHINGTON, UNIVERSITY OF (VA) ....umw.edu **1225/1840/27**
Amer St, Bio, Bus Admin, Chem, Classics, Comp Sci, Econ, English, Geog, Geol, Hist, Math, Poli Sci, Pre-Med/Pre-Dental, Psych

MARYWOOD UNIVERSITY (PA) .... marywood.edu **1030/1540/22**
Art, Ed, Home Ec, Music, Psych, Reli Stu

MASSACHUSETTS, UNIVERSITY OF (MA) .... umass.edu **1130/1700/25**
Anthro, Astro, Bus Admin, Chem, Communic, Comp Sci, Econ, Engine, English, Forest, Geol, Hist, Music, Nurs, Poli Sci, Pre-Law, Pre-Med/Pre-Dental, Psych, Zoo

MASSACHUSETTS, UNIVERSITY OF (BOSTON) (MA) . umb.edu **1030/1550/22**
Amer St, Anthro, Bus Admin, Chem, Classics, English, Geog, Hist, Music, Nurs, Philo, Physics, Poli Sci, Pre-Law, Psych, Soc

MASSACHUSETTS, UNIV. OF (DARTMOUTH) (MA) .... umassd.edu **1070/1605/23**
Art, Bus Admin, Chem, Engine, Nurs, Psych, Soc

MASSACHUSETTS, UNIV. OF (LOWELL) (MA) .... uml.edu **1065/1600/23**
Art, Art Hist, Bus Admin, Chem, Comp Sci, Engine, Math, Music, Nurs, Physics

MASSACHUSETTS COLLEGE OF ART (MA) .... massart.edu **1100/1650/24**
Art

MASSACHUSETTS COLL. OF LIBERAL ARTS (NO. ADAMS)(MA).. mcla.edu **1050/1575/22**
Bus Admin, Communic, Ed, English, Hist, Philo, Physics, Soc

MASSACHUSETTS COLLEGE OF PHARMACY (MA) .... mcp.edu **1040/1560/22**
Pharm

MASSACHUSETTS INSTITUTE OF TECHNOLOGY (MA) ... mit.edu **1480/2215/33**
Anthro, Arch, Astro, Biochem, Bio, Bus Admin, Chem, Comp Sci, Econ, Engine, Geol, Hist, Math, Physics, Poli Sci, Pre-Law, Pre-Med/Pre-Dental

MASSACHUSETTS MARITIME ACADEMY (MA) .... mma.edu **1040/1560/22**
Engine

MASSACHUSETTS STATE COLLEGE SYSTEM (MA) **1020/1530/22**
Ed

MASTER'S COLLEGE, THE (CA) .... masters.edu **1100/1650/24**
Bus Admin, Communic, English, Home Ec, Music, Reli Stu

McDANIEL COLLEGE (MD) .... mcdaniel.edu **1130/1700/25**
Art Hist, Bio, Bio Chem, Bus Admin, Drama, Ed, English, Music, Physics, Poli Sci, Pre-Med/Pre-Dental, Soc

McKENDREE COLLEGE (IL) .... mckendree.edu **1120/1680/24**
Bio, Chem, Comp Sci, Ed, English, Hist, Nurs

McMURRY UNIVERSITY (TX) .... mcm.edu **1000/1500/21**
Bus Admin, Chem, Hist, Nurs, Reli Stu

McPHERSON COLLEGE (KS) .... mcpherson.edu **1000/1500/21**
Art, Drama, Ed, Hist, Music

MEMPHIS COLLEGE OF ART (TN) .... mca.edu **1000/1500/21**
Art

MEMPHIS, UNIVERSITY OF (TN) .... memphis.edu **1070/1600/23**
Art, Communic, Ed, Engine, English, Music, Nurs

MERCER UNIVERSITY (GA) .... mercer.edu **1170/1755/26**
Bus Admin, Chem, Comp Sci, Econ, Ed, Engine, English, Music, Nurs, Pharm, Psych, Reli Stu

MERCY COLLEGE (NY) .... mercy.edu **1000/1500/21**
Ed, Nurs, Psych

MERCYHURST COLLEGE (PA) .... mercyhurst.edu **1080/1620/23**
Anthro, Art, Bus Admin, Chem, Ed, English, Poli Sci, Pre-Law, Reli Stu

MEREDITH COLLEGE (NC) .... meredith.edu **1050/1575/22**
Art, Bio, Bus Admin, Drama, English, Math, Music, Psych, Reli Stu

MERRIMACK COLLEGE (MA) .... merrimack.edu **1080/1620/23**
Bio, Bus Admin, Chem, English, Philo, Poli Sci, Psych, Reli Stu, Soc

MESSIAH COLLEGE (PA) .... messiah.edu **1160/1740/25**
Art, Bio, Bus Admin, Ed, Engine, English, Math, Philo, Reli Stu

MIAMI UNIVERSITY (OH) .... muohio.edu **1210/1810/27**
Arch, Bot, Bus Admin, Comp Sci, Econ, Ed, Engine, English, Geog, Hist, Math, Music, Physics, Poli Sci, Pre-Law, Pre-Med/Pre-Dental, Psych, Zoo

MIAMI, UNIVERSITY OF (FL) .... miami.edu **1250/1875/28**
Arch, Bio, Biochem, Bus Admin, Chem, Communic, Comp Sci, Drama, Ed, English, Hist, Music, Nurs, Pre-Law, Pre-Med/Pre-Dental, Psych

MICHIGAN, UNIVERSITY OF (MI) .... umich.edu **1300/1950/29**
*Amer St, Anthro, Arch, Art, Art Hist, Astro, Bot, Bus Admin, Chem, Classics, Communic,
Comp Sci, Drama, Econ, Ed, Engine, English, Forest, For Lang, Geog, Geol, Hist, Math, Music,
Nurs, Pharm, Philo, Physics, Poli Sci, Pre-Law, Pre-Med/Pre-Dental, Psych, Soc, Zoo*

MICHIGAN, UNIVERSITY OF (DEARBORN) (MI) .... umd.umich.edu **1090/1635/24**
*Bus Admin, Chem, Comp Sci, Econ, Engine, Hist, Math, Philo, Physics, Pre-Law,
Pre-Med/Pre-Dental*

MICHIGAN STATE UNIVERSITY (MI) .... msu.edu **1140/1710/25**
*Ag, Anthro, Biochem, Bio, Bot, Bus Admin, Chem, Communic, Econ, Ed, Engine, English,
Forest, Geog, Geol, Hist, Home Ec, Math, Music, Nurs, Philo, Physics, Poli Sci, Pre-Law,
Pre-Med/Pre-Dental, Psych, Soc, Zoo*

MICHIGAN TECHNOLOGICAL UNIVERSITY (MI) .... mtu.edu **1170/1755/26**
Bus Admin, Comp Sci, Engine, Forest, Geol, Math, Physics

MIDDLEBURY COLLEGE (VT) .... middlebury.edu **1400/2100/31**
*Art, Art Hist, Bio, Classics, Chem, Comp Sci, Drama, Econ, English, For Lang, Geog,
Hist, Math, Physics, Poli Sci, Pre-Law, Pre-Med/Pre-Dental, Reli Stu*

MIDDLE TENNESSEE STATE UNIVERSITY (TN) .... mtsu.edu **1050/1575/22**
Bio, Bus Admin, Chem, Ed, English, Hist, Math, Music, Nurs, Psych

MIDWESTERN STATE UNIVERSITY (TX) .... mwsu.edu **1000/1500/21**
Art, Comp Sci, Math, Nurs

MILLERSVILLE UNIV. OF PENNSYLVANIA (PA) ..... millersville.edu **1060/1590/23**
*Art, Bio, Bus Admin, Chem, Comp Sci, Econ, Ed, English, Hist, Math,
Poli Sci, Physics, Pre-Law, Psych, Soc*

MILLIGAN COLLEGE (TN) .... milligan.edu **1070/1600/23**
Bio, Bus Admin, Chem, Communic, Ed, Hist, Music, Nurs, Philo, Psych, Reli Stu

MILLIKIN UNIVERSITY (IL) .... millikin.edu **1080/1620/23**
Art, Drama, Ed, English, Music, Nurs

MILLS COLLEGE (CA) .... mills.edu **1140/1710/25**
Art, Art Hist, Communic, Ed, English, For Lang, Music, Psych

MILLSAPS COLLEGE (MS) .... millsaps.edu **1185/1775/26**
*Bio, Bus Admin, Chem, Classics, Comp Sci, Drama, Ed, English, Geol, Hist,
Math, Music, Poli Sci, Pre-Law, Pre-Med/Pre-Dental*

MILWAUKEE SCHOOL OF ENGINEERING (WI) .... msoe.edu **1185/1770/26**
Arch, Bus Admin, Engine, Nurs

MINNESOTA STATE UNIVERSITY (MANKATO) (MN) ... mnsu.edu **1020/1530/22**
Astro, Comp Sci, Drama, Engine

MINNESOTA STATE UNIVERSITY (MOORHEAD) (MN) mnstate.edu **1040/1560/22**
Anthro, Art, Bio, Ed, Math, Music, Physics, Psych

MINNESOTA, UNIVERSITY OF (MN) .... umn.edu **1200/1800/26**
*Ag, Amer St, Arch, Art Hist, Biochem, Bus Admin, Classics, Communic, Drama, Econ, Ed,
Engine, English, For Lang, Forest, Geog, Geol, Hist, Music, Nurs, Pharm, Philo, Poli Sci,
Pre-Law, Psych, Soc*

MINNESOTA, UNIVERSITY OF (DULUTH) (MN) ...... d.umn.edu **1070/1600/23**
Art, Bio, Communic, Comp Sci, Ed, Engine, Geol, Music, Pharm, Psych, Soc

MINNESOTA, UNIVERSITY OF (MORRIS) (MN) .... mrs.umn.edu **1140/1710/25**
Art, Bio, Chem, Comp Sci, Ed, English, For Lang, Geol, Hist, Philo, Poli Sci,
Pre-Law, Pre Med/Pre-Dental, Psych

COLLEGE MISERICORDIA (PA) .... miseri.edu **1010/1515/21**
Biochem, Bio, Bus Admin, Chem, Communic, Ed, English, Hist, Nurs

MISSISSIPPI COLLEGE (MS) ....mc.edu **1095/1645/24**
Art, Bus Admin, Comp Sci, Ed, Music, Nurs, Reli Stu

MISSISSIPPI STATE UNIVERSITY (MS) .... msstate.edu **1090/1635/24**
Ag, Arch, Art, Biochem, Bus Admin, Comp Sci, Ed, Engine, Forest, Math,
Physics, Pre-Med/Pre-Dental, Soc

MISSISSIPPI, UNIVERSITY OF (MS) .... olemiss.edu **1090/1635/24**
Bus Admin, Classics, Communic, Econ, Ed, Engine, English, Hist, Pharm,
Physics, Pre-Law, Pre-Med/Pre-Dental

MISSISSIPPI UNIVERSITY FOR WOMEN (MS) .... muw.edu **1090/1635/24**
Bus Admin, Communic, Ed, English, Nurs

MISSOURI BAPTIST UNIVERSITY (MO)................... mobap.edu **1000/1500/21**
Ed, Music

MISSOURI SOUTHERN STATE UNIVERSITY (MO) ..... mssc.edu **1030/1545/22**
Art, Bio, Bus Admin, Communic, Ed, English, Nurs

MISSOURI STATE UNIVERSITY (MO) .... missouristate.edu **1095/1645/24**
Classics, Comp Sci, Drama, Ed, Math, Poli Sci, Pre-Law, Soc

MISSOURI, UNIVERSITY OF (MO) .... missouri.edu **1165/1750/25**
Ag, Art Hist, Biochem, Bus Admin, Classics, Communic, Econ, Ed, Engine, English,
Forest, Hist, Music, Nurs, Philo, Poli Sci, Pre-Law, Pre-Med/Pre-Dental, Psych

MISSOURI, UNIVERSITY OF (KANSAS CITY) (MO) ...umkc.edu **1100/1650/24**
Art, Art Hist, Bio, Bus Admin, Chem, Communic, Comp Sci, Drama, Econ,
Ed, English, Hist, Music, Pharm, Psych

MISSOURI, UNIVERSITY OF (ROLLA) (MO) .... umr.edu **1230/1840/27**
Bio, Chem, Comp Sci, Engine, Hist, Physics

MISSOURI, UNIVERSITY OF (ST. LOUIS) .... umsl.edu **1080/1620/23**
Bus Admin, Chem, Communic, Ed, Nurs, Philo, Poli Sci, Psych

MOBILE, UNIVERSITY OF (AL) .... umobile.edu **1050/1575/23**
Bio, Bus Admin, Comp Sci, Ed, Music, Nurs

MOLLOY COLLEGE (NY) .... molloy.edu **1010/1515/21**
Nurs, Philo, Pre-Law, Psych

MONMOUTH COLLEGE (IL) ....monm.edu **1070/1610/23**
Biochem, Bio, Bus Admin, Chem, Econ, Ed, Hist, Pre-Med/Pre-Dental

MONMOUTH UNIVERSITY (NJ) ....monmouth.edu **1070/1600/23**
Art, Bus Admin, Communic, Comp Sci, Math, Music, Poli Sci

MONTANA TECH OF THE UNIV. OF MONTANA (MT) ... mtech.edu **1100/1650/24**
Bio, Chem, Comp Sci, Engine, Math, Nurs

MONTANA, UNIVERSITY OF (MT) ....umt.edu **1080/1620/23**
Astro, Bot, Bus Admin, Chem, Classics, Communic, Comp Sci, Drama, Ed, English, Forest, Geol, Math, Music, Pharm, Poli Sci, Soc, Zoo

MONTANA STATE UNIVERSITY (BILLINGS) (MT) . msubillings.edu **1000/1500/21**
Art, Bus Admin, Ed, Math, Soc

MONTANA STATE UNIVERSITY (MT) ....montana.edu **1090/1630/24**
Ag, Arch, Art, Bus Admin, Chem, Comp Sci, Econ, Engine, For Lang, Math, Nurs, Physics, Poli Sci

MONTCLAIR STATE (NJ) ....montclair.edu **1030/1550/22**
Art, Bus Admin, Classics, Ed, English, Home Ec, Math, Music, Psych

MONTEVALLO, UNIVERSITY OF (AL) .... montevallo.edu **1020/1530/22**
Art, Communic, Ed, English, Hist, Home Ec, Math, Music

MONTSERRAT COLLEGE OF ART (MA) .... montserrat.edu **1000/1500/21**
Art

MONTREAT COLLEGE (NC)................................... montreat.edu **1050/1570/22**
Bus Admin, Music, Reli Stu

MOORE COLLEGE OF ART (PA) .... moore.edu **1000/1500/21**
Art, Art Hist

MORAVIAN COLLEGE (PA) .... moravian.edu **1130/1700/25**
Art, Biochem, Bus Admin, Communic, Comp Sci, Econ, Ed, Math, Music, Nurs, Pre-Med/Pre-Dental, Psych, Soc

MOREHOUSE COLLEGE (GA) ....morehouse.edu **1080/1620/23**
Bus Admin, Comp Sci, English, Hist, Math, Poli Sci, Reli Stu, Soc

MORGAN STATE UNIVERSITY (MD) .... morgan.edu **1000/1500/21**
Arch, Bio, Engine, English, Hist

MORNINGSIDE COLLEGE (IA) .... morningside.edu **1050/1575/22**
Art, Bio, Bus Admin, Chem, Communic, Ed, Music, Nurs, Pre-Med/Pre-Dental, Psych

MOUNT HOLYOKE COLLEGE (MA) ....mtholyoke.edu **1260/1890/28**
Art Hist, Astro, Biochem, Bio, Chem, Comp Sci, Drama, Econ, English, For Lang, Geol, Hist, Math, Music, Philo, Physics, Poli Sci, Pre-Law, Pre-Med/Pre-Dental, Psych, Reli Stu

MOUNT MERCY COLLEGE (IA) .... mtmercy.edu **1050/1575/22**
Art, Bio, Bus Admin, Ed, English, Nurs, Philo, Soc

MOUNT ST. JOSEPH, COLLEGE OF (OH) .... msj.edu **1020/1530/22**
Art, Bio, Bus Admin, Chem, Comp Sci, Ed, English, Math, Music, Nurs, Pre-Law, Pre-Med/Pre-Dental, Psych, Reli Stu, Soc

MOUNT ST. MARY'S COLLEGE (CA) .... msmc.la.edu **1055/1580/23**
Art, Bio, Bus Admin, Music, Nurs, Reli Stu

MOUNT ST. MARY'S UNIVERSITY (MD) .... msmary.edu **1080/1620/23**
Bus Admin, Ed, Hist, Philo, Poli Sci, Pre-Law, Pre-Med/Pre-Dental

MOUNT ST. MARY COLLEGE (NY) .... msmc.edu **1040/1560/22**
Comp Sci, Ed, Nurs

MOUNT UNION COLLEGE (OH) .... muc.edu **1050/1575/22**
Bus Admin, Comp Sci, Ed, English, Music, Poli Sci

MUHLENBERG COLLEGE (PA) .... muhlenberg.edu **1225/1840/27**
*Amer St, Art, Bio, Biochem, Bus Admin, Chem, Communic, Drama, Econ, English,
Hist, Math, Philo, Poli Sci, Pre-Law, Pre-Med/Pre-Dental, Psych, Reli Stu*

MURRAY STATE UNIVERSITY (KY) .... murraystate.edu **1070/1600/23**
Ag, Art, Bio, Bus Admin, Chem, Communic, Comp Sci, Ed, English, Hist, Math, Music, Nurs

MUSEUM OF FINE ARTS, SCHOOL OF THE (MA) ..... smfa.edu **1070/1600/23**
Art

MUSKINGUM COLLEGE (OH) .... muskingum.edu **1060/1590/23**
*Bus Admin, Chem, Communic, Comp Sci, Ed, English, Geol, Hist, Music,
Physics, Poli Sci, Psych, Reli Stu*

NAZARETH COLLEGE OF ROCHESTER (NY) .... naz.edu **1135/1700/25**
Art, Bio, Bus Admin, Ed, English, For Lang, Math, Music, Nurs, Philo, Reli Stu

NEBRASKA, UNIVERSITY OF (NE) .... unl.edu **1130/1700/25**
*Ag, Arch, Astro, Biochem, Bus Admin, Classics, Communic, Econ, Ed, Engine,
For Lang, Hist, Home Ec, Music, Physics, Pre-Law*

NEBRASKA, UNIVERSITY OF (KEARNEY) (NE) .... unk.edu **1040/1560/22**
Art, Bus Admin, Econ, Ed

NEBRASKA, UNIVERSITY OF (OMAHA) (NE) ...... unomaha.edu **1070/1600/23**
Bus Admin, Comp Sci, Econ, Ed, Poli Sci

NEBRASKA WESLEYAN UNIVERSITY (NE) .... nebrwesleyan.edu **1110/1660/24**
Bio, Chem, Drama, Pre-Med/Pre-Dental, Psych

NEVADA, UNIVERSITY OF, AT:
    LAS VEGAS .... unlv.edu **1020/1530/22**
    *Anthro, Arch, Art, Bus Admin, Drama, Ed, Engine, English, Geol, Hist,
    Music, Nurs, Poli Sci, Psych, Soc*
    RENO .... unr.edu **1060/1590/23**
    *Ag, Biochem, Bus Admin, Communic, Comp Sci, Ed, Engine, English,
    Geol, Home Ec, Music, Nurs, Physics, Poli Sci, Pre-Med/Pre-Dental, Soc*

NEW COLLEGE OF FLORIDA (FL) .... ncf.edu **1330/2000/30**
*Anthro, Bio, Chem, English, Hist, Math, Philo, Physics, Pre-Law,
Pre-Med/Pre-Dental, Psych, Reli Stu, Soc*

NEW ENGLAND CONSERVATORY (MA) newenglandconservatory.edu **1100/1650/24**
Music

NEW HAMPSHIRE, UNIVERSITY OF (NH) .... unh.edu **1115/1675/24**
*Ag, Bio, Bus Admin, Chem, Communic, Comp Sci, Drama, Ed, Engine, English, For Lang,
Forest, Home Ec, Hist, Music, Nurs, Philo, Physics, Pre-Law, Pre-Med/Pre-Dental, Psych, Zoo*

NEW JERSEY, COLLEGE OF (NJ) .... tcnj.edu   **1250/1875/28**
Art, Bus Admin, Chem, Cmp Sci, Ed, Engine, English, Hist, Math,
Nurs, Physics, Pre-Law, Pre-Med/Pre-Dental, Psych, Soc

NEW JERSEY INSTITUTE OF TECHNOLOGY (NJ) .... njit.edu   **1150/1725/25**
Arch, Chem, Comp Sci, Engine, Math

NEWMAN UNIVERSITY (KS) .... newmanu.edu   **1100/1650/24**
Bus Admin, Math, Nurs, Psych, Reli Stu

NEW MEXICO INST. OF MINING & TECHNOLOGY (NM) .. nmt.edu   **1200/1800/26**
Chem, Comp Sci, Engine, Geol, Math, Physics

NEW MEXICO STATE UNIVERSITY (NM) .... nmsu.edu   **1030/1545/22**
Ag, Anthro, Bio, Bus Admin, Chem, Comp Sci, Ed, Engine, English, Geol,
Hist, Home Ec, Math, Music, Nurs, Poli Sci

NEW MEXICO, UNIVERSITY OF (NM) ....unm.edu   **1080/1620/23**
Amer St, Anthro, Art, Bio, Bus Admin, Comp Sci, Drama, Econ, Ed, Engine,
For Lang, Geol, Hist, Nurs, Pharm, Psych, Soc

NEW ORLEANS, UNIVERSITY OF (LA) ....uno.edu   **1050/1575/22**
Bus Admin, Ed, English, Engine, Geog, Hist, Physics, Poli Sci, Soc

NEW SCHOOL UNIV. (EUGENE LANG COLL.) (NY) ..newschool.edu   **1200/1800/26**
Drama, Ed, English, Psych

NEW YORK, CITY UNIVERSITY OF, AT
      BARUCH COLLEGE ....baruch.cuny.edu   **1060/1590/23**
      Bus Admin, Comp Sci, Econ, English, Hist
      BROOKLYN COLLEGE ....brooklyn.cuny.edu   **1010/1515/22**
      Bio, Chem, Classics, Comp Sci, Drama, Ed, Geol, Music, Philo,
      Physics, Pre-Med/Pre-Dental, Psych
      CITY COLLEGE ....ccny.cuny.edu   **1000/1500/21**
      Anthro, Arch, Art Hist, Chem, Ed, Econ, Engine, English, Hist, Math,
      Philo, Physics, Poli Sci, Pre-Law, Pre-Med/Pre-Dental, Soc
      HERBERT LEHMAN COLLEGE ....lehmman.cuny.edu   **1000/1500/21**
      Ed, English, For Lang, Math, Nurs, Philo, Psych, Soc
      HUNTER COLLEGE .... hunter.cuny.edu   **1020/1530/22**
      Anthro, Art, Art Hist, Bio, Chem, Classics, Communic, Comp Sci, Drama, Ed,
      English, For Lang, Geog, Nurs, Poli Sci, Pre-Law, Psych, Soc
      JOHN JAY COLL. OF CRIMINAL JUSTICE .jjay.cuny.edu   **1000/1500/21**
      Poli Sci, Psych
      QUEENS COLLEGE ....qc.edu   **1040/1560/22**
      Amer St, Anthro, Art Hist, Chem, Comp Sci, Econ, Ed, English, Music,
      Philo, Poli Sci, Psych, Soc
      STATEN ISLAND .... csi.cuny.edu   **1050/1575/22**
      Psych

NEW YORK INSTITUTE OF TECHNOLOGY (NY) ....nyit.edu   **1130/1700/25**
Arch, Comp Sci, Engine

NEW YORK, STATE UNIVERSITY OF, AT
      ALBANY.. albany.edu   **1170/1755/26**
      Anthro, Art, Art Hist, Bio, Bus Admin, Chem, Comp Sci, Econ, English, For Lang,
      Geol, Hist, Math, Philo, Physics, Poli Sci, Pre-Law, Pre-Med/Pre-Dental, Psych, Soc

NEW YORK, STATE UNIVERSITY OF, AT *(Continued)*

      BINGHAMTON .... binghamton.edu **1270/1900/28**
*Anthro, Art, Art Hist, Bio, Biochem, Bus Admin, Chem, Comp Sci, Drama,
Econ, English, Engine, For Lang, Geol, Hist, Math, Music, Nurs, Philo,
Physics, Poli Sci, Pre-Law, Pre-Med/Pre-Dental, Psych, Soc*

      BROCKPORT, COLLEGE AT .... brockport.edu **1080/1620/23**
*Bus Admin, Chem, Communic, Comp Sci, Drama, Ed, English, Geol,
Hist, Nurs, Poli Sci, Pre-Law, Psych*

      BUFFALO .... buffalo.edu **1180/1770/26**
*Amer St, Anthro, Arch, Art, Bio, Bus Admin, Chem, Classics, Comp Sci,
Drama, Ed, Engine, English, Geog, Hist, Math, Music, Nurs, Pharm,
Physics, Pre-Law, Pre-Med/Pre-Dental, Psych*

      FREDONIA, COLLEGE AT .... fredonia.edu **1120/1680/24**
Amer St, Art, Bus Admin, Communic, Drama, Ed, English, Hist, Music

      GENESEO, COLLEGE AT .... geneseo.edu **1235/1850/27**
*Bio, Biochem, Bus Admin, Ed, English, Geol, Hist, Math, Music, Philo,
Physics, Pre-Med/Pre-Dental, Soc*

      MARITIME COLLEGE .... sunymaritime.edu **1080/1620/23**
Engine

      NEW PALTZ, COLLEGE AT .... newpaltz.edu **1130/1700/25**
Art Hist, Bus Admin, Communic, Ed, Engine, English, For Lang, Geog, Philo, Psych

      ONEONTA, COLLEGE AT ....oneonta.edu **1080/1620/23**
Econ, Ed, English, Geog, Geol, Hist, Home Ec, Music, Philo, Physics, Pre-Law

      OSWEGO, COLLEGE AT .... oswego.edu **1090/1635/24**
Bio, Bus Admin, Communic, Comp Sci, Ed, English, Hist, Poli Sci, Pre-Law, Psych, Zoo

      PLATTSBURGH, COLLEGE AT .... plattsburgh.edu **1060/1590/23**
Anthro, Art, Bus Admin, Communic, Geol, Hist, Nurs, Psych

      POTSDAM, COLLEGE AT .... potsdam.edu **1060/1590/23**
Anthro, Art, Bus Admin, Comp Sci, Ed, Math, Music, Psych

      PURCHASE, COLLEGE AT .... purchase.edu **1090/1635/24**
*Art, Communic, Drama, English, Hist, Music, Philo, Poli Sci,
Pre-Law, Pre-Med/Pre-Dental, Psych*

      STONY BROOK .... sunysb.edu **1170/1755/26**
*Anthro, Art Hist, Astro, Biochem, Bio, Chem, Comp Sci, Engine, English, For Lang, Geol,
Hist, Music, Philo, Physics, Poli Sci, Pre-Law, Pre-Med/Pre-Dental, Psych, Reli Stu, Soc*

NEW YORK UNIVERSITY (NY) .... nyu.edu **1340/2000/30**
*Anthro, Art, Art Hist, Bus Admin, Classics, Communic, Comp Sci, Drama,
Econ, For Lang, Hist, Math, Music, Nurs, Philo, Physics, Pre-Med/Pre-Dental, Psych*

NIAGARA UNIVERSITY (NY) .... niagara.edu **1055/1580/23**
Bus Admin, Drama, Ed, English, Pre-Law, Reli Stu

NICHOLLS STATE UNIVERSITY (LA) .... nichols.edu **1000/1500/21**
Art, Bio, Bus Admin, Chem, Ed, English, Home Ec, Nurs

NORTH CAROLINA SCHOOL OF THE ARTS (NC) ...... ncarts.edu **1130/1700/25**
Drama, Music

NORTH CAROLINA, UNIVERSITY OF, AT

      ASHEVILLE .... unca.edu **1180/1770/26**
Art, Classics, Ed, Hist, Psych, Soc

      CHAPEL HILL .... unc.edu **1300/1950/29**
*Amer St, Anthro, Art Hist, Bio, Bot, Bus Admin, Chem, Classics, Communic, Drama, Ed,
English, For Lang, Hist, Nurs, Pharm, Poli Sci, Pre-Law, Pre-Med/Pre-Dental, Reli Stu, Soc*

NORTH CAROLINA, UNIVERSITY OF, AT *(Continued)*
    CHARLOTTE .... uncc.edu   **1080/1620/23**
    Bus Admin, Chem, Engine, For Lang, Geog, Nurs, Poli Sci, Pre-Law,
    Pre-Med/Pre-Dental, Psych, Reli Stu
    GREENSBORO .... uncg.edu   **1050/1575/22**
    Art, Bus Admin, Classics, Communic, Comp Sci, Drama, Ed, Hist,
    Home Ec, Music, Nurs, Psych
    PEMBROKE .... uncp.edu   **1000/1500/21**
    Art, Bio, Bus Admin, Communic, Soc
    WILMINGTON .... uncwil.edu   **1100/1650/24**
    Bio, Bus Admin, Chem, English, Geol, Nurs, Pre-Law, Psych, Soc

NORTH CAROLINA STATE UNIVERSITY (NC) .... ncsu.edu   **1200/1800/26**
Ag, Arch, Astro, Bot, Chem, Comp Sci, Econ, Ed, Engine, English, Forest,
Math, Physics, Pre-Law, Psych, Zoo

NORTH CENTRAL COLLEGE (IL) .... noctrl.edu   **1120/1680/24**
Bio, Bus Admin, Chem, Communic, Comp Sci, English, Poli Sci, Pre-Law,
Pre-Med/Pre-Dental, Zoo

NORTH DAKOTA STATE UNIVERSITY (ND) .... ndsu.edu   **1100/1650/24**
Ag, Arch, Chem, Ed, Engine, Home Ec, Math, Pharm

NORTH DAKOTA, UNIVERSITY OF (ND) .... und.edu   **1070/1600/23**
Art, Bio, Bus Admin, Chem, Communic, Comp Sci, Ed, Engine, English, Math, Nurs

NORTH FLORIDA, UNIVERSITY OF (FL) .... unf.edu   **1130/1700/25**
Bus Admin, Communic, Comp Sci, Ed, Math, Music, Nurs

NORTH GEORGIA COLLEGE & STATE UNIV. (GA) .. ngcsu.edu   **1080/1620/23**
Bio, Bus Admin, Ed

NORTH TEXAS, UNIVERSITY OF (TX) .... unt.edu   **1100/1650/24**
Art, Bus Admin, Communic, Music, Poli Sci, Soc

NORTHEASTERN ILLINOIS UNIVERSITY (IL) .... neiu.edu   **1000/1500/21**
Comp Sci, Ed, English, Philo

NORTHEASTERN STATE UNIVERSITY (OK) .... nsuok.edu   **1000/1500/21**
Ed, English, Math, Psych

NORTHEASTERN UNIVERSITY (MA) .... neu.edu   **1220/1830/27**
Arch, Bus Admin, Chem, Communic, Comp Sci, Engine, English, Hist, Pharm, Philo, Psych

NORTHERN ARIZONA (AZ) .... nau.edu   **1050/1575/22**
Astro, Bot, Bus Admin, Ed, Forest, Geol, Nurs, Psych

NORTHERN COLORADO, UNIVERSITY OF .... unco.edu   **1060/1590/23**
Bus Admin, Econ, Ed, English, Hist, Music, Nurs, Soc

NORTHERN ILLINOIS UNIVERSITY (IL) .... niu.edu   **1050/1575/22**
Art, Bio, Biochem, Bus Admin, Chem, Communic, Ed, Engine, Home Ec, Geol,
Math, Nurs, Physics, Philo

NORTHERN IOWA, UNIVERSITY OF (IA) .... uni.edu   **1080/1620/23**
Art, Bus Admin, Ed, Psych

NORTHERN KENTUCKY UNIVERSITY (KY) .... nku.edu **1000/1500/21**
Bus Admin, Chem, Communic, Ed, English

NORTHERN MICHIGAN UNIVERSITY (MI) .... nmu.edu **1070/1600/23**
Art, Bio, Chem, Comp Sci, Econ, Ed, English, Math, Nurs, Physics, Soc

NORTHLAND COLLEGE (WI) ....northland.edu **1130/1695/25**
Bio, Geol, Pre-Law

NORTHWEST MISSOURI STATE UNIVERSITY (MO) .nwmissouri.edu **1055/1580/23**
Ag, Communic

NORTHWESTERN COLLEGE (IA) .... nwciowa.edu **1120/1680/24**
Bio, Chem, Drama, Ed, English, For Lang, Hist, Music, Philo, Physics, Psych, Reli Stu

NORTHWESTERN COLLEGE (MN) .... nwc.edu **1100/1660/24**
Art, Bus Admin, Ed, Music, Psych, Reli Stu

NORTHWESTERN STATE UNIV. OF LOUISIANA (LA) .... nsula.edu **1000/1500/21**
Bus Admin, Comp Sci, Ed, Hist, Math, Music, Nurs, Pharm

NORTHWESTERN UNIVERSITY (IL) ....northwestern.edu **1398/2095/31**
Amer Stu, Anthro, Astro, Chem, Classics, Communic, Drama, Econ, Engine, English, For Lang, Hist, Math, Music, Poli Sci, Pre-Law, Pre-Med/Pre-Dental, Psych, Reli Stu, Soc

NORTHWOOD UNIVERSITY (MI) .... northwood.edu **1000/1500/21**
Bus Admin, Econ

NORWICH UNIVERSITY (VT) .... norwich.edu **1040/1560/22**
Arch, Engine

NOTRE DAME, UNIVERSITY OF (IN) .... nd.edu **1360/2040/31**
Anthro, Arch, Bio, Bus Admin, Chem, Classics, Engine, English, For Lang, Hist, Math, Philo, Physics, Poli Sci, Pre-Med/Pre-Dental, Pre-Law, Psych, Reli Stu, Soc

NOVA SOUTHEASTERN UNIVERSITY (FL) .... nova.edu **1040/1560/22**
Bus Admin, Pharm, Pre-Med/Pre-Dental

NYACK COLLEGE (NY) .... nyackcollege.edu **1000/1500/21**
Bus Admin, Ed, Music, Psych, Reli Stu

OAKLAND CITY UNIVERSITY (IN)..................................oak.edu **1000/1500/21**
Bus Admin, Ed, Music, Psych, Reli Stu

OAKLAND UNIVERSITY (MI) .... oakland.edu **1040/1560/22**
Art Hist, Bus Admin, Chem, Communic, Comp Sci, Econ, Ed, Engine, Math, Physics, Nurs

OBERLIN COLLEGE (OH) ....oberlin.edu **1350/2030/30**
Art Hist, Bio, Chem, Classics, Drama, Econ, English, Geol, Hist, Math, Music, Philo, Physics, Poli Sci, Pre-Law, Pre-Med/Pre-Dental, Reli Stu, Soc

OCCIDENTAL COLLEGE (CA) ....oxy.edu **1200/1800/26**
Bio, Chem, Drama, Econ, English, Ed, Math, Physics, Poli Sci, Pre-Law, Pre-Med/Pre-Dental, Psych, Reli Stu

OGLETHORPE UNIVERSITY (GA) ....ogelthorpe.edu **1150/1725/25**
Bio, Bus Admin, Econ, English, Hist, Poli Sci, Pre-Law, Pre-Med/Pre-Dental

OHIO NORTHERN UNIVERSITY (OH) .... onu.edu **1140/1710/25**
Bio, Biochem, Bus Admin, Chem, Ed, Engine, Math, Nurs, Pharm

OHIO STATE UNIVERSITY (OH) .... osu.edu **1200/1800/26**
Ag, Arch, Art, Astro, Biochem, Bus Admin, Chem, Classics, Communic, Comp Sci, Drama, Econ, Ed, Engine, English, For Lang, Geog, Geol, Hist, Math, Music, Nurs, Pharm, Philo, Physics, Poli Sci, Pre-Law, Pre-Med/Pre-Dental, Psych

OHIO UNIVERSITY (OH) .... ohio.edu **1100/1650/24**
Art, Bot, Bus Admin, Classics, Communic, Comp Sci, Drama, Ed, Engine, English, Hist, Math, Music, Physics, Pre-Law, Psych, Soc, Zoo

OHIO WESLEYAN UNIVERSITY (OH) .... owu.edu **1210/1820/27**
Bio, Bot, Chem, Communic, Econ, Ed, English, Poli Sci, Pre-Med/Pre-Dental, Pre-Law, Psych, Zoo

OKLAHOMA BAPTIST UNIVERSITY (OK) .... okbu.edu **1130/1690/25**
Ed, English, Hist, Music, Nurs, Philo, Psych, Reli Stu

OKLAHOMA CHRISTIAN UNIVERSITY (OK) .... oc.edu **1080/1620/23**
Bio, Comp Sci, Ed, English, Reli Stu

OKLAHOMA CITY UNIVERSITY (OK) .... okcu.edu **1130/1700/25**
Bio, Bus Admin, Communic, Comp Sci, Drama, English, Hist, Music, Nurs, Poli Sci, Pre-Law, Psych, Reli Stu

OKLAHOMA, UNIVERSITY OF (OK) .... ou.edu **1170/1750/26**
Anthro, Arch, Astro, Bot, Bus Admin, Chem, Classics, Communic, Comp Sci, Drama, Econ, Ed, Engine, English, Geog, Geol, Hist, Math, Pharm, Poli Sci, Pre-Law, Psych, Zoo

OKLAHOMA STATE UNIVERSITY (OK) .... okstate.edu **1130/1700/25**
Ag, Arch, Biochem, Bio, Botany, Bus Admin, Drama, Ed, Engine, English, Forest, Geog, Geol, Hist, Home Ec, Math, Music, Physics, Poli Sci, Psych, Soc, Zoo

OLD DOMINION UNIVERSITY (VA) .... odu.edu **1050/1575/22**
Art, Bus Admin, Comp Sci, Econ, Ed, Engine, Hist, Nurs, Physics, Soc

OLIN COLLEGE OF ENGINEERING (MA) .... olin.edu **1490/2220/34**
Engine

OLIVET NAZARENE UNIVERSITY (IL) .... olivet.edu **1100/1650/24**
Ed, Nurs, Reli Stu

ORAL ROBERTS UNIVERSITY (OK) .... oru.edu **1060/1590/23**
Bus Admin, Ed, Music, Nurs, Reli Stu

OREGON, UNIVERSITY OF (OR) .... uoregon.edu **1110/1665/24**
Anthro, Arch, Art, Art Hist, Bio, Bus Admin, Chem, Communic, Comp Sci, Ed, English, For Lang, Geog, Math, Music, Poli Sci, Pre-Law, Pre-Med/Pre-Dental, Psych, Soc

OREGON INSTITUTE OF TECHNOLOGY (OR) .... oit.edu **1040/1560/22**
Bus Admin, Engine

OREGON STATE UNIVERSITY (OR) .... orst.edu **1080/1620/23**
Ag, Biochem, Bot, Econ, Engine, Forest, Geol, Hist, Home Ec, Philo, Physics, Zoo

OTIS ART INSTITUTE (CA) .... otis.edu   **1000/1500/21**
Art

OTTERBEIN COLLEGE (OH) .... otterbein.edu   **1080/1620/23**
Art, Chem, Drama, English, Music, Nurs, Psych

OUACHITA BAPTIST UNIVERSITY (AR) .... obu.edu   **1090/1630/24**
Chem, Ed, Music, Reli Stu

OZARKS, COLLEGE OF THE (MO) .... cofo.edu   **1050/1575/22**
Ag, Art, Bus Admin, Comp Sci, Ed, Hist, Math, Philo, Physics, Psych

PACE UNIVERSITY (NY) .... pace.edu   **1100/1650/24**
Bus Admin, Comp Sci, Drama, English, Nurs, Psych, Soc

PACIFIC LUTHERAN UNIVERSITY (WA) .... plu.edu   **1120/1680/24**
Anthro, Bio, Bus Admin, Comp Sci, Ed, Music, Nurs, Pre-Med/Pre-Dental, Reli Stu

PACIFIC UNIVERSITY (OR) .... pacificu.edu   **1120/1680/24**
Art, Bio, Bus Admin, Comp Sci, English, For Lang, Physics, Pre-Med/Pre-Dental

PACIFIC, UNIVERSITY OF THE (CA) .... uop.edu   **1185/1775/26**
Art, Bus Admin, Chem, Ed, Engine, Music, Pharm

PALM BEACH ATLANTIC UNIVERSITY (FL) .... pba.edu   **1060/1600/23**
Bus Admin, Ed, Pharm, Psych

PARSONS SCHOOL OF DESIGN (NY) .... parsons.edu   **1080/1620/23**
Arch, Art

PAUL SMITH'S COLLEGE (NY) .... paulsmiths.edu   **1000/1500/21**
Forest

PENNSYLVANIA ACAD. OF THE FINE ARTS (PA) ..... pafa.edu   **1000/1500/21**
Art

PENNSYLVANIA, UNIVERSITY OF (PA) .... upenn.edu   **1420/2130/32**
Amer St, Anthro, Art, Art Hist, Astro, Biochem, Bus Admin, Classics, Econ, Engine, English, For Lang, Geol, Hist, Math, Nurs, Philo, Physics, Poli Sci, Pre-Law, Psych, Reli Stu, Soc

PENNSYLVANIA STATE UNIV. (ERIE)(PA) .... pserie.psu.edu   **1080/1620/23**
Bus Admin, English, Math, Physics

PENNSYLVANIA STATE UNIV. (HARRISBURG)(PA)   hbg.psu.edu   **1060/1590/23**
Comp Sci, Engine, Psych

PENNSYLVANIA STATE UNIVERSITY (PA) .... psu.edu   **1210/1815/27**
Ag, Arch, Astro, Biochem, Bot, Bus Admin, Chem, Communic, Comp Sci, Ed, Engine, Forest, Geog, Geol, Home Ec, Nurs, Pre-Med/Pre-Dental, Zoo

PEPPERDINE UNIVERSITY (CA) .... pepperdine.edu   **1240/1860/28**
Art, Bio, Bus Admin, Communic, Comp Sci, For Lang

PERU STATE COLLEGE (NE) .... peru.edu   **1000/1500/21**
Bus Admin, Ed, Music, Psych

PHILADELPHIA BIBLICAL UNIVERSITY (PA)..............pbu.edu **1070/1600/23**
Ed, Music, Reli Stu

PHILADELPHIA UNIVERSITY (PA)...........................philau.edu **1070/1600/23**
Arch, Bus Admin

PIEDMONT COLLEGE (GA)..............................piedmont.edu **1100/1650/24**
Ed, Soc

PINE MANOR COLLEGE (MA).......................................pmc.edu **900/1350/19**
Amer St, Art, Bio, Bus Admin, Communic, Poli Sci, Psych

PITTSBURG STATE UNIVERSITY (KS)....................pittstate.edu **1030/1550/22**
Bus Admin, Ed, Music, Nurs

PITTSBURGH, UNIVERSITY OF (PA)...........................pitt.edu **1220/1830/27**
Anthro, Art Hist, Astro, Biochem, Bus Admin, Chem, Classics, Communic, Comp Sci, Econ, Ed, Engine, English, For Lang, Hist, Math, Nurs, Pharm, Philo, Physics, Poli Sci, Pre-Law, Pre-Med/Pre-Dental, Psych, Reli Stu

PITTSBURGH, UNIV. OF (BRADFORD) (PA)............upb.pitt.edu **1010/1510/22**
Bio, Comp Sci, Nurs, Soc

PITTSBURGH, UNIV. OF (GREENSBURG) (PA)......upg.pitt.edu **1040/1560/22**
Anthro, Bus Admin, English, Hist, Poli Sci, Psych

PITTSBURGH, UNIV. OF (JOHNSTOWN) (PA)........upj.pitt.edu **1040/1560/22**
Bus Admin, Chem, Comp Sci, Ed, Engine, Math

PITZER COLLEGE (CA).......................................pitzer.edu **1300/1950/29**
Anthro, Bio, Chem, English, Hist, Pre-Med/Pre-Dental, Pre-Law, Psych, Soc

PLYMOUTH STATE COLLEGE (NH).....................plymouth.edu **1000/1500/21**
Art, Ed, English

POINT LOMA NAZARENE UNIVERSITY (CA)...........ptloma.edu **1120/1680/24**
Bus Admin, Ed, Home Ec, Music, Nurs

POINT PARK UNIVERSITY (PA)...........................pointpark.edu **1020/1530/22**
Bio, Drama, Ed, English, Psych

POLYTECHNIC UNIVERSITY OF NEW YORK (NY)......poly.edu **1230/1850/27**
Comp Sci, Engine

POMONA COLLEGE (CA).......................................pomona.edu **1450/2175/32**
Amer St, Anthro, Art Hist, Bio, Chem, Communic, Drama, Econ, English, For Lang, Geol, Hist, Math, Music, Philo, Physics, Poli Sci, Pre-Law, Pre-Med/Pre-Dental, Psych, Reli Stu, Soc

PORTLAND STATE UNIVERSITY (OR)........................pdx.edu **1050/1575/22**
Art, Bus Admin, Comp Sci, Engine, English, For Lang, Music, Pre-Law, Psych, Soc

PORTLAND, UNIVERSITY OF (OR)................................up.edu **1160/1740/25**
Bus Admin, Chem, Ed, Engine, Hist, Math, Nurs, Philo, Poli Sci, Reli Stu

PRATT INSTITUTE (NY)...pratt.edu **1140/1710/25**
Arch, Art

PRESBYTERIAN COLLEGE (SC) .... presby.edu **1140/1710/25**
Bio, Bus Admin, English, Hist, Physics, Poli Sci, Pre-Law, Pre-Med/Pre-Dental, Reli Stu

PRESENTATION COLLEGE (SD) .... presentation.edu **1000/1500/21**
Bus Admin, Nurs

PRINCETON UNIVERSITY (NJ) .... princeton.edu **1480/2220/33**
Anthro, Arch, Art Hist, Bio, Biochem, Chem, Classics, Comp Sci, Drama, Econ, Engine, English, For Lang, Geol, Hist, Math, Music, Philo, Physics, Poli Sci, Pre-Law, Pre-Med/Pre-Dental, Psych, Reli Stu, Soc

PRINCIPIA COLLEGE (IL) .... prin.edu/college **1160/1740/25**
Art, Bus Admin, Ed, English, Philo, Pre-Law, Soc

PROVIDENCE COLLEGE (RI) .... providence.edu **1210/1815/27**
Bio, Bus Admin, Chem, Ed, English, Hist, Math, Philo, Poli Sci, Pre-Law, Reli Stu

PUERTO RICO, UNIV. OF (PR) .... upr.clu.edu **1100/1650/24**
Arch, Bus Admin, Ed

PUERTO RICO, UNIV. OF (CAYEY) (PR) ..... wwwcuc.upr.clu.edu **1000/1500/21**
Bio, Bus Admin, Chem, Ed

PUERTO RICO, UNIV. OF (MAYAGUEZ) (PR) .... uprm.edu **1170/1750/26**
Ag, Chem, Engine, For Lang, Math

PUGET SOUND, UNIVERSITY OF (WA) .... ups.edu **1250/1875/28**
Bio, Bus Admin, Chem, Classics, Econ, English, Music, Poli Sci, Pre-Law, Pre-Med/Pre-Dental, Soc

PURDUE UNIVERSITY (IN) .... purdue.edu **1140/1710/25**
Ag, Biochem, Bot, Bus Admin, Chem, Comp Sci, Engine, Forest, Geol, Home Ec, Nurs, Pharm

QUEENS UNIVERSITY OF CHARLOTTE (NC) .... queens.edu **1100/1650/24**
Amer St, Bus Admin, English, Hist, Music, Pre-Law

QUINCY UNIVERSITY (IL) .... quincy.edu **1050/1575/22**
Bus Admin, Hist, Nurs, Reli Stu

QUINNIPIAC UNIVERSITY (CT) .... quinnipiac.edu **1110/1670/24**
Bus Admin, Communic, Comp Sci, Nurs, Psych, Soc

RADFORD UNIVERSITY (VA) .... radford.edu **1000/1500/21**
Bus Admin, Ed, Geog, Pre-Law, Psych

RAMAPO COLLEGE OF NEW JERSEY (NJ) .... ramapo.edu **1180/1770/26**
Amer St, Biochem, Bus Admin, Communic, Comp Sci, Hist, Math, Physics, Poli Sci, Psych

RANDOLPH-MACON COLLEGE (VA) .... rmc.edu **1115/1675/24**
Bio, Classics, Econ, English, For Lang, Pre-Law, Pre-Med/Pre-Dental, Psych

RANDOLPH COLLEGE (VA) .... randolphcollege.edu **1170/1755/26**
Amer St, Art, Bio, Classics, Communic, English, Pre-Law, Pre-Med/Pre-Dental, Psych

REDLANDS, UNIVERSITY OF (CA) .... redlands.edu **1160/1740/25**
Art, Bus Admin, Ed, English, Music, Philo, Poli Sci, Pre-Law, Pre-Med/Pre-Dental

REED COLLEGE (OR) .... reed.edu **1370/1960/31**
*Anthro, Art Hist, Bio, Chem, Classics, Econ, English, For Lang, Hist, Math, Philo,
Physics, Pre-Law, Pre-Med/Pre-Dental, Psych*

REGIS COLLEGE (MA) .... regiscollege.edu **1000/1500/21**
Biochem, Communic, English, Nurs, Poli Sci

REGIS UNIVERSITY (CO) .... regis.edu **1080/1620/23**
*Bus Admin, Communic, Comp Sci, Ed, Hist, Nurs, Philo, Poli Sci,
Pre-Med/Pre-Dental, Psych, Reli Stu, Soc*

REINHARDT COLLEGE (GA) .... reinhardt.edu **1000/1500/21**
Bio, Bus Admin, Communic, Ed

RENSSELAER POLYTECHNIC INSTITUTE (NY) .... rpi.edu **1310/1975/29**
Arch, Bio, Bus Admin, Chem, Comp Sci, Econ, Engine, Geol, Math, Physics

RHODE ISLAND COLLEGE (RI) .... ric.edu **1000/1500/21**
Bio, Econ, Ed, Hist, Math, Music, Nurs, Philo, Psych

RHODE ISLAND SCHOOL OF DESIGN (RI) .... risd.edu **1200/1800/26**
Arch, Art

RHODE ISLAND, UNIVERSITY OF (RI) .... uri.edu **1100/1650/24**
*Anthro, Bio, Communic, Comp Sci, Econ, Engine, English, Geol, Home Ec,
Music, Nurs, Pharm, Poli Sci, Pre-Law, Psych*

RHODES COLLEGE (TN) .... rhodes.edu **1270/1905/28**
*Art, Bio, Bus Admin, Chem, Classics, Econ, English, For Lang, Hist, Math,
Music, Philo, Physics, Poli Sci, Pre-Law, Pre-Med/Pre-Dental, Psych, Reli Stu*

RICE UNIVERSITY (TX) .... rice.edu **1430/2145/32**
*Anthro, Arch, Biochem, Bio, Chem, Comp Sci, Econ, Engine, English, Hist,
Math, Music, Physics, Poli Sci, Pre-Law, Pre-Med/Pre-Dental*

RICHARD STOCKTON COLL. OF NEW JERSEY (NJ) .. stockton.edu **1132/1700/25**
Bus Admin, Chem, Econ, Hist, Math, Philo, Physics, Poli Sci, Pre-Med/Pre-Dental

RICHMOND, UNIVERSITY OF (VA) .... richmond.edu **1300/1950/29**
Bio, Bus Admin, Chem, Comp Sci, English, Hist, Poli Sci, Pre-Law, Pre-Med/Pre-Dental, Reli Stu

RIDER UNIVERSITY (NJ) .... rider.edu **1040/1560/22**
Amer St, Bio, Bus Admin, Chem, Communic, Comp Sci, Ed, Music, Pre-Med/Pre-Dental

RIPON COLLEGE (WI) .... ripon.edu **1120/1680/24**
*Anthro, Bio, Biochem, Bus Admin, Chem, Econ, English, Hist, Poli Sci, Pre-Law,
Pre-Med/Pre-Dental*

ROANOKE COLLEGE (VA) .... roanoke.edu **1130/1700/25**
Art, Bio, Bus Admin, Chem, Comp Sci, English, Hist, Math, Music, Poli Sci, Pre-Law, Psych, Reli Stu, Soc

ROBERT MORRIS UNIVERSITY (PA) .... rmu.edu **1020/1530/22**
Bus Admin, Comp Sci, Communic, Econ, Ed, English

ROCHESTER, UNIVERSITY OF (NY) .... rochester.edu **1340/2010/30**
*Art, Art Hist, Biochem, Bio, Chem, Comp Sci, Econ, Engine, English, For Lang, Geol,
Hist, Math, Music, Nurs, Philo, Physics, Poli Sci, Pre-Law, Pre-Med/Pre-Dental, Psych*

ROCHESTER INSTITUTE OF TECHNOLOGY (NY) .... rit.edu **1230/1840/27**
Bio, Bus Admin, Chem, Comp Sci, Econ, Engine, Math, Physics

ROCKFORD COLLEGE (IL) .... rockford.edu **1070/1605/23**
Art, Bio, Bus Admin, Drama, English, Nurs, Pre-Law, Psych

ROCKHURST UNIVERSITY (MO) .... rockhurst.edu **1140/1710/25**
Bus Admin, Chem, Ed, Math, Nurs, Philo, Psych, Reli Stu

ROCKY MOUNTAIN COLLEGE (MT) .... rocky.edu **1060/1590/22**
Art, Bio, Drama, Ed, English, Music

ROGER WILLIAMS UNIVERSITY (RI) .... rwu.edu **1080/1620/23**
Arch, Bio, Bus Admin, Communic, Ed, Engine, Psych

ROLLINS COLLEGE (FL) .... rollins.edu **1180/1770/26**
Chem, Classics, Drama, Econ, English, Physics, Psych, Reli Stu

ROOSEVELT UNIVERSITY (IL) .... roosevelt.edu **1060/1590/23**
Bus Admin, Communic, Comp Sci, Music, Psych

ROSE-HULMAN INST. OF TECHNOLOGY (IN) . rose-hulman.edu **1310/1980/30**
Chem, Comp Sci, Econ, Engine, Math, Physics

ROSEMONT COLLEGE (PA) .... rosemont.edu **1060/1590/22**
Art, Art Hist, English, For Lang, Hist, Pre-Law, Psych, Soc

ROWAN UNIVERSITY (NJ) .... rowan.edu **1140/1710/25**
*Art, Bio, Bus Admin, Communic, Ed, Engine, Hist, Music, Philo, Physics,
Pre-Law, Pre-Med/Pre-Dental, Reli Stu*

RUSSELL SAGE COLL. (THE SAGE COLLEGES) (NY) ...... sage.edu **1070/1600/23**
Nurs, Psych

RUTGERS UNIVERSITY (NJ) .... rutgers.edu **1220/1830/27**
*Ag, Anthro, Art Hist, Biochem, Bio, Bus Admin, Chem, Drama, Econ, Ed, Engine, English, For Lang,
Hist, Music, Pharm, Philo, Physics, Poli Sci, Pre-Law, Pre-Med/Pre-Dental, Psych, Reli Stu, Soc*

RUTGERS UNIVERSITY (CAMDEN) (NJ) .... rutgers.edu **1120/1680/24**
Comp Sci, English, Hist, Pre-Law, Soc

RUTGERS-NEWARK (NJ) .... rutgers-newark.rutgers.edu **1130/1700/25**
Bus Admin, Nurs, Psych

SACRED HEART UNIVERSITY (CT) .... sacredheart.edu **1070/1600/23**
Biochem, Bus Admin, Psych

SAGINAW VALLEY STATE UNIVERSITY (MI) .... svsu.edu **1000/1500/21**
Ed, Nurs

ST. AMBROSE UNIVERSITY (IA) .... sau.edu **1030/1545/22**
Bus Admin, Communic, Comp Sci, Ed, Hist, Nurs, Philo, Psych, Reli Stu

ST. ANDREWS PRESBYTERIAN COLLEGE (NC) .... sapc.edu **1000/1500/21**
Biochem, Bus Admin, Ed, Philo

ST. ANSELM COLLEGE (NH) .... anselm.edu **1120/1680/24**
Classics, Econ, English, For Lang, Nurs, Pre-Law, Psych, Soc,

ST. BONAVENTURE UNIVERSITY (NY) .... sbu.edu **1060/1590/23**
Bus Admin, Communic, Ed, English, Philo, Poli Sci, Pre-Law, Reli Stu

ST. CATHERINE, COLLEGE OF (MN) .... stkate.edu **1130/1700/25**
Bus Admin, Ed, English, Music, Nurs, Philo, Reli Stu, Soc

ST. CLOUD STATE UNIVERSITY (MN) .... stcloudstate.edu **1020/1530/22**
Communic, Comp Sci, Ed, Philo, Poli Sci, Pre-Law

ST. EDWARD'S UNIVERSITY (TX) .... stedwards.edu **1100/1650/24**
Art, Bus Admin, Communic, Comp Sci, Drama, Ed, English, Psych, Reli Stu

ST. FRANCIS COLLEGE (NY) .... stfranciscollege.edu **1000/1500/21**
Bus Admin, Psych

ST. FRANCIS, UNIVERSITY OF (IN) .... sf.edu **1020/1530/22**
Art, Ed, Nurs, Reli Stu

ST. FRANCIS UNIVERSITY (PA) .... francis.edu **1040/1560/22**
Bio, Chem, Nurs, Philo, Pre-Law, Pre-Med/Pre-Dental, Soc

ST. JOHN FISHER COLLEGE (NY) .... sjfc.edu **1065/1600/23**
Bus Admin, Communic

ST. JOHN'S UNIVERSITY (NY) .... stjohns.edu **1060/1600/23**
Bus Admin, Chem, Pharm, Philo, Poli Sci, Psych, Reli Stu, Soc

SAINT JOHN'S UNIV./COLL. OF SAINT BENEDICT (MN) .... csbsju.edu **1170/1755/26**
Bio, Bus Admin, Chem, Classics, Comp Sci, Econ, Ed, Hist, Nurs, Philo,
Physics, Poli Sci, Pre-Law, Pre-Med/Pre-Dental, Reli Stu

SAINT JOSEPH COLLEGE (CT) .... sjc.edu **1000/1500/21**
Ed

ST. JOSEPH'S COLLEGE (IN) .... saintjoe.edu **1020/1530/22**
Bus Admin, Ed, Psych

ST. JOSEPH'S COLLEGE (ME) .... sjcme.edu **1000/1500/21**
Ed, Nurs

ST. JOSEPH'S COLLEGE (NY) .... sjcny.edu **1060/1600/23**
Bus Admin, Comp Sci, Ed, Hist, Math, Psych

SAINT JOSEPH'S UNIVERSITY (PA) .... sju.edu **1220/1830/27**
Bus Admin, English, Hist, Poli Sci, Pre-Med/Pre-Dental, Reli Stu

ST. LAWRENCE UNIVERSITY (NY) .... stlawu.edu **1190/1785/26**
Econ, English, Geol, Poli Sci, Pre-Law, Psych, Soc

ST. LOUIS COLLEGE OF PHARMACY (MO) .... stlcop.edu **1180/1770/26**
Pharm, Pre-Med/Pre-Dental

SAINT LOUIS UNIVERSITY (MO) .... slu.edu **1195/1795/26**
Bio, Bus Admin, Chem, Communic, Comp Sci, Ed, Engine, English, Math, Nurs,
Philo, Pre-Law, Pre-Med/Pre-Dental, Psych, Reli Stu

SAINT MARTIN'S COLLEGE (WA) .... stmartin.edu **1000/1500/21**
Bus Admin, Ed, Engine, Psych

SAINT MARY, COLLEGE OF (NE) .... csm.edu **1020/1530/22**
Comp Sci, Ed, Nurs

SAINT MARY, UNIVERSITY OF (KS) .... stmary.edu **1010/1515/21**
Comp Sci, Ed, English, Psych

SAINT MARY'S COLLEGE (IN) .... saintmarys.edu **1140/1710/25**
Art, Bus Admin, Communic, Ed, English, Nurs, Philo, Pre-Law, Reli Stu

SAINT MARY'S COLLEGE OF CALIFORNIA (CA) ..stmarys-ca.edu **1100/1650/24**
Bus Admin, Ed, Psych, Soc

ST. MARY'S COLLEGE OF MARYLAND (MD) ....smcm.edu **1230/1845/27**
Anthro, Bio, Econ, English, Hist, Math, Music, Poli Sci, Pre-Med/Pre-Dental, Psych

ST. MARY'S UNIVERSITY OF MINNESOTA (MN) .... smumn.edu **1050/1575/22**
Bus Admin, Chem, Communic, Comp Sci, Drama, Ed, Hist, Philo, Reli Stu

ST. MARY'S UNIVERSITY (TX) .... stmarytx.edu **1070/1600/23**
Bus Admin, English, Poli Sci, Pre-Law, Pre-Med/Pre-Dental, Soc

SAINT MICHAEL'S COLLEGE (VT) .... smcvt.edu **1115/1670/24**
Bio, Bus Admin, Chem, Communic, Ed

SAINT NORBERT COLLEGE (WI) .... snc.edu **1130/1700/25**
Bio, Bus Admin, Communic, Comp Sci, Ed, English, Hist

SAINT OLAF COLLEGE (MN) .... stolaf.edu **1230/1845/27**
*Amer St, Art, Bio, Chem, Classics, Drama, Econ, English, Hist, Math, Music,
Nurs, Philo, Physics, Pre-Law, Pre-Med/Pre-Dental, Psych, Reli Stu*

SAINT PETER'S COLLEGE (NJ) .... stpeters.edu **1000/1500/21**
Bus Admin, English, Reli Stu

SAINT ROSE, COLLEGE OF (NY) .... strose.edu **1060/1600/23**
Art, Bus Admin, Ed, Soc

ST. SCHOLASTICA, COLLEGE OF (MN) ....css.edu **1100/1650/24**
Bio, Bus Admin, Chem, Comp Sci, Ed, English, Nurs, Pre-Med/Pre-Dental, Psych, Reli Stu

SAINT THOMAS AQUINAS COLLEGE (NY) ....stac.edu **1060/1600/23**
Ed, Psych

SAINT THOMAS, UNIVERSITY OF (MN) .... stthomas.edu **1145/1720/25**
Bus Admin, Chem, Communic, Econ, Ed, Geol, Philo, Reli Stu

SAINT THOMAS, UNIVERSITY OF (TX) .... stthom.edu **1160/1740/25**
Chem, Philo, Pre-Med/Pre-Dental, Psych, Reli Stu

ST. VINCENT COLLEGE (PA) .... stvincent.edu **1100/1650/24**
Bio, Bus Admin, Chem, Pre-Med/Pre-Dental, Psych, Reli Stu

SALEM COLLEGE (NC) .... salem.edu **1120/1680/24**
Art, Art Hist, Bus Admin, Econ, English, Pre-Law, Soc

SALEM STATE COLLEGE (MA) .... sscmass.edu **1000/1500/21**
Art, Chem, Comp Sci, Drama, Ed, Geog, Geol, Hist, Nurs, Psych, Soc

SALISBURY UNIVERSITY (MD) .... ssu.edu **1140/1710/25**
Ed, English, Geog, Philo, Pre-Law, Psych

SAMFORD UNIVERSITY (AL) .... samford.edu **1140/1700/25**
Bus Admin, Communic, Music, Nurs, Pharm, Reli Stu

SAN DIEGO STATE UNIVERSITY (CA) .... sdsu.edu **1100/1650/24**
*Art, Art Hist, Astro, Bus Admin, Chem, Communic, Ed, Engine, English, Geog,
Geol, Hist, Nurs, Psych, Soc*

SAN DIEGO, UNIVERSITY OF (CA) .... sandiego.edu **1180/1780/26**
Bus Admin, Math, Nurs, Poli Sci, Pre-Law, Pre-Med/Pre-Dental, Reli Stu

SAN FRANCISCO ART INSTITUTE (CA) .... sfai.edu **1000/1510/21**
Art

SAN FRANCISCO CONSERVATORY OF MUSIC (CA) .. sfcm.edu **1160/1750/25**
Music

SAN FRANCISCO, UNIVERSITY OF (CA) .... usfca.edu **1130/1700/25**
Bus Admin, Econ, Nurs, Pre-Law, Pre-Med/Pre-Dental, Psych

SAN FRANCISCO STATE UNIVERSITY (CA) .... sfsu.edu **1010/1515/21**
Anthro, Astro, Communic, Drama, English, Hist, Pre-Law, Soc

SAN JOSE STATE UNIVERSITY (CA) .... sjsu.edu **1060/1600/23**
*Art, Bus Admin, Chem, Communic, Comp Sci, Engine, Math, Music, Nurs, Physics,
Pre-Med/Pre-Dental, Zoo*

SANTA CLARA UNIVERSITY (CA) .... scu.edu **1205/1810/27**
*Bus Admin, Communic, Comp Sci, Drama, Engine, English, Hist, Music, Philo, Physics,
Poli Sci, Pre-Law, Psych, Reli Stu*

SANTA FE, COLLEGE OF (NM) .... csf.edu **1100/1650/24**
Art, Drama, Ed

SARAH LAWRENCE COLLEGE (NY) .... slc.edu **1270/1900/28**
Amer St, Art, Art Hist, Drama, English, Geog, Hist, Music, Pre-Law

SCHOOL OF THE ART INSTITUTE OF CHICAGO (IL) .. saic.ed **1100/1660/24**
Art

SCHREINER UNIVERSITY (TX) .... schreiner.edu **1000/1500/21**
Bus Admin, English

SCIENCES IN PHILADELPHIA, UNIV. OF THE (PA) ...... usip.edu **1120/1680/24**
Bio, Biochem, Bus Admin, Chem, Comp Sci, Pharm

SCRANTON, UNIVERSITY OF (PA) .... scranton.edu **1120/1680/24**
Bio, Bus Admin, Communic, Pre-Med/Pre-Dental

SCRIPPS COLLEGE (CA) .... scrippscol.edu **1350/2025/30**
*Art, Art Hist, Bio, Classics, Drama, English, For Lang, Music, Poli Sci, Pre-Law, Pre-Med/
Pre-Dental, Psych*

SEATTLE PACIFIC UNIVERSITY (WA) .... spu.edu **1170/1760/26**
Bio, Chem, Drama, Ed, Engine, English, Nurs

SEATTLE UNIVERSITY (WA) .... seattleu.edu **1150/1725/25**
Bus Admin, Chem, Drama, Econ, Engine, English, Hist, Math, Nurs, Philo, Pre-Law

SETON HALL UNIVERSITY (NJ) .... shu.edu **1120/1680/24**
Bus Admin, Communic, Ed, Nurs, Philo, Pre-Law, Pre-Med/Pre-Dental, Psych, Reli Stu

SETON HILL COLLEGE (PA) .... setonhill.edu **1000/1500/21**
Art, Drama, Music

SHAW UNIVERSITY (NC) .... shawuniversity.edu **1010/1510/21**
Bus Admin, Soc

SHAWNEE STATE UNIVERSITY (OH) .... shawnee.edu **1000/1500/21**
Art, Ed

SHENANDOAH UNIVERSITY (VA) .... su.edu **1010/1510/21**
Music, Nurs

SHEPHERD UNIVERSITY (WV) .... shepherd.edu **1020/1530/22**
Art, Bus Admin, Chem, Ed, English, Hist, Music, Psych

SHIPPENSBURG UNIVERSITY (PA) .... ship.edu **1060/1590/23**
Bio, Bus Admin, Chem, Comp Sci, Econ, Ed, English, Hist, Physics, Psych, Soc

SHORTER COLLEGE (GA) .... shorter.edu **1050/1575/22**
Chem, Ed, Music

SIENA COLLEGE (NY) .... siena.edu **1125/1690/24**
Bio, Biochem, Bus Admin, Chem, Poli Sci, Pre-Law, Pre-Med/Pre-Dental, Psych

SIENA HEIGHTS UNIVERSITY (MI) .... sienaheights.edu **1000/1500/21**
Art, Psych

SILVER LAKE COLLEGE (WI) .... sl.edu **1000/1500/21**
Bus Admin, Ed, Reli Stu

SIMMONS COLLEGE (MA) .... simmons.edu **1110/1660/24**
Bus Admin, Communic, Ed, Math, Nurs, Psych, Soc

SIMPSON COLLEGE (IA) .... simpson.edu **1120/1680/24**
Bus Admin, Ed, Math, Music, Psych, Reli Stu, Soc

SKIDMORE COLLEGE (NY) .... skidmore.edu **1320/1980/29**
Amer St, Anthro, Art, Art Hist, Bio, Biochem, Bus Admin, Chem, Classics, Drama, Ed,
English, For Lang, Geol, Music, Philo, Poli Sci, Pre-Law, Pre-Med/Pre-Dental, Psych

SLIPPERY ROCK UNIVERSITY (PA) .... sru.edu **1000/1500/21**
Communic, Drama, Ed, English, For Lang, Music

SMITH COLLEGE (MA) .... smith.edu **1270/1905/28**
Amer St, Anthro, Art, Art Hist, Bio, Econ, Engine, English, For Lang, Geol, Hist,
Music, Philo, Physics, Poli Sci, Pre-Law, Pre-Med/Pre-Dental, Psych

SONOMA STATE UNIVERSITY (CA) .... sonoma.edu **1075/1615/23**
Anthro, Art Hist, Bus Admin, Chem, Geog, Music, Nurs, Physics, Psych, Soc

SOUTH, UNIVERSITY OF THE (TN) .... sewanee.edu **1230/1845/27**
*Amer St, Anthro, Bio, Chem, Econ, Drama, English, Forest, For Lang, Geol, Hist,
Poli Sci, Physics, Pre-Law, Pre-Med/Pre-Dental, Reli Stu*

SOUTH ALABAMA, UNIVERSITY OF (AL) .... usouthal.edu **1060/1590/23**
Bio, Bus Admin, Communic, English, For Lang, Nurs, Philo, Soc

SOUTH CAROLINA, UNIVERSITY OF (SC) .... sc.edu **1150/1725/25**
*Bus Admin, Communic, Comp Sci, Drama, Ed, Engine, English, For Lang, Geog, Geol,
Hist, Nurs, Pharm, Physics, Poli Sci, Pre-Law*

SOUTH DAKOTA, UNIVERSITY OF (SD) .... usd.edu **1050/1575/22**
Art, Bio, Bus Admin, English, Hist, Music, Nurs, Poli Sci, Pre-Law, Pre-Med/Pre-Dental, Psych

SOUTH DAKOTA SCHOOL OF MINES AND TECH. (SD) .... sdsmt.edu **1120/1680/24**
Chem, Comp Sci, Engine, Geol, Math, Physics

SOUTH DAKOTA STATE UNIVERSITY (SD) .... sdstate.edu **1060/1590/23**
Econ, Engine, Math, Nurs, Pharm, Soc

SOUTH FLORIDA, UNIVERSITY OF (FL) .... usf.edu **1150/1725/25**
Amer St, Anthro, Bus Admin, Chem, Drama, Ed, Engine, For Lang, Music, Nurs, Philo

SOUTHEAST MISSOURI STATE UNIV. (MO) .... semo.edu **1040/1560/22**
Bus Admin, Ed

SOUTHEASTERN LOUISIANA STATE UNIV. (LA) .... selu.edu **1000/1500/21**
Communic, Comp Sci, Ed, English

SOUTHEASTERN OKLAHOMA STATE UNIV. (OK) ..... sosu.edu **1000/1500/21**
Bot, Bus Admin, Zoo

SOUTHERN CALIFORNIA, UNIVERSITY OF (CA) .... usc.edu **1360/2040/31**
Astro, Arch, Bus Admin, Communic, Drama, Ed, Engine, Math, Music, Pharm, Psych

SOUTHERN CONNECTICUT STATE UNIV. (CT) .... southernct.edu **1000/1500/21**
Chem, Communic, Comp Sci, Econ, Ed, English, Geog, Physics, Poli Sci, Psych, Soc

SOUTHERN ILLINOIS UNIV. (CARBONDALE) (IL) .... siuc.edu **1030/1545/22**
Bot, Bus Admin, Chem, Communic, Engine, Forestry, Geog, Hist, Music, Poli Sci, Psych, Zoo

SOUTHERN ILLINOIS UNIV. (EDWARDSVILLE) (IL) .... siue.edu **1060/1590/23**
Ed, Engine, Nurs, Poli Sci

SOUTHERN MAINE, UNIVERSITY OF (ME) .... usm.maine.edu **1030/1550/22**
Art, Bus Admin, Chem, Communic, Comp Sci, Drama, Engine, Music, Nurs

SOUTHERN METHODIST UNIVERSITY (TX) .... smu.edu **1210/1805/27**
Anthro, Art, Art Hist, Bus Admin, Communic, Drama, Econ, Engine, Hist, Reli Stu

SOUTHERN MISSISSIPPI, UNIVERSITY OF (MS) .... usms.edu **1010/1515/21**
Bus Admin, Drama, Ed, Hist, Music, Nurs

SOUTHERN NAZARENE UNIVERSITY (OK) ....snu.edu **1050/1575/22**
Ed, English, Nurs, Reli Stu

SOUTHERN OREGON UNIVERSITY (OR) .... sou.edu **1040/1560/22**
Art, Bio, Bus Admin, Chem, Ed, For Lang, Soc

SOUTHERN POLYTECHNIC UNIVERSITY (GA) .... spsu.edu **1100/1650/24**
Arch, Comp Sci, Engine, Math

SOUTHERN UTAH UNIVERSITY (UT) .... suu.edu **1020/1530/22**
Communic, Drama, Econ, Ed, English

SOUTHWEST BAPTIST UNIVERSITY (MO) .... sbuniv.edu **1060/1590/23**
Ed, Music, Reli Stu

SOUTHWESTERN COLLEGE (KS) .... sckans.edu **1040/1560/22**
English, Music, Nurs

SOUTHWESTERN OKLAHOMA STATE UNIV. (OK) .. swosu.edu **1000/1500/21**
Bus Admin, Chem, Ed, Pharm

SOUTHWESTERN UNIVERSITY (TX) .... southwestern.edu **1230/1845/27**
Art, Bio, Bus Admin, Chem, Communic, Drama, Econ, English, For Lang, Hist, Music,
Philo, Poli Sci, Pre-Law, Pre-Med/Pre-Dental, Psych, Reli Stu, Soc

SPELMAN COLLEGE (GA) .... spelman.edu **1080/1630/24**
Bio, Chem, Comp Sci, Econ, English, Poli Sci, Pre-Law, Pre-Med/Pre-Dental, Soc

SPRING HILL COLLEGE (AL) .... shc.edu **1100/1650/24**
Bio, Bus Admin, Chem, Communic, English, Hist, Poli Sci, Pre-Law, Pre-Med/Pre-Dental

SPRINGFIELD COLLEGE (MA) .... spfldcol.edu **1030/1545/22**
Drama, Ed, English, Psych, Soc

STANFORD UNIVERSITY (CA) .... stanford.edu **1450/2175/32**
Amer St, Anthro, Art, Art Hist, Bio, Chem, Classics, Communic, Comp Sci, Drama,
Econ, Ed, Engine, English, For Lang, Math, Music, Physics, Poli Sci, Pre-Law,
Pre-Med/Pre-Dental, Psych, Reli Stu, Soc

STEPHEN F. AUSTIN STATE UNIVERSITY (TX) .... sfasu.edu **1010/1515/21**
Forest

STEPHENS (MO) .... stephens.edu **1090/1640/24**
Bus Admin, Communic, Drama, Ed, Pre-Law, Psych

STERLING COLLEGE (KS) .... sterling.edu **1040/1560/22**
Drama, Ed, Music

STETSON UNIVERSITY (FL) .... stetson.edu **1130/1700/25**
Bus Admin, Chem, Comp Sci, Ed, English, Hist, Math, Music, Pre-Law,
Pre-Med/Pre-Dental, Psych, Reli Stu

STEVENS INSTITUTE OF TECHNOLOGY (NJ) . stevens-tech.edu **1330/2000/30**
Comp Sci, Engine

STONEHILL COLLEGE (MA) .... stonehill.edu **1160/1740/25**
Bio, Bus Admin, Chem, Comp Sci, Poli Sci, Pre-Law, Psych

SUFFOLK UNIVERSITY (MA) .... suffolk.edu   **1040/1560/22**
Bus Admin, Communic, Poli Sci, Soc

SUNY COLL. OF ENVIRONMENTAL SCIENCE & FORESTRY (NY) esf.edu   **1160/1740/25**
Forest

SUSQUEHANNA UNIVERSITY (PA) ....susqu.edu   **1160/1740/25**
Bio, Biochem, Bus Admin, Chem, Communic, Drama, Econ, Ed, English,
Music, Poli Sci, Pre-Med/Pre-Dental, Psych

SWARTHMORE COLLEGE (PA) ....swarthmore.edu   **1420/2130/32**
Art Hist, Biochem, Bio, Classics, Econ, Ed, Engine, English, Hist,
Philo, Physics, Poli Sci, Pre-Law, Pre-Med/Pre-Dental, Psych

SWEET BRIAR COLLEGE (VA) .... sbc.edu   **1140/1710/25**
Anthro, Art Hist, Chem, Drama, Engine, For Lang, Math, Poli Sci, Pre-Law, Psych

SYRACUSE UNIVERSITY (NY) .... syracuse.edu   **1200/1800/26**
Anthro, Arch, Art, Art Hist, Bus Admin, Chem, Communic, Comp Sci, Drama,
Engine, Forest, Geog, Music, Physics, Poli Sci, Pre-Law, Psych, Reli Stu, Soc

TABOR COLLEGE (KS) .... tabor.edu   **1060/1600/23**
Ed

TAMPA, UNIVERSITY OF (FL) .... utampa.edu   **1095/1645/23**
Bus Admin, Communic, Music

TARLETON STATE UNIVERSITY (TX) .... tarleton.edu   **1000/1500/21**
Ag, Drama, English, Hist, Music, Soc

TAYLOR UNIVERSITY (IN) .... taylor.edu   **1150/1725/25**
Bus Admin, Comp Sci, Psych, Reli Stu

TEMPLE UNIVERSITY (PA) .... temple.edu   **1100/1650/24**
Arch, Art, Biochem, Bio, Bus Admin, Chem, Communic, Comp Sci, Drama, English,
For Lang, Music, Pharm, Pre-Law, Pre-Med/Pre-Dental, Soc

TENNESSEE TECHNOLOGICAL UNIVERSITY (TN) .. tntech.edu   **1060/1590/23**
Ed, Engine

TENNESSEE, UNIVERSITY OF
       CHATTANOOGA .... utc.edu   **1020/1530/22**
       Chem, English, Math, Psych
       KNOXVILLE .... utk.edu   **1130/1700/25**
       Ag, Anthro, Arch, Art, Bot, Bus Admin, Chem, Classics, Ed, Engine, English,
       Forest, Hist, Physics, Poli Sci, Pre-Law, Pre-Med/Pre-Dental, Reli Stu, Zoo
       MARTIN ....utm.edu   **1030/1550/22**
       Ag, English, Math

TEXAS, UNIVERSITY OF, AT
       ARLINGTON .... uta.edu   **1060/1590/23**
       Arch, Bio, Bus Admin, Communic, Comp Sci, Engine, Nurs, Poli Sci
       AUSTIN .... utexas.edu   **1250/1875/28**
       Amer St, Arch, Astro, Bio, Bot, Bus Admin, Classics, Communic, Comp Sci,
       Drama, Ed, Engine, For Lang, Geog, Geol, Hist, Math, Music, Pharm, Philo,
       Physics, Poli Sci, Pre-Med/Pre-Dental, Psych, Zoo

TEXAS, UNIVERSITY OF, AT *(Continued)*

    DALLAS .... utdallas.edu **1250/1875/28**
    Bus Admin, Comp Sci, Econ, Engine, Hist, Physics

    EL PASO .... utep.edu **1000/1500/21**
    Art, Bus Admin, Communic, Drama, Ed, Engine, Music, Nurs, Psych

    SAN ANTONIO .... utsa.edu **1000/1500/21**
    Arch, Art, Bio, Bus Admin, Engine, English, Hist, Music, Pre-Med/Pre-Dental, Psych

    SAN ANTONIO (HEALTH SCIENCE CENTER) .. uthscsa.edu **1100/1650/24**
    Nurs (No Frosh - Transfers Only)

    TYLER .... uttyl.edu **1050/1575/22**
    Bus Admin, Comp Sci, Engine, English, Math, Nurs, Psych

TEXAS A&M (TX) .... tamu.edu **1200/1800/26**
Ag, Anthro, Arch, Bus Admin, Chem, Communic, Econ, Ed, Engine, English, Forest, Geol, Hist, Philo, Poli Sci, Pre-Med/Pre-Dental, Zoo

TEXAS A&M - COMMERCE (TX) .... tamu-commerce.edu **1020/1530/22**
Bus Admin

TEXAS A&M - CORPUS CHRISTI (TX) .... tamucc.edu **1000/1500/21**
Art, Bio, Bus Admin, Chem, Ed, English, Geog, Geol, Hist, Math, Nurs, Psych

TEXAS A&M - GALVESTON (TX) .... tamug.edu **1110/1665/24**
Bus Admin

TEXAS A&M - KINGSVILLE (TX) .... tamuk.edu **1000/1500/21**
Engine

TEXAS CHRISTIAN UNIVERSITY (TX) .... tcu.edu **1160/1740/25**
Bio, Bus Admin, Communic, Drama, Ed, Geol, Hist, Music, Nurs, Reli Stu

TEXAS LUTHERAN UNIVERSITY (TX) .... tlu.edu **1040/1560/22**
Bio, Bus Admin, Chem, Ed, Hist, Music, Reli Stu

TEXAS STATE UNIVERSITY - SAN MARCOS (TX) .... txstate.edu **1050/1575/22**
Ag, Anthro, Bio, Bus Admin, Comp Sci, Drama, Ed, Geog, Hist, Math

TEXAS TECH UNIVERSITY (TX) .... ttu.edu **1110/1665/24**
Ag, Arch, Art, Bus Admin, Ed, Engine, English, Hist, Home Ec, Math

TEXAS WESLEYAN UNIVERSITY (TX) .... txwesleyan.edu **1010/1510/21**
Bus Admin, Communic, Ed, Psych

THOMAS MORE COLLEGE (KY) .... thomasmore.edu **1040/1560/22**
Bio, Bus Admin, Chem, Comp Sci, Ed, Nurs, Physics, Pre-Med/Pre-Dental

TOLEDO, UNIVERSITY OF (OH) .... utoledo.edu **1040/1560/22**
Bus Admin, Econ, Engine, Hist, Pharm

TOUGALOO COLLEGE (MS) .... tougaloo.edu **1000/1500/21**
Bio, Ed

TOWSON UNIVERSITY (MD) .... towson.edu **1095/1645/24**
Anthro, Art, Bus Admin, Chem, Communic, Drama, Ed, Math, Music, Nurs, Psych, Soc

TRANSYLVANIA UNIVERSITY (KY) .... transy.edu **1200/1800/26**
Bio, Bus Admin, Chem, Comp Sci, Ed, Philo, Pre-Med/Pre-Dental, Psych

TRINITY COLLEGE (CT) .... trincoll.edu **1310/1965/29**
Amer St, Art Hist, Bio, Bus Admin, Chem, Econ, Engine, English, Hist, Math,
Philo, Pre-Law, Pre-Med/Pre-Dental, Reli Stu

TRINITY COLLEGE (DC) .... trinitydc.edu **1050/1575/22**
Bus Admin, For Lang, Math, Poli Sci, Pre-Law, Soc

TRINITY UNIVERSITY (TX) .... trinity.edu **1290/1935/29**
Art, Art Hist, Bio, Bus Admin, Chem, Classics, Communic, Econ, Ed, English,
For Lang, Hist, Philo, Physics, Poli Sci, Pre-Law, Pre-Med/Pre-Dental, Soc

TRI-STATE UNIVERSITY (IN) .... tristate.edu **1060/1590/23**
Engine

TROY STATE UNIVERSITY (AL) .... troy.edu **1000/1500/21**
Bus Admin. Ed, English, Nurs

TRUMAN STATE UNIVERSITY (MO) .... truman.edu **1220/1830/27**
Bio, Bus Admin, Chem, Econ, Ed, English, For Lang, Math, Nurs, Pre-Med/Pre-Dental

TUFTS UNIVERSITY (MA) .... tufts.edu **1380/2070/31**
Bio, Chem, Classics, Drama, Econ, Engine, English, Hist, Philo, Poli Sci,
Pre-Law, Pre-Med/Pre-Dental, Psych

TULANE UNIVERSITY (LA) .... tulane.edu **1270/1900/28**
Amer St, Anthro, Arch, Art, Bio, Biochem, Bus Admin, Drama, Engine, For Lang, Hist,
Math, Philo, Poli Sci, Pre-Law, Pre-Med/Pre-Dental, Psych

TULSA, UNIVERSITY OF (OK) .... utulsa.edu **1230/1850/27**
Anthro, Art, Bio, Bus Admin, Communic, Comp Sci, Engine, English, Geol, Hist, Music,
Physics, Psych

TUSKEGEE UNIVERSITY (AL) .... tuskegee.edu **1000/1500/21**
Ag, Arch, Engine, Nurs, Physics, Pre-Law, Pre-Med/Pre-Dental

UNION COLLEGE (NE) .... ucollege.edu **1050/1575/22**
Nurs, Reli Stu

UNION COLLEGE (NY) .... union.edu **1300/1950/30**
Astro, Biochem, Bio, Chem, Comp Sci, Econ, Engine, English, Geol, Hist,
Math, Poli Sci, Pre-Law, Pre-Med/Pre-Dental, Psych, Soc

UNION UNIVERSITY (TN) .... uu.edu **1100/1650/24**
Art, Chem, Music, Nurs, Physics, Reli Stu

U. S. AIR FORCE ACADEMY (CO) .... usafa.edu **1300/1950/29**
Bus Admin, Comp Sci, Engine, Math, Physics, Poli Sci

U. S. COAST GUARD ACADEMY (CT) .... cga.edu **1270/1905/28**
Engine

U. S. MILITARY ACADEMY (NY) .... usma.edu **1280/1920/29**
Econ, Engine, Hist, Poli Sci

U. S. NAVAL ACADEMY (MD) .... usna.edu **1325/1980/30**
Chem, Engine, Poli Sci

URSINUS COLLEGE (PA) .... ursinus.edu **1210/1815/26**
Bio, Bus Admin, Chem, Drama, Econ, Ed, Physics, Poli Sci, Pre-Law, Pre-Med/Pre-Dental

UTAH, UNIVERSITY OF (UT) .... utah.edu **1100/1650/24**
Art, Art Hist, Bio, Bus Admin, Chem, Comp Sci, Drama, Engine, English, For Lang, Geol, Hist, Home Ec, Pharm, Philo, Poli Sci, Pre-Law, Pre-Med/Pre-Dental

UTAH STATE UNIVERSITY (UT) .... usu.edu **1100/1650/24**
Ag, Bio, Chem, Drama, Ed, Engine, English, Forest, Home Ec, Music, Poli Sci

UTICA COLLEGE (NY) .... ucsu.edu **1010/1510/22**
Bus Admin

VALPARAISO UNIVERSITY (IN) .... valpo.edu **1160/1740/26**
Bio, Bus Admin, Ed, Engine, For Lang, Math, Music, Nurs, Pre-Med/Pre-Dental, Psych, Reli Stu

VANDERBILT UNIVERSITY (TN) .... vanderbilt.edu **1370/2055/31**
Anthro, Art Hist, Bio, Classics, Econ, Ed, Engine, English, Geol, Hist, Music, Nurs, Philo, Physics, Poli Sci, Pre-Law, Pre-Med/Pre-Dental, Psych

VASSAR COLLEGE (NY) .... vassar.edu **1360/2040/30**
Art, Art Hist, Astro, Bio, Comp Sci, Drama, Econ, English, Hist, Math, Music, Philo, Pre-Law, Pre-Med/Pre-Dental, Psych

VERMONT, UNIVERSITY OF (VT) .... uvm.edu **1160/1740/25**
Ag, Bio, Bot, Bus Admin, Chem, Econ, For Lang, Geog, Geol, Hist, Nurs, Physics, Poli Sci, Pre-Law, Pre-Med/Pre-Dental, Reli Stu, Psych, Zoo

VILLA JULIE COLLEGE (MD) .... vjc.edu **1050/1575/22**
Nurs

VILLANOVA UNIVERSITY (PA) .... villanova.edu **1260/1890/28**
Astro, Bio, Bus Admin, Communic, Econ, Engine, Math, Nurs, Philo, Poli Sci, Pre-Law, Pre-Med/Pre-Dental

VIRGINIA, UNIVERSITY OF (VA) .... virginia.edu **1330/2000/30**
Amer St, Arch, Art, Astro, Bio, Biochem, Bus Admin, Chem, Classics, Econ, Engine, English, For Lang, Hist, Music, Nurs, Poli Sci, Pre-Law, Pre-Med/Pre-Dental, Psych, Reli Stu, Soc

VIRGINIA COMMONWEALTH UNIVERSITY (VA) .... vcu.edu **1070/1605/23**
Art, Bus Admin, Drama, Engine, For Lang, Music, Nurs, Pharm, Pre-Med/Pre-Dental, Pre-Law, Psych, Reli Stu

VIRGINIA MILITARY INSTITUTE (VA) .... vmi.edu **1140/1710/25**
Bus Admin, Chem, Econ, Engine, Hist, Pre-Law

VIRGINIA POLYTECHNIC INSTITUTE (VA) .... vt.edu **1230/1845/26**
Ag, Arch, Bio, Biochem, Bus Admin, Chem, Communic, Comp Sci, Engine, Forest, Hist, Psych

VIRGINIA WESLEYAN UNIVERSITY (VA) .... vwc.edu **1030/1545/22**
Bio, Bus Admin, Communic, Poli Sci, Pre-Law, Pre-Med/Pre-Dental, Psych, Reli Stu, Soc

VISUAL ARTS, SCHOOL OF (NY) .... schoolofvisualarts.edu **1064/1600/23**
Art, Bus Admin

VITERBO UNIVERSITY (WI) .... viterbo.edu **1055/1590/23**
Chem, Drama, Music, Nurs

WABASH COLLEGE (IN) .... wabash.edu **1190/1790/26**
Bio, Chem, Classics, Econ, English, Hist, Math, Philo, Poli Sci, Pre-Law, Pre-Med/Pre-Dental, Psych, Reli Stu

WAGNER COLLEGE (NY) .... wagner.edu **1130/1695/25**
Amer St, Bus Admin, Drama, Ed, Soc

WAKE FOREST UNIVERSITY (NC) .... wfu.edu **1310/1965/29**
Bio, Bus Admin, Chem, Drama, Econ, English, For Lang, Hist, Math, Physics, Poli Sci, Pre-Law, Pre-Med/Pre-Dental, Psych, Reli Stu, Soc

WALLA WALLA COLLEGE (WA) .... wwc.edu **1030/1550/22**
Communic, Engine, English, Nurs, Pre-Med/Pre-Dental

WALSH UNIVERSITY (OH) .... walsh.edu **1020/1530/22**
Ed, English, Nurs

WARREN WILSON COLLEGE (NC) .... warren-wilson.edu **1150/1725/25**
English, Hist, Pre-Law

WARTBURG COLLEGE (IA) .... wartburg.edu **1120/1680/24**
Bio, Bus Admin, Communic, Drama, Ed, English, Hist, Music, Pre-Med/Pre-Dental, Reli Stu

WASHBURN UNIVERSITY (KS) .... washburn.edu **1140/1700/25**
Ed, Nurs, Physics

WASHINGTON COLLEGE (MD) .... washcoll.edu **1155/1715/25**
Amer St, Bio, Bus Admin, Hist, Pre-Med/Pre-Dental, Psych

WASHINGTON & JEFFERSON COLLEGE (PA) ..... washjeff.edu **1140/1700/25**
Art, Bio, Bus Admin, Chem, Econ, Ed, English, Hist, Poli Sci, Pre-Law, Pre-Med/Pre-Dental, Psych

WASHINGTON & LEE UNIVERSITY (VA) .... wlu.edu **1370/2055/31**
Art, Bio, Bus Admin, Chem, Communic, Econ, English, For Lang, Geol, Hist, Math, Physics, Poli Sci, Pre-Law, Pre-Med/Pre-Dental

WASHINGTON UNIVERSITY IN ST. LOUIS (MO) .... wustl.edu **1380/2070/31**
Anthro, Arch, Art, Art Hist, Bio, Bus Admin, Chem, Comp Sci, Engine, English, For Lang, Geol, Math, Philo, Physics, Pre-Law, Pre-Med/Pre-Dental, Psych

WASHINGTON STATE UNIVERSITY (WA) .... wsu.edu **1100/1650/24**
Amer St, Ag, Anthro, Arch, Biochem, Bus Admin, Communic, Econ, Ed, Engine, English, Hist, Home Ec, Pharm, Physics, Soc, Zoo

WASHINGTON, UNIVERSITY OF (WA) .... washington.edu **1195/1795/26**
Anthro, Arch, Art, Art Hist, Astro, Biochem, Bio, Bot, Bus Admin, Chem, Classics, Comp Sci, Drama, Econ, Ed, Engine, English, Forest, Geog, Geol, Hist, Math, Music, Nurs, Philo, Physics, Poli Sci, Pre-Law, Pre-Med/Pre-Dental, Psych, Soc, Zoo

WAYNE STATE COLLEGE (NE) .... wsc.edu **1000/1500/21**
Chem, Ed, Psych

WAYNE STATE UNIVERSITY (MI) .... wayne.edu **1000/1500/21**
Art, Art Hist, Bio, Bus Admin, Chem, Comp Sci, Drama, Ed, Engine, For Lang, Music, Nurs, Pharm, Pre-Med/Pre-Dental, Psych

WAYNESBURG COLLEGE (PA) .... waynesburg.edu   **1000/1500/21**
Communic, Nurs

WEBER STATE UNIVERSITY (UT) ....weber.edu   **1020/1530/22**
Art, Bus Admin, Communic, Comp Sci, Drama, Econ, Ed, Math, Music, Nurs, Physics, Zoo

WEBSTER UNIVERSITY (MO) ....webster.edu   **1120/1680/24**
Comp Sci, Drama, Hist, Music, Nurs, Philo, Poli Sci, Psych

WELLESLEY COLLEGE (MA) .... wellesley.edu   **1360/2040/30**
*Art, Art Hist, Bio, Chem, Econ, Ed, English, For Lang, Hist, Math, Physics,
Poli Sci, Pre-Law, Pre-Med/Pre-Dental, Reli Stu*

WELLS COLLEGE (NY) .... wells. edu   **1120/1680/24**
*Amer St, Bio, Bus Admin, Chem, Drama, Ed, English, For Lang, Hist, Music,
Pre-Law, Pre-Med/Pre-Dental, Psych, Soc*

WESLEYAN COLLEGE (GA) ....wesleyan-college.edu   **1115/1670/24**
Amer St, Art, Bus Admin

WESLEYAN UNIVERSITY (CT) .... wesleyan.edu   **1400/2100/31**
*Amer St, Art, Astro, Bio, Chem, Drama, Econ, English, Hist, Math, Poli Sci,
Pre-Law, Pre-Med/Pre-Dental, Psych, Reli Stu*

WEST CHESTER UNIVERSITY (PA)......................... wcupa.edu   **1070/1600/23**
*Art, Bio, Bus Admin, Chem, Communic, Comp Sci, English, For Lang, Music, Philo,
Poli Sci, Pre-Law, Soc*

WEST FLORIDA, UNIVERSITY OF (FL) .... uwf.edu   **1120/1680/24**
Bio, Bus Admin, Chem, Communic, Comp Sci, Ed, Pre-Med/Pre-Dental, Psych

WEST VIRGINIA UNIVERSITY (WV) ....wvu.edu   **1060/1600/23**
*Arch, Art, Bio, Bus Admin, Chem, Communic, Comp Sci, Drama, Engine, Forest,
Geol, Music, Physics, Poli Sci, Pre-Law, Pre-Med/Pre-Dental, Psych, Soc*

WEST VIRGINIA WESLEYAN COLLEGE (WV) .... wvwc.edu   **1040/1560/22**
Art, Bio, Comp Sci, Drama, Ed, English, Hist, Physics

WESTERN CAROLINA UNIVERSITY (NC) ....wcu.edu   **1030/1545/22**
Bus Admin, Chem, Comp Sci, Ed, English, Math, Music, Nurs

WESTERN CONNECTICUT STATE UNIV. (CT) .... wcsu.ctstateu.edu   **1000/1500/21**
Amer St, Anthro, Art, Astro, Bus Admin, Ed, English, Music, Nurs, Soc

WESTERN ILLINOIS UNIVERSITY (IL) ....wiu.edu   **1010/1515/21**
Ag, Chem, Communic, Ed, English, Geog, Music, Soc

WESTERN KENTUCKY UNIVERSITY (KY) ....wku.edu   **1040/1560/22**
Ag, Bio, Comp Sci, Ed, Hist, Nurs, Physics, Psych, Soc

WESTERN MICHIGAN UNIVERSITY (MI) ....wmich.edu   **1060/1590/22**
*Art, Bus Admin, Communic, Comp Sci, Drama, Ed, English, Engine, For Lang, Hist,
Home Ec, Music, Nurs, Physics, Psych*

WESTERN NEW ENGLAND COLLEGE (MA).............. wnec.edu   **1060/1590/23**
Bus Admin, Communic, Comp Sci, Ed, Engine, Pre-Law, Psych

WESTERN STATE COLLEGE OF COLORADO .... western.edu **1000/1500/21**
Bio, Bus Admin, Drama, English, Hist, Geol, Music

WESTERN WASHINGTON UNIVERSITY (WA) .... wwu.edu **1120/1680/24**
Anthro, Art, Communic, Ed, English, Geog, Poli Sci, Pre-Law, Psych, Soc

WESTFIELD STATE COLLEGE (MA) .... wsc.mass.edu **1020/1530/22**
Ed, English, Music, Poli Sci, Psych

WESTMINSTER COLLEGE (MO) .... wcmo.edu **1120/1680/24**
Bio, Bus Admin, Econ, English, Hist, Poli Sci, Pre-Law, Pre-Med/Pre-Dental, Psych

WESTMINSTER COLLEGE (PA) .... westminster.edu **1080/1620/24**
Bio, Comp Sci, Pre-Med/Pre-Dental, Soc

WESTMINSTER COLLEGE (UT) .... westminstercollege.edu **1100/1650/24**
*Art, Bio, Bus Admin, Chem, Communic, Comp Sci, Ed, Engine, English, Hist, Nurs,
Philo, Physics, Poli Sci, Psych*

WESTMONT COLLEGE (CA) .... westmont.edu **1220/1830/27**
Bio, Chem, Econ, Hist, Pre-Law, Pre-Med/Pre-Dental, Psych, Reli Stu

WHEATON COLLEGE (IL) .... wheaton.edu **1340/2010/30**
*Art, Bio, Chem, Communic, Ed, English, Hist, Math, Music, Philo, Physics,
Pre-Law, Pre-Med/Pre-Dental, Psych, Reli Stu, Soc*

WHEATON COLLEGE (MA) ....wheatonma.edu **1210/1815/26**
*Art, Art Hist, Astro, Bio, Drama, Econ, English, For Lang, Hist, Math,
Poli Sci, Pre-Law, Pre-Med/Pre-Dental, Psych, Soc*

WHEELING JESUIT (WV) .... wju.edu **1045/1570/22**
Bio, Bus Admin, Chem, English, Hist, Math, Nurs, Philo, Psych, Reli Stu

WHEELOCK COLLEGE (MA) .... wheelock.edu **1020/1530/22**
Ed

WHITMAN COLLEGE (WA) .... whitman.edu **1340/2010/30**
*Art, Astro, Bio, Chem, Classics, Drama, Econ, English, For Lang, Geol, Hist, Math, Music,
Philo, Physics, Poli Sci, Pre-Law, Pre-Med/Pre-Dental, Psych, Soc*

WHITTIER COLLEGE (CA) .... whittier.edu **1090/1640/24**
Bus Admin, Chem, Econ, Ed, English, Poli Sci, Pre-Law

WHITWORTH COLLEGE (WA) .... whitworth.edu **1160/1740/26**
Art, Bus Admin, Chem, Communic, Ed, English, Hist, Music, Physics, Psych, Reli Stu

WICHITA STATE UNIVERSITY (KS) .... wichita.edu **1080/1620/23**
Bus Admin, Communic, English

WIDENER UNIVERSITY (PA) ....widener.edu **1140/1710/25**
Bus Admin, Ed, Engine, Nurs

WILBERFORCE UNIVERSITY (OH) .... wilberforce.edu **1000/1500/21**
Bus Admin, Poli Sci, Pre-Law

WILKES UNIVERSITY (PA) .... wilkes.edu **1080/1620/23**
Bio, Comp Sci, Engine, English, Hist, Math, Nurs, Pre-Med/Pre-Dental, Psych

WILLAMETTE UNIVERSITY (OR) ....willamette.edu   **1230/1845/27**
Art Hist, Bio, Chem, Classics, Econ, English, Hist, Math, Music, Philo,
Poli Sci, Pre-Law, Pre-Med/Pre-Dental, Psych, Reli Stu, Soc

WILLIAM JEWELL COLLEGE (MO) ....jewell.edu   **1160/1740/25**
Bio, Bus Admin, Chem, Comp Sci, Ed, English, Music, Nurs, Physics

WILLIAM & MARY, COLLEGE OF (VA)..........................wm.edu   **1350/2030/30**
Amer St, Bio, Bus Admin, Classics, Comp Sci, Drama, Econ, Ed, English,
For Lang, Geol, Hist, Philo, Physics, Poli Sci, Pre-Med/Pre-Dental, Reli Stu

WILLIAM PATERSON UNIVERSITY (NJ)....................wpunj.edu   **1040/1560/22**
Anthro, Bus Admin, Comp Sci, English, Hist, Music, Nurs, Soc

WILLIAMS COLLEGE (MA) ....williams.edu   **1410/2120/32**
Amer St, Art, Art Hist, Astro, Bio, Chem, Classics, Comp Sci, Drama, Econ,
English, Hist, Poli Sci, Pre-Law, Pre-Med/Pre-Dental, Psych

WILMINGTON COLLEGE (OH) ....wilmington.edu   **1000/1500/21**
Ag, Ed, English, Hist

WILSON COLLEGE (PA) ....wilson.edu   **1040/1560/22**
Econ, Pre-Law, Psych, Soc

WINGATE UNIVERSITY (NC) ....wingate.edu   **1000/1500/21**
Art, Communic, Hist, Music

WINONA STATE UNIVERSITY (MN) .... winona.msus.edu   **1090/1635/24**
Bio, Bus Admin, Chem, Communic, Comp Sci, Ed, English, Hist, Pre-Med/Pre-Dental, Soc

WINTHROP UNIVERSITY (SC) .... winthrop.edu   **1055/1585/22**
Art, Bio, Bus Admin, Chem, Drama, Ed, English, Hist, Math, Poli Sci, Psych

WISCONSIN LUTHERAN COLLEGE (WI) ....wlc.edu   **1100/1650/24**
Art, Chem, Communic, Ed, Math, Music, Reli Stu

WISCONSIN, UNIVERSITY OF, AT
        EAU CLAIRE ....uwec.edu   **1099/1650/24**
        Bio, Bus Admin, Chem, English, Math, Nurs
        GREEN BAY .... uwgb.edu   **1060/1590/23**
        Art, Bus Admin, Hist, Psych
        LA CROSSE ....uwlax.edu   **1130/1700/25**
        Astro, Bus Admin, Chem, Communic, Comp Sci, Geog, Soc
        MADISON .... wisc.edu   **1250/1875/27**
        Ag, Anthro, Art, Art Hist, Astro, Biochem, Bot, Bus Admin, Chem, Classics, Communic,
        Comp Sci, Drama, Ed, Engine, English, For Lang, Forest, Geog, Geol, Hist, Home Ec, Math,
        Music, Nurs, Pharm, Philo, Physics, Poli Sci, Pre-Law, Pre-Med/Pre-Dental, Psych, Soc, Zoo
        MILWAUKEE .... uwm.edu   **1080/1620/23**
        Anthro, Arch, Bio, Bus Admin, Chem, Drama, Econ, Ed, English, For Lang,
        Hist, Nurs, Physics, Poli Sci, Pre-Law
        PLATTEVILLE .... uwplatt.edu   **1050/1575/22**
        Ag, Bio, Chem, Ed, Engine, English
        RIVER FALLS .... uwrf.edu   **1040/1560/22**
        Ag, Ed
        STEVENS POINT .... uwsp.edu   **1100/1650/24**
        Art, Bio, Bus Admin, Chem, Communic, Drama, Ed, Home Ec, Math, Music, Soc

WISCONSIN, UNIVERSITY OF, AT *(Continued)*
    STOUT .... uwstout.edu **1000/1500/21**
    Bus Admin, Home Ec, Psych
    SUPERIOR .... uwsuper.edu **1000/1500/21**
    Art, Ed, Music
    WHITEWATER .... uww.edu **1000/1500/21**
    Bus Admin, Communic

WITTENBERG UNIVERSITY (OH) .... wittenberg.edu **1150/1725/25**
Art, Bio, Bus Admin, Chem, Ed, English, Geog, Hist, Music, Poli Sci,
Pre-Law, Pre-Med/Pre-Dental, Psych, Reli Stu

WOFFORD COLLEGE (SC) .... wofford.edu **1210/1815/27**
Bio, Chem, Comp Sci, Econ, Ed, English, For Lang, Hist, Math, Philo,
Pre-Law, Pre-Med/Pre-Dental, Psych, Soc

WOODBURY UNIVERSITY (CA) .... woodburyu.edu **1000/1500/21**
Arch, Bus Admin

WOOSTER, COLLEGE OF (OH) .... wooster.edu **1190/1785/26**
Art Hist, Bio, Chem, Classics, Drama, Econ, English, Geol, Hist, Math, Music,
Poli Sci, Pre-Law, Pre-Med/Pre-Dental, Reli Stu, Soc

WORCESTER POLYTECHNIC INSTITUTE (MA) .... wpi.edu **1300/1950/29**
Bio, Biochem, Bus Admin, Chem, Comp Sci, Econ, Engine, Math, Physics, Pre-Law

WORCESTER STATE COLLEGE (MA) .... worcester.edu **1015/1525/22**
Bus Admin, Chem, Communic, Ed, Nurs, Philo, Psych

WRIGHT STATE UNIVERSITY (OH) .... wright.edu **1010/1515/21**
Econ, Engine, Geol, Nurs

WYOMING, UNIVERSITY OF (WY) .... uwyo.edu **1080/1620/24**
Ag, Amer St, Anthro, Astro, Bio, Bot, Bus Admin, Chem, Econ, Ed, Engine,
English, Geog, Geol, Nurs, Pharm, Pre-Law, Pre-Med/Pre-Dental, Psych, Zoo

XAVIER UNIVERSITY (OH) .... xu.edu **1170/1755/26**
Bio, Bus Admin, Chem, Classics, Communic, Econ, Hist, Philo, Physics, Psych, Reli Stu

XAVIER UNIVERSITY OF LOUISIANA (LA) .... xula.edu **1040/1560/22**
Bio, Bus Admin, Chem, Ed, Music, Pharm, Pre-Med/Pre-Dental, Psych

YALE UNIVERSITY (CT) .... yale.edu **1480/2220/33**
Amer St, Anthro, Arch, Art, Art Hist, Bio, Biochem, Classics, Drama, Econ, English, For Lang,
Hist, Math, Music, Philo, Physics, Poli Sci, Pre-Law, Pre-Med/Pre-Dental, Psych, Reli Stu, Soc

YESHIVA UNIVERSITY (NY) .... yu.edu **1200/1800/26**
Bio, Bus Admin, Comp Sci, Hist, Physics, Poli Sci, Pre-Med/Pre-Dental, Psych

YORK COLLEGE (NE) .... york.edu **1050/1575/22**
 Ed, Psych, Reli Stu

YORK COLLEGE OF PENNSYLVANIA (PA) .... ycp.edu **1090/1635/24**
Bus Admin, Communic, Ed, Nurs

YOUNGSTOWN STATE UNIVERSITY (OH) .... ysu.edu **1000/1500/21**
Art, Bus Admin

SECTION FOUR

APPENDICES

APPENDIX A

The 1100 Colleges Used In This Study

A   **Abilene Christian University**
Abilene, Texas 79699

Adelphi University
Garden City, NY 11530

Adrian College
Adrian, Michigan 49221

◆ **Agnes Scott College**
Decatur, Georgia 30030

Akron, University of
Akron, Ohio 44325

◆ **Alabama, University of**
Tuscaloosa, Alabama 35487

Alaska Pacific University
Anchorage, Alaska 99508

Alaska, University of
Anchorage, Alaska 99508

Alaska, University of
Fairbanks, Alaska 99775

Albany College of Pharmacy
Albany, New York 12208

Albertson College of Idaho
Caldwell, Idaho 83605

◆ **Albion College**
Albion, Michigan 49224

Albright College
Reading, Pennsylvania 19612

Alderson-Broaddus College
Phillipi, West Virginia 26416

◆ **Alfred University**
Alfred, New York 14802

◆ **Allegheny College**
Meadville, Pennsylvania 16335

◆ **Alma College**
Alma, Michigan 48801

Alverno College
Milwaukee, Wisconsin 53234

American Academy of Dramatic Arts
New York, New York 10016

American International College
Springfield, Massachusetts 01109

◆ **American University**
Washington, DC 20016

◆ **Amherst College**
Amherst, Massachusetts 01002

Anderson University
Anderson, Indiana 46012

Andrews University
Berrien Springs, Michigan 49104

Anna Maria College
Paxton, Massachusetts 01612

Appalachian State University
Boone, North Carolina 28608

Aquinas College
Grand Rapids, Michigan 49506

Arcadia University
Glenside, Pennsylvania 19038

◆ **Arizona, University of**
Tucson, Arizona 85721

◆ **Arizona State University**
Tempe, Arizona 85287

◆ **Arkansas, University of**
Fayetteville, Arkansas 72701

Art Center College of Design
Pasadena, California 91103

Art Institute of Chicago, School of the
Chicago, Illinois 60603

Arts, University of the
Philadelphia, Pennsylvania 19102

Asbury College
Wilmore, Kentucky 40390

Ashland University
Ashland, Ohio 44805

Assumption College
Worcester, Massachusetts 01609

◆ **Auburn University**
Auburn University, Alabama 36849

Augsburg College
Minneapolis, Minnesota 55454

Augusta State University
Augusta, Georgia 30964

◆ **Augustana College**
Rock Island, Illinois 61201

Augustana College
Sioux Falls, South Dakota 57197

◆ **Austin College**
Sherman, Texas 75091

Averett University
Danville, Virginia 24541

Avila University
Kansas City, Missouri 64145

◆ Phi Beta Kappa Schools   ▮ Predominantly African-American Institutions

B

Azusa Pacific University
Azusa, California 91702

Babson College
Wellesley, Massachusetts 02157

Baker University
Baldwin City, Kansas 66006

Baldwin-Wallace College
Berea, Ohio 44017

Ball State University
Muncie, Indiana 47306

Bard College,
Annandale-on-Hudson, New York 12504

Barry University
Miami Shores, Florida 33161

◆ **Bates College**
Lewiston, Maine 04240

Bay Path College
Longmeadow, MA 01106

◆ **Baylor University**
Waco, Texas 76798

Belhaven College
Jackson, Mississippi 39202

Bellarmine University
Louisville, Kentucky 40205

Belmont Abbey College
Belmont, North Carolina 28012

Belmont University
Nashville, Tennessee 37212

◆ **Beloit College**
Beloit, Wisconsin 53511

Bemidji State University
Bemidji, Minnesota 56601

Benedictine College
Atchison, Kansas 66002

Benedictine University
Lisle, Illinois 60532

▌ **Bennett College**
Greensboro, North Carolina 27401

Bennington College
Bennington, Vermont 05201

Bentley College
Waltham, Massachusetts 02154

Berea College
Berea, Kentucky 40404

Berklee College of Music
Boston, Massachusetts 02215

Berry College
Rome, Georgia 30149

Bethany College
Lindsborg, Kansas 67456

Bethany College
Bethany, West Virginia 26032

Bethany College
North Newton, Kansas 67117

Bethel College
Mishawaka, Indiana 46545

Bethel College
St. Paul, Minnesota 55112

Biola University
La Mirada, California 90639

◆ **Birmingham-Southern College**
Birmingham, Alabama 35254

Blackburn College
Carlinville, Illinois 62626

Bloomsburg University
Bloomsburg, Pennsylvania 17815

Bluffton College
Bluffton, Ohio 45817

Boise State University
Boise, Idaho 83725

Boston Architectural Center
Boston, Massachusetts 02115

◆ **Boston College**
Chestnut Hill, Massachusetts 02167

Boston Conservatory
Boston, Massachusetts 02215

◆ **Boston University**
Boston, Massachusetts 02215

◆ **Bowdoin College**
Brunswick, Maine 04011

◆ **Bowling Green State University**
Bowling Green, Ohio 43403

Bradley University
Peoria, Illinois 61625

◆ **Brandeis University**
Waltham, Massachusetts 02254

Brescia University
Owensboro, Kentucky 42301

Briar Cliff University
Sioux City, Iowa 51104

Bridgewater College
Bridgewater, Virginia 22812

Bridgewater State College
Bridgewater, Massachusetts 02325

Brigham Young University
Provo, Utah 84602

◆ **Brown University**
Providence, Rhode Island 02912

Bryan College
Dayton, Tennessee 37321

Bryant University
Smithfield, Rhode Island 02917

Bryn Athyn College of the New Church
Bryn Athyn, Pennsylvania 19009

Bryn Mawr College
Bryn Mawr, Pennsylvania 19010

◆ **Bucknell University**
Lewisburg, Pennsylvania 17837

Buena Vista University
Storm Lake, Iowa 50588

Butler University
Indianapolis, Indiana 46208

C **Caldwell College**
Caldwell, New Jersey 07006

California College of the Arts
San Francisco, California 94107

California Institute of the Arts
Valencia, California 91355

California Institute of Technology
Pasadena, California 91125

California, University of, at
◆ **Berkeley,** California 94720
◆ **Davis,** California 95616
◆ **Irvine,** California 92717
◆ **Los Angeles,** California 90024
◆ **Merced,** California 95344
◆ **Riverside,** California 92521
◆ **San Diego,** California 92093
◆ **Santa Barbara,** California 93106
◆ **Santa Cruz,** California 95064

California Lutheran University
Thousand Oaks, California 91360

California Maritime Academy
Vallejo, California 94590

California Polytechnic State University
Pomona, California 91768

California Polytechnic State University
San Luis Obispo, California 93407

California, State University of, at
Bakersfield, California 93311
Camarillo, California 93012
◆ **Chico,** California 95929
Dominguez Hills, Carson, California 90747
East Bay, California 94542
Fresno, California 93740

California, State University of, at (*Cont.*)
Fullerton, California 92834
Long Beach, California 90840
Los Angeles, California 90032
Monterey Bay, California 93955
Northridge, California 91330
Sacramento, California 95819
San Bernardino, California 92407
San Jose, California 95192
San Marcos, California 92096
Stanislaus, California 95382

Calvin College
Grand Rapids, Michigan 49456

Campbell University
Buies Creek, North Carolina 27506

Capital University
Columbus, Ohio 43209

◆ **Carleton College**
Northfield, Minnesota 55057

◆ **Carnegie Mellon University**
Pittsburgh, Pennsylvania 15213

Carroll College
Helena, Montana 59625

Carroll College
Waukesha, Wisconsin 53186

Carson-Newman College
Jefferson City, Tennessee 37760

Carthage College
Kenosha, Wisconsin 53140

◆ **Case Western Reserve University**
Cleveland, Ohio 44106

Catawba College
Salisbury, North Carolina 28144

Catholic University of America
Washington, DC 20064

Cedar Crest College
Allentown, Pennsylvania 18104

Cedarville University
Cedarville, Ohio 45314

Centenary College of Louisiana
Shreveport, Louisiana 71104

Central Arkansas, University of
Conway, Arkansas 72035

Central College
Pella, Iowa 50219

Central Connecticut State University
New Britain, Connecticut 06050

Central Florida, University of
Orlando, Florida 32816

Central Michigan University
Mount Pleasant, Michigan 48859

Central Missouri State University
Warrensburg, Missouri 64093

Central Oklahoma, University of
Edmond, Oklahoma 73034

Centre College
Danville, Kentucky 40422

Chaminade University
Honolulu, Hawaii 96816

Champlain College
Burlington, Vermont 05402

Chapman College
Orange, California 92866

Coastal Carolina University
Conway, South Carolina 29528

College of Charleston
Charleston, South Carolina 29424

Charleston Southern University
Charleston, South Carolina 29423

Charleston, University of
Charleston, West Virginia 25304

◆ **Chatham College**
Pittsburgh, Pennsylvania 15232

Chestnut Hill College
Philadelphia, Pennsylvania 19118

Cheyney University of Pennsylvania
Cheyney, Pennsylvania 19319

◆ **Chicago, University of**
Chicago, Illinois 60637

Chowan College
Murfreesboro, North Carolina 27855

Christian Brothers University
Memphis, Tennessee 38104

Christopher Newport University
Newport News, Virginia 23606

Christendom College
Front Royal, Virginia 22630

◆ **Cincinnati, University of**
Cincinnati, Ohio 45221

Citadel, The
Charleston, South Carolina 29409

▪ **Claflin University**
Orangeburg, South Carolina 29115

◆ **Claremont McKenna College**
Claremont, California 91711

▪ **Clark Atlanta University**
Atlanta, Georgia 30314

◆ **Clark University**
Worcester, Massachusetts 01610

Clarke College
Dubuque, Iowa 52001

Clarkson University
Potsdam, New York 13676

Clemson University
Clemson, South Carolina 29634

Cleveland Institute of Art
Cleveland, Ohio 44106

Cleveland Institute of Music
Cleveland, Ohio 44106

◆ **Coe College**
Cedar Rapids, Iowa 52402

Cogswell Polytechnic College
Sunnyvale, California 94089

Coker College
Hartsdale, South Carolina 29550

◆ **Colby College**
Waterville, Maine 04901

Colby-Sawyer College
New London, New Hampshire 03257

◆ **Colgate University**
Hamilton, New York 13346

◆ **Colorado College**
Colorado Springs, Colorado 80903

◆ **Colorado, University of**
Boulder, Colorado 80309

Colorado, University of
Colorado Springs, Colorado 80933

Colorado, University of
Denver, Colorado 80217

Colorado School of Mines
Golden, Colorado 80401

◆ **Colorado State University**
Fort Collins, Colorado 80523

Columbia College
Chicago, Illinois 60605

Columbia College
Columbia, Missouri 65216

Columbia College
Columbia, South Carolina 29203

◆ **Columbia University**
New York, New York 10027
  ◆ **Barnard College,** New York, NY 10027

◆ Phi Beta Kappa Schools ▪ Predominantly African-American Institutions

Concordia University
Irvine, California 92612

Concordia College
Moorhead, Minnesota 56560

Concordia University
Seward, Nebraska 68434

◆ **Connecticut, University of**
Storrs, Connecticut 06269

◆ **Connecticut College**
New London, Connecticut 06320

Converse College
Spartanburg, South Carolina 29302

Cooper Union College, The
New York, New York 10003

◆ **Cornell College**
Mount Vernon, Iowa 52314

◆ **Cornell University**
Ithaca, New York 14853

Cornish College of the Arts
Seattle, Washington 98102

Covenant College
Lookout Mountain, Georgia 30750

Creighton University
Omaha, Nebraska 68178

Culver-Stockton College
Canton, Missouri 63435

Cumberland College
Williamsburg, Kentucky 40769

Curtis Institute of Music
Philadelphia, Pennsylvania 19103

D **Daemen College**
Amherst, New York 14226

◆ **Dallas, University of**
Irving, Texas 75062

Dana College
Blair, Nebraska 68008

◆ **Dartmouth College**
Hanover, New Hampshire 03755

◆ **Davidson College**
Davidson, North Carolina 28036

Dayton, University of
Dayton, Ohio 45469

Delaware State University
Dover, Delaware 19901

◆ **Delaware, University of**
Newark, Delaware 19716

Delaware Valley College of Pennsylvania
Doylestown, Pennsylvania 18901

◆ **Denison University**
Granville, Ohio 43023

◆ **Denver, University of**
Denver, Colorado 80208

DePaul University
Chicago, Illinois 60604

◆ **DePauw University**
Greencastle, Indiana 46135

DeSales University
Center Valley, Pennsylvania 18034

Detroit Mercy, University of
Detroit, Michigan 48221

◆ **Dickinson College**
Carlisle, Pennsylvania 17013

▮ **Dillard University**
New Orleans, Louisiana 70122

Dixie State College
Saint George, Utah 84770

Doane College
Crete, Nebraska 68333

Dominican University
River Forest, Illinois 60305

Dominican University of California
San Rafael, California 94901

Dordt College
Sioux Center, Iowa 51250

◆ **Drake University**
Des Moines, Iowa 50311

◆ **Drew University**
Madison, New Jersey 07940

Drexel University
Philadelphia, Pennsylvania 19104

Drury University
Springfield, Missouri 65802

Dubuque, University of
Dubuque, Iowa 52001

◆ **Duke University**
Durham, North Carolina 27706

Duquesne University
Pittsburgh, Pennsylvania 15282

D'Youville College
Buffalo, New York 14201

E ◆ **Earlham College**
Richmond, Indiana 47374

East Carolina University
Greenville, North Carolina 27858

East Central University
Ada, Oklahoma 74820

East Stroudsburg University
East Stroudsburg, Pennsylvania 18301

East Tennessee State University
Johnson City, Tennessee 37614

Eastern University
St. Davids, Pennsylvania 19087

Eastern Connecticut State University
Willimantic, Connecticut 06226

Eastern Kentucky University
Richmond, Kentucky 40475

Eastern Illinois University
Charleston, Illinois 61920

Eastern Mennonite University
Harrisonburg, Virginia 22802

Eastern Michigan University
Ypsilanti, Michigan 48197

Eastern Nazarene College
Quincy, Massachusetts 02170

Eastern Oregon University
La Grande, Oregon 97850

Eastern Washington University
Cheney, Washington 99034

◆ **Eckerd College**
St. Petersburg, Florida 33733

Edgewood College
Madison, Wisconsin 53711

Edinboro University of Pennsylvania
Edinboro, Pennsylvania 16444

Elizabethtown College
Elizabethtown, Pennsylvania 17022

Elon University
Elon University, North Carolina 27244

Elmhurst College
Elmhurst, Illinois 60126

◆ **Elmira College**
Elmira, New York 14901

Elms College
Chicopee, Massachusetts 01013

Embry-Riddle Aeronautical University
Daytona Beach, Florida 32114

Emerson College
Boston, Massachusetts 02116

Emmanuel College
Boston, Massachusetts 02115

Emory and Henry College
Emory, Virginia 24327

◆ **Emory University**
Atlanta, Georgia 30322

Endicott College
Beverly, MA 01915

Erskine College
Due West, South Carolina 29639

Eureka College
Eureka, Illinois 61530

Evansville, University of
Evansville, Indiana 47722

F ◆ **Fairfield University**
Fairfield, Connecticut 06430

Fairleigh Dickinson University
Teaneck, New Jersey 07666

Fairmont State University
Fairmont, West Virginia 26554

Faulkner University
Montgomery, Alabama 36109

Ferris State University
Big Rapids, Michigan 49307

Findlay, University of
Findlay, Ohio 45840

◆■ **Fisk University**
Nashville, Tennessee 37208

Fitchburg State College
Fitchburg, Massachusetts 01420

Five Towns College
Dix Hills, New York 11746

Flagler College
St. Augustine, Florida 32085

◆ **Florida, University of**
Gainesville, Florida 32611

◆ **Florida A&M University**
Tallahassee, FL 32307

Florida Atlantic University
Boca Raton, Florida 33431

Florida Gulf Coast University
Fort Myers, Georgia 33965

Florida Institute of Technology
Melbourne, Florida 32901

◆ **Florida International University**
Miami, Florida 33199

Florida Southern College
Lakeland, Florida 33801

◆ **Florida State University**
Tallahassee, Florida 32306

◆ Phi Beta Kappa Schools   ■ Predominantly African-American Institutions

Fontbonne University
St. Louis, Missouri 63105

◆ **Fordham University**
Bronx, New York 10458

Fort Hays State University
Hays, Kansas 67601

Fort Lewis College
Durango, Colorado 81301

Framingham State College
Framingham, Massachusetts 01701

Franciscan University of Steubenville
Steubenville, Ohio 43952

Franklin College
Franklin, Indiana 46131

◆ **Franklin & Marshall College**
Lancaster, Pennsylvania 17604

Freed-Hardeman University
Henderson, Tennessee 38340

Friends University
Wichita, Kansas 67213

Frostburg State University
Frostburg, Maryland 21532

◆ **Furman University**
Greenville, South Carolina 29613

G **Gannon University**
Erie, Pennsylvania 16541

Gardner-Webb University
Boiling Springs, North Carolina 28017

Geneva College
Beaver Falls, Pennsylvania 15010

Georgetown College
Georgetown, Kentucky 40324

◆ **Georgetown University**
Washington, DC 20057

George Fox University
Newberg, Oregon 97132

George Mason University
Fairfax, Virginia 22030

◆ **George Washington University**
Washington, DC 20052

◆ **Georgia, University of**
Athens, Georgia 30602

Georgia Institute of Technology
Atlanta, Georgia 30332

Georgia Southern University
Statesboro, Georgia 30460

Georgia Southwestern University
Americus, Georgia 31704

Georgia State University
Atlanta, Georgia 30303

◆ **Gettysburg College**
Gettysburg, Pennsylvania 17325

Gonzaga University
Spokane, Washington 99258

Gordon College
Wenham, Massachusetts 01984

Goshen College
Goshen, Indiana 46526

◆ **Goucher College**
Towson, Maryland 21204

Graceland University
Lamoni, Iowa 50140

Grambling State University
Grambling, Louisiana 71245

Grand Valley State University
Allendale, Michigan 49401

Great Falls, University of
Great Falls, Montana 59405

Greensboro College
Greensboro, North Carolina 27401

◆ **Grinnell College**
Grinnell, Iowa 50112

Grove City College
Grove City, Pennsylvania 16127

Guilford College
Greensboro, North Carolina 27410

◆ **Gustavus Adolphus College**
St. Peter, Minnesota 56082

Gwynedd-Mercy College
Gwnedd Valley, Pennsylvania 19437

H ◆ **Hamilton College**
Clinton, New York 13323

◆ **Hamline University**
St. Paul, Minnesota 55104

◆ **Hampden-Sydney College**
Hampden-Sydney, Virginia 23943

◆ **Hampton University**
Hampton, Virginia 23668

Hannibal-La Grange College
Hannibal, Missouri 63401

Hanover College
Hanover, Indiana 47243

Harding University
Searcy, Arkansas 72149

Hardin-Simmons University
Abilene, Texas 79698

Harrisburg University
Harrisburg, Pennsylvania 17101

Hartford, University of
Hartford, Connecticut 06117

Hartwick College
Oneonta, New York 13820

◆ **Harvard University**
Cambridge, Massachusetts 02138

Harvey Mudd College
Claremont, California 91711

Hastings College
Hastings, Nebraska 68901

◆ **Haverford College**
Haverford, Pennsylvania 19041

Hawaii Pacific University
Honolulu, Hawaii 96813

Hawaii, University of
Hilo, Hawaii 96720

◆ **Hawaii, University of**
Manoa, Honolulu, Hawaii 96822

Heidelberg College
Tiffin, Ohio 44883

Henderson State University
Arkadelphia, Arkansas 71999

◆ **Hendrix College**
Conway, Arkansas 72032

High Point University
High Point, North Carolina 27262

Hillsdale College
Hillsdale, Michigan 49242

◆ **Hiram College**
Hiram, Ohio 44234

◆ **Hobart & William Smith Colleges**
Geneva, New York 14456

◆ **Hofstra University**
Hempstead, New York 11550

◆ **Hollins University**
Roanoke, Virginia 24020

◆ **Holy Cross, College of the**
Worcester, Massachusetts 01610

Holy Names University
Oakland, California 94619

Hood College
Frederick, Maryland 21701

◆ **Hope College**
Holland, Michigan 49423

Houghton College
Houghton, New York 14744

Houston Baptist University
Houston, Texas 77074

Houston, University of
Houston, Texas 77004

◆■ **Howard University**
Washington, DC 20059

Humboldt State University
Arcata, California 95521

Huntingdon College
Montgomery, Alabama 36106

Huntington University
Huntington, Indiana 46750

Husson College
Bangor, Maine 04401

I ◆ **Idaho, University of**
Moscow, Idaho 83844

Idaho State University
Pocatello, Idaho 83209

Illinois, University of, at
◆ **Urbana-Champaign,** Illinois 61801
◆ **Chicago,** Illinois 60680

◆ **Illinois College**
Jacksonville, Illinois 62650

Illinois Institute of Technology
Chicago, Illinois 60616

Illinois State University
Normal, Illinois 61761

◆ **Illinois Wesleyan University**
Bloomington, Illinois 61702

Immaculata University
Immaculata, Pennsylvania 19345

Indiana State University
Terre Haute, Indiana 47809

◆ **Indiana University**
Bloomington, Indiana 47405

Indiana University of Pennsylvania
Indiana, Pennsylvania 15705

I.U. - P.U. - Indianapolis University
Indianapolis, Indiana 46202

Indiana University of Technology
Fort Wayne, Indiana 46803

Indiana Wesleyan University
Marion, Indiana 46953

Iona College
New Rochelle, New York 10801

◆ **Iowa, University of**
Iowa City, Iowa 52242

◆ **Iowa State University of Science
& Technology**
Ames, Iowa 50011

Ithaca College
Ithaca, New York 14850

J   **Jacksonville State University**
Jacksonville, Alabama 36265

Jacksonville University
Jacksonville, Florida 32211

James Madison University
Harrisonburg, Virginia 22807

Jamestown College
Jamestown, North Dakota 58405

John Brown University
Siloam Springs, Arkansas 72761

John Carroll University
Cleveland, Ohio 44118

◆ **Johns Hopkins University**
Baltimore, Maryland 21218

Johnson State College
Johnson, Vermont 05656

Johnson C. Smith University
Charlotte, North Carolina 28216

Judson College
Marion, Alabama 36756

Juilliard School
New York, New York 10023

Juniata College
Huntingdon, Pennsylvania 16652

K   ◆ **Kalamazoo College**
Kalamazoo, Michigan 49006

Kansas City Art Institute
Kansas City, Missouri 64111

◆ **Kansas, University of**
Lawrence, Kansas 66045

◆ **Kansas State University**
Manhattan, Kansas 66506

Kean University of New Jersey
Union, New Jersey 07083

Keene State College
Keene, New Hampshire 03435

Kennesaw State College
Marietta, Georgia 30144

◆ **Kent State University**
Kent, Ohio 44242

◆ **Kentucky, University of**
Lexington, Kentucky 40506

Kentucky Wesleyan College
Owensboro, Kentucky 42301

◆ **Kenyon College**
Gambier, Ohio 43022

Kettering University
Flint, Michigan 48504

King College
Bristol, Tennessee 37620

King's College
Wilkes-Barre, Pennsylvania 18711

◆ **Knox College**
Galesburg, Illinois 61401

Kutztown University
Kutztown, Pennsylvania 19530

L   ◆ **Lafayette College**
Easton, Pennsylvania 18042

◆ **Lake Forest College**
Lake Forest, Illinois 60045

Lamar University
Beaumont, Texas 77710

Lambuth University
Jackson, Tennessee 38301

LaSalle University
Philadelphia, Pennsylvania 19141

Lasell College
Newton, Massachusetts 02466

La Verne, University of
La Verne, California 91750

◆ **Lawrence University**
Appleton, Wisconsin 54912

Lebanon Valley College
Annville, Pennsylvania 17003

◆ **Lehigh University**
Bethlehem, Pennsylvania 18015

LeMoyne College
Syracuse, New York 13214

Lenoir Rhyne College
Hickory, North Carolina 28603

Lesley University
Cambridge, Massachusetts 02138

LeTourneau College
Longview, Texas 75607

◆ **Lewis & Clark College**
Portland, Oregon 97219

Lewis-Clark State College
Lewiston, Idaho 83501

Liberty University
Lynchburg, Virginia 24502

Lindenwood University
St. Charles, Missouri 63301

Linfield College
McMinnville, Oregon 97128

Lipscomb University
Nashville, Tennessee 37204

Lock Haven University of Pennsylvania
Lock Haven, Pennsylvania 17745

Long Island University-Brooklyn
Brooklyn, New York 11201

Long Island University-C.W. Post
Brookville, New York 11548

Longwood University
Farmville, Virginia 23909

Loras College
Dubuque, Iowa 52001

Louisiana College
Pineville, Louisiana 71360

Louisiana-Lafayette, University of
Lafayette, Louisiana 70504

Louisiana-Monroe, University of
Monroe, Louisiana 71209

◆ **Louisiana State University**
Baton Rouge, Louisiana 70803

Louisiana Tech University
Ruston, Louisiana 71272

Louisville, University of
Louisville, Kentucky 40292

Lowell, University of
Lowell, Massachusetts 01854

◆ **Loyola College**
Baltimore, Maryland 21210

◆ **Loyola Marymount University**
Los Angeles, California 90045

◆ **Loyola University of Chicago**
Chicago, Illinois 60611

Loyola University
New Orleans, Louisiana 70118

◆ **Luther College**
Decorah, Iowa 52101

Lycoming College
Williamsport, Pennsylvania 17701

Lynchburg College
Lynchburg, Virginia 24501

Lyndon State College
Lyndonville, Vermont 05851

Lyon College
Batesville, Arkansas 72503

M ◆ **Macalester College**
St. Paul, Minnesota 55105

MacMurray College
Jacksonville, Illinois 62650

Maine, University of
Farmington, Maine 04938

◆ **Maine, University of**
Orono, Maine 04469

Malone College
Canton, Ohio 44709

Manchester College
North Manchester, Indiana 46962

◆ **Manhattan College**
Riverdale, New York 10471

Manhattan School of Music
New York, New York 10027

Manhattanville College
Purchase, New York 10577

Mannes School of Music
New York, New York 10024

Mansfield University of Pennsylvania
Mansfield, Pennsylvania 16933

◆ **Marietta College**
Marietta, Ohio 45750

Marist College
Poughkeepsie, NY 12601

◆ **Marquette University**
Milwaukee, Wisconsin 53201

Marshall University
Huntington, West Virginia 25755

◆ **Mary Baldwin College**
Staunton, Virginia 24401

▮ **Marygrove College**
Detroit, Michigan 48221

Maryland Institute-College of Art
Baltimore, Maryland 21217

◆ **Maryland, University of Baltimore County**
Baltimore, Maryland 21250

◆ **Maryland, University of**
College Park, Maryland 20742

◆ Phi Beta Kappa Schools   ▮ Predominantly African-American Institutions

Marymount Manhattan College
New York, New York 10021

Marymount University
Arlington, Virginia 22207

Maryville College
Maryville, Tennessee 37804

Maryville University-Saint Louis
St. Louis, Missouri 63141

◆ **Mary Washington, University of**
Fredericksburg, Virginia 22401

Marywood University
Scranton, Pennsylvania 18509

Massachusetts College of Art
Boston Massachusetts 02215

Massachusetts College of Liberal Arts
North Adams, Massachusetts 01247

Massachusetts College of Pharmacy
Boston, Massachusetts 02115

◆ **Massachusetts, University of**
Amherst, Massachusetts 01003

Massachusetts, University of
Boston, Massachusetts 02125

Massachusetts, University of
Lowell, Massachusetts 01854

Massachusetts, University of
North Dartmouth, Massachusetts 02747

◆ **Massachusetts Institute of Technology**
Cambridge, Massachusetts 02139

Massachusetts Maritime Academy
Buzzards Bay, Massachusetts 02532

Master's College, The
Santa Clarita, California 91321

McDaniel College
Westminster, Maryland 21157

◆ **McKendree College**
LeBaron, Illinois 62254

McMurry University
Abilene, Texas 79697

McPherson College
McPherson, Kansas 67460

Memphis College of Art
Memphis, Tennessee 38112

Memphis, University of
Memphis, Tennessee 38152

Mercer University
Macon, Georgia 31207

Mercy College
Dobbs Ferry, New York 10522

Mercyhurst College
Erie, Pennsylvania 16546

Meredith College
Raleigh, North Carolina 27607

Merrimack College
No. Andover, Massachusetts 01845

Messiah College
Grantham, Pennsylvania 17027

◆ **Miami University**
Oxford, Ohio 45056

◆ **Miami, University of**
Coral Gables, Florida 33124

◆ **Michigan, University of**
Ann Arbor, Michigan 48109

Michigan, University of
Dearborn, Michigan 48128

◆ **Michigan State University**
East Lansing, Michigan 48824

Michigan Technological University
Houghton, Michigan 49931

◆ **Middlebury College**
Middlebury, Vermont 05753

Middle Tennessee State University
Murfreesboro, Tennessee 37132

Midwestern State University
Wichita Falls, Texas 76308

Millersville University of Pennsylvania
Millersville, Pennsylvania 17551

Milligan College
Milligan College, Tennessee 37682

Millikin University
Decatur, Illinois 62522

◆ **Mills College**
Oakland, California 94613

◆ **Millsaps College**
Jackson, Mississippi 39210

Milwaukee School of Engineering
Milwaukee, Wisconsin 53201

Minnesota State University - Mankato
Mankato, Minnesota 56001

Minnesota State University - Moorhead
Moorhead, Minnesota 56563

Minnesota, University of
Duluth, Minnesota 55812

◆ **Minnesota, University of**
Minneapolis, Minnesota 55455

Minnesota, University of
Morris, Minnesota 56267

Misericordia, College
Dallas, Pennsylvania 18612

Mississippi College
Clinton, Mississippi 39058

Mississippi State University
Mississippi State, Mississippi 39762

◆ **Mississippi, University of**
University, Mississippi 38677

Mississippi University for Women
Columbus, Mississippi 39701

Missouri Baptist University
St. Louis, Missouri 63141

Missouri Southern State University
Joplin, Missouri 64801

Missouri State University
Springfield, Missouri 65897

◆ **Missouri, University of**
Columbia, Missouri 65211

Missouri, University of
Kansas City, Missouri 64110

Missouri, University of
Rolla, Missouri 65401

Missouri, University of
St. Louis, Missouri 63121

Mobile, University of
Mobile, Alabama 36663

Molloy College
Rockville Centre, New York 11571

Monmouth College
Monmouth, Illinois 61462

Monmouth University
West Long Branch, New Jersey 07764

Montana Tech. of the U. of Montana
Butte, Montana 59701

Montana, University of
Missoula, Montana 59812

Montana State University
Billings, Montana 59101

Montana State University
Bozeman, Montana 59717

Montevallo, University of
Montevallo, Alabama 35115

Montclair State College
Upper Montclair, New Jersey 07043

Montreat College
Montreat, North Carolina 28757

Montserrat College of Art
Beverly, Massachusetts 01915

Moore College of Art
Philadelphia, Pennsylvania 19103

Moravian College
Bethlehem, Pennsylvania 18018

◆■ **Morehouse College**
Atlanta, Georgia 30314

■ **Morgan State University**
Baltimore, Maryland 21257

Morningside College
Sioux City, Iowa 51106

◆ **Mount Holyoke College**
South Hadley, Massachusetts 01075

Mount Mercy College
Cedar Rapids, Iowa 52402

Mount St. Joseph, College of
Cincinnati, Ohio 45233

Mount St. Mary's University
Emmitsburg, Maryland 21727

Mount St. Mary's College
Los Angeles, California 90049

Mount St. Mary College
Newburgh, New York, 12550

Mount Union College
Alliance, Ohio 44601

◆ **Muhlenberg College**
Allentown, Pennsylvania 18104

Murray State University
Murray, Kentucky 42071

Museum of Fine Arts, School of the
Boston, Massachusetts 02115

Muskingum College
New Concord, Ohio 43762

N **Nazareth College of Rochester**
Rochester, New York 14618

Nebraska, University of
Kearney, Nebraska 68849

◆ **Nebraska, University of**
Lincoln, Nebraska 68588

Nebraska, University of
Omaha, Nebraska 68182

Nebraska Wesleyan University
Lincoln, Nebraska 68504

◆ Phi Beta Kappa Schools ■ Predominantly African-American Institutions

Nevada, University of, at
Las Vegas, Nevada 89154
Reno, Nevada 89557

New College of Florida
Sarasota, Florida 34243

New England Conservatory of Music
Boston, Massachusetts 02115

◆ **New Hampshire, University of**
Durham, New Hampshire 03824

New Jersey, College of
Ewing, New Jersey 08628

New Jersey Institute of Technology
Newark, New Jersey 07102

Newman University
Wichita, Kansas 67213

New Mexico Institute of Mining
and Technology
Socorro, New Mexico 87801

New Mexico State University
Las Cruces, New Mexico 88003

◆ **New Mexico, University of**
Albuquerque, New Mexico 87131

New Orleans, University of
New Orleans, Louisiana 70148

New School University -
Eugene Lang College
New York, New York 10011

New York, City University of, at
◆ **Baruch College,** New York, NY 10010
◆ **Brooklyn College,** Brooklyn, NY 11210
◆ **City College,** New York, New York 10031
◆ **Herbert H. Lehman Coll.,** Bronx, NY 10468
◆ **Hunter College,** New York, NY 10021
  John Jay College, New York, NY 10019
◆ **Queens College,** Flushing, NY 11367

New York Institute of Techology
Old Westbury, New York 11568

New York, State University of, at
◆ **Albany,** New York 12222
◆ **Binghamton,** New York 13902
  Brockport, New York 14420
◆ **Buffalo,** New York 14214
  Fredonia, New York 14063
◆ **Geneseo,** New York 14454
  Maritime College (TNS), New York 10465
  New Paltz, New York 12561
  Oneonta, New York 13820
  Oswego, New York 13126
  Plattsburgh, New York 12901
  Potsdam, New York 13676
  Purchase, New York 10577
  Staten Island, New York 10314
◆ **Stony Brook,** New York 11794

◆ **New York University**
New York, New York 10011

Niagara University
Niagara Falls, New York, 14109

Nichols State University
Thibodaux, Louisiana 70310

North Carolina School of the Arts
Winston-Salem, North Carolina 27117

North Carolina, University of, at
  Asheville, North Carolina 28804
◆ **Chapel Hill,** North Carolina 27599
  Charlotte, North Carolina 28223
◆ **Greensboro,** North Carolina 27412
  Pembroke, North Carolina 28372
  Wilmington, North Carolina 28403

◆ **North Carolina State University**
Raleigh, North Carolina 27695

North Central College
Naperville, Illinois 60566

North Dakota State University
Fargo, North Dakota 58105

◆ **North Dakota, University of**
Grand Forks, North Dakota 58202

North Florida, University of
Jacksonville, Florida 32216

North Georgia College & State Univ.
Dahlonega, Georgia 30597

North Texas, University of
Denton, Texas 76203

Northeastern Illinois University
Chicago, Illinois 60625

Northeastern State University
Tahlequah, Oklahoma 74464

Northeastern University
Boston, Massachusetts 02115

Northern Arizona University
Flagstaff, Arizona 86011

Northern Colorado University
Greeley, Colorado 80639

Northern Illinois University
DeKalb, Illinois 60115

Northern Iowa, University of
Cedar Falls, Iowa 50614

Northern Kentucky University
Highland Heights, Kentucky 41099

Northern Michigan University
Marquette, Michigan 49855

Northwest Missouri State University
Maryville, Missouri 64468

Northwestern College
Orange City, Iowa 51041

Northwestern College
St. Paul, Minnesota 55113

◆ **Northwestern University**
Evanston, Illinois 60204

Northwestern University of Louisiana
Natchitoches, Louisiana 71497

Northwood University
Midland, Michigan 48640

Norwich University
Northfield, Vermont 05663

◆ **Notre Dame, University of**
Notre Dame, Indiana 46556

Nova Southeastern University
Ft. Lauderdale, Florida 33314

Nyack College
Nyack, New York 10960

O **Oakland City University**
Oakland City, Indiana 47660

Oakland University
Rochester, Michigan 48309

◆ **Oberlin College**
Oberlin, Ohio 44074

◆ **Occidental College**
Los Angeles, California 90041

Oglethorpe University
Atlanta, Georgia 30319

Ohio Northern University
Ada, Ohio 45810

◆ **Ohio State University**
Columbus, Ohio 43210

◆ **Ohio University**
Athens, Ohio 45701

◆ **Ohio Wesleyan University**
Delaware, Ohio 43015

Oklahoma Baptist University
Shawnee, Oklahoma 74801

Oklahoma Christian University
Olahoma, City, Oklahoma 73136

Oklahoma City University
Oklahoma City, Oklahoma 73106

◆ **Oklahoma, University of**
Norman, Oklahoma 73069

Oklahoma State University
Stillwater, Oklahoma 74078

Old Dominion University
Norfolk, Virginia 23529

Olivet Nazarene University
Bourbonnais, Illinois 60914

Olin College of Engineering
Needham, Massachusetts 02492

Oral Roberts University
Tulsa, Oklahoma 74171

Oregon Institute of Technology
Klamath Falls, Oregon 97601

◆ **Oregon, University of**
Eugene, Oregon 97403

Oregon State University
Corvallis, Oregon 97331

Otis College of Art and Design
Los Angeles, California 90045

Otterbein College
Westerville, Ohio 43081

Ouachita Baptist University
Arkadelphia, Arkansas 71998

Ozarks, College of the
Point Lookout, Missouri 65726

P **Pace University**
New York, New York 10038

Pacific Lutheran University
Tacoma, Washington 984473

Pacific, U. of the
Stockton, California 95211

Pacific University
Forest Grove, Oregon 97116

Palm Beach Atlantic University
West Palm Beach, Florida 33416

Parsons School of Design
New York, New York 10011

Paul Smith's College
Paul Smiths, New York 12970

Pennsylvania Academy of the Fine Arts
Philadelphia, Pennsylvania 19102

Pennsylvania State University at Erie
Erie, Pennsylvania 16563

Pennsylvania State University at Harrisburg
Harrisburg, Pennsylvania 17057

◆ **Pennsylvania State University**
University Park, Pennsylvania 16802

◆ **Pennsylvania, University of**
Philadelphia, Pennsylvania 19104

Pepperdine University
Malibu, California 90263

Philadelphia Biblical University
Langhorne, Pennsylvania 19047

Philadelphia University
Philadelphia, Pennsylvania 19144

Piedmont College
Demorest, Georgia 30535

Pine Manor College
Chestnut Hill, Massachusetts 02167

Pittsburg State University
Pittsburg, Kansas 66762

Pittsburgh, University of
Bradford, Pennsylvania 16701

Pittsburgh, University of
Greensburg, Pennsylvania 15601

Pittsburgh, University of
Johnstown, Pennsylvania 15904

◆ **Pittsburgh, University of**
Pittsburgh, Pennsylvania 15260

Pitzer College
Claremont, California 91711

Plymouth State College
Plymouth, New Hampshire 03264

Point Loma Nazarene University
San Diego, California 92106

Point Park University
Pittsburgh, Pennsylvania 15222

Polytechnic Institute of New York
Brooklyn, New York 11201

◆ **Pomona College**
Claremont, California 91711

Portland State University
Portland, Oregon 97200

Portland, University of
Portland, Oregon 97203

Pratt Institute
Brooklyn, New York 11205

Presbyterian College
Clinton, South Carolina 29325

Presentation College
Aberdeen, South Dakota 57401

◆ **Princeton University**
Princeton, New Jersey 08544

Principia College
Elsah, Illinois 62028

Providence College
Providence, Rhode Island 02918

Puerto Rico, University of
Cayey, Puerto Rico 00736

Puerto Rico, University of
Mayaguez, Puerto Rico 00680

Puerto Rico, University of
Rio Piedras, Puerto Rico 00931

◆ **Puget Sound, University of**
Tacoma, Washington 98416

◆ **Purdue University**
W. Lafayette, Indiana 47907

Q **Queens University of Charlotte**
Charlotte, North Carolina 28274

Quincy University
Quincy, Illinois 62301

Quinnipiac University
Hamden, Connecticut 06518

R **Radford University**
Radford, Virginia 24142

Ramapo College
Mahwah, New Jersey 07430

Randolph College
Lynchburg, Virginia 24503

◆ **Randolph-Macon College**
Ashland, Virginia 23005

◆ **Redlands, University of**
Redlands, California 92373

◆ **Reed College**
Portland, Oregon 97202

Regis College
Weston, Massachusetts 02193

Regis University
Denver, Colorado 80221

Reinhardt College
Waleska, Georgia 30183

Rensselaer Polytechnic Institute
Troy, New York 12180

Rhode Island College
Providence, Rhode Island 02908

Rhode Island School of Design
Providence, Rhode Island 02903

◆ **Rhode Island, University of**
Kingston, Rhode Island 02881

◆ **Rhodes College**
Memphis, Tennessee 38112

◆ **Rice University**
Houston, Texas 77251

Richard Stockton College of New Jersey
Pomona, New Jersey 08240

◆ **Richmond, University of**
Richmond, Virginia 23173

Rider University
Lawrenceville, New Jersey 08648

◆ **Ripon College**
Ripon, Wisconsin 54971

◆ **Roanoke College**
Salem, Virginia 24153

Robert Morris University
Moon Township, Pennsylvania 15108

◆ **Rochester, University of**
Rochester, New York 14627

Rochester Institute of Technology
Rochester, New York 14623

◆ **Rockford College**
Rockford, Illinois 61108

Rockhurst University
Kansas City, Missouri 64110

Rocky Mountain College
Billings, Montana 59102

Roger Williams University
Bristol, Rhode Island 02809

Rollins College
Winter Park, Florida 32789

Roosevelt University
Chicago, Illinois 60605

Rose-Hulman Institute of Technology
Terre Haute, Indiana 47803

Rosemont College
Rosemont, Pennsylvania 19010

Rowan University
Mahwah, New Jersey 08028

◆ **Rutgers University**
New Brunswick, New Jersey 08854

Rutgers University
Camden, New Jersey 08101

Rutgers-Newark
Newark, New Jersey 07102

S **Sacred Heart University**
Fairfield, Connecticut 06432

Sage Colleges
Troy, New York 12180

Saginaw Valley State University
University Center, Michigan 48710

St. Ambrose University
Davenport, Iowa 52803

St. Andrews Presbyterian College
Laurinburg, North Carolina 28352

St. Anselm College
Manchester, New Hampshire 03102

St. Bonaventure University
St. Bonaventure, New York 14778

◆ **St. Catherine, College of**
St. Paul, Minnesota 55105

St. Cloud University
St. Cloud, Minnesota 56301

St. Edward's University
Austin, Texas 78704

St. Francis College
Brooklyn, New York 11201

St. Francis, University of
Fort Wayne, Indiana 46808

St. Francis University
Loretto, Pennsylvania 15940

St. John Fisher College
Rochester, New, York 14618

St. John's University
Jamaica, New York 11439

**Saint John's University/College
of Saint Benedict**
Collegeville, Minnesota 56321

Saint Joseph College
W. Hartford, Connecticut 06117

St. Joseph's College
Rensselaer, Indiana 47978

St. Joseph's College
Standish, Maine 04084

St. Joseph's College
Patchogue, New York 11772

◆ **Saint Joseph's University**
Philadelphia, Pennsylvania 19131

◆ **St. Lawrence University**
Canton, New York 13617

St. Louis College of Pharmacy
St. Louis, Missouri 63110

◆ **Saint Louis University**
St. Louis, Missouri 63103

Saint Martin's College
Lacey, Washington 98503

Saint Mary, College of
Omaha, Nebraska 68124

Saint Mary's College
Notre Dame, Indiana 46556

◆ Phi Beta Kappa Schools   ▮ Predominantly African-American Institutions

Saint Mary's College of California
Moraga, California 94575

Saint Mary, University of
Leavenworth, Kansas 66048

◆ **St. Mary's College of Maryland**
St. Mary's City, Maryland 20686

St. Mary's University of Minnesota
Winona, Minnesota 55987

St. Mary's University
San Antonio, Texas 78228

◆ **Saint Michael's College**
Colchester, Vermont 05439

St. Norbert College
DePere, Wisconsin 54115

◆ **St. Olaf College**
Northfield, Minnesota 55057

St. Peter's College
Jersey City, New Jersey 07306

Saint Rose, College of
Albany, New York 12203

St. Scholastica, College of
Duluth, Minnesota 55811

St. Thomas Aquinas College
Sparkhill, New York 10976

Saint Thomas, University of
St. Paul, Minnesota 55105

St. Thomas, University of
Houston, Texas 77006

St. Vincent College
Latrobe, Pennsylvania 15650

Salem College
Winston-Salem, North Carolina 27108

Salem State College
Salem, Massachusetts 01970

Salisbury University
Salisbury, Maryland 21801

Samford University
Birmingham, Alabama 35229

◆ **San Diego State University**
San Diego, California 92182

◆ **San Diego, University of**
San Diego, California 92110

San Francisco Art Institute
San Francisco, California 94133

San Francisco Conservatory of Music
San Francisco, California 94122

San Francisco, University of
San Francisco, California 94117

◆ **San Francisco State University**
San Francisco, California 94132

San Jose State University
San Jose, California 95192

◆ **Santa Clara University**
Santa Clara, California 95053

Santa Fe, College of
Santa Fe, New Mexico 87501

Sarah Lawrence College
Bronxville, New York 10708

School of the Art Institute of Chicago
Chicago, Illinois 60603

Schreiner University
Kerrville, Texas 78028

Sciences in Philadelphia, University of the
Philadelphia, Pennsylvania 19104

Scranton, University of
Scranton, Pennsylvania 18510

◆ **Scripps College**
Claremont, California 91711

Seattle Pacific University
Seattle, Washington 98119

Seattle University
Seattle, Washington 98122

Seton Hall University
South Orange, New Jersey 07079

Seton Hill College
Greensburg, Pennsylvania 15601

■ **Shaw University**
Raleigh, North Carolina 27601

Shawnee State University
Portsmouth, Ohio 45662

Shenandoah University
Winchester, Virginia 22601

Shepherd University
Shepherdstown, West Virginia 25443

Shippensburg University
Shippensburg, Pennsylvania 17257

Shorter College
Rome, Georgia 30165

Siena College
Loudonville, New York 12211

Siena Heights University
Adrian, Michigan 49221

Silver Lake College
Mantiowoc, Wisconsin 54220

◆ Phi Beta Kappa Schools   ■ Predominantly African-American Institutions

Simmons College
Boston, Massachusetts 02115

Simpson College
Indianola, Iowa 50125

◆ **Skidmore College**
Saratoga Springs, New York 12866

Slippery Rock University
Slippery Rock, Pennsylvania 16057

◆ **Smith College**
Northampton, Massachusetts 01063

◆ **South, University of the**
Sewanee, Tennessee 37383

South Alabama, University of
Mobile, Alabama 36688

◆ **South Carolina, University of**
Columbia, South Carolina 29208

◆ **South Dakota, University of**
Vermillion, South Dakota 57069

**South Dakota School of Mines
and Technology**
Rapid City, South Dakota 57701

South Dakota State University
Brookings, South Dakota 57006

South Florida, University of
Tampa, Florida 33620

Southeast Missouri State University
Cape Girardeau, Missouri 63701

Southeastern Louisiana State
Hammond, Louisiana 70402

**Southeastern Oklahoma State
University**
Durant, Oklahoma 74701

◆ **Southern California, University of**
Los Angeles, California 90089

Southern Connecticut State University
New Haven, Connecticut 06515

Southern Illinois University
Carbondale, Illinois 62901

Southern Illinois University
Edwardsville, Illinois 62026

Southern Maine, University of
Portland, Maine 04103

◆ **Southern Methodist University**
Dallas, Texas 75275

Southern Mississippi, University of
Hattiesburg, Mississippi 39406

Southern Nazarene University
Bethany, Oklahoma 73008

Southern Oregon University
Ashland, Oregon 97520

Southern Polytechnic University
Marietta, Georgia 30060

Southern Utah University
Cedar City, Utah 84720

Southwest Baptist University
Bolivar, Missouri 65613

Southwestern College
Winfield, Kansas 67156

◆ **Southwestern University**
Georgetown, Texas 78627

Southwestern Oklahoma State Univ.
Weatherford, Oklahoma 73096

◆∎ **Spelman College**
Atlanta, Georgia 30314

Spring Hill College
Mobile, Alabama 36608

◆ **Stanford University**
Stanford, California 94305

Stephen F. Austin State University
Nagogdoches, Texas 75962

Sterling College
Sterling, Kansas 67579

◆ **Stetson University**
Deland, Florida 32720

Stevens Institute of Technology
Hoboken, New Jersey 07030

Stonehill College
North Easton, Massachusetts 02357

Suffolk University
Boston, Massachusetts 02108

Susquehanna University
Selinsgrove, Pennsylvania 17870

◆ **Swarthmore College**
Swarthmore, Pennsylvania 19081

◆ **Sweet Briar College**
Sweet Briar, Virginia 24595

◆ **Syracuse University**
Syracuse, New York 13210

T **Tabor College**
Hillsboro, Kansas 67063

Tampa, University of
Tampa, Florida 33606

Tarleton State University
Stephenville, Texas 76402

Taylor University
Upland, Indiana 46989

◆ **Temple University**
Philadelphia, Pennsylvania 19122

Tennessee Tech University
Cookeville, Tennessee 38505

Tennessee, University of, at
  Chattanooga, Tennessee 37403
  ◆ **Knoxville,** Tennessee 37996
  Martin, Tennessee 38238

Texas, University of, at
  Arlington, Texas 76019
  ◆ **Austin,** Texas 78712
  Dallas, Richardson, Texas 75083
  Health Science Center
    San Antonio, Texas 78284
  San Antonio, Texas 78249
  Tyler, Texas 75799

◆ **Texas A & M**
College Station, Texas 77843

Texas A & M - Commerce
Commerce, Texas 75429

Texas A & M - Corpus Christi
Corpus Christi, Texas 78412

Texas A & M - Galveston
Galveston, Texas 77553

Texas A & M - Kingsville
Kingsville, Texas 78363

◆ **Texas Christian University**
Fort Worth, Texas 76129

Texas Lutheran University
Seguin, Texas 78155

Texas State University-San Marcos
San Marcos, Texas 78666

Texas Tech University
Lubbock, Texas 79409

Texas Wesleyan University
Fort Worth, Texas 76105

Thomas College
Waterville, Maine 04901

Thomas More College
Crestview Hills, Kentucky 41017

Toledo, University of
Toledo, Ohio 43606

■ **Tougaloo College**
Tougaloo, Mississippi 39174

Towson University
Towson, Maryland 21204

Transylvania University
Lexington, Kentucky 40508

◆ **Trinity College**
Hartford, Connecticut 06106

◆ **Trinity College**
Washington, DC 20017

◆ **Trinity University**
San Antonio, Texas 78212

Tri-State University
Angola, Indiana 46703

◆ **Truman State University**
Kirksville, Missouri 63501

◆ **Tufts University**
Medford, Massachusetts 02155

◆ **Tulane University**
New Orleans, Louisiana 70118

◆ **Tulsa, University of**
Tulsa, Oklahoma 74104

■ **Tuskegee University**
Tuskegee, Alabama 36088

U **Union College**
Lincoln, Nebraska 68506

◆ **Union College**
Schenectady, New York 12308

Union University
Jackson, Tennessee 38305

U.S. Air Force Academy
Colorado Springs, Colorado 80840

U.S. Coast Guard Academy
New London, Connecticut 06320

U.S. Military Academy
West Point, New York 10996

U.S. Naval Academy
Annapolis, Maryland 21402

◆ **Ursinus College**
Collegeville, Pennsylvania 19426

◆ **Utah, University of**
Salt Lake City, Utah 84112

Utah State University
Logan, Utah 84322

Utica College
Utica, New York 13502

V ◆ **Valparaiso University**
Valparaiso, Indiana 46383

◆ **Vanderbilt University**
Nashville, Tennessee 37240

◆ Phi Beta Kappa Schools ■ Predominantly African-American Institutions

◆ **Vassar College**
Poughkeepsie, New York 12601

◆ **Vermont, University of**
Burlington, Vermont 05401

Villa Julie College
Stevenson, Maryland 21153

◆ **Villanova University**
Villanova, Pennsylvania 19085

◆ **Virginia, University of**
Charlottesville, Virginia 22904

Virginia Commonwealth University
Richmond, Virginia 23284

Virginia Military Institute
Lexington, Virginia 24450

◆ **Virginia Polytechnic Institute**
Blacksburg, Virginia 24061

Virginia Wesleyan College
Norfolk, Virginia 23502

Visual Arts, School of
New York, New York 10010

Viterbo University
La Crosse, Wisconsin 54601

W ◆ **Wabash College**
Crawfordsville, Indiana 47933

Wagner College
Staten Island, New York 10301

◆ **Wake Forest University**
Winston-Salem, North Carolina 27109

Walla Walla College
College Place, Washington 99324

Walsh University
North Canton, Ohio, 44720

Warren Wilson College
Asheville, North Carolina 28815

Wartburg College
Waverly, Iowa 50677

Washburn University
Topeka, Kansas 66621

Washington College
Chestertown, Maryland 21620

◆ **Washington & Jefferson College**
Washington, Pennsylvania 15301

◆ **Washington & Lee University**
Lexington, Virginia 24450

◆ **Washington University in St. Louis**
St. Louis, Missouri 63130

◆ **Washington, University of**
Seattle, Washington 98195

◆ **Washington State University**
Pullman, Washington 99164

◆ **Wayne State College**
Wayne, Nebraska 68787

Wayne State University
Detroit, Michigan 48202

Waynesburg College
Waynesburg, Pennsylvania 15370

Weber State University
Ogden, Utah 84408

Webster University
St. Louis, Missouri 63119

◆ **Wellesley College**
Wellesley, Massachusetts 02481

◆ **Wells College**
Aurora, New York 13026

Wesleyan College
Macon, Georgia 31210

◆ **Wesleyan University**
Middletown, Connecticut 06457

West Chester University
West Chester, Pennsylvania 19383

West Florida, University of
Pensacola, FL 32514

◆ **West Virginia University**
Morgantown, West Virginia 26506

West Virginia Wesleyan College
Buckhannon, West Virginia 26201

Western Carolina University
Cullowhee, North Carolina 28723

Western Connecticut State University
Danbury, Connecticut 06810

Western Illinois University
Marcomb, Illinois 61455

Western Kentucky University
Bowling Green, Kentucky 42101

◆ **Western Michigan University**
Kalamazoo, Michigan 49008

Western New England College
Springfield, Massachusetts 01119

Western State College of Colorado
Gunnison, Colorado 81231

Western Washington University
Bellingham, Washington 98225

Westfield State College
Westfield, Massachusetts 01086

◆ Phi Beta Kappa Schools   ▌ Predominantly African-American Institutions

Westminster College
Fulton, Missouri 65251

Westminster College
Wilmington, Pennsylvania 16172

Westminster College
Salt Lake City, Utah 84105

Westmont College
Santa Barbara, California 93108

Wheaton College
Wheaton, Illinois 60187

◆ **Wheaton College**
Norton, Massachusetts 02766

Wheeling Jesuit University
Wheeling, West Virginia 26003

Wheelock College
Boston, Massachusetts 02215

◆ **Whitman College**
Walla Walla, Washington 99362

Whittier College
Whittier, California 90608

Whitworth College
Spokane, Washington 99251

Wichita State University
Wichita, Kansas 67260

Widener University
Chester, Pennsylvania 19013

■ **Wilberforce University**
Wilberforce, Ohio 45384

Wilkes University
Wilkes-Barre, Pennsylvania 18766

◆ **Willamette University**
Salem, Oregon 97301

William Jewell College
Liberty, Missouri 64068

◆ **William & Mary, College of**
Williamsburg, Virginia 23187

William Paterson University
Wayne, New Jersey 07470

◆ **Williams College**
Williamstown, Massachusetts 01267

Wilmington College
Wilmington, Ohio 45177

◆ **Wilson College**
Chambersburg, Pennsylvania 17201

Wingate University
Wingate, North Carolina 28174

Winona State University
Winona, Minnesota 55987

Winthrop University
Rock Hill, South Carolina 29733

Wisconsin Lutheran College
Milwaukee, Wisconsin 53226

◆ **Wisconsin, University of, at**
Eau Claire, Wisconsin 54701
Green Bay, Wisconsin 54311
LaCrosse, Wisconsin 54601
◆ **Madison,** Wisconsin 53706
◆ **Milwaukee,** Wisconsin 53201
Platteville, Wisconsin 53818
River Falls, Wisconsin 54022
Stevens Point, Wisconsin 54481
Stout, Menomonie, Wisconsin 54751
Superior, Wisconsin 54880
Whitewater, Wisconsin 53190

◆ **Wittenberg University**
Springfield, Ohio 45501

◆ **Wofford College**
Spartanburg, South Carolina 29303

Woodbury University
Burbank, California 91510

◆ **Wooster, College of**
Wooster, Ohio 44691

Worcester Polytechnic Institute
Worcester, Massachusetts 01609

Worcester State College
Worcester, Massachusetts 01602

Wright State University
Dayton, Ohio 45435

◆ **Wyoming, University of**
Laramie, Wyoming 82071

Xavier University
Cincinnati, Ohio 45207

X ■ **Xavier University of Louisiana**
New Orleans, Louisiana 70125

◆ **Yale University**
New Haven, Connecticut 06520

Y ✡ **Yeshiva University**
New York, New York 10033

York College
York, Nebraska 68467

York College of Pennsylvania
York, Pennsylvania 17403

Youngstown State University
Youngstown, Ohio 44555

APPENDIX B

The Miscellaneous Majors Colleges Used In This Study

Aeronautics, College of
Flushing, NY 11369

Andrews University
Berrien Springs, MI 49104

Atlantic, College of the
Bar Harbor, ME 04609

Aurora University
Aurora, Il 60506

Bellevue University
Bellevue, NE 68005

Black Hills State University
Spearfish, SD 57799

Bradford College
Haverhill, MA 01835

Brooks Institute of Photography
Santa Barbara, CA 93108

Cabrini College
Radnor, PA 19087

Carlow College
Pittsburgh, PA 15213

Central Oklahoma University
Edmond, OK 73034

■ **Central State University**
Wilberforce, OH 45384

Centenary College
Hackettstown, NJ 07840

Chadron State University
Chadron, Nebraska 69337

Cincinnati College of Mortuary Science
Cincinnati, OH 45224

Clarion University of Pennsylvania
Clarion, PA 16214

Cleveland State University
Cleveland, OH 44115

Columbia College - Hollywood
Tarzana, CA 91356

Columbus College of Art & Design
Columbus, OH 43215

Cortland State College
Cortland, NY 13045

Curry College
Milton, MA 02186

Daniel Webster College
Nashua, NH 03063

Davis & Elkins College
Elkins, WV 26241

Deep Springs College
Deep Springs Via Dyer, NV 89010

Defiance College, The
Defiance, OH 43512

Eastern Montana College
Billings, MT 59101

Eastern New Mexico University
Portales, NM 88130

Eugene Lang College
(New School Social Research)
New York, NY 11743

Fashion Institute of Technology
New York, NY 10001

Hampshire College
Amherst, MA 01002

Holy Family College
Philadelphia, PA 19114

Johnson & Wales University
Providence , Rhode Island 02903

Kendall College of Art and Design
Grand Rapids, MI 49503

Lake Erie College
Painesville, OH 44077

Landmark College
Putney, VT 05346

Langston University
Langston, OK 73050

Lees-McRae College
Banner Elk, NC 28604

Loma Linda University
Loma Linda, CA 92350

Lourdes College
Sylvania, OH 43560

Madonna University
Livonia, MI 48150

Maine Maritime
Castine, Maine 04420

Maine, University of
Machias, Maine 04654

Marian College of Fond du Lac
Fond du Lac, WI 54935

Mesa State College
Grand Junction, CO 81502

APPENDIX B (Continued)

The Miscellaneous Majors Colleges Used In This Study

Metropolitan State College
Denver, CO 80204

Midwestern State University
Wichita Falls, TX 76308

Mitchell College
New London, CT 06320

Mount Ida College
Newton Centre, Massachusetts 02459

Mt. St. Claire
Clinton, IA 52732

Neumann College
Aston, PA 19014

University of New England
Biddeford, ME 04005

New Haven, University of
New Haven, CT 06516

New School for Social Research
New York, NY 11743

New York School of Interior Design
New York, NY 10021

North Carolina Wesleyan College
Rocky Mount, NC 27804

Northeastern Louisiana University
Monroe, LA 71209

Northwestern Oklahoma State University
Alva, OK 73717

Park University
Cahokia, IL 62206

Pfeiffer College
Misenheimer, NC 28109

Prescott College
Prescott, AZ 86301

Ringling School of Art & Design
Sarasota, FL 34234

St. Elizabeth, College of
Convent Station, NJ 07960

Saint John's College
Annapolis, MD 21404

Saint Leo College
Saint Leo, FL 33574

Saint Thomas University
Miami, FL 33054

Salem International University
Salem, WV 26426

Salve Regina-The Newport College
Newport, RI 02840

Sam Houston State University
Huntsville, TX 77341

Science and Arts of Oklahoma
Chickasha, Oklahoma 73018

Simon's Rock College of Bard
Great Barrington, MA 01230

Southern Illinois, U. of
Edwardsville, IL 62026

Southern New Hampshire, University of
Manchester, NH 03106

Spring Arbor College
Spring Arbor, MI 49283

SUNY-Farmingdale
Farmingdale, NY 11735

■ **Texas Southern University**
Houston, TX 77004

Texas Woman's University
Denton, TX 76204

Thomas Aquinas College
Santa Paula, CA 93060

Tusculum College
Greenville, TN 37743

United States Merchant Marine Academy
Kings Point, NY 11024

Unity College
Unity, ME 04988

Virginia Intermont College
Bristol, VA 24201

Webb Institute
Glen Cove, NY 11542

APPENDIX C

Single Sex Colleges Included In This Study

WOMEN'S COLLEGES

Agnes Scott College (GA)
Alverno (WI)
Bay Path College (MA)
Bennett College (NC)
Bryn Mawr College (PA)
Cedar Crest College (PA)
Chatham College (PA)
Converse College(SC)
Hollins College (VA)
Judson College (AL)
Mary Baldwin College (VA)
Meredith College (NC)

Mills College (CA)
Mount Holyoke College (MA)
Pine Manor College (MA)
Rosemont College (PA)
St. Catherine, College of (MN)
Saint Joseph's (CT)
Saint Mary's College (IN)
Salem College (NC)
Scripps College (CA)
Seton Hill (PA)
Simmons College (MA)
Smith College (MA)

Spelman College (GA)
Sweet Briar College (VA)
Texas Woman's College
Trinity College (DC)
Wellesley College (MA)
Wesleyan College (GA)

MEN'S COLLEGES

Hampden-Sydney College (VA)
Morehouse College (GA)
Wabash College (IN)

APPENDIX D

Anyone who has been touched by the problem of alcohol or substance abuse, or who has worked with those struggling in recovery, knows that higher education will increasingly have to meet the needs of these persons. Several colleges are trying to address the needs of these students, and The Wellness Institute at Ball State has published a list of wellness dorms. Unfortunately, the grant for this no longer exists, but Ball State in Muncie, Indiana has done a fine job with young people in this area. You might call them at 765-285-8259.

Respectfully submitted,
Joseph W. Streit
Long-time Secondary School Counselor in New Jersey

APPENDIX E

A Simplified Timetable and Checklist for Seniors Planning on College*

SEPTEMBER - OCTOBER	Write for college catalogs, applications, financial aid information and pick up a financial aid booklet, continuing from your junior year.
SEPTEMBER - OCTOBER	Inquire at your high school Guidance Office about upcoming college nights.
SEPTEMBER - NOVEMBER	Continue campus visits as senior year academic commitments permit.
SEPTEMBER	Deadline for mailing in the late October or early November National College Exam Forms.
OCTOBER	Think about which two teachers you will ask to write college recommendations for you.
LATE OCTOBER	Deadline for mailing in the December National College Exam Forms.
NOVEMBER	Prepare a final list of colleges. Talk to your counselor about need-based funds. And look into merit-based money awarded by the colleges themselves.
	Talk to your counselor and/or a favorite teacher - show them your completed college essay, if your colleges require one.
NOVEMBER 1-15	Many early applications due.
NOVEMBER OR DECEMBER	Attend, with your parents, a local financial aid night given by an area high school.
NOVEMBER - DECEMBER	Apply to colleges. But always check deadlines. Some may be earlier.
DECEMBER 1	ROTC Scholarship applications to be in.
EARLY DECEMBER	Last call for mailing in the National College Exam Forms (SAT/ACT).
DECEMBER 15	Profile of Financial Aid Form (Step 1) due to College Scholarship Service (CSS).
JANUARY	Fill out the Financial Aid Form (FAF/FAFSA/PROFILE) or Family Financial Statement. Your counselor has it, and has advice for filling it out. This form will probably help you get a good deal of your total scholarships, jobs, and loans. It is the big one. Apply. Apply. Apply. Even if your family earns over $250,000. Everything flows from these federal forms.
JANUARY - FEBRUARY	Send mid-year reports to colleges.
FEBRUARY 1	Profile application (Step 2) to College Scholarship Service (CSS).
MARCH	Local scholarship forms available in the guidance office.
EARLY APRIL	All colleges will notify you by this time if they will accept you or not. The more competitive colleges usually deliberate longer and many of these top schools wait until the first week of April to notify you.
MID-APRIL	If unhappy with the financial aid package at any of the colleges where you have been accepted, you, the student, call that office and discuss it.
LATE APRIL	Send deposit to selected college.
MAY 1	Inform all colleges which accepted you whether or not you plan to attend.
MAY 1	Notify Guidance Office of your choice of college.
MAY - JUNE	Apply for summer jobs so that you can meet summer earnings expectations.
	Don't forget to graduate from high school!
SUMMER	Attend college orientation.
LATE SUMMER	Write Thank You notes to organizations that awarded you money.

NOTE: Before your senior year, prepare preliminary list of colleges you're interested in and those you would like to visit. Spring visits in the junior year are advised.

APPENDIX F

The Get-Going Form

A simple, useful form to use with the college-bound to get them started applying to colleges. The student and/or counselor and/or parent should fill in four colleges below, complete with address and zip codes.

Dear Student:

Within the next two weeks, please write to the Director of Admissions at the schools listed below, requesting information. A sample letter is included at the bottom of the page.

1. _____
_____
_____

2. _____
_____
_____

3. _____
_____
_____

4. _____
_____
_____

SAMPLE LETTER

Date

Director of Admissions
Name of College
Address of College and Zip Code

Dear Director:

   I am a student of Northampton High School in Northampton, Massachusetts and expect to graduate in June, 2010.

   I am interested in your school and would appreciate your sending me an application for admission and information concerning your financial aid program, and your _____ program of studies. Thank you.

   Very truly yours,

Your signature
Your Name
Your Address and Zip Code

COUNSELOR'S NOTES

COUNSELOR'S NOTES

COUNSELOR'S NOTES

COUNSELOR'S NOTES

COUNSELOR'S NOTES

ABOUT THE AUTHOR

Fred Rugg

Raised by an older sister, FRED RUGG was one of a handful of "Huckleberry Finn" cases that the top universities accepted in the mid-1960's. He is a writer, speaker, workshop presenter, and author. Unlike virtually all other college guidebook people, Rugg is one of the true professionals, having directed secondary college counseling programs for 20 years in all types of communities. A 1967 Applied Math graduate from Brown, Rugg is the holder of advanced degrees in secondary school guidance and administration. Early in his career he was employed as a statistician for two New England companies and worked his way through Ivy League Brown - the only member of his class to enter public school teaching. Offering dozens of workshops yearly from coast to coast, Fred is an often animated, charismatic and humorous speaker, and is the only one giving monthly seminars who draws a crowd. In addition, he has become well known for his evening speaking engagements for parents and students, which are informative and fun. He has lived and worked just about everywhere in America, has been married for over 40 years, and has two daughters. Beginning with his first volunteer assignment (Brown Youth Guidance), Rugg has been a perennial volunteer, and he's taught courses at four colleges. A native of New England, he has been based in Colorado and Florida, and now resides in California. As always, he is totally independent of the colleges.

FROM RUGG'S RECOMMENDATIONS...

INFORMATION THAT IS TO THE POINT, THAT YOU CAN USE IMMEDIATELY

Saving the college counselor enormous time with lists and answers found nowhere else - presented from the secondary school point of view!

FROM RUGG, YOU ALWAYS GET A NEW SLANT ON THE COLLEGES

1. *THE NEW BOOK: RUGG'S RECOMMENDATIONS ON THE COLLEGES 25th Ed.*
Locating Quality Undergraduate Colleges For Counselors, Parents & Students.
ISBN #1-883062-71-3 • LC89-062896 • $25.95 • © 2008 by Frederick E. Rugg

★ **Over 1000 Entry Changes in the New SILVER Book** ★

Rugg's Recommendations on the Colleges recommends quality departments at quality colleges. It is the primary brainstorming source for secondary public school counselors in creating a student's initial college list. Two new majors have been added and there are wholesale changes on over 30 others. Rugg's 25th edition is available listing 13,000 quality departments at 1100 quality colleges. The guidebook has been designated nationally as "a revered staple, the book parents and students must start with" in the search for a college to attend. The 25th edition is the accumulation of 35 years of work in the undergraduate college admissions process, and as always, *Rugg's* is independent of the colleges. There are over 1000 entry changes since the 24th edition, 114 majors, 160 recommended departments per major.

"You make it too easy for the 21st - century guidance counselor. So much information, yet so easy to use. Great job!"

—Ralph Strycharz
Long-time teacher and counselor
Hampshire Reg. H.S. (MA)

"A Revered Staple."

—West Coast Library Reviewer

"I love your book!"

—Carol Gill, Educational Consultants
Dobbs Ferry, NY

"A gem."

—College Bound, Evanston, Illinois

2. *THE SPECIAL REPORT: TWENTY MORE TIPS ON THE COLLEGES, Revised*
Twenty new behind the scenes tips. Ideal for counselors, parents, and students. 14th Edition.
ISBN #1-883062-72-1 • $8.95 • © 2008

Brutally honest information about colleges and the application process. This Special Report, *Twenty More Tips on the Colleges,* offers insights into assessing a college or university from the first "hello." Author Rugg succinctly presents 20 key tips to assist counselors, parents and students in selecting the best college for a student. Tips include colleges with high success rates for medical school acceptance, and what to consider before deciding to attend a military school. Overlooked state institutions, as well as other important and helpful comments, are included. The college search and selection process is incomplete without reading the valuable information contained within this Special Report.

"I have known Fred Rugg for nearly forty years, since we were on the staff together at Bristol (RI) High School. Fred has developed an uncanny insight and he is able to ask the right questions of both student and admission officer. Always up-to-date; never disappointing. Read his material; attend the seminars. They are great!"

—Robert Jeffrey, Independent Consultant
Orlando, FL

"I have used your information for years. It is a wonderful resource."

—Harriet Gershman, Academic
Counseling Services, Evanston, IL

3. *FORTY TIPS ON THE COLLEGES: THE REVISED SPECIAL REPORT 14th edition*
For all college bound students, parents, and their counselors. 20 pages. Over 35 college entry changes for 2008.
ISBN # 1-883062-73-x • $11.95 (money back guarantee) • Revised 2008

Get the "insider's" advice on college admissions. In *Forty Tips on the Colleges,* author Rugg shares with the reader 40 key tips on the college admissions process. Rugg spent in excess of 3000 hours visiting with over 9000 secondary school counselors in 48 states, to compile the information contained in this transcript. These insightful suggestions provide the reader with some of the unwritten do's and don'ts in the college admissions process. Rugg presents his 40 tips, accompanied by his personal observations of the campuses, with honesty and a sense of humor. *Forty Tips on the Colleges* offers straight talk about selecting a college and gaining admission. The special report contains helpful advice for the student, parent and school counselor alike. Topics include previously unpublished tips on which colleges care the most about their students; colleges with good learning disabilities programs; and how to choose a college where the student "fits in." The tips also contain helpful information concerning financial aid, college applications and SAT/ACT scores. This **must read** is our most popular special report.

*"I give **Rugg's Recommendations** five stars. This reference book for college search is a good place to start. Each year Mr. Rugg updates information for the college clients and counselors themselves, not ivy-towered college presidents. He lists "Quality departments in quality colleges." He includes schools by major and highlights miscellaneous majors such as art therapy, criminal justice, atmospheric sciences, orthotics and prosthetics, alternative colleges and mortuary science. This is by far the best starting place for students who know or don't know a preferred major or possible college "fit." The book is easy to use and full of current information on 1100 colleges. Take a look for yourself.*

—Jan Livingston, Independent Counselor
Northridge, CA

4. THE SPECIAL REPORT: *THIRTY QUESTIONS ON THE COLLEGES, Revised 14th Edition*

For all college bound students, parents and their counselors. 21 pages.

ISBN # 1-883062-74-8• $9.95 • Revised 2008 • Over 45 college entry changes

Thirty frequently asked questions with some answers even Deans of Admissions can't give you. This Special Report includes: 180 recommended colleges where black youngsters will maximize their education • What makes individuals happy at college? • Community college graduates – how do top colleges really view them at transfer time? • The best of the best journalism schools • Understanding student body make-up. And 23 other topics based on over 400 counselor meetings across the country. Counselors and parents find this transcript form extremely useful (yes, it's O.K. to copy it with appropriate acknowledgement).

> *"Your college guide is my #1 book when I visit junior classes every spring."*
> —Dr. Jim Burke
> East Brunswick H.S. (NJ)

> *"I have used **Rugg's Recommendations on the Colleges** for many years, as a Guidance Counselor and School Administrator. The research is excellent, up-to-date, and a most wonderful resource."*
> —Helen Unger
> Long-time N.J. Director of Pupil Personnel Services and College Counselor Consultant

5. THIRTY SEMINAR SHEETS $25

Our most popular lists are now available separately. Includes all of the rankings in #6 below, plus colleges where the following youngsters maximize their education: Jewish (125), Hispanic (150), Asian (130), and Black (170).

> *"I rely on your seminar sheets and book constantly."*
> —Sharon Barkins-Wasson
> Director of Counseling
> Crespi Carmelite HS, Encino, CA

6. THE COLLEGE SEMINAR SUBSTITUTE

For Secondary School Counselors, public and private • $55 (lists updated monthly)

Can't make it to a college seminar? Do the next best thing: Order this special package. *The College Seminar Substitute* provides you with 90% of the 60 items covered in our seminar agenda. In this package you receive Rugg's three Special Reports, *Twenty More Tips on the Colleges, Forty Tips on the Colleges, Thirty Questions and Answers,* plus 30 seminar handouts. These handouts contain over 2400 entries—a wealth of information. Topics covered include: a listing of safe campuses, snob schools; prestigious school rankings; underrated schools, the top 250 schools for the learning disabled, the most generous schools, new information on financial aid; advice on school recommendations; a listing of intense (rigorous) schools; big colleges that play small; rated Catholic colleges; and four minority lists. This package gives the counselor a foundation in understanding and navigating the admission game. See why over 9000 secondary school counselors have attended Rugg's College Admission Seminars.

> *"It is the best single source of information that we have. It answers the questions most frequently asked by parents. Your college materials help both the beginning and experienced counselor. The various ratings and lists inspire both students and their parents to further research the college scene. When parents and students are clueless, your information provides direction and humor in beginning the college selection process."*
> —Ira Lipton, Counselor, E. Hampton (NY)

7. SPECIAL! SEND IT ALL! $75

Includes 1 book, 3 special reports, 30 seminar sheets—all our products.

> *"As always, I find your reports and book invaluable."*
> —Michelle Koetke, Ind. College Counselor
> Newbury Park, CA

➡ *ORDER FORM ON REVERSE*

Rugg's advice and comments have appeared in such diverse publications as USA TODAY, ROLLING STONE, COLLEGE BOUND, THE BOSTON GLOBE, THE CLEVELAND PLAIN DEALER, NEW JERSEY MONTHLY, THE WASHINGTON POST, ROCKY MOUNTAIN NEWS and BUSINESS WEEK.

2008 PRODUCT ORDER FORM

ITEM #	TITLE OR DESCRIPTION	PRICE	QTY	AMOUNT
1	*Rugg's Recommendations on the Colleges:* The Book (25th ed.)	$25.95		
2	*20 More Tips on the Colleges:* Revised Special Report (14th ed.)	$ 8.95		
3	*Forty Tips on the Colleges:* Revised Special Report (14th ed.)	$11.95		
4	*Thirty Questions & Answers:* Revised Special Report (14th ed.)	$ 9.95		
5	*Thirty Seminar Sheets: Colleges*	$25.00		
6	*College Seminar Substitute:* Includes 2 thru 5	$55.00		
7	**SEND IT ALL!!!** Send one of each (Items 1-5)	$75.00		

Order 5 or more books:	Only $23.00 each! Discount price available only on the book.	**SUBTOTAL**	
Prepaid Orders over $89:	Subtract $4 from total.	Less $4 for prepaid orders over $89	
International Orders:	Shipping and handling cost: Actual Cost.	Sales Tax (CA only) 7.75%	
California Residents:	Please add 7.75% sales tax.		
SHIPPING CHARGES: (all orders mailed first class)	$ 0-15 Postage $2 $16-35 Postage $5 $36+ Postage $6	**Shipping**	
		TOTAL ENCLOSED	

Name _____

Address _____

City _____ State _____ Zip _____

Send to:
RUGG'S RECOMMENDATIONS
P.O. Box 417 • Fallbrook, CA 92088

For information on our 2008 COLLEGE ADMISSIONS SEMINARS,
call us at 760-728-4558 or Fax 760-728-4467 OR visit our Website at http://www.ruggsrecs.com